Books are to be returned on or b
the last date below

A DICTIONARY OF ENGLISH COSTUME

900–1900

Other works by
C. Willett & Phillis Cunnington

HANDBOOK OF ENGLISH MEDIAEVAL COSTUME

HANDBOOK OF ENGLISH COSTUME
IN THE SIXTEENTH CENTURY

HANDBOOK OF ENGLISH COSTUME
IN THE SEVENTEENTH CENTURY

HANDBOOK OF ENGLISH COSTUME
IN THE EIGHTEENTH CENTURY

HANDBOOK OF ENGLISH COSTUME
IN THE NINETEENTH CENTURY

A HISTORY OF UNDERCLOTHES

By C. Willett Cunnington

ENGLISH WOMEN'S CLOTHING
IN THE NINETEENTH CENTURY

ENGLISH WOMEN'S CLOTHING
IN THE PRESENT CENTURY

FEMININE ATTITUDES
IN THE NINETEENTH CENTURY

WHY WOMEN WEAR CLOTHES

THE PERFECT LADY

THE ART OF ENGLISH COSTUME

WOMEN : AN ANTHOLOGY

Queen Elizabeth I in a bodice with long stomacher front and trunk sleeves, with immense hanging sleeves behind ; the frounced skirt over a French farthingale. Fan-shaped ruff and behind it a wired head rail. Folded fan in the right hand. Date 1592.

A DICTIONARY
OF ENGLISH COSTUME

BY

C. WILLETT CUNNINGTON
PHILLIS CUNNINGTON

AND

CHARLES BEARD

WITH COLOUR FRONTISPIECE
AND 303 LINE ILLUSTRATIONS
BY CECIL EVERITT AND
PHILLIS CUNNINGTON

LONDON
ADAM & CHARLES BLACK

FIRST PUBLISHED 1960
REPRINTED 1965 AND 1968
BY A. AND C. BLACK LTD.
4, 5 AND 6 SOHO SQUARE, LONDON, W.1

© 1960 C. WILLETT CUNNINGTON
AND PHILLIS CUNNINGTON
SBN 7136 0370 4

PRINTED IN GREAT BRITAIN
BY R. & R. CLARK, LTD., EDINBURGH

7,483

PREFACE

THE authorship of this dictionary requires a word of explanation. For a number of years the late Charles Beard had been collecting material for an encyclopaedic work on English Costume on the lines and dimensions of Planché's familiar volumes. As a mediaevalist Mr. Beard's chief interest lay in the early centuries with particular attention to armour and heraldry. At his death it appeared that the later centuries had not yet been adequately explored by him. We, on the other hand, unaware of his researches, had started to make a concise reference dictionary of English Costume; and now, invited to incorporate as much of Mr. Beard's material as might be relevant to our design, we have gladly accepted his mediaeval items as authoritative while reluctantly discarding much that lay outside our own plan.

At a rough computation about a sixth of the text of this volume may be attributed to him while for the rest we alone are responsible. In PART I the name of each garment is followed by the date when it came into use (in England) with, in many cases the date when, approximately it ceased to be fashionable; and the sex—M. or F.—which wore it.

PART 2 is a glossary of materials with the dates when they came into use.

C. WILLETT CUNNINGTON
PHILLIS CUNNINGTON

'We are ill informed even of the names of the articles we wear. People come to years of discretion scarce know the difference between a plain Hat and a Lunardi; and I have heard a lady, who I was told had a very good education, mistake a Parachute for a Fitzherbert.'

1786. THE LOUNGER no. 76

A

ABILLEMENTS, HABILLEMENTS
See Billiments.

ACCORDION-PLEATING
C. 1889, on. (F.) A form of close-pleating which enabled the garment to expand its shape on movement, inspiring the fashion for 'skirt-dancing' introduced by Loie Fuller. Also used for sleeves of some day dresses, the pleating ending at the elbow, the fullness gathered into a close long cuff.

ADELAIDE BOOTS
1830's to 1860. (F.) Boots of which the tops were edged with fur or fringe.

ADONIS
18th c. (M.) A long bushy white wig, 'like the twigs of a gooseberry bush in a deep snow' (1734). *The London Magazine*, 'A fine flowing Adonis or white periwig.' (1773, R. Graves, *The Spiritual Quixote.*)

ADONISING
1807. The fashionable expression for 'dressing for dinner'.

AESTHETIC DRESS
1878 to *c.* 1882. (F.) An attempt by a small group of the cultured class to revive in modified form the 'artistic' dress of the 14th c. It took the form of a high-waisted flowing dress with sleeves puffed at the shoulders; of patterned materials in 'indescribable tints'. Satirised by W. S. Gilbert as the 'Greenery-yallery, Grosvenor Gallery' costume and depicted by Du Maurier in *Punch*. The essential feature of its many variations was to appear limp and lank and too, too utterly intense.

Aesthetic Costume

AGGRAFES, AGGRAPES
16th c. on. Hooks and eyes; also clasp or buckle.

19th c. An ornamental clasp or a hook, known as Agrafe.

AGGRAVATORS
C. 1830–50. (M.) 'His hair carefully twisted into the outer corner of each eye till it formed that description of semi-curls usually known as "aggravators".' (1835–6, *Sketches by Boz.*)

AGLETS, AIGLETS, AIGULETS
15th to mid 17th c. (M.) Ornamental metal tags to the ties called 'points', used to join hose to doublet in 15th c. Often of gold or silver or sometimes cut into the shape of little

images; hence the term 'aglet-baby' meant a diminutive person. From 16th c., aglets were used by both sexes as trimming, either as tags to short lengths of ribbon or sewn on in pairs or bunches.

AGNES SOREL BODICE

1861. (F.) For day, the neckline half-high, cut square front and back, with full bishop sleeves.

AGNES SOREL CORSAGE

1851. (F.) Corsage of a pelisse-robe (redingote) in the form of a day jacket with a basque, plain or tabbed; worn closed to the neck or open, showing a waistcoat-front.

AGNES SOREL STYLE

1861. (F.) French term for the English 'Princess' style of dress, the bodice and skirt cut in one without a seam at the waist.

AIGRET, EGRET, AIGRETTE

18th and 19th c's. (F.) An upright plume of feathers or a jewelled ornament in the shape of feathers, worn on the head.

'A bracelet or a well-fancied aigret.' (1772, S. Foote, *The Nabob*.)

Fashionable in the last quarter of the 18th c. and in the 1880's and 1890's when aigrettes were worn on hats for day and also on the evening head-dress.

The favourite feathers (19th c.) were osprey and heron.

AILE DE PIGEON

1750's–1760's. (M.) The pigeon-wing periwig, a toupee with one or two stiff horizontal roll curls projecting above the ears, with the foretop and sides smooth and plain.

ALBERT BOOTS

1840's on. (M.) Side-lacing boots with cloth tops and patent-leather toe-caps; often with 'a close row of little mother-of-pearl buttons down the front; not for any purpose, for the real method of fastening being by the humble lace and tag at the side'.

(1847, Albert Smith, *The Natural History of the Gent.*)

A style which survived until *c*. 1870.

ALBERT COLLAR

C. 1850. (M.) separate stand collar of starched white linen, fastened at the back to a button attached to the shirt.

ALBERT DRIVING-CAPE or SAC

1860. (M.) A very loose form of Chesterfield overcoat, sometimes called simply DRIVING-CAPE or the SAC. The back usually made without a seam down the centre. S-B or D-B. 'Sometimes these coats are cut without a seam under the arms in which case there must of course be a back-seam.' (Minister's *Complete Guide to Practical Cutting*, 3rd ed.)

ALBERT JACKET

C. 1848. (M.) A very short skirted coat, S-B and slightly waisted, with or without a seam at the waist, and with or without side pleats. No breast pocket.

ALBERT OVERCOAT

1877. (M.) A loose overcoat, fly-front fastening; a half-circle cape cut to lie flat on the shoulders. Vertical slit pockets on each breast; flapped pocket on hips. Deep back vent closed by buttons under a fly. Length to mid-calf. Close sleeves with stitched cuffs.

ALBERT RIDING COAT

1841. (M.) S-B. 'The fronts slanted rather like the Newmarket style.' Full skirts with rounded corners. Broad collar, narrow lapels. Pockets on the hips. Buttoned high on the chest.

ALBERT TOP FROCK

1860's to 1900. (M.) An overcoat in the form of a frock coat; velvet collar 3″ deep, short waist, long skirts; flapped pockets on the hips. Collar, lapels and cuffs broader than the ordinary Top Frock and material usually heavy. In 1893 made D-B, very long and close-fitting.

2

ALBERT WATCH-CHAIN

C. 1870, on. (M.) A heavy chain worn across the front of the waistcoat from one pocket to the opposite, the watch at one end, a 'guard' (short rod of the metal) at the other; the chain passed through a button-hole; after c. 1888 through a special 'chain-hole' in the waistcoat.

ALEXANDRA JACKET

1863. (F.) A day jacket with postillions; the back with no centre seam, the front with small revers, and a collar. Sleeves with epaulettes and cuffs.

ALEXANDRA PETTICOAT

1863. (F.) An under-garment of poplin with a broad plaid border above the hem. Day wear.

ALGERIAN BURNOUSE

See BURNOUSE.

ALL-ROUNDER

1854. (M.) A rigid stand-collar attached to the shirt and completely encircling the neck. 'No military stock ever strangled an unfortunate soldier half so cruelly as these all-round collars.' (1854, *Punch*.)

ALMAIN COAT or JACKET

2nd half 15th c. into 16th c. (M.) A short close-fitting jacket with short flared skirts and long pendant sleeves open in the front seams; worn over the doublet.

ALMAIN or GERMAN HOSE

Late 16th c. (M.) Very baggy paned hose with voluminous pullings-out. See PLUDERHOSE.

ALPINE HAT

1890's. (M.) A soft felt hat with low round crown slightly depressed circularly.

ALPINE JACKET

1876. (M.) An 'improved' form of Norfolk jacket, made D-B, with a pleat down the centre of the back skirt; vertical pockets in the side seams, ornamented with side edges. Worn fastened up to the neck, often without a waistcoat under.

AMADIS SLEEVE

1830. (F.) A term denoting a sleeve with a tight cuff at the wrist. Fashionable for day wear in the 1830's; revived in the 1850's when the tightness extended to the elbow and was closed by buttons. To be distinguished from the turned-back cuff-end. *See* MOUSQUETAIRE CUFF.

AMAZON CORSAGE

1842. (F.) A plain high bodice tightly buttoned up to the throat, with a small cambric collar and cuffs; for day wear.

AMAZON CORSET

1850's. (F.) A riding corset with elastic lacings. 'By pulling a concealed cord can be shortened 3" for riding.'

AMERICAN COAT

1829. (M.) 'A new kind of coat called an "American", has very broad collar, narrow lapels, skirt flaps, very long and wide, and is made S-B. It may be in black cloth.'

AMERICAN NECK-CLOTH, YANKEE NECKCLOTH

1818 to 1830's. (M.) A form of Stock with vertical pleatings on each side of the central portion in front; and narrow ends brought forward and tied low down in a small knot called a Gordian Knot.

American Neckcloth and Gordian Knot

AMERICAN SHOULDERS

1875. (M.) The padding inserted in the shoulders of men's coats to produce the effect of 'square' broad shoulders. 'In New York they place the thickest part of the wadding about 2" in front of the shoulder seam.' (*The Tailor & Cutter*.)

AMERICAN TROUSERS

1857 on. (M.) The cloth gathered into a narrow waistband with a strap and buckle behind; worn without braces.

AMERICAN VEST
1860's on. (M.) A waistcoat made S-B, without collar or lapels and buttoned high. Later, known also as the 'French Vest', *q.v.*

ANADEME
Late 16th and early 17th c's. (F.) A fillet or garland of flowers or leaves for the head.

ANDALOUSE CAPE
1846. (F.) An outdoor cape of silk trimmed with broad volants of *crêpe lisse* fringed; the front borders cut straight, the arms being free.

ANDALUSIAN CASAQUE
1809. (F.) A tunic worn with evening dress; fastened down the centre and sloping away to knee-level behind.

ANGEL OVERSKIRT
1894. (F.) Day wear; a short upper-skirt made with two deep points on each side.

ANGEL SLEEVE
1889. (F.) Name applied to long square panels reaching nearly to the ground and covering the arm-holes; attached to some mantles.

ANGLAISE, THE
1840 on. (M.) Term denoting 'the collar and fold of the turnover' of a coat or waistcoat.

ANGLE-FRONTED COAT, UNIVERSITY COAT
1870–80. (M.) A variation of the morning coat fashionable in those years. Instead of the fronts sloping away in a curve from the 2nd button, the fronts were so cut that the gap between them formed an angle exposing much of the waistcoat. The bottoms were cut into obtuse angles instead of being rounded. Usually S-B, occasionally D-B.

ANGLESEA HAT
C. 1830. (M.) Hat with a high cylindrical crown and flat brim.

D-B Angle-fronted Coat, 1870

ANGLO-GREEK BODICE
1820's. (F.) A bodice made with fichu-robings, the lapels broad and wide apart, often edged with lace. For day or evening.

ANGOULÊME BONNET
1814. (F.) Of straw with high crown and broad front brim, tied on one side.

ANKLE-BREECHES
1st half 17th c. (M.) A nickname for SPANISH BREECHES, generally called Spanish hose, *q.v.*

ANKLE-JACKS
Chiefly 1840's. (M.) Short boots fitting round the ankles and laced up in front through eyelets five a side. Much worn in the East End of London.

ANSLET
See HANSLET.

ANTIGROPOLIS
1850's. (M.) A form of high gaiter 'adapted to either walking or riding; generally of leather, similar in shape

4

to the mud boot but fastens at the side by means of a spring. The back part is cut away at the ham and the front is raised to protect the thigh.' (1855, *The Gentleman's Magazine of Fashion.*)

ANTIQUE BODICE
1830's and 1840's. (F.) An evening bodice with a low décolletage and deeply pointed waist.

APOLLO CORSET
C. 1810. (M. and F.) A form of whalebone corset worn by dandies of the period; a rival of the Brummell Bodice and the Cumberland Corset.

Also 'worn by the ladies to make their waists look slender and genteel'. (1813, *Spirit of the Public Journals.*)

APOLLO KNOT
1824 to 1832. (F.) False hair plaited into a loop or loops and wired up to stand erect on the evening or sometimes day coiffure.

Apollo Knot, 1829

APPAREL
A term used from the early 14th c. to denote clothing, in particular a suit of clothes. In the late 14th c. it was also applied to embroidered borders of ecclesiastical garments and to embellishment of harness or armour.

APRON
13th c. on. (M. and F.) Also APORNE and NAPRON, the latter term used in 14th and first half of 15th c's.; subsequently APRON.

(1) MALE APRON: worn by artisans and workmen to protect the front of their clothing; tied at the waist and often cut in one to spread up over the chest. 'Checkered apron men' denoted barbers in 16th c. who wore check-patterned aprons. 'Blue-aproned men' was applied to tradesmen 16th to 18th cs. 'Green-aproned men' applied to London porters, 18th c., and green baize aprons were worn by furniture removers and in auction-rooms, 19th c.

Male Apron, 13th c.

(2) FEMALE APRON: sometimes served to protect the clothing but also much used as a decorative feature. Gathered into a waistband and tied round the waist; some working aprons had an attached bib extending up from the waist to protect the bodice.

Decorative aprons were of fine materials, usually without bibs, and often embroidered; fashionable from end of 16th c. to *c.* 1640 and very fashionable throughout the 18th c.; and again in the 1870's. These latter were very small, of black silk

5

sometimes embroidered in colours and popularly known as 'fig-leaves'.

AQUATIC SHIRT
C. 1830, on. (M.) Early form of 'Sports' shirt for boating; also for country and seaside wear. Of cotton in coloured stripes or checks or in whole colours (red, blue, green). Decorated with sporting designs and popular in 1840's and 1850's with the class known as 'the Gent'.

ARAGONESE BONNET
1834. (F.) Mainly of silk, with arched front brim, and pyramidal crown.

ARMENIAN MANTLE
1847. (F.) A loose pelisse without a cape; the front trimmed with passe-menterie.

ARTIFICIAL CRINOLINE
See CRINOLINE.

ARTOIS BUCKLE
End of 18th c. (M.) The very large decorative shoe buckle fashionable between 1775 and 1788.

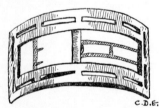

Artois Shoe Buckle, c. *1777*

ASCOT JACKET
1876. (M.) D-B. The skirts rounded off in front at the bottom, and a belt of the same material passing through loops at the sides, drawing in the fullness.

ASCOT TIE
1876 on. (M.) The plain form similar to the OCTAGON (*q.v.*). The 'Puffed Ascot' was puffed out in the centre. Both kinds usually self-tied but some were ready-made up. Of patterned silk.

ASOOCH, ASWASH
17th c. (M.) A term signifying sash-wise or scarf-wise; a garment worn 'asooch' or 'aswash' was draped diagonally across the body instead of hanging normally; a fashionable style for cloaks and sometimes for shamews in 17th c.

ASSASIN or VENEY-A-MOY
Late 17th c. (F.) 'A certain Breast-knot, as much as to say, Come to me, Sir.' (1690, J. Evelyn, *Fop-Dictionary.*)

ATTIRE
15th c. on. (F.) (1) A head-dress of goldsmithry and gems, worn on occasions of state. Later, curtailed to 'Tire'.
(2) Apparel.

AULMONIERE, AUMONIERE, ALMONER, AUMER
Med. A pouch or purse suspended from the girdle and worn by nobles. The first two names are modern pseudo-archaic forms.

AURUM POTABILE
16th and 17th c's. A cosmetic; 'a red dye for the tongue furred by too much indulgence.' 'A blood-red, gummie or honey-like substance.' (1678, Phillips.)

B

BABET BONNET
1838. (F.) A small bonnet of tulle covering the back of the head and descending over the ears. For evening wear.

BABET CAP
1836–1840's. (F.) A morning cap of muslin with a small round caul, the sides descending over the cheeks; trimmed with ribbon.

BABY BODICE
1878 to end of c. (F.) A day bodice with a square neck and vertical pleats down the centre and a large basque extending below the waistband. In 1897 the neck drawn in with threaded ribbons and a wide sash with hanging ends replaced the belt.

BABY CAP
Late 16th and early 17th c's. (F.) Term then used for a fashionable woman's coif of lawn or lace resembling a baby's bonnet.

BACHLICK
1868. (F.) A fichu with a hood-like point behind having a tassel; of cashmere edged with swansdown. Worn over the day dress.

BACK, BAK
14th c. Term then used loosely for any outer garment; in the plural for clothing in general. 'Oure bakkes . . . that moth-etan be. (1377, Langland, *Piers Plowman.*)

BACK BREADTH
19th c. (M.) Tailor's term for the combined width of the two back pieces of a man's coat, at waist level.

BACK PIECE
19th c. (M.) Tailor's term for the part of the back of a coat between the midline seam and the side seam.

BACK STRING
18th c. A child's leading strings attached to the shoulders of the dress.
'Misses at whose age their mother wore
The back-string and the bib.'
(1785, Cowper, *The Task.*)

BAG
(1) Late Mediaeval and 16th c. Term for the girdle pouch.
(2) 16th c. Term sometimes used for the padding of doublets.
(3) 18th c. A wig. *See* BAG-WIG.

BAG BODICE
1883. (F.) A blouse bodice the front of which sagged pouch-like over the waistband. For day wear.

BAG BONNET
Early 19th c. (F.) An outdoor day Capote of which the soft crown loosely covered the back of the head.

BAGGING SHOE
16th and 17th c's. (M.) A loose shoe roughly made for country wear; the term sometimes applied to STARTUPS (*q.v.*).

BAG-IRONS, rarely BAG-RINGS
15th and early 16th c's. (M.) The cross-bar and swivel for suspension of a pouch and the pendant concentric semicircular rings which acted as stiffeners for the pouch-mouth and the covering flap. The bag-irons might also be of bronze, silver or latten and were occasionally engraved with posies or mottoes.

BAGPIPE SLEEVES, POKYS
15th c. (M. and F.) Very wide sleeves deeply pendant from a closed

wrist, and forming a huge hanging pouch, often used as a pocket. These sleeves were peculiar to HOUPPE-LANDES (*q.v.*).

Bagpipe Sleeves (early 15th cent.)

BAG PLASTRON
1884. (F.) A plastron or front panel of a day bodice, the plastron sagging in front and forming a 'bag'. Sometimes worn instead of a waistcoat-front.

BAGS
19th c. (M.) Slang term for trousers. *See* UNMENTIONABLES.

BAG-WAISTCOAT
1883. (F.) A day waistcoat sagging in front to form a pouch.

BAG-WIG or BAG
18th c. (M.) The queue of the wig was enclosed in a square black silk bag drawn in at the nape of the neck with a running string, concealed by a stiff black bow. Worn with 'dress' and 'full dress'.

BAHUT
18th c. A masquerade dress or domino.

Bag Plastron, 1883

BALANDRANA
12th and 13th c's. A wide cloak or mantle worn by travellers.

BALAYEUSE
1870's on. (F.) A frilling of stiff white muslin protecting the inner surface of the hem of a skirt.

BALDRICK
13th c. to 1700. (M.) A belt worn diagonally across the chest or sometimes across the abdomen for suspending the sword, dagger, bugle, horn or pouch. In the 16th c. the bugle baldrick was called the 'Corse'. In the 17th c. the term 'shoulder-belt' was used; it suspended a rapier.

BALLET-SKIRT
1883. (F.) For evening dress, a skirt of tulle composed of three or four skirts diminishing from below upwards and mounted on a silk or satin foundation; the uppermost skirt spotted with stars, pearls or beetle-wings. Worn with a velvet, plush or satin bodice.

8

BALLOON HAT, LUNARDI, PARACHUTE HAT

1783–5. (F.) A hat with a large ballooned crown and wide brim, made of gauze or sarcenet over a wire or chip foundation. Very fashionable in those years as a compliment to Lunardi and his balloon.

Balloon or Lunardi Hat, c. 1787

BALL-ROOM NECKCLOTH

1830's. (M.) A white starched neckcloth, the ends crossing in front in broad folds and secured to the braces. A brilliant brooch or pin in the centre held the neckcloth in place.

BALMORAL BODICE

1867. (F.) The name then given to the postillion corsage with two short basques falling over the upper part of the back of the day skirt.

BALMORAL BOOT

Late 1850's to 1870's. (F.) A short black boot lacing up the front often with coloured laces and generally worn with country or walking dress.

BALMORAL CLOAK

1852. (F.) A short sleeveless cloak with a narrow hood. The name given in the year that Queen Victoria bought Balmoral Castle.

BALMORAL JACKET

(1) 1867. (F.) A jacket simulating a waistcoat with pointed fronts and long pointed ends behind; buttoned up to the throat. For day wear.

(2) 1870. (F.) Tailor-made version: 'Resembles the Riding Habit but not made to fit so close; the back cut without a centre seam; side bodies added; D-B foreparts with lapels. The fronts rounded off; pocket flaps on the front of the skirts of the jacket. Sleeves with small gauntlet cuffs. Band or belt round the waist.' (*The Tailor & Cutter.*)

BALMORAL MANTLE

1866. (F.) Made like an Inverness Cape, of velvet, cashmere, or cloth; for outdoor wear.

BAND

16th and 17th c's. (M. and F.) A white collar, the word being transferred from the shirt-band to a separate collar. A 'falling-band' or 'fall' was a turned-down collar whether raised or flat. A 'standing-band' was an upright collar without a turnover. 'Short bands' were a pair of short narrow pendants of white linen worn by ministers of religion, barristers and collegians. After *c.* 1850 gradually discarded by High Church clergy and later by all Church of England clergy but still used by Evangelicals and Nonconformist ministers to the end of the 19th c.

BANDANA HANDKERCHIEF

18th and 19th c's. (M.) Originally of silk, later of cotton having a dark ground commonly of Turkey red or blue with little white or yellow spots. Imported from India and used, in 18th c., for neckcloths; later as snuff-handkerchiefs.

BAND-BOX

16th and 17th c's. A box in which collars and ruffs were kept.

BANDELET

16th c. 'Any sort of scarf.' (1598, Florio.)

BANDORE and PEAK

1700–*c.* 1730. (F.) A widow's headdress, a black bonnet curving to a point over the forehead; worn with a black veil flowing behind.

BAND-STRINGS

16th and 17th c's. (M. and F.) Tasselled ties to fasten bands or ruffs in front; sometimes several pairs were used. 'Snake-bone' band-strings were woven to resemble the backbone of a snake. (17th c.)

BANG

1880's. (F.) An Americanism for the hair cut in a straight fringe across the forehead.

BANGING CHIGNON

1770's. (F.) A wide flat loop of hair dressed to hang from the top down to the nape of the neck; sometimes tied round with ribbon.

BANIAN, BANYAN, BANJAN, INDIAN NIGHTGOWN. (M.)

2nd half of 17th c. to early 19th c. A loose-skirted coat, knee-length, with a short back vent and fastened by a clasp or buttoned or hooked down the front; sleeves close and slit. Worn domestically and in 1780's often out of doors, when it was very fashionable and of costly materials. In the early 19th c. it had become a superior kind of dressing-gown, made without a back vent but with a Banyan pleat and ankle-length.

Banyan, c. 1800

BANYAN PLEAT

19th c. (M.) Tailor's term for a back-pleat made with a tackover but without a back vent.

BARBE

14th to late 16th c. (F.) A long piece of vertically pleated linen encircling the chin and falling to the bosom; worn with a black hood and pendant veil behind. The head-dress of widows and mourners. The barbe covered the chin with ladies of high rank; by all other gentlewomen it was worn with the chin exposed.

Barbe (Widow's), 1519

BARBETTE

13th and 1st half of 14th c. (F.) A French term for the wimple and also for the linen band worn under the chin and pinned on the top or sides of the head; usually worn with a white fillet.

BARCELONA HANDKERCHIEF

18th and 19th c's. Of soft twilled silk often coloured but usually black; used as a neckerchief. 'A Barcelona black and tight' pinned round the neck. (Peter Pindar.)

But also used as a handkerchief: 'Barcelona silk snuff-handkerchiefs'. (1734, Essex Record Office, Inventory.)

BARME CLOTH, BARMHATRE

Early Med. An apron; a term used to end of 14th c. and then gradually replaced by APRON.

BARMFELL, BARMSKIN

14th to 17th c. A leather apron.

BAROUCHE COAT

1809. (F.) A ¾-length close-fitting outdoor coat, with round bosom and full sleeves; fastened down the front with barrel-snaps and a buckled girdle round the waist.

BARREL HOSE

1570 to 1620. (M.) Breeches voluminous throughout; after 1610 heavily pleated or gathered from top to bottom. (Certain Cambridge students) 'waring greate Galligaskins and Barreld hooese stuffed with horse tayles, with Skabilonians and knitt netherstockes too fine for schollers'. (1570, MS. in Corpus Christi College, Cambridge.)

BARREL-SNAPS

1800 to 1830. Tubular snap-fastenings of gilt metal; fashionable for cloaks and pelisses.

BARROW

19th c. A baby's flannel wrapped round the body and turned up over the feet.

BASE COAT

C. 1490 to 1540. (M.) A jacket or jerkin with deep skirts called 'bases' hanging in tubular pleats to just above the knees; neck square; sleeves short. The Half-base coat was a military garment.

Base Coat (Worn under Gown), 1544

BASES

C. 1490 to 1540. (M.) The tubular pleated skirts of jacket or jerkin; sometimes separate items especially when worn with armour.

BASE SOCKS

16th c. (M.) Under-socks.

BASKET

2nd half 16th c. (F.) A tall wickerwork hat. 'Their maried Women weare on their heades fine wickre Basquettes of a foot and a half long.' (1555, *Fardle of Facions*.)

BASKET BUTTONS

18th and 19th c's. Buttons covered with an interlacing pattern or a metal imitation thereof; especially fashionable on men's coats in 18th c.

BASQUE

19th c. (F.) Fashionable term for an extension of the corsage below the waist.

BASQUE-HABIT

1860's on. (F.) A corsage with square-cut basques.

BASQUE-WAISTBAND

1867 on. (F.) A waistband with five vandyked tabs; for afternoon dress style.

BASQUIN-BODY

1850's. (F.) A day bodice with basques sometimes cut in one piece with the bodice.

BASQUINE, BASQUIN

(1) 1857. (F.) A coat with deep basques, fringed trimming, a bertha and pagoda sleeves.

(2) 1860's. A new name for the outdoor jacket then worn.

BAST HAT

17th c. A hat made of plaited bast or bass, the inner bark of the lime or linden. 'Bast or Straw-Hats both knotted and plain.' (1670–5, *Book of Rates*.)

BATHING COSTUME

(1) MALE. Voluminous flannel gowns, spoken of as 'flannels', were worn at

public baths (e.g. at Bath) in 18th and early 19th c's. But for seaside bathing nothing was worn by men until *c.* 1870 when brief triangular trunks became the mode.

(2) FEMALE. Until 1865 a loose flannel gown, ankle-length, with sleeves. In that year 'the Zouave Marine Swimming Costume' with 'body and trousers cut in one', of stout brown holland or dark-blue serge, came into vogue. In 1868 an attached knee-length skirt was added; in 1878 the skirt was shorter and a separate item. By 1880 the garment became combinations often of stockinette, knee-length, sleeveless, with short detachable skirt. Torchon lace trimming was often added.

BATSWING TIE
1896. (M.) A bow-tie, the ends shaped to resemble bats' wings; for day wear.

BATTENBURG JACKET
1880's. (F.) An outdoor short jacket with loose fronts, large buttons and a turned-down collar.

BATTS
17th c. Heavy low shoes laced in front; for country wear.

BAVARETTE
17th c. 'A bib, mocet or mocheter to put before the bosom of a child.' (1611, Cotgrave.)

BAVARIAN DRESS STYLE
1826. (F.) A carriage dress decorated with rows of bands down the front.

BAVARIAN PELISSE-ROBE
1826. (F.) A pelisse-robe with two lines of trimming descending from the shoulders to the bottom of the skirt *en tablier*.

BAVAROY, BEVEROY
Early 18th c. (M.) A coat the exact nature of which is unknown. 'A sandy colour Beveroy broadcloth coat.' (1711, *London Gazette*.)

BAVOLET
1830 on. (F.) The 'curtain' at the back of a bonnet shading the neck.

BAYADERE TRIMMING
1850's. (F.) Flat trimming of velvet woven in or sewn on to the dress material.

BEARD
(1) Although the beard was worn by men at various periods previously, it was from the mid-16th to the mid-17th c. that it acquired a peculiar social significance; in that hundred years there were over fifty named cuts of beard in fashion. The traveller returning from 'foreign lands' would sport a style of beard indicating the country he had visited; his beard might reveal his social rank or occupation, or express 'every man in his humour'. The following are the more important styles:

(1) CADIZ BEARD. Sometimes called CADS BEARD. From the Expedition to Cadiz in 1596. A large and disordered growth. 'His face, Furr'd with Cads-beard.' (1598, E. Guilpin, *Skialetheia.*)

(2) GOAT BEARD. 'How, Sir, will you be trimmed? Your moustachios sharp at the ends like a shoemaker's awls, or hanging down to your mouth like goat's flakes?' (1591, J. Lyly, *Midas.*)

(3) PEAK. A common name for the beard, exclusive of the moustache. The beard cut to a point and often starched. 'Some spruce yonker with a starcht beard and his whiskers turned up.' (1623, J. Mabbe, *The Rogue.*)

(4) PENCIL BEARD. A slight tuft of hair on the point of the chin. 'Sir, you with the pencil on your chin.' (1599, Ben Jonson, *Cynthia's Revels.*)

(5) PICK-A-DEVANT, OR BARBULA. So called 'when it ends in a point under the chin and on the higher lip, chin, and cheeks'. (1688, R. Holme, *Armourie.*)

(6) PISA BEARD. Synonymous with STILETTO BEARD. 'Play with your Pisa beard! Why, where's your

Pickdevant, 1588

Spade, 1561

brush, pupil?' (1618, Fletcher, *Queen of Corinth.*)

(7) ROMAN T BEARD, also called HAMMER CUT. 1618 to 1650. A straight tuft under the lower lip, forming the 'handle', the waxed moustache horizontal forming the cross-piece of the hammer or T.

Square Cut, 1571

(10) MARQUISETTO. 1570's. Cut close to the chin.

(11) STILETTO BEARD. 1610–40. 'Some sharpe steletto fashion, dagger like.' (1621, J. Taylor, *Superbiae Flagellum.*)

(12) SWALLOW'S TAIL BEARD. 1560 to 1600. A version of the forked but with the ends longer and more widely spread.

Roman T, 1620–5

(8) ROUND BEARD, or BUSH BEARD. 'Some made round like a rubbing brush.' (1587, Harrison's *England.*)

(9) SPADE BEARD. 1570 to 1605. The shape of a pioneer's spade (that of an ace of spades on a playing card), broad above with curved sides to a point below. Thought to give a martial appearance and favoured by soldiers. '. . . whether he will have his peake cut broade pendant like a spade, to be terrible like a warrior?' (1592, R. Greene, *Quip for an Upstart Courtier.*) 'His spade peake is as sharpe as if he had been a Pioneer.' (1592, T. Nashe, *Piers Pennilesse.*) Beards 'Some like a spade, some like a fork, some square'. (1621, J. Taylor, *Superbiae Flagellum.*)

BEARD-BRUSH

1st half 17th c. (M.) A small brush for the beard; very popular and used in public.

BEARD-COMB

1st half 17th c. (M.) A small comb for the beard; uncommon.

BEARER

(1) 17th c. (M.) Stiffening for boot-hose tops. '. . . a paire of bearers for my toppes.' (1656, Sir M. Stapleton's *Household Books.*)

(2) 2nd half 17th and early 18th c's. (F.) Padded rolls acting as bustles, worn 'under the skirts of gowns at their setting on at the bodies, which raise up the skirt at that place to what breadth the wearer pleaseth

and as the fashion is'. (1688, R. Holme, *Armourie*.)

(3) 19th c. (M.) A band buttoned across the inside of the top of breeches or trousers which were made with falls. The bearer, placed behind the ralls flap, was deeper at the sides than in the centre where the two parts were buttoned together; rising a couple of inches above the top of the flap.

(*a*) BILSTON BEARER. The bearer band of the breeches cut extra wide to give more abdominal support; a type used by labourers.

(*b*) FRENCH BEARER. The bearer band cut very narrow.

BEARING CLOTH
17th and 18th c's. The mantle or cloth used to cover an infant when carried to baptism. 'For 5 yeard of dameske to mak a bearing cloth £3 : 6 : 6.' (1623, Lord William Howard of Naworth, *Household Books*.)

BEAU
C. 1680 to mid 19th c. (M.) A gentleman very particular as to his dress; not necessarily as effeminate as a Fop.

BEAUFORT COAT
1880. (M.) Also known as JUMPER COAT, a lounge jacket, 4 button, and closing high; seams raised or double-stitched; narrow straight sleeves.

BEAVER, BEAVER HAT
14th c. on. (M. and F.) A hat originally made of beaver skin but from 16th c. of felted beaver fur wool. In 19th c. 'the bodies of beaver hats are made of a firm felt wrought up of fine wool, rabbits' hair etc. . . . over this is placed the nap prepared from the hair of the beaver'. (1862, Mayhew, *London Labour and the London Poor*.)

BEBE BONNET
1877. (F.) A very small outdoor bonnet, the border turned up to show a cap; trimming of tulle, ribbons and flowers.

BECK
Late 15th and early 16th c's. (F.) A beak-shaped accessory to a mourning hood.

BEDGOWN
18th c. (M. and F.) A loose-sleeved dressing-gown, worn only as négligée in the bedroom or for comfort.
'Why must the wrapping bed-gown hide
Your snowy bosom's swelling pride?'
(*c*. 1744, Edward Moore.)

BEEHIVE HAT, HIVE BONNET
1770's and 1780's. (F.) A hat with a tall rounded crown, beehive-shaped, and a narrow brim.

BELCHER, BELCHER HANDKER-CHIEF
1st half 19th c. (M.) A blue neckerchief with large white spots, each with a dark-blue 'eye'; as worn by the pugilist of that name.

BELETTE, BILETT
1300 to mid 16th c. A jewel or ornament.

BELL
Late 13th into 15th c. (M. and F.) A travelling cloak with a circular cut; some hooded, some buttoned at the neck and sometimes made with side vents and back vent.

BELL HOOP, CUPOLA COAT
1710 to 1780. (F.) An under-petticoat distended with whalebone hoops to the shape of a bell.

BELLIED DOUBLET
See LONG-BELLIED DOUBLET.

BELLOWS POCKET
Late 19th c. (M.) A patch-pocket with side folds capable of expanding or lying flat, like a bellows. Common in Norfolk jackets from 1890 on.

BELL SKIRT
1891. (F.) A gored skirt, the front breadth made to the shape with darts. The foot of the skirt stiffened with muslin lining or, for walking, lined throughout. The skirt sometimes buttoned up on each side

14

instead of having a placket hole behind. Commonly tailor-made.

BELL SLEEVE
2nd half 19th c. (F.) Close-fitting to mid-forearm and there expanding into a bell-shaped opening.

BELLY-CHETE
16th c. Slang for Apron.

BELLY-PIECE
C. 1620 to 1660's. (M.) A triangular stiffening of pasteboard or whalebone and buckram sewn into the lining of the doublet in front, on each side of the opening at waist-level, with the base of the triangle placed vertically along the front border; thus forming a corset-like ridge down the belly.

BELOW
See FURBELOW.

BELT
Military Belt of Knightly Girdle (q.v.).
Shoulder Belt or Baldrick (q.v.).
Waistbelt: a strip of leather or material to confine or support clothes or weapons.

BEND
C. A.D. 1000 to end of 15th c. Primarily a band of material worn in association with dress. Special uses:
(1) A fillet or other circular ornament worn on the head or as a hat-band. 'My bende for an hat of black sylk and silver.' (1463, Bury Wills.)
(2) Synonym for a stripe.

BENDEL
15th c. Not identified. 'She wyped it . . . with a bendel of sylk.' (1483, Caxton, Golden Legend.)

BENDIGO
19th c. (M.) A rough fur cap worn by the working classes.

BENJAMIN
19th c. (M.) A loose overcoat worn by the working classes.

BENJY
19th c. (M.) Slang term for a waistcoat.

BENOITON CHAINS
1866. (F.) Chains of metal or jet hanging from the head over the chignon to the bosom; so named from Sardou's play, La Famille Benoîton, of that year.

BENTS
Late 16th and early 17th c's. Strips of whalebone or rushes used to distend bum rolls or farthingales. 'Their bents of whalebone to beare out their bummes.' (1588, W. Averell, Combat Contrar . . .')

BERET
1820's, 1830's and 1840's. (F.) A cap with a large flat halo crown extensively trimmed. Usually of velvet; worn with evening dress.

Beret, 1826

BERET HAT
1872. (F.) An outdoor hat of white chip, shaped like a small mob cap, trimmed with roses and pendant ribbons behind.

BERET SLEEVE
1829. (F.) An evening dress shoulder sleeve, short, circular and widely distended so as to resemble a beret head-dress. It was closed by a band round the arm, and the shape sustained by a stiff lining of book muslin. Occasionally the beret was double, one above the other.

BERGER
17th c. (F.) A lock of hair. 'A small lock (à la Shepherdess) turned up with a puff.' (1690, J. Evelyn, Mundus Muliebris.)

15

Beret Sleeves, 1834

BERGÈRE HAT, MILKMAID HAT.
1730 to 1800, and in 1860's. (F.) A large straw hat with flexible brim and low crown.

Bergère Hat, 1750–60

BERLIN GLOVES
1830 on. (M.) 'Made of a kind of strong cotton which should be very thin and neat.' Washable. Worn by the lower middle class.

BERMUDA HAT
1st half 18th c. (F.) Of straw for country wear. 'Women's Hatts made

of fine Bermuda Platt.' (1727, *New England Weekly Journal.*)

BERNHARDT MANTLE
1886. (F.) A short outdoor cape, the back shaped, the front loose, and having a turned-down collar and sling sleeves.

BERTHA
From 1839 on. (F.) A deep fall of lace or silk encircling the neck and shoulders or merely the shoulders, in a low decolletage; a Victorian 'revival' of the mid 17th c. fashion.

Bertha, 1853

BERTHA-PELERINE
1840's. (F.) A bertha carried down the centre front to the waist; worn with evening dress.

BETEN
Med. Embroidered with fancy subjects.

BEWDLEY CAP
1570 to *c.* 1825. (M.) A MONMOUTH CAP (*q.v.*) made at Bewdley, Worcs., and used by country-folk as late as 19th c.

BIAS, BYESSE
Med. A term used from 15th c. on for material cut on the cross, a method used for the early kind of hose in order to obtain a close fit. 'Hozen knitte at ye knees and lyned within with Lynnen cloth *byesse* as the hose is.' (1434, John Hyll's *Traytese upon Worship in Armes.*)

BIB

From 16th c. A small square of linen hung in front of a child's neck to protect the clothes from being soiled.

BIB-APRON

17th c. on. An apron with a bib extension.

BIB-CRAVAT

End of 17th c. (M.) A broad bib-like cravat usually edged with lace; secured at the neck by a cravat-string or knot, of ribbon usually coloured.

BIBI BONNET

1831 to 1836. (F.) Also known as ENGLISH COTTAGE BONNET. A bonnet of which the sides projected forward with an upward tilt.

BIBI CAPOTE

1830's. (F.) Name applied to any capote with a projecting brim in front, sloping down to a small crown at the back of the head and shaped like a baby's bonnet.

BIGGIN, BIGGON

(1) 16th and 17th c's. A term used in Scotland as early as 1329, for a child's cap shaped like a coif.

(2) 2nd half 16th and 17th c's. (M.) A man's night-cap worn in bed.

(3) Early 19th c. (F.) A large form of mob cap worn without ties under the chin.

BIGOTE

17th c. A moustache (rare).

BILBOQUETS

See ROULETTES.

BILLIMENT, BILLMENT, HABIL-LEMENT, ABILLEMENT

16th c. (F.) (1) The decorated border to a French hood. The Upper Billiment adorned the crown, the Nether Billiment the front of the bonnet. 'Upper and nether habil-ments of goldsmith's work for the French hood.' (1541, Letters and Papers of Henry VIII.)

(2) A head ornament popular with brides.

D.C.—2

BILLYCOCK

19th c. (M.) A colloquial term for a low-crowned flexible felt hat with wide curving brim. Two explana-tions of the name have been offered:

(1) Derived from the 'bully-cocked' hat of 18th c.

(2) 'First used by Billy Coke [Mr. William Coke] at the great shooting parties at Holkham.' (Dr. Cobham Brewer, 1894.)

But see BULLY-COCKED for quota-tion of 1721.

BILSTON BEARER

See BEARER.

BINDING CLOTH

17th c. (F.) A rare synonym for FOREHEAD CLOTH (*q.v.*). 'When shall I have my binding cloth for my forehead? Shall I have no forehead cloth?' (1605, Peter Erondell, *French Garden.*)

BIRLET, BURLET, BOURRELET

15th c. (M.) A circular padded roll as worn with chaperons.

BIRTHDAY SUIT

18th c. (M.) A Court suit for wear-ing on a Royal birthday.

BISHOP SLEEVE

19th c. (F.) A day sleeve in light materials, very full from the shoulder to wrist where it was gathered into a closed cuff. Worn from 2nd decade off and on to end of century. In 1850's the 'full bishop' was very large; in the 1890's the 'small bishop' was preferred and popular for blouses.

BIVOUAC MANTLE

1814. (F.) A large loose mantle descending nearly to the feet and having a high collar; made of scarlet cloth wadded and lined with ermine.

BLACKING

16th c. on. A composition containing lamp-black and oil, applied to the surface of shoes and boots. 'Shoes that stink of blacking.' (1611, Middle-ton, *The Roaring Girl.*)

17

BLACKS

Med. to end of 18th c. (M. and F.) Mourning apparel for both sexes. In the Middle Ages only the cloak had to be black, the rest might be coloured. From the end of 15th c. all surface garments were black.

BLACK-WORK

1530's to 1630's. Embroidery in black silk, generally on linen; often worked in an all-over pattern in continuous scrolling. Very popular for collars, wristbands, smocks and handkerchiefs.

Black-Work, 1589

BLANCHET

12th to 14th c. BLANCH, 17th c. BLANC, 18th c. Terms denoting white paint or powder used as cosmetic for the skin.

BLAZER

C. 1890. (M.) Originally a scarlet jacket worn with cricketing or boating costume; later applied to any brightly striped jacket similarly worn.

BLIAUT, BLIAUNT, BLEHANT, BLEHAND

12th to early 14th c. (M. and F.)
(1) A loose ankle-length super-tunic, usually having wide sleeves.
(2) A costly material.

BLISTERED

Late 16th and early 17th c's. Synonymous with 'slashed', a form of decoration.

BLOOMERS

(1) Name applied to those young ladies who dared to imitate Mrs. Amelia Bloomer (1851) in wearing a modified form of trousers. 'A young lady of a certain age—an ardent Bloomer.' (1853, Surtees, *Mr. Sponge's Sporting Tour.*)

(2) 1890. Name given to the baggy knickerbockers worn by some women cyclists.

Bloomers, 1890

BLOUSE

2nd half 19th c. (F.) A loose separate bodice of different material from the skirt, always worn with a belt, and with or without a jacket over it. An early form was the GARIBALDI SHIRT (1863, *q.v.*). Usually for day wear but in 1895 evening blouses were introduced.

BLOUSE-BODICE

1877. (F.) A day bodice in blouse form, falling over the hips and worn with a belt.

BLOUSE DRESS

1870's. (M.) For boys; a loose sac-like blouse worn outside the trousers and confined round the

18

waist by a belt. A vertical pleat down each side of the front.

Blouse Dress (Boys)

BLUCHERS
C. 1820 to 1850. (M.) Half-boots, close-fitting and laced up in front over a tongue; having six eyelet holes on each side.

BLUE BILLY
C. 1800 to 1820. (M.) A blue neck-cloth with white spots, as worn by the pugilist William Mace.

BLUE COAT
End of 16th to end of 17th c. (M.) A coat of blue worn by apprentices and serving men, and therefore a colour avoided by gentlemen.

BOAS
19th c. (F.) Long round tippets, called by the French 'Boas' (1829) but worn all through the century; specially fashionable in the 1890's. Made of swansdown, feathers or fur.

BOATER
19th c. (M.) A stiff straw hat with moderately deep flat-topped crown and straight narrow brim with hat-band of petersham ribbon. The Henley Boater (1894) was a blue or drab felt hat of similar shape.

BOB, BOB-WIG
18th c. (M.) A wig without a queue. The Long Bob covered the back of the neck; the Short Bob ended above the neck. Always an 'undress' wig.

Bob-Wigs. Long Bob, 18th c.

Bob-Wigs. Short Bob, 18th c.

BODICE
19th c. (F.) The upper part of a woman's dress. Many named varieties:

(1) *En Blouse.* (1822.) The front gathered and pouched; the neck half high and round.

(2) *En Cœur.* (1820's on.) The front heart-shaped descending to a slight point in front and having a number of narrow pleats along the upper edge of a low neck.

(3) *à l'Edith.* A variation of the Roxalane and Sévigné.

(4) *à l'Enfant.* (1820's.) The neck half high and round, gathered by a draw-string.

(5) *en Gerbe.* The front folds pleated fan-wise from the shoulders.

(6) *à la Polonese.* (1828 on.) A

19

cross-over front, the folds crossing high up.

(7) *à la Roxalane*. (1829 on.) Similar to the Sévigné, the pleats across the top, sloping down towards the central vertical bone of the bodice.

(8) *à la Sévigné*. The bodice with pleated folds crossing the bosom nearly horizontally, divided by a central bone in the lining, down to the waist.

BODIES, PAIR OF

17th c. (M. and F.) An under-bodice stiffened with whalebone, wood or steel, and sometimes padded; corresponding to a pair of stays.

BODKIN

16th, 17th and 18th c's. (F.) A long pin used for dressing ladies' hair.

BODKIN-BEARD

1520 to early 17th c. A long pointed beard decorating the centre of the chin only.

BODY

15th to 17th c. (F.) A term denoting the bodice; Fore-body was the front portion of the bodice.

BODY COAT

19th c. (M.) Tailoring term to distinguish the upper garment of a suit from the outdoor 'overcoat' or 'top coat'.

BOISSON

1780's. (F.) A short cloak with a hood. 'Small boissongs, craped with a small handkerchief and hood, made very narrow round the shoulders', for half-dress. (1782, *The Lady's Magazine*.)

BOLERO

1853 on. (F.) A loose-fitting jacket with basques cut in points and fringed. (From the Spanish, inspired by the Empress Eugénie.) Revived in the 1890's and then made very short without basques, the fronts curved away just above waist-level. Some with narrow revers peaked up over the shoulders. With or without sleeves.

BOLERO BODICE

1896. (F.) A day bodice trimmed to simulate the wearing of a bolero rounded in front.

BOLERO COAT or JACKET

1890's. (F.) A short jacket, worn open over a blouse.

Bolero Coat, 1892

BOLERO MANTLE

1899. (F.) A short mantle with bolero-shaped fronts.

BOLERO TOQUE

1887. (F.) A small toque of velvet, dress material or astrakhan or fur, with back trimming rising over the crown.

BOLLINGER

1858 to 1860's. (M.) 'THE HEMI-SPHERICAL HAT' (*q.v.*) with bowl-shaped crown and narrow circular brim. A knob on the centre of the crown. Originally worn by cab-drivers, becoming adopted by gentlemen for country wear.

BOLSTER

15th to 17th c. Term denoting a pad

inserted into a garment to produce the required shape.

BOMBAST
16th and 17th c's. (M. and F.) Padding used to distend garments, especially trunk-hose and sleeves; using horsehair, flock, wool, rags, flax, bran and cotton.

BONGRACE
16th and early 17th c's. (F.) (1) As a separate article it was a flat, stiffened oblong head covering projecting over the forehead in front and falling down over the back of the head to the shoulders. It could be worn alone or over a coif.

(2) As part of the French hood, it was the pendant flap behind, which was turned up over the crown and fixed so as to project forward above the forehead. '(My face) was spoiled for want of a bongrace when I was young.' (1612, Beaumont and Fletcher, *The Captain.*)

Bongrace, 1530

BONNET
Med. and on. (M. and F.) A term loosely used for any small head-covering. 19th c. (F.) Usually implied a form of hat of which the brim at the back was absent or greatly diminished; generally tied by ribbon-strings under the chin.

BOOT CUFF
1727 to c. 1740. (M.) A very deep, closed, turned-back cuff to a man's coat. The cuff frequently reached the bend of the elbow. The term 'Boot sleeve' was applied to one with a boot-cuff. 'These boot-sleeves were certainly intended to be the receivers of stolen goods.' (1733, H. Fielding, *The Miser.*)

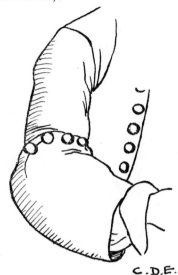

Boot Cuff, 1730

BOOT GARTERS
18th c. (M.) Straps fixed to the back of a riding boot and then passed round the leg above the knee, over the breeches, to keep the boot in position.

BOOT HOSE
2nd half of 15th to 18th c. (M., rarely F.) Stockings worn inside boots to protect the more elegant under-stockings from wear and dirt. Usually of coarse material but in the late 16th and early 17th c's. some were very fine. 'They have also boot-hose to be wondered at; for they be of the finest cloth that may be got.' (1583, Stubbes, *Anatomie of Abuses.*)

In 18th c. they were called 'Boot stockings'.

BOOT HOSE TOPS, or TOPS
16th and 17th c's. (M.) A decorated upper border to boot-hose; the tops might be of thread lace or gold or

silver lace, ruffled linen, or fringed with silk. 'For a quarter of an ounce of gold lace to laye on the toppes of those boot-hose.' (1590, Petre Accts., Essex Record Office.)

Boot Hose Tops, c. 1635

BOOTIKIN
18th c. (M.) A soft boot worn by sufferers from gout.

BOOT JACK
18th and 19th c's. (M.) An implement of wood or iron to hold the boot while the wearer withdraws his foot, an office previously performed by a servant. Used chiefly for removing any form of high boot.

BOOTS
From early Anglo-Saxon on. (M. and F.) Footwear of leather or stout material extending up beyond the ankles; many varieties of height and style. In 15th c. 'Single boots' indicated unlined as opposed to lined boots.

BOOT SLEEVE
See Boot Cuff.

BOOT STOCKING
See Boot Hose.

BOPEEPER
17th c. A mask.

BORDERS
16th c. (F.) Another name for the Billiments, upper and nether, of the French hood; often costly. 'To my Ladie Scudamore a pair of Borders of Golde of the beste, to mrs. Goringe a paire of Borders with pearle . . .' (1594, Will of Lady Dacre, Essex Record Office.)

BOREL
14th c. Clothing.

BOSOM BOTTLES
2nd half 18th c. (F.) Small vessels of tin or glass holding water and worn by ladies to keep their bouquets fresh. 'Bosom Bottles, pear-shaped, flat, 4 inches long, of ribbed glass for bouquets.' (1770, *Boston Evening Post*.)

BOSOM FLOWERS
18th c. (F., also M.) Artificial nosegays worn by women in full dress; also by Macaronies in day dress.

BOSOM FRIENDS
Late 18th and early 19th c's. (F.) Chest protectors, of wool, flannel or fur, which also served as bust-improvers. 'The fashionable belles have provided themselves with *bosom friends* for the winter. Their province is to protect that delicate region from assault of every kind; and they may be had at all the furriers shops in town. A modern lady, with her feet in a *fur-basket*, and her *bosom-friend*, is as impregnable as the Rock of Gibraltar.' (Dec. 26, 1789, *Norfolk Chronicle*.) 'Some persons do not hollow out bosom friends but knit them square or oblong.' (1838, *Workwoman's Guide*.)

BOSOM KNOT
Synonymous with Breast-Knot, *q.v.*

BOSSES
Late 13th to end of 14th c. (F.) Decorative cauls of net-work or linen covering thick coils of plaited hair, generally artificially enlarged and arranged on each side of the head above the temples. Usually worn with a veil (coverchief). *See* Templers.

Bosses, c. 1340

BOTEWS
15th c. (M.) Buskins.

BOTTINE
16th c. (F.) A knee-high riding boot. 'Ryding botines lyned with cloth.' (1503, List of boots and shoes for the Queen of Scots.)

BOUFFANT
19th c. Term denoting a puffed-out part of a dress.

BOUFFANT MÉCANIQUE
1828. (F.) A spring attached to the top of the corset and projecting into the top of the sleeve to distend it.

BOUFFANTE SLEEVE
19th c. (F.) A term used for named varieties throughout the 19th c. A puffed-out shoulder sleeve for evening wear, puffed out to the elbow for day wear.

BOUILLON
19th c. (F.) A puffed-out applied trimming.

BOURBON LOCK
A LOVE LOCK, *q.v.*

BOURGOGNE, BURGUNDY
Late 17th c. (F.) A lady's cap, the form unidentified.

BOURRELET, BURLET
15th c. (M.) (1) A circular padded roll worn as a head-dress or as the base of one, as in the roll of the Chaperon.
(2) 19th c. (F.) A pad inserted into a dress.

BOURSE, BURSE
C. 1440 to 18th c. (1) A large purse or bag. The form 'bourse' was usual until mid 18th c. when 'burse' became commoner.
(2) 18th c. The black silk bag of a bag-wig, a French term seldom used.

BOWDY, BOW-DYE
17th c. Scarlet; from the dye-house at Bow, established in 1643.

BOWLER
C. 1860 on. (M.) A hard felt hat with domed crown and narrow brim rolled up at the sides. The name derived from a hatter, William Bowler, *c.* 1850–60, but the shape was much older, being worn in the 1820's. Usually black but brown and fawn were worn with Norfolk jackets (1883).

Bowler Hat, 1896

BOW TIE
19th c. (M.) A necktie worn with a bow in front, having a great many named varieties, some ready made up.

BOX BOTTOMS
19th c. (M.) The close-fitting extensions of breeches fastened below the knees and there stiffened with lining.

BOX COAT
End of 18th to end of 19th c. (M.) A heavy caped overcoat, the capes often multiple, worn by coachmen, travellers and those riding outside the coach.

BOXES
17th c. (M.) Galloshes. '. . . walk the streets with a dainty pair of Boxes neatly buckl'd on.' (1676, Sir G. Etherege, *The Man of Mode.*)

BRACES, GALLOWSES
From *c.* 1787 on. (M.) The term 'gallowses' survived among country-folk to mid 19th c., while the American term was 'Suspenders'. Braces

23

Box Coat, 1812

having been in Saxon times an outer garment, became concealed by the Norman tunic (mid 12th c.) and so converted into an under-garment. The legs were wide, loose and short, and the garment was pulled in by the braie-girdle, a running string which emerged at intervals from the deep hem at the waist. By mid 13th c. the legs were tied at the knees with strings. By the 15th c. braies had shrunk to mere loin-cloths, and by 1500 they resembled shorts

Braies (12th c.)

at first consisted of a pair of straps, often of morocco leather, passing over the shoulders and attached to a single button on each side in front and behind, to support the breeches or trousers. From 1825 a double-tongued pattern to attach to two buttons on each side in front, began to be used. Fancy designs in embroidered braces became fashionable. By 1850 the two straps were united at the point where they crossed under the shoulder blades and indiarubber braces came in. By 1860 'the plain elastic web with double sliding ends' had become the conventional mode.

BRAEL
14th c. (M.) The breech girdle.

BRAIE-GIRDLE, BREGIRDLE, BRAYGIRDLE
Other spellings of Breech Girdle.

BRAIER
Med. (M.) The French equivalent to Braie-girdle, used for pulling in the waist of the braies and tied in front.

BRAIES, BRÈCHES
Med. to 15th c. (M.) A primitive form of male drawers which,

BRANDENBOURG, BRANDEN-BURGS
18th c. on. Trimming of transverse cording and tassel in the military style.

BRANDENBURG
1674 to c. 1700. (M.) A long loose overcoat for winter wear, generally trimmed with cord and fastened with frogs, i.e. with loops and frog-buttons (olive-shaped 'olivettes').

BRASSARD
19th c. (F.) A ribbon bow attached to the outer side of the elbow of an evening dress sleeve.

Brandenburg Overcoat, late 17th c.

BRATT
(1) 9th and 10th c's. An Irish mantle or coarse cloak worn by peasants.

(2) A wrap such as might be used to wrap an infant in arms.

'. . . had they but a shete
Which they might wrappen hem in a-night,
And a bratt to walken in by daylight.'

(*C.* 1386, Chaucer, *The Chanonnes Yemannes Tale.*)

BRAYETTE
End of 14th c. (M.) A narrow braie-girdle buckled in front.

BREAST-HOOK
See STAY-HOOK.

BREAST-KERCHIEF
Late 15th to mid 16th c. (F., sometimes M.) A kerchief wrapped about the shoulders and folded across the breast for warmth. Worn under the doublet or gown.

BREAST-KNOT, BOSOM KNOT
18th and early 19th c's. (F.) A ribbon bow or bunch of ribbons worn at the breast of a woman's gown.

BREAST POCKET
(M.) (1) 1770 on. An inside pocket in the lining of the right breast of a man's coat.

(2) A horizontal slit pocket outside the left breast of a man's coat; fashionable, off and on, from *c.* 1830.

BREASTS
18th c. (M.) Tailor's term, commonly used in bills, for waistcoat buttons; usually combined with 'coats', for coat buttons.

BREECH, BREECHES
(1) Early Med. (M.) The term BREECH corresponded to BRAIES, *q.v.*

(2) End of 14th to early 16th c. The term BREECH represented the upper part of the long hose which then combined stockings and breeches in the form of tights. In the 16th c. the breech was usually of a different colour and material from the rest of the hose. 'A payre of hosen, black, with purple breche embroidered and underlayd with cloth of silver.' (1521, *Inventory of Henry, Earl of Stafford,* Camden Soc.)

The waistbelt of the breech, when this was the upper portion of the joined long hose (in the form of tights), was then known as the BREECH BELT.

(3) End of 16th c. on. (M.) An outer covering for the legs ending just above or more usually just below the knees; the terms 'breeches' and 'hose' were interchangeable until *c.* 1660 when 'hose' began to signify stockings. In the 17th c. might be closed or open at the knee. A large number of named varieties were known; *see* CLOAK-BAG Breeches, KNEE Breeches, GALLIGASKINS, SLOPS, PETTICOAT Breeches, SPANISH Hose, VENETIANS.

The front opening: a vertical opening down the midline closed by buttons; a method persisting so long as the front was concealed by the long waistcoat descending over the thighs. As the waistcoat shortened, *c.* 1760, exposing the front of the breeches the vertical opening was replaced by Falls (*q.v.*), which remained in fashion for evening dress breeches to *c.* 1840, and for riding breeches the general rule to the end of the 19th c. The fly-front opening was used for evening dress breeches from *c.* 1840.

The introduction of braces, *c.* 1790, led to a change in construction of breeches; previously cut very full in the seat they hung on the hip-bones, the waistband tightened by strings at the back of the waist.

When held up by braces the general fit was closer but the waistband was no longer drawn in as tightly.

BREECH BELT
See BREECH.

BREECH FARTHINGALE
C. 1580 to 1620's. (F.) An unusual term for the 'Roll Farthingale' which bore out the gown's skirt at the back and sides.

BREECH GIRDLE
13th to 15th c. (M.) A girdle threaded *en coulisse* through the wide hem at the top of the breech to secure it about the waist—or more usually just below. *See* BRAIER.

BRETELLE
19th c. (F.) A strap-shaped trimming.

BRIDAL VEIL
See WEDDING VEIL.

BRIDE-LACE
16th and 17th c's. A length of blue ribbon binding sprigs of rosemary, used as wedding favours. In the 16th c. such sprigs were tied to the arm but later worn in the hat. The bride of Jack of Newbury (mid 16th c.) 'was led to church between two boys with bride laces and rosemary tied about their sleeves.' 'With nosegay and bride laces in their hats.' (1603, Heywood, *A Woman killed with Kindness.*)

BRIDES
1830's and 1840's. (F.) The name then commonly given to the broad ribbon-strings attached inside the brim of the open bonnet and occasionally the broad-brimmed hat of the period, and allowed either to float free or tied loosely under the chin. A rosette of ribbon was often used to cover the point of attachment.

BRIDLES
18th c. (F.) The strings for tying a mob cap under the chin. *See* 'KISSING STRINGS'.

BRIGADIER WIG
2nd half 18th c. (M.) This was identical with the 'Major wig', a military style with a double queue. 'Brigadier' was the name used in France, but seldom in England.

'Hence we hear of the Brigadier or the Major for the Army.' (1782, James Stewart, *Plocacosmos.*) *See* MAJOR WIG.

BRISTOL DIAMOND or STONE
C. 1590 to end of 18th c. Rock crystals found at Clifton, near Bristol, and used as imitation diamonds in jewellery.

BROAD BEARD
16th and early 17th c's. (M.) Identical with CATHEDRAL BEARD, *q.v.*

BRODEKIN, BRODKIN, BROTIKEN
15th to late 17th c. (M.) A boot reaching to the middle of the calf or just below the knee. The name is chiefly Scottish though used in English accounts; the English form was Buskin.

BRODEQUIN
1830's. (F.) Boots of velvet or satin, trimmed with a fringe round the top edge.

BROGS
Late 16th and 17th c's. (M.) Long breeches or trousers worn by native Irish.

26

BROGUES

16th and early 17th c's. (M. and F.) Rough shoes of undressed leather with the hair side out, tied on with thongs. Worn by the poor in the wilder parts of Ireland and the Scottish Highlands.

BROWN GEORGE

Late 18th c. (M.) Colloquial term for a brown wig said to resemble a loaf of coarse brown bread.

BRUMMELL BODICE

1810–20. (M.) A whalebone corset worn by dandies of the Regency.

BRUNSWICK GOWN or SACK, GERMAN GOWN

1760–80. (F.) A sack-backed gown with front-buttoned bodice and long sleeves to the wrists, an unusual feature with Sacks.

Brunswick Gown, c. 1760

BRUTUS HEAD or WIG

C. 1790 to 1820. (M.) A cropped head of hair or brown unpowdered wig, both dishevelled in appearance; inspired by the French Revolution. ' "I suppose, Sir," said a London hair-dresser to a gentleman from the country, "You would like to be dressed in the Brutus style—all over frizzley, Sir, like the Negers—they be Brutus you know ".' (1807, Manuel Alvarez Espriella, *Letters from England.*)

BUCK CLOTHES

16th and 17th c's. Clothes taken in buck baskets to be washed; the domestic laundry being a bi-annual event. 'One woman to wash their buck clothes.' (1625, *Statutes of Uppingham Hospital.*)

BUCKINGAMO

Mid 17th c. (M.) A MONTERO, *q.v.* 'When I must be covered I infinitely prefer the Buckingamo or Montero, lately reformed.' (1661, J. Evelyn, *Tyrranus, or the Mode.*)

BUCKLE

(1) A clasp consisting of a rectangular or curved rim with one or more movable tongues secured to the chape at one side or in the middle and long enough to rest on the opposite side. Used to fasten straps or as ornaments. *See* ARTOIS BUCKLE.

(2) Buckle from the French 'boucle'; a curl of hair associated with men's wigs of the 18th c.

BUCKLED WIG

18th c. (M.) One having tightly rolled curls generally arranged horizontally above or about the ears.

BUCKSKIN

15th to 19th c. (1) Meaning gloves of buckskin.

(2) Occasionally meaning breeches of buckskin, chiefly from *c.* 1790 to *c.* 1820.

BUDGET

17th c. A wallet. 'A budget or pocket to hang by their sides to put their nails in.' (1677, Moxon, *Mechanick Exercises.*)

BUFF COAT, BUFF JERKIN, LEATHER JERKIN

16th and 17th c's. (M.) A military garment adopted by civilians; a jacket made of ox hide (originally buffalo hide) and very strong. Worn over the doublet and followed the fashion style of the day; sometimes sleeveless having wings only.

In 17th c. it might have sleeves of other material than leather.

BUFFINS, PAIR OF
16th c. (M.) A North Country term for a pair of wide breeches such as slops, or possibly round hose.

BUFFON, BUFFONT
Chiefly 1780's. (F.) A large diaphanous neckerchief of gauze or fine linen swathed round the neck and shoulders and puffed out over the bosom. 'A large buffont of white gauze carried up near the chin.' (1787, *Ipswich Journal*.)

Buffont, 1788

BUGLES
16th c. on. Tubular glass beads, generally black but also white or blue, very popular in 16th c. for decorating ladies' dresses, cloaks, hats and hair. Less popular in 17th and 18th c's. but much used from 1870 on.

BULGARE PLEAT
1875. (F.) A form of pleating used on skirts, being a double box-pleat narrow at the waist and expanding

downwards, the folds being kept in place by strips of elastic sewn on the under side.

BULL HEAD, BULL-TOUR
1670's–1680's. (F.) A female coiffure with a forehead fringe of thick curls. 'Some term this curled forehead a bull-head from the French Taure, a bull. It was the fashion of women to wear bull-heads or bull-like foreheads, anno 1674 and about that time.' (R. Holme, *Armourie*.)

BULLION-HOSE
16th c. (M.) I.e. BOULOGNE or FRENCH HOSE, *q.v.*

BULLY-COCKED
18th c. (M.) A hat cocked in the style favoured by the bullies of the period; generally a broad-brimmed hat. (The Oxford Smart) 'easily distinguished by . . . a broad bully-cocked hat'. (1721, Amherst, *Terrae Filius*.)

BUM-BARREL
2nd half 16th and early 17th c's. (F.) A padded roll for distending the skirt at the hips.

BUM ROLL, BUM
2nd half 16th and early 17th c's. Similar to BUM-BARREL but the more usual term.

Bum Roll, early 17th c.

BURDASH, BERDASH
Late 17th and early 18th c's. A fringed sash worn round the waist over the coat; favoured by the beaux.

BURLET
15th c. (M.) A circular padded roll worn as a head-dress or as part of the chaperon. *See* BOURRELET.

Burlet or Roll of Chaperon, c. 1420–70

BURNET
17th c. (1) 'A hood or attire for the head'. (1616, John Bullokar, *An English Expositor*.) Thus defined by H. Cockeram, 1623, and by Phillips, 1678.
(2) 13th to 15th c. A material.

BURN-GRACE
Synonym of BONGRACE.

BURNOUSE
1830's to 1860's. (F.) An evening wrap of cashmere, usually knee-length, fastened at the neck; sometimes with a small hood, or imitation of one, attached.
The ALGERIAN BURNOUSE (1858) was of wool with broad satin stripes.

BURRAIL COLLAR
1832. (M.) A collar (of a great-coat) made 'to stand up or fall down at pleasure'. (*Gentleman's Magazine of Fashion*.)

BURSE
See BOURSE.

BUSH, BUSH BEARD
Late 16th and 17th c's. (M.) Jocular synonyms for a thick mop of hair or full beard.

BUSH-WIG
A similar term.

BUSK
16th, 17th, 18th and 19th c's. (F., sometimes M.) (1) 'Buc, a buske, plated (pleated) bodie or other quilted thing worne to make or keepe the bodie straight'. (1611, Cotgrave.) But the usual meaning of the word was the stiffener of a bodice; the busk being a flat length of bone, whalebone, wood or in 17th c. sometimes horn, attached to the front of a bodice (or stays) to render it inflexible. In the 18th c. the busk was sometimes carved with emblems and worn pushed down into a busk sheath in front of the bodice. In 19th c. stay busks were often of steel.
(2) BUSK, BUSKE. A material.

BUSKINS
14th to end of 17th c. (M. and F.) High boots sometimes reaching to the knees. In Middle Ages often made of silk in various designs. In 16th c. those worn at Court might be of silk or cloth.
Leather buskins were mainly riding boots.
Women's buskins worn for travelling were of velvet, satin or Spanish leather.

BUSK POINT
A tie for securing the Busk.

BUST BODICE
1889 on. (F.) A breast support of white coutil, laced front and back with bones on each side of lace holes. Worn above the corset. Prototype of the modern brassière.

BUST IMPROVER
1840 on. (F.) Bosom pads of wool and cotton. Various structures intro-

duced such as a patent of 1860—'an improved inflated undulating artificial bust to improve the female figure'. 1896. Flexible celluloid bust improvers were advertised.

BUSTLE

From 14th c. on. (F.) (Name not used until *c.* 1830.) A device for thrusting out the skirt at the back of the waist. Innumerable forms and materials have been adopted through the centuries, from foxes' tails (1343) to kitchen dusters (1834, Mrs. Carlyle), from down cushions to wire cages. Until the 19th c. padded rolls were the usual form. (*See* BUM ROLL, BEARERS, RUMP-FURBELOWS, CORK RUMPS.)

19th c.: 1806–20. A small pad or narrow roll, sometimes known as a 'Nelson'.

1815–19. An outside bustle called a 'Frisk' helped to produce the 'Grecian bend'. (The Frisk was more of a French than an English fashion.)

1830–50. A huge pad stuffed with wool, spreading from the back round the sides of the waist.

1857–65. Bustle omitted during the Crinoline period.

1865–76. Bustles of steel half-hoops known as 'Crinolettes'.

1876–82. Bustles omitted.

1882–9. Bustles again fashionable, the maximum size in 1885, the shape now projecting backwards like a shelf and variously constructed. The Bustle then known as a 'Dress Improver' or 'Tournure'. It finally disappeared in 1889.

Bustle, 1872

BUTTERFLY BOW SLEEVE

1895. (F.) An evening dress sleeve with pleats on the outer side forming wings.

BUTTERFLY CAP, FLY CAP

1750–60's. (F.) A small lace cap wired into the form of a butterfly and worn perched above the forehead. Lappets, jewels and flower trimming were sometimes added for Court wear.

Bustle worn with 'Grecian Bend', 1819

BUTTERFLY HEAD-DRESS

2nd half 15th c. (F.) A 16th-c. term for the head-dress of the previous century, which had consisted of a wire frame supporting a gauze veil spreading out above the head on each side, like a pair of diaphanous wings, with a V-shaped dip over the forehead. It was fixed to a small ornamental cap, fez-shaped, worn on the back of the head.

'These were called by some "Great Butterflies" from having two large wings on each side resembling those of that insect.' (1591, Paradin.)

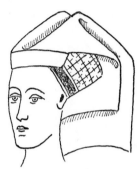

Butterfly Head-dress, 1457

BUTTON

At least from 13th c. on. (M. and F.) As fastenings or dress ornaments. A knob or disc sewn or affixed to a garment to fasten it by passing through a button-hole. *See* named types: BASKET B., COVERED B., DEATH'S HEAD B., DORSET THREAD B., HIGH TOPS, LEEK B., OLIVE B., SNAIL B., STALK B.

BUTTON BOOTS

1837. (M.) 1860's, (F.) on to end of 19th c. Short boots fastened up the

Button Boot (F.), 1890

outer side with buttons, usually black japanned. Mother-of-pearl buttons (1830's) were ornamental. Light jack-boots might be buttoned, from 17th c., but the term 'button boot' was not applied to them.

BUTTONED CAP

16th c. (M.) A cap with a round or square close beret-shaped crown, and a button on the top for securing the side flaps when present.

Buttoned Cap, c. 1530

BUTTONED HANDKERCHIEF

C. 1590 to 1700. (M. and F.) Pocket handkerchief trimmed at the corners with buttons acting as tassels.

BUTTONER

14th c. (M. and F.) A close row of buttons down the front of the Houppelande, serving as an ornament.

BUTTON HOOK

19th c. (1) A metal hook on a handle; used to engage the buttons of tight gloves or boots into their respective button-holes.

(2) BUTTON-HOOKS. 1865-6. (M.) These were metal eyelet hooks replacing eyelet holes up the fronts of boots. The boot-laces were caught in the hooks and criss-crossed from side to side, thus fastening up the boot.

In 1897 they became brass oval hooks called 'Lacing Studs'.

BUTTON STAND

19th c. Tailor's term for a separate

31

piece of material carrying the buttons and button-holes of a coat (usually D-B) or waistcoat, and seamed on to the margin of the forepart. A device invented by George IV, c. 1820.

BYRON TIE

C. 1840's and 1850's. (M.) A small narrow necktie such as 'a bit of mousselaine de laine a few inches long or a bit of broad shoe-string'.

C

CABAN
(1) 14th and 15th c's. (M.) A loose cloak with arm-holes.
(2) 1840's. (M.)
Also known as TEMPLAR CLOAK. A loose wrapper with turned-down collar, and wide enough to be worn without using the sleeves. Sometimes in the form of a PALETOT-SAC.

CABBAGE-RUFF
Early 17th c. (M.) A large ruff with informal convolutions not in the organ-pipe style.
'Hiss cabbage Ruffe of the outragious sise,
Starched in colour to beholders eyes.'
(*C.* 1620, S. Rowlands, *A Roaring Boyes Description.*)

CABBAGE SHOE-STRING
C. 1610 to 1680. (M.) A large cabbage-shaped shoe-rose (i.e. rosette).

CABLE HATBAND
See HATBAND.

CABRIOLE, CAPRIOLE HEAD-DRESS
1755 to 1757. (F.) A head-dress in the shape of 'some kind of carriage'. 'Those heads which are not able to bear a coach-and-six . . . make use of a post-chaise.' (1756, *The Connoisseur.*)

CADDIE
1890's. (M.) A hip-pocket, i.e. a cross-pocket at the back of the hip of trousers.

CADOGAN
Late 18th c. (M. and F.) Rare term for CLUB WIG and CATOGAN, *q.v.*

CAFTAN
1844. (F.) An outdoor garment 'between a Paletot and a Mantle'.

CAGE
1856 to end of 1860's. (F.) Short name for the 'artificial crinoline' composed of a coarse petticoat distended with graduated hoops of whalebone, wire or watch-spring.

CAGE-AMÉRICAINE
1862 to 1869. (F.) A cage petticoat of which only the lower half was covered with material, the upper half being in skeleton form to reduce the weight.

CAGE EMPIRE
1861 to 1869. (F.) Cage for wearing under a ball-dress; the cage slightly trained and composed of 30 steel hoops increasing in width downwards.

CAGE PETTICOAT, ARTIFICIAL CRINOLINE
1856 to 1868. (F.) A structure composed of hoops, at first of whalebone but after 1857 of wire or watch-spring, joined together at intervals by vertical bands of tape or braid. The hoops increased in size from the waistband down, forming a dome-shaped petticoat resembling a cage, to be worn under a wide skirt to distend it to the required size. The cage was tied round the waist in front and below the ties a short gap in the hoops enabled the cage to be put on. The number of hoops, their size and shape varied. At first dome-shaped, becoming by 1860 pyramidal; by 1866 the front flattened with the main projection behind; by 1868 the cage shrank and became the CRINOLETTE, *q.v.*

CAKE HAT
1890's. (M.) A soft felt hat with a low round crown slightly depressed circularly; similar to the Alpine hat.

'A blue cake hat.' (1895, *The Babe, B.A.*)

CALASH, CALÈCHE
C. 1770 to 1790; revived 1820 to 1839. (F.) A large folding hood, hooped, being built up on arches of whalebone or cane covered with soft silk; named after the hood of the French carriage called a Calèche. Worn out of doors to protect the high head-dresses fashionable in those two periods. Its original French name was a 'Thérèse'.

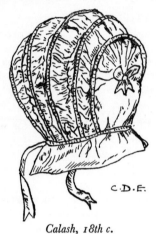

Calash, 18th c.

Calash, 1770 (as worn)

CALCARAPEDES
1860's. (M.) 'Self-adjusting galoshes' of rubber. (1861, *Our Social Bees.*)

CALICO BUTTON
1840's on. A flat button consisting of a metal ring covered with calico and sewn on by piercing the calico; some had two metal eyelets in the centre. Both types appeared about the same date. Used for underclothing.

CALOTTE, CALLOT
17th c. (M.) (1) An under-cap. 'An ordinary callotte or cap which we wear under our hats.' (1670, Lassels, *Voyage to Italy.*)
(2) A plain skull-cap.

CALVES, FALSE
17th, 18th and 19th c's. (M.) Pads worn inside the stockings to improve the shape of the legs. 'They say he puts off the calves of his legs with stockings every night.' (1601, B. Jonson, *Cynthia's Revels.*)

CALYPSO CHEMISE
1790's. (F.) A round gown of coloured muslin worn with a loose robe over it.

CAMAIL
1842. (F.) A waist-length or $\frac{3}{4}$-length cloak with arm-holes and small falling collar. Rounded or pointed below and lined with silk (summer) or wadded cashmere, satin or velvet (winter).

CAMARGO
1879. (F.) A day-jacket, the basques of which were rounded off and draped into panniers on the hips; worn over a waistcoat. Named after Marie Camargo, a celebrated French dancer of the 18th c.

CAMARGO HAT
1836. (F.) An evening dress-hat, small, with brim raised in front.

CAMARGO PUFF
1868. (F.) A puff formed by looping up high the back of the overskirt of a pannier dress.

CAMBRIDGE COAT
1870 on. (M.) A lounge coat, S-B or D-B, usually a 'THREE-SEAMER' (*q.v.*) with central back vent. Made to button 3. At first 'cut sharply off from the 1st or 2nd button producing an opening at the waist.' From 1876

34

made closer and longer with 4 patch-pockets having buttoned flaps.

By 1880 identical with the S-B Reefer.

CAMBRIDGE PALETOT

1855. (M.) A large and full knee-length overcoat with wide sleeves having immense turned-back cuffs; wide cape-collar and broad lapels descending nearly to the hem.

CAMELEONS

C. 1859. (F.) Ladies' boots and shoes having the uppers perforated with ornamental holes revealing coloured stockings.

CAMISE, CAMES, (M.E.) KEMES, KEMSE

See CHEMISE.

CAMISIA

Med. (M. and F.) A shirt or smock.

CAMISOLE

1820's on. (F.) A short-sleeved or sleeveless under-bodice of white long-cloth, worn over the stays to protect the tight-fitting dress. Sometimes called a 'waistcoat' and by 1890 a 'petticoat-bodice'.

Camisole, 1876

CAMPAIGN COAT

17th c. (M.) A long military coat worn by the rank and file from c. 1667. 'Campaign-coat, originally only such as soldiers wore, but afterwards a mode in Cities.' (1690, B.E., *Dictionary of the Canting Crew*.)

In 18th c. a term used for any old tattered coat worn by beggars and gypsies to arouse compassion.

CAMPAIGNE WIG, TRAVELLING WIG

C. 1675 to 1750's; subsequently old-fashioned. (M.) A bushy wig with short side locks usually with knotted ends and a very short queue behind. The side locks were sometimes tied back for travelling. A kind of wig popular with the elderly.

CANE

Early 16th c. on. (M., occasionally also F.) The stem of a plant similar to bamboo and used as a walking-stick; the finer kinds usually carried under the arm. The fashionable periods for canes (as distinct from sticks) were 17th and 18th c's.; of very variable length; in 2nd half of 18th c. often very long and carried by ladies as well as by gentlemen. Types: Malacca or 'Clouded' cane. Rattan, a species of palm from the East Indies.

'. . . a little black rattoon painted and gilt.' (1660, *Diary of Samuel Pepys*.)

CANEZOU

1820's to 1850's. (F.) In 1820's a white sleeveless spencer.

In 1830's a short pointed cape covering the front and back but not the arms. By 1850's the Canezou had become an elaborate fichu of muslin, lace and ribbons covering the front and back of the chest.

CANEZOU-PELERINE

1830's. (F.) A Canezou with long pelerine extensions down the front.

CANIONS

C. 1570 to 1620. (M.) Thigh-fitting extensions from trunk-hose to the knees or just below, and often of a different colour and material from the trunk-hose. Stockings were drawn up over them.

CANNONS, CANONS, PORT CANONS

Mainly 1660's and 1670's. (M.) Wide decorative frills to the tops of stockings worn with petticoat breeches or breeches not confined at the knee.

35

Canions, c. 1595

These borders were turned down over the garters and fell in a broad flounce below the knee. 'He walks in his Portcannons like one that stalks in long grass.' (C. 1680, Samuel Butler, *Genuine Remains*.)

Cannons, c. 1660

CANNON SLEEVES, TRUNK SLEEVES

C. 1575 to 1620. (F.) Gown sleeves, moderately wide above and sloping to be closed at the wrist. They were made rigid with padding, and sometimes distended with reed, wire or whalebone sewn into a lining of fustian or holland, thus producing their shape of a cannon.

CANTAB HAT

1806. (F.) A day-hat of straw, with a rectangular crown, flat on the top, and a narrow rolled brim.

CAP

From Med. on. (M. and F.) (1) MALE. A small head-covering usually of soft material and often fitting more closely than a hat. For named varieties *see* under their names.

The un-named Cap began in 16th c. to imply social inferiority (as in the servant, apprentice or schoolboy). When in the 19th c. the gentleman began to wear it in the country or for outdoor sports, he made it a rule never to wear it 'in Town'. The cap with a stiff vizor was an improvement of the 1880's; the 'hook-down' Cap in which the front of the crown hooked on to the top of the vizor appeared in the 1890's, especially favoured for tennis and golf.

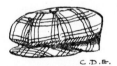

Cap, 1899

(2) FEMALE. The domestic Cap worn indoors dates from *c.* 1500 and survived as such nearly to the end of the 19th c.; usually as named varieties (*q.v.*), e.g. CAUL, LETTICE CAP, CORNET, RAIL, FONTANGE, ROUND-EARED CAP, PULTENEY CAP, MOB, BUTTERFLY CAP, MARIE STUART CAP, BABET, CORDAY.

The wearing of caps by ladies began to decline in the 1850's and in 1857 'young married ladies need not wear caps until they have acquired the endearing name of "Mother"'. By 1880 'young women no longer wear caps' and by the 1890's they were

36

worn only by the elderly and by
female domestic servants.

CAPA PLUVIALIS, CHAPE A PLUIE
Med. (F.) A large cloak, generally
hooded, to protect from the rain.

CAPE
(1) From 12th to 14th c. Known as
a COPE, q.v.

(2) From 15th to end of 18th c.
A turned-down collar, whether large
or small.

(3) A short shoulder-cloak. The
old meaning of turned-down collar
remained, however, as a tailor's term
in the 19th c.

CAPE COAT
17th c. (M.) An overcoat with a
cape collar.

CAPELINE
2nd half 18th c. (F.) A woman's
hat adorned with feathers.

1863. A light hood with attached
cape; usually of cashmere or barege.
For country wear.

CAP-HOOD
See CAPOUCH.

CAPE-PALETOT
1859 on. (M.) A sleeved cloak with
a deep cape; known as the Inverness,
q.v.

CAPOT, CAPOTE
18th c. (M.) A loose coat. 'Wrapped in their thick capots or loose
coats.' (1775, R. Chandler, *Travels
in Asia Minor*.)

CAPOTE
Mainly 1830's. (F.) A bonnet with
a soft crown shaped to the head and
having a rigid brim round the face.

CAPOTE ANGLAISE
1830's. (F.) See BIBI or ENGLISH
COTTAGE BONNET.

CAPOUCH, CAPUCHE
17th c. (M. and F.) A hood attached
to a cloak. 'His Hood or Capuch
(which was part of the Cloak) and
served to cover the Head.' (1658,
J. Cleveland, *Rustick Rampant*.)

CAPRICE
1846. (F.) A loose sleeveless evening jacket, sloped away behind to a
rounded point below the waist.

CAPUCHE
1852. (F.) A muslin sun-bonnet
lined with silk.

CAPUCHIN, CAPUCHON
16th, 17th and 18th c's. (F.) A soft
hood worn out of doors. In the 18th
c. it was known as a Riding hood and
was worn in the country and when
travelling by coach. It had a coloured lining and a deep cape.

CAPUCHIN COLLAR
Late 18th and early 19th c's. (F.)
A roll collar following a V-neckline
of the high-waisted dress of the period.

CAPUCHON
(1) See CAPUCHIN.

(2) or CARMEILLETTE. 1837. (F.)
A waist-length evening mantlet with
a hooped hood and long sleeves;
worn out of doors.

(3) 1877. (F.) A bonnet composed entirely of flowers mounted on
a slight foundation, covering only a
small part of the head.

CARACALLA WIG
Late 18th and early 19th c's. (M.)
A black wig.

CARACO
Late 18th and 19th c's. (F.) In
18th c. a thigh-length waisted jacket
worn as the bodice of a gown and
forming with the skirt the 'Caraco
dress'.

In 19th c., mainly 1840's to 1860's,
a similar garment but varying according to the fashion of the day. Always
a day dress in both centuries.

CARACO CORSAGE
1848 to 1860's. (F.) The bodice of
a day dress made to resemble a jacket.

CARAVAN
1765. (F.) A small and early form
of the CALASH, q.v. 'It consists of
whalebone formed in large rounds,
which at a touch throws down over

the face a blind of white sarcenet.'
(1764, *Universal Magazine.*)

CARCAN
16th c. (M.) A collar wide enough
to rest on the shoulders.

CARDIGAN
Early 1890's. (M.) A short, close-
fitting, knitted jacket of Berlin wool
or English worsted; no collar or a
velvet one; by 1896 some had a short
roll collar.

CARDINAL
18th and 19th c's. (F.) In 18th c.
a ¾-length hooded cloak, usually of
scarlet cloth. In 19th c. fashionable
in 1840's, a shorter cloak ending about
waist-level and without hood or collar.

CARDINAL PELERINE
1840's. (F.) A deep lace bertha
cleft in the centre front and worn with
evening dress.

CARDOWS
Late 16th and early 17th c's. (M.)
The tasselled cords of a ceremonial
robe.

CARELESS
1830's. (M.) A loose overcoat with
a large full cape and spreading collar :
without a seam at the waist.

CARMEILLETTE
1830's. (F.) *See* CAPUCHON.

CAROLINE CORSAGE
1830's. (F.) An evening corsage
having a narrow fall of lace and
drapery forming a 'V' *en pèlerine.*

CAROLINE HAT
1680's to mid 18th c. (M.) A hat
made of Carolina Beaver; the fur
imported from Carolina and, owing to
the climate, inferior to the Canadian
fur known as 'French Beaver'. Caroline hats were therefore usually worn
by servants and generally black.
'Two Caroline hats for the servants.'
(1742, *Purefoy Letters.*)

CAROLINE SLEEVE
1830's. (F.) A day dress sleeve very
full to the elbow; thence close-
fitting to the wrist.

CARPET SLIPPERS
C. 1840 on. (M.) Bedroom slippers, the uppers made either of
German wool woven like carpet
material, or by hand in cross stitch
of Berlin woolwork.

CARRICK
1877 on. (F.) A long dust-cloak
with triple capes. *See* ULSTER.

Carrick, 1890

CARTHAGE CYMAR
1809. (F.) A fancy scarf of silk or
net with gold embossed border; worn
with evening dress, attached to one
shoulder and hanging down the back
to about knee-level.

CARTOOSE COLLAR
17th c. A standing collar with small
pickadills about its upper edge on
which the ruff was supported.

CASAQUE
1855 to 1860's. (F.) A close-fitting
jacket buttoned up to the neck and
having a deep basque forming an
overskirt.

CASAQUE BODICE
1873. (F.) A close-fitting bodice with a deep basque in front.

CASAQUIN BODICE
1878. (F.) A tight-fitting day bodice shaped like a gentleman's tail-coat, and buttoned down the front, some having a waistcoat, 'actual or simulated'. Worn with a 'short skirt' untrained and 2" off the ground. Usually tailor-made.

CASAWECK
1836 to c. 1850. (F.) A short quilted outdoor mantle having sleeves and a close-fitting collar of velvet, satin or silk. A trimming of fur, velvet or lace bordered the garment.

CASCADE WAISTBAND
1860's. (F.) A waistband fringed with jet pendants arranged in vandykes.

CASED BODY
(1) 2nd half 16th c. (M.) A sleeveless Jerkin worn over the Doublet, fitting it closely.
(2) 1810–20. (F.) A bodice with a series of transverse pleats or gauging across the front.

CASED SLEEVE
1810–20. (F.) A long sleeve divided into 'compartments' by bands of insertion.

CASQUETTE
1863–4. (F.) A straw hat shaped like a Glengarry, the brim low in front and behind; trimmed with black velvet and ostrich feather.

CASSOCK
Late 16th and 17th c.'s. (M. and F.) A long loose overcoat buttoned down the front, some having cape collars. Described, contemporarily, as 'a horseman's coat'; and also worn by farmers and rustics, shortened.

CASSOCK MANTLE
1880's. (F.) A cloak with short sleeves and reaching to below the knees; gathered on the shoulders and down the centre of the back. 'No-

thing could be more peculiar or unbecoming.' (1880.)

CASSOCK VEST
1850's. (M.) The New form of clerical waistcoat, at first fastened on the right shoulder; later, nearer the midline. Worn by Tractarian High Church clergy and so thought to savour of 'Popery'; hence its nickname, the 'Mark of the Beast' or 'M. B. waistcoat'. Worn with a white 'dog-collar' fastened behind.

CASTOR
17th c. and 19th c. (M. and F.) A beaver hat, but towards the end of the century the castor was often made of other materials. 'The Castor . . . is made of Coney wooll mixt with Polony wooll.' (1688, R. Holme, *Armourie.*) *See* DEMI-CASTOR.

CATAGAN
1870–5. (F.) A chignon of ringlets or plaits of hair hanging at the back of the head, tied above with a wide ribbon and forming a resemblance to the male CATOGAN of the 18th c.

CATAGAN HEAD-DRESS
1889. (F.) The hair plaited behind and turned up with a wide ribbon bow; a style suitable for older schoolgirls.

CATAGAN NET
1870's. (F.) A hair-net frequently used to contain the plaited catagan.

CATER-CAP
16th and 17th c.'s. (M.) The four-cornered square cap worn by Academicians (cater = quatre.)

CATHEDRAL BEARD
16th and early 17th c.'s. (M.) Broad and long. *See* BEARD.

CATHERINE WHEEL FARTHINGALE
1580 to c. 1620. (F.) A farthingale producing a tub-shaped hang of the skirt. 'A short Dutch waist with a round Catherine wheel fardingale.' (1607, Dekker and Webster, *Northward Hoe.*) *See* WHEEL FARTHINGALE.

Cathedral Beard, c. 1547

CATOGAN, CLUB WIG

1760 to 1790's. (M.) A wig with a broad flat queue turned up on itself and tied round the middle with black ribbon.

Catogan or Club Wig, c. 1770

CAUDEBEC HAT

End of 17th c. and 18th c. (M.) A felt hat imitating a beaver; said to have originated from Caudebec in Normandy. Known in England as CAWDEBINK or CORDYBACK HAT. 'For a black Cawdebink hat.' (1680, W. Cunningham, *Diary*.)

CAUL

(1) 14th, 15th, 16th and occasionally 17th c's. (F.) The mediaeval caul was generally called a 'FRET', *q.v.*

A trellis-work coif or skull cap of silk thread or goldsmithry, sometimes lined with silk. More often worn by maidens, the matrons wearing veils, i.e. head kerchiefs.

(2) Late 17th and 18th c's. (M.) The network foundation on which the wig was built. 'To the foretop of his Wig . . . Down to the very net-work, named the caul.' (1786, Peter Pindar.)

(3) 18th and 19th c's. (F.) The soft pliable crown of a bonnet or cap.

CAULIFLOWER WIG

2nd half 18th c. (M.) A closely curled bob-wig, commonly worn by coachmen.

CAVALIER SLEEVE

1830's. (F.) A day sleeve, full down to the elbow, thence half tight to the wrist; closed along the outer side by a series of ribbon bows.

CAXON

18th c. (M., rarely F.) A tie-wig, usually white or pale-coloured but occasionally black. Worn with 'undress', chiefly by the professional classes.

'All were attention fix'd upon the stage,
And slighting Beaux in Tetes, in Queues and Bags,
Preferr'd old Lear's Caxon and his rags.' (1768, E. Lloyd.)
'Some wives there are . . .
Invade man's province, bluster and look big;
Nor wear the breeches only but the wig;
The red-hair'd lass, to hide her golden nob
Tucks up her tresses in a nut-brown mob,
And full-blown dames, thro' time a a little flaxen,
Conceal that outrage by a coal-black caxen.'
(1798, Thomas Morton, *Secrets worth Knowing*.)

CEINT, SEINT

14th and 15th c's. (M. and F.) A girdle.

CERUSE

16th, 17th and 18th c's. A cosmetic used by both sexes to whiten the face. Originally made of white lead.

CHAFFERS

16th c. (F.) The embroidered lapels of the English (gable-shaped) hood.

CHAIN BUCKLE

Mid 18th c. (M.) A variety of curled wig ('buckle' meaning 'curl').

CHAIN-HOLE

1879 on. (M.) An additional hole, for the watch-chain, resembling a button-hole, placed vertically between two button-holes of the waistcoat. First mentioned in 1879 but common from 1888 and general in lounge suits from 1895.

CHAMBARD MANTLE

1850's. (F.) A ¾-length sleeved mantle with hood or collar, and deep hollow folds at the back.

CHAMMER, CHYMER, SHAMEW

Late 15th to early 17th c. (M.) A rich sleeved gown worn open in front. 'A chammer of black satin with three borders of black velvet and furred with sables.' (1517, Wardrobe Inventory of Henry VIII.)

The Chammer of 14th and 15th c's. was mainly academical.

CHANCELLOR

18th c. (M.) A variety of wig, possibly the full-bottom form.

CHAPEAU BRAS

(1) 1760's to 1830's. (M.) A dress hat made to be carried under the arm. In the 18th c. it was a flat tricorne; in the 19th, a flat crescent-shaped hat usually carried under the arm but occasionally worn, the peaks pointing fore and aft. By the 1830's it was generally called an 'opera hat'.

(2) 1814. (F.) A satin calash, small enough when folded flat to be carried in a handbag.

CHAPERON

(1) 14th c. (M.) The Anglo-French term for a hood with 'gole' or cape and dangling LIRIPIPE (q.v.).

(2) 15th c. (M.) The chaperon, derived from the hood, was a head-dress consisting of a circular roll or 'burlet', a liripipe or tippet, sometimes left dangling, sometimes twisted round the head, and the cockscomb-like flopping crown.

Chaperon, 15th c.

(3) CHAPERONE. 17th c. (F.) A small soft hood for informal wear.

Chaperone, 1642

41

CHAPLET

(1) Originally and generally a garland of flowers for the head. In Anglo-Saxon times worn by both sexes on festive occasions such as May Day, Whitsun and weddings. In 15th c. the chaplet of flowers was worn by the bride only.

(2) 14th, 15th and early 16th c's. A circlet set with gems, also called a 'Coronal of goldsmithry'; worn by both sexes on festive occasions, and in 16th c. by brides.

(3) Late 14th and 15th c's. (F., sometimes M.) A wreath of twisted silk or satin or made up of an ornamental padded roll not confined to festive occasions. 'White and blod (red) taffata and red tartryn for chaplets for the Earl of Derby's daughters.' (1397, Duchy of Lancaster Records. White and red were the livery colours of the House of Plantagenet.)

Chaplets, 14th c.

(4) 17th c. A term used to describe a short rosary or set of beads. 'A chaplet hanging down on her neck.' (1653, H. Cogan, *Pinto's Traveles*, ed. 1663.)

CHARLOTTE CORDAY BONNET

1870's and 1880's. (F.) An outdoor head-dress with an upstanding crown of soft material, drawn to a narrow frilled brim, the join covered by broad ribbon band with pendant strings behind. In 1889 it was flattened.

CHARLOTTE CORDAY CAP

1870's. (F.) An indoor day cap with small puffed muslin crown gathered under a ribbon band with a lace frill below. Small lace lappets behind and long dangling ribbons.

CHATELAINE

1840's on. (F.) An ornamental chain attached at the waist (usually hooked) from which hung various articles of domestic use such as scissors, penknife, tape - measure, thimble-case, button hook. In the 1840's usually of cut steel; in the 1870's of oxidised silver, steel or electroplate.

CHAUSONS

The equivalent of the English 'Braies'.

CHAUSSEMBLES, CHAUXSIM-LEZ, CHASEMBLES, CASH-AMBLES (O.F. CHAUSSESE-MALÉES)

Med. (M.) Hose with leather or whalebone soles stitched under the feet to obviate the use of boots or shoes.

From 2nd half of 14th c. to mid 15th c. these were in general use by the nobility.

From mid 15th c. to early 17th c. they were garments proper to the Robes of the Bath. 'Cloth stockings soled with white leather called Cashambles but no shoes.' (1610, Brit. Mus. Harl. MS. 5176.)

CHAUSSES

See HOSE. An Anglo-French term for the mediaeval hose; but as soon as Anglo-French gave way to English as the language of knighthood and nobility, in the 15th c. the word 'chausses' was abandoned in favour of 'hose', which had been in use since the 11th c. Later uses of the term 'chausses' were concessions.

CHEATS

17th c. (M.) Waistcoats with rich foreparts but with cheap material at the back.

19th c. (M.) A term sometimes applied to a shirt-front with collar attached, worn as a DICKEY, *q.v.*

CHECK

See CUT-IN.

CHECKERED-APRON MEN
16th c. *See* APRON.

CHEEKS AND EARS
See COIF.

CHEEK WRAPPERS
2nd half 18th c. (F.) The side flaps of the DORMEUSE or FRENCH NIGHT-CAP, *q.v.*

CHEMISE, CAMISE, M.E. KEMES, KEMSE
From early Med. to end of 19th c. The undermost garment, usually of linen, worn by both sexes in the early Mediaeval period.

In the 13th and early 14th c's. the Chemise and Smock were often recorded together as distinct garments. 'Hire chemise smal and hwit . . . and hire smoc hwit.' (*c.* 1200. Trinity College Homilies, 163.) The Chemise then was sometimes coloured and worn over the Smock. Subsequently the Chemise was known as a Smock when a woman's garment and a Shirt when a man's.

From the 14th c. the term Chemise disappeared until imported from France in the late 18th c. as a refined name for 'smock' or 'shift'.

Made of linen, homespun or cotton, very voluminous and knee-length; without trimming, oblong in shape and with short sleeves. Until *c.* 1850

the square neck often had a front flap which fell over the top of the corset. In 1876 pleated gussets were introduced to allow for the shape of the breasts. Subsequently it became elaborately trimmed with frills, tucks and lace. In the 1890's it was being replaced by combinations.

CHEMISE DRESS, GOWN, ROBE
1780 to *c.* 1810. (F.) In 18th c. the top drawn in round a low neck and always worn with a sash; long tight sleeves. The English Chemise gown, known as the 'Perdita Chemise', was closed down the front from bosom to hem with buttons or a series of ribbon bows; a sash was essential.

In the 19th c. the neckline might be drawn in high with a falling frill or cut low. Buttons down the front were usual, and a small train was optional. Sleeves short and melon-shaped; no sash.

Chemise gowns were always of thin muslin, cambric, or coloured silk and cut with the waist-line according to the fashion of the day.

CHEMISETTE
19th c. (F.) A white muslin or cambric 'fill-in' to the bodice of a day gown cut low in front.

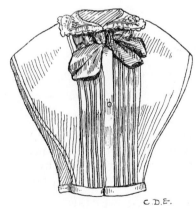

Chemisette, 1862

CHESTERFIELD
Later, in tailors' parlance, CHESTER. 1840 on. (M., and towards the end of the c. also F.) An overcoat,

Chemise, c. 1700

named after the 6th Earl of Chesterfield, a leader of fashion in the 1830's and 1840's. A slightly waisted overcoat, S-B or D-B, having a short back vent and centre back seam but no seam at the waist, or side vents. Velvet collar usual. Side flapped pockets and pocket outside left breast. By 1859 a small ticket pocket was added above the pocket on right side. 4 or 5 covered buttons to waist-level, occasionally under a fly. In the 1850's this form of overcoat was known in France as a 'Twine' and corresponded to the PARDESSUS, *q.v.*

Chesterfield, 1891–2

CHEVESAILLE
(From O.F. 'Chevecaille'.) Med. The border round the neck of a garment. Rare. Used by Chaucer in *Romaunt of the Rose. c.* 1400.

CHEVEUX-DE-FRISE
18th c. A vandyked frill or edging.

CHEVRONS
1826 on. (F.) 'A new form of trimming above the hem of a skirt', applied in a zigzag pattern.

CHICKEN-SKIN GLOVES
From end of 17th to early 19th c. (F.)
'Some of chicken-skin at night
To keep her Hands plump, soft, and white.'
(1690, J. Evelyn, *Mundus Muliebris*.)
But though retaining the name the gloves were frequently made of other materials: 'The name induced some to think they were made from the skins of chickens; but on the contrary they are made of a thin strong leather which is dressed with almonds and spermaceti.' (1778. From a shop bill of Warren the Perfumer.) *See* LIMERICK GLOVES.

CHIGNON
2nd half of 18th c. to end of 19th c. (F.) Term denoting a mass of hair arranged at the back of the head. 'Chignon flottant' (1790's) was made up of loops of hair or ringlets arranged to hang down from the back of the head over the neck. *See* also BANGING CHIGNON.

Chignon, 1777

In the 19th c. the chignon reached its maximum in the late '60's to '70's composed mainly of artificial hair and formal rows of curls ('marteaux') pinned down. 'False hair is worn in incredible quantities and chignons are made of these marteaux all ready

44

to be fastened on with a comb.'
(1866.) 'Chignons often weigh five
or more ounces.' (1868.)

Chignon, 1864

CHIMNEY-POT HAT
1830's on. (M.) A high-crowned
hat with narrow brim, replacing the
high-crowned Beaver hat previously
fashionable. 'The surface covering
being of silk faced with a felting of
rabbit hair which has received a
smooth satin-like surface.' (1862,
Mayhew, *London Labour and the London
Poor.*)
Synonyms: POT HAT, TOP HAT,
TOPPER, SILK HAT, PLUG HAT
(American).

CHIN CLOAK, CHIN CLOUT, CHIN CLOTH, CHINNER
C. 1535 to 1660's. Synonyms for
MUFFLER, *q.v.*

CHINESE SLIPPER
1786. (F.) *See* KAMPSKATCHA SLIP-
PER.

CHINESE SPENCER
1808. (F.) A very short jacket or
spencer with two long points in front.

CHIN STAYS
End of 1820's to end of 1830's. (F.)
Frills of tulle or lace added to the
insertion of bonnet strings, forming a
frill round the chin when tied. *See*
MENTONNIÈRES.

CHITTERLINGS
18th and 19th c's. (M.) Popular
term for the frills down the front of a
shirt.

Chitterlings of Shirt, late 18th c.

CHOPINE, CHOPIN, CHAPINEY
C. 16th century. (F.) An over-shoe
consisting of a toe-cap fixed to a high
stump-like sole of cork or wood,
variously decorated. Rare in England; but 'there are many of these
chapineys of a great height, even half
a yard high'. (1611, T. Coryate,
Crudities.)

Chopines, late 17th c.

CHOUX
Late 17th c. term. (F.) A lady's
chignon. 'The great round boss or
bundle (of hair) resembling a cabbage.' (1690, J. Evelyn, *Mundus
Muliebris.*)

CICLATON, CINGLATON, SYGLATON
See CYCLAS.

CIRCASSIAN BODICE
1829 on. (F.) A gown bodice with
cross-over folds descending from the
shoulders and crossing at the waist.

CIRCASSIAN WRAPPER
1813. (F.) A loose day wrap cut like a night-chemise; made of muslin and lace, the sleeves of muslin and lace in alternating strips.

CIRCLET, SERCLETT
14th and 16th c's. term. Denoting a decorative circular head roll or chaplet of goldsmithry. 'For a serclett to marry maidens in.' (1540, Churchwardens' Accts., St. Margaret's, Westminster.)

CIRCULAR SKIRT
1895. (F.) A tailor-made gored skirt with sewn-down pleats over the hips and back; the hem 18 feet round.

CIRCUMFOLDING HAT
1830's. (M.) A round dress-hat, the crown moderately low and made to fold flat for carrying under the arm.

CLARENCE
19th c. (M.) A kind of boot, made with a triangular gusset of soft folded leather and eyelet holes for lacing across it; a forerunner of the elastic-sided boot.

CLARISSA HARLOWE BONNET
1879. (F.) A large bonnet of Leghorn straw, the brim brought forward on the forehead; lined with velvet.

CLARISSA HARLOWE CORSAGE
1847. (F.) An evening dress style, with neckline off the shoulders and folds caught in at the waist with a band of ribbon. Short sleeves with 2 or 3 lace falls.

CLOAK
Anglo-Saxon period on. (M. and F.) A loose outer garment of varying length falling from the neck over the shoulders. Very many named styles, which *see* under their respective headings.

CLOAK BAG, PORTMANTEAU
16th and 17th c's. (M.) A receptacle in which a valuable cloak could be packed for travelling.

CLOAK-BAG BREECHES
Early 17th c. (M.) Full and oval in shape, drawn in above the knee; encircled with decorative points (metal-tipped laces or ribbons) or closed below the knee with a ribbon rosette or bow on the outer side.

Cloak-Bag Breeches, 1625

CLOCHE
End of 13th c. CLOCHER, 14th into 15th c. A travelling cloak. *See* BELL.

CLOCK
16th c. on. (1) A gore or triangular insertion into a garment to widen it at that point, as with collars, stockings, etc. 'Of a band (collar) the clocks (are) the laying in of the cloth to make it round.' (1688, R. Holme, *Armourie*.) In the 16th c. the cape portions of some of the hoods worn by women were with or without clocks.

(2) Since the seams forming the triangular insertion began to be embroidered the term 'clock' was transferred to this form of embroidery and

46

the clocks of stockings came to mean embroidery at the ankles, whether gored or not.

Clocks (Embroidered), 1616

CLOGS
Med. to mid 19th c. (M. and F.) (1) Wooden-soled over-shoes to raise the wearer above the dirt. Until the 17th c. the term was synonymous with PATTENS, *q.v.* The shape followed the fashion of foot-wear of the day. 'Clogges or Pattens to keepe them out of the durt.' (1625, Purchas, *Pilgrimage.*)

Clog, 18th c.

(2) In 17th and 18th c.'s. the term was applied to ladies' leather-soled over-shoes with merely instep-straps, and generally matching the shoe. (On arrival of the guests) 'the Gentlemen were to put their hats and sticks in one corner and the Ladies their clogs in another'. (1780, *The Mirror*, no. 93.)
(3) All-wooden shoes worn by country-folk.

CLOSE COAT
18th and 19th c.'s. (M.) Term for a coat worn buttoned up. '. . . dress'd in a drab colour'd close Great Coat.' (1757, Dec., *Norwich Mercury.*)

CLOT, CLOUT-SHOEN
15th c. (M.) A heavy shoe shod with thin iron plates; worn by labourers.

CLOUD
1870's. (F.) A long scarf worn as an outdoor head-covering, with evening dress. '. . . in a swans-down cloak with a white cloud.' (1888, R. Kipling, *Plain Tales from the Hills.*)

CLUB
(1) Med. on. (M.) A heavy stick; fashionable instead of a cane in the 1730's and *c.* 1800 to 1810.
(2) An alternative name for the CATOGAN WIG, *q.v.* 'In an undress, unless you have a club as thick as both your double fists, you are not fit to be seen.' (1769, G. Colman, *Man and Wife.*)

CLY
16th c. on. Slang for a pocket.

COAT, M.E. COTE
From 13th c. (1) 13th c. (M. and F.). The everyday loose tunic, being the main garment worn by both sexes, though 'Kirtle' was more usual for women.
14th and 15th c.'s. A male garment, the term being largely replaced by Gipon or Doublet.
16th c. (M.) A short-sleeved or sleeveless jacket or jerkin worn over the doublet.

47

Mid 17th c. (M.) The name beginning to acquire its modern meaning of a sleeved body garment, varying in style according to the fashion of the period and worn as a body coat or as an upper garment (overcoat).

18th c. (M.) Distinguished from the Frock by having no turned-down collar; towards the end of the century the full E.D. coat had a stand collar. By that date the day Coat and Frock merged into the FROCK COAT (q.v.) and the Dress Coat (day or evening) began to replace the former COAT, q.v.

(2) 16th to end of 18th c. (F.) The name 'Coat', shortened from 'petticoat', was the term commonly used either for the under-petticoat or for the skirt of the gown.

COAT-BODICE

1880's. (F.) A day bodice made with long basques and pleated at the back like a man's frock coat with 2 hip buttons; cut high in the neck, having outside pockets and fastened all down the front. Sometimes made D-B. Usually tailor-made.

COAT-HANGER

19th c. (M.) The early name for the loop attached within the neck of a coat by which it could be hung up; the device used from 1830. Chain coat-hangers from c. 1850.

COATLET

1899. (F.) A short coat of velvet or fur with a fan-shaped spreading collar and large revers. Some were of cloth, frogged and braided.

COATS

18th c. A tailor's term for coat-buttons. See BREASTS.

COAT SHIRT

1890's. (M.) A shirt opening all down the front and closed by buttons; a device to avoid having to put the shirt on over the head; an American novelty, becoming later the Tunic shirt.

COAT-SLEEVE

C. 1864 on. (F.) Cut like the sleeve of a man's coat, straight and tubular, with a slight curve about the elbow and slight narrowing towards the wrist. Used for women's bodices and jackets. In the early 1870's a Mousquetaire cuff was often added.

COCK

From end of 17th to early 19th c. (M.) (1) The turn-up of the brim of a hat; various named forms such as the DENMARK COCK, the MONMOUTH COCK, DETTINGEN COCK, q.v.

(2) Later the term was used to denote the angle at which the hat was worn.

COCKERED CAP

16th c. (M.) A cap with a turned-up brim.

COCKERS, COKERS, COCURS

14th on into 19th c. (M.) From 14th to 16th c., a knee-high boot of rough make, worn by labourers, shepherds and country-folk. In the 17th c. the term was also applied to a sea-boot. 'Fishermen's great boots with which they wade into the sea, are called cokers.' (1695, Kennet, Par. Antiq. Gloss.)

From the 18th c., possibly earlier, the term was generally applied to leggings buckled or buttoned at the side and strapped under the foot. See OKERS.

COCKLE

17th c. (F.) A curl or ringlet.
'Instant she sped
To curl the Cockles of her new-bought head.'
(1608, Sylvester, Du Bartas.)

COD

Med. to 16th c. A bag. In 18th c. a cant term for a purse.

CODOVEC

17th c. (M.) A fancy trade name for a CASTOR (hat), q.v.

CODPIECE

15th and 16th c's. (M.) In 15th c. the front flap forming a pouch at the

48

fork of the long hose (tights) worn at that period. 'A kodpese like a pokett.' (*C.* 1460, *Townley Mysteries.*) In the 16th c. worn with trunk-hose, the codpiece was padded and very prominent; in the 17th c. when the projecting pouch was discarded the term was often applied to the front fastening of the breeches, and in the 18th c. occasionally to the front fall of the breeches.

COD-PLACKET
16th to 18th-c. (M.) Term denoting the front opening of the breeches.

Cod-Placket, 18th-c. breeches

CODRINGTON
1840's. (M.) A wrapper or loose overcoat, D-B or S-B, somewhat resembling a Chesterfield. Named after the Admiral, the victor of Navarino in 1827.

COGGERS
18th and early 19th c's. (M.) Gaiters of stiff leather or cloth buttoned up the side with a strap under the instep. *See* COCKERS.

COIF
(1) End of 12th c. to mid 15th c. (M.) A close-fitting plain linen cap, resembling a baby's bonnet, covering the ears and tied under the chin. In the 16th c. worn by the learned professions or the aged, as under caps or alone, for warmth; sometimes then of black cloth.

(2) 16th c. to 18th c. (F.) In 16th c. worn as an under cap; in late 16th and early 17th c's. the coif was often embroidered in coloured

silks, the sides made to curve forwards over the ears (popularly known as 'cheeks and ears') and often worn with a FOREHEAD CLOTH, *q.v.* In 18th c. the term was sometimes applied to indoor caps, particularly the ROUND-EARED CAP.

Coif, 13th c.

COIN DE FEU
1848. (F.) A short coat with wide sleeves and closed at the neck. Made of velvet, cashmere or silk, and generally worn indoors over a 'home dress'.

COINTISE, QUAINTISE
13th and 14th c's. Term denoting the curious or extravagant in fashion. Also used in connection with 14th-c. armour.

COLLAR
From *c.* 1300 on. A piece of material attached to the neck opening of a garment or added separately, to form a covering for the neck. In the 2nd half of 16th and throughout the 17th c. the more usual term was 'BAND', *q.v.*

The social significance of the collar restricting the free movements of the neck, as a symbol of Class Distinction, persisted through the centuries. For named forms see PRUSSIAN C., MASHER C., STAND-FALL C., ROSEBERY C., ETON C., DUX C., PICCADILLY C., POLO C.

COLLAR OF ESSES, SS COLLAR
The Livery collar of the House of Lancaster instituted by John of Gaunt, Duke of Lancaster, *c.* 1360.

COLLEEN BAWN CLOAK

1861. (F.) A cloak of white grenadine with a large cape caught up in the middle of the back with two rosettes. (Named after Dion Boucicault's famous melodrama.)

COLLEGIANS, OXONIANS

1830's. (M.) Short boots with 'a wedge cut out from each side of the top so as to enable the boot to be pulled on easily'.

COLLEY-WESTONWARD

16th c. (M.) A term denoting 'worn awry', and applied to the mandilion, a form of jacket fashionably worn sideways with one sleeve hanging down in front and the other behind.

Colley-Westonward Wearing of Mandilion, 1585–90

COLOURED SHIRT

1840's on. (M.) Developed from the AQUATIC SHIRT, *q.v.*, pink being a common colour. In 1860 French printed cambrics in various coloured patterns supplied shirts for informal wear. By 1894 coloured shirts had become 'perfectly good form even with frock coats', provided that the collar was white. 'Solid colours are barred; neat stripes in pink and blue are favourites.'

COMBINATIONS

2nd half 19th c. (M. and F.) (1) MALE. A vest and drawers in one, of woollen material; patented 1862; commonly worn in 1880's and 1890's.

(2) FEMALE. Chemise and drawers in one, introduced in 1877. Sometimes with high neck and long sleeves, for day wear. Of linen, merino, calico, nainsook and washing silks. In 1885 of natural wool introduced by Jaeger & Co. In the 1890's becoming more elegant with lace trimming, and the neck sometimes drawn in with coloured 'baby-ribbon'.

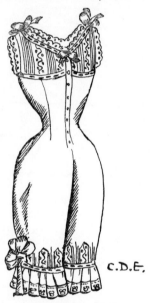

Combinations, 1898

COMFORTER

1840's on. (M.) A woollen scarf for wrapping round the neck in cold weather.

COMFORTS

1800. (F.) Double-soled sandals.

COMMODE

Late 17th and early 18th c's. (F.) A wire frame supporting the high fontange head-dress, *q.v.* 'The Commode is a frame of Wire cover'd with silk, on which the whole Head Attire is adjusted.' (1690, J. Evelyn, *Fop-Dictionary*.)

COMPASS CLOAK
16th and 17th c's. (M.) One style of the French cloak, being circular in cut; the 'Half Compass Cloak' was semicircular.

CONFIDANTS
Late 17th c. (F.) 'Smaller curles next the eares.' (1690, J. Evelyn, *Mundus Muliebris.*)

CONSTABLES
1830–40. (M.) 'Very small canes without handles, the top covered with gold plate.' (1830, *Gentleman's Magazine of Fashion.*)

CONVERSATION BONNET
1806. (F.) A poke bonnet with one side of the brim projecting beyond the cheek, the other side being turned back from the cheek.

CONVERSATION HAT
1803. (F.) Similar to the Conversation Bonnet but with brim complete at the back.

Conversation Hat, 1804

COPE
Med. (M. and F.) Originally and throughout the mediaeval period a voluminous semicircular cloak with a hood and open down the front. Worn by both sexes as a protection against cold and rain. Distinguished from the Mantle which had no hood. 'A route of ladies . . . in kirtles and in copes riche. . . . The cloth when fresh and new may make either a cope or a mantle, but in order of time it is first a cope—when it becomes old it

is beheaded, and being beheaded it becomes a mantle.' (1393, Gower, *Confessio Amantis.*)
(Cope also a monastic and ecclesiastical garment.)

COPOTAIN, COPINTANK, COPATAIN, COPPINTANKE, COPYTANK, COPTANK
16th, 17th c's. (M. and F.) First mentioned in 1508 but very fashionable from 1560 to 1620. A hat with a high conical crown and moderate brim often rolled up at the sides. Revived 1640's to 1665 as the 'Sugarloaf Hat'.

Copotain, 1575

COPPED HAT or CAP
Similar to Copotain. 'Sometyme men were coppid cappis like a sugar lofe.' (1519, Horman, *Vulgaria.*)

COPPED SHOE
2nd half 15th c. (M.) A piked shoe.

CORAL CURRANT BUTTON
1850's. (M.) A coral button shaped like a red currant and used on waistcoats.

CORAZZA
1845 on. (M.) A shirt made to button down the back, cut to the shape of the body, with narrow sleeves; of cambric or cotton.

CORDYBACK HAT
See CAUDEBEC HAT.

51

CORK

15th c. (M.) Apparently identical with the early galoshe and patten except that the sole was made of cork and not aspen.

CORK RUMP, or RUMP

Late 18th c. (F.) A bustle in the form of a large crescentic pad stuffed with cork.

CORK SHOE, CORKED SHOE, CORK-HEELED SHOE

16th and early 17th c's. (M. and F.) Shoes with wedge-shaped cork heels. Also worn for swimming.

CORK SOLES

(1) 16th and 17th c's. Shoes soled with cork.

(2) 19th c. (M.) Thin soles of cork for inserting into boots. Patent 1854. (F.) Thin soles of cork lined with wool for inserting into boots in cold weather. 1862.

CORK WIG

1760's. (M.) Cork, one of the many materials used for making wigs. 'John Light, peruke maker, has brought to great perfection the best method of making Cork Wigs, either smooth or in curls; and also Cork-Bag-wigs in the neatest manner.' (1763, *The Salisbury Journal*.)

CORNED SHOE

C. 1510 to 1540. The broad-toed shoe of the period. 'So many garded hose, such cornede shoes . . .' (1529, Skelton.)

CORNET

16th, 17th and 19th c's. (F.) (1) 16th and 17th c's. The Cornet was similar to the Bongrace and generally made of dark-coloured velvet when worn with a French hood; otherwise of lawn. 'Cornet, a fashion of shadow or Boongrace.' (1611, Cotgrave.)

(2) Late 17th c. The term applied to a lace or lawn day cap with lappets falling about the ears and sometimes a pendant flap behind.

(3) 19th c. 1st half: a cornet or (usually) cornette was a white day cap with rounded or slightly pointed caul, and tied under the chin.

Cornet, 1806

CORNET or FRENCH SKIRT

1892. (F.) A day skirt made with a seam at each side and slightly trained. The front piece slightly gored to measure 40″ at hem diminishing to 20″, and shaped with darts at the waist. The back cut on the cross in one piece 20″ at the hem diminishing up to 10″ at the waist; the train being a segment of a circle. No foundation skirt worn under it.

CORNETTE

See CORNET.

CORONET, CRONET, Med. CORONAL

14th c. The open crown of nobility.

CORSAGE

The upper or bodice portion of a woman's dress.

CORSE

See BALDRICK.

CORSELET

1860's on. (F.) A deep form of SWISS BELT, *q.v.*

CORSET or CORSE

14th and 15th c's. (M. and F.) (1) A close-fitting sleeveless bodice, often very decorative.

(2) CORSET or STAYS. End of 18th

52

c. on. (M. and F.) An under-garment with whalebone or steel ribs
embracing the chest and compressing
the natural waist-level. The French
word 'corset' was beginning to be
used as a refinement for 'stays' at the
close of the 18th c.; but both terms
were in common use. 'Neat stays
and corsets.' (1800, adv. *Ipswich
Journal.*)

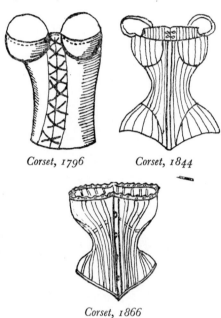

Corset, 1796   *Corset, 1844*

Corset, 1866

Named styles: (F.) (*a*) Demi-
corset. 1820's. Eight to ten inches
long with light whalebones, worn by
day for domestic duties.

(*b*) Glove - fitting corset. 1867.
Front fastening; held by spring latch.

(*c*) Long corset. 1800 to 1810.
Supported the breasts, covered the
hips and was laced up the back.

(*d*) Short corset. 1820's. Metal-
bound eyelet holes introduced; back-
laced. 'Stays are bound with iron
in the holes through which the laces
are drawn, so as to bear the tremen-
dous tugging which is intended to
reduce so important a part of the
human frame to a third of its natural
proportion.' (1828.)

(*e*) Skeleton corset. 1899. A belt
corset with a few crossed straps.

(*f*) Swan-bill corset. 1876. The
long metal busk in front had a marked
curve below and by 1878 suspenders
were added, replacing garters for
keeping up stockings.

Front fastening for all corsets of a
better quality became general after
c. 1851. *See* also STAYS.

CORSICAN NECKTIE
1830's. (M.) *See* NAPOLEON NECK-
TIE.

COSSACKS
1814 to c. 1850. (M.) Trousers
pleated into a waistband and tied
round the ankles with a ribbon draw-
string. Inspired from the Cossacks
accompanying the Czar of Russia at
the Peace celebrations of 1814. At
first very baggy but becoming less so
in 1820 when the drawstrings were
usually omitted; double straps under
the instep were added in 1830 and
from c. 1840 a single strap, when the
garment began to be called simply
'pleated trousers'.

Cossacks, 1819

COSTUME

1860's on. (F.) A dressmaker's term denoting a day dress of one material designed for outdoor activities; by 1868 also applied to afternoon dresses with long trains.

COSTUME RASTERRE

1870's. (F.) A walking dress of which the skirt just brushed the ground.

COTE

See COAT.

COTE-HARDIE, COTE-HARDY

14th to mid 15th c. (M. and F.)
(1) MALE. Earliest reference 1333. Its exact nature remains obscure; the cote-hardie is thought to have been a close-fitting, knee-length overgarment with low neck; buttoned down the front to a low waist. Elbow-length sleeves with a tongue-shaped extension behind. After c. 1350 the cote-hardie was shortened and the elbow flap lengthened into a long narrow hanging band known as a 'tippet' or French 'coudière'. Tippets and skirts were often dagged. A belt was always worn at hip-level, and the Knightly Girdle worn by nobles.

Cote-hardie (F.), 14th c.

(2) FEMALE. A close-fitting waisted garment worn over the kirtle, long; low neck; sleeves with tippets. With or without buttons down the front. Fitchets (placket holes) in the skirt were common. No girdle.

COTTAGE BONNET

1808 to 1870's. (F.) A close-fitting straw bonnet, the brim projecting beyond the cheeks. Modified through these decades, and in the 1870's the brim rolled upwards, with lining of pleated satin.

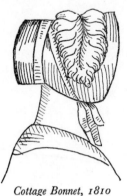

Cottage Bonnet, 1810

COTTAGE FRONT

1800 to 1820. (F.) A day bodice made with a gap in front and fastened by lacing across from one edge to the other over a habit shirt.

COUCHED

Med. Trimmed.

COUDIÈRES

See TIPPET and COTE-HARDIE.

COUNTER-FILLET

Late 14th and early 15th c's. (F.) The fillet securing the veil.

COURTEPYE

14th and 15th c's. (M. and F.) An upper garment akin to the Surcoat. Exact nature unknown. The male garment was short and in 15th c. may have been the same as the short Houppelande.

COUTENANCE, COUNTENANCE

Late 16th and early 17th c's. A

small muff. 'A snuffkin or muffe.'
(1611, Cotgrave.)

COVERCHIEF
Med. into 16th c. (F.) The Norman term for the Saxon Head-Rail or Veil. A draped head-covering varying in size, worn by all classes but largely discarded by the higher ranks from the 15th c. or worn with other head-dresses. Made of various materials and colours. In 13th c. those worn by royalty or nobles were of silk or cloth of gold.

COVERT COAT, COVER COAT
1880's on. (M.) A short fly-fronted overcoat with strapped seams, made with whole back, no centre back vent, but short vents in the side seams. Popular 'with horsey young gentlemen' and at first designed for riding but soon adopted for general wear. In 1897 made with Raglan sleeves and known as a 'Raglan Covert'.

Covert Coat, 1891

COXCOMB, COCKSCOMB
Late 16th and early 17th c's. (M.) A professional fool's hood with its apex in the shape of a cock's comb.

CRACOWES, CRAKOWS, CRAW-CAWS
1360, but commoner 1390 to 1410 and again 1450 to 1480. (M. and F.) Long piked shoes, later called POULAINES, *q.v.*

CRAN
1830's on. (M.) The V-shaped gap between the turned-over collar and the lapel of a coat.

CRANTS, CRAUNCE, GRAUNDICE
Med. to end of 18th c. (F.) A chaplet or garland of flowers or of goldsmithry and gems. 'The Funeral Crants' was a symbolic garland carried at the funeral of a virgin. (*See* Hamlet, V, i.) These were sometimes made of paper flowers and a framework of linen or iron to which the flowers, real or sham, were attached. Subsequently the Crants were hung over the deceased's seat in church or chancel, together with her collar, girdle and one white glove.

CRAVAT
Mentioned in 1643 but commonly worn from 1660 to end of 19th c. with periods when it was unfashionable. (M. and F.) (1) MALE. A neckcloth of lawn, muslin or silk, folded round the neck, the ends tied in a knot or bow in front.

In 19th c. often starched and supported on a 'stiffener'. From *c.* 1840 the large form covering the shirt-front above the waistcoat was called a 'Scarf', the smaller a 'Necktie'.

(2) FEMALE. From 1830's on with sporting costumes.

CRAVATE COCODES
1863. (F.) A large bow cravat worn with a habit shirt and stand collar.

CRAVAT STRINGS
1665 to 1680's. (M.) A length of coloured ribbon passed round the two ends of the cravat and tied in a bow under the chin. Later it was often a made-up stiffened bow with several loops, fixed on behind the cravat which was loosely tied, the ends falling over the centre of the bow.

CREPINE, CREPYN, CRIPPEN, CRESPINE

A crimped or pleated frill. 'Crespine, the crepine of a French hood.' (1611, Cotgrave.) N.B.—'Crespine' has not been found in any MSS. of the Middle Ages. 'Crepine' occurs once in 1347. The identification of the Crepine with the Caul must be discarded. The word 'Crepine' was revived at the beginning of the 16th c. (spelt in 1532 'Crispyne'); apparently a crimped material.

CRÊVE-CŒUR

End of 17th c. (F.) Curled locks at the nape of the neck.

CREWEL CAP

17th c. (M.)

'The crewel cap is knit like hose
For them whose zeale takes cold i'
    th' nose;
Whose purity doth judge it meete
To clothe alike both head and feete.'
    (C. 1620, *The Ballad of the Caps.*)

CRICKET SHOES

See SPIKED SHOES.

CRINOLETTE

1868 to *c.* 1873. (F.) A small form of cage crinoline hooped behind only; 'of steel half hoops with horsehair or crinoline flounces forming a bustle'.

Crinolette, 1873

CRINOLETTE PETTICOAT

C. 1870, revived 1883. (F.) A petticoat plain in front with half circle steel hoops round the upper part behind and flounces below.

Crinolette Petticoat with detachable Flounce, 1871

CRINOLINE

1829. *See* TEXTILES. In 1840 made of horsehair warp and wool weft, used for making stiff under-petticoats to expand the skirt. In 1856 the Artificial Crinoline or Cage Petticoat appeared with whalebone hoops added, replaced in '57 by watch-spring hoops. Henceforth the name 'Crinoline' was applied to this cage petticoat. The number of hoops varied and also the shape; in 1857–9 domed, then pyramidal. By 1862 the size began to diminish; in 1866 the front became flat and the back

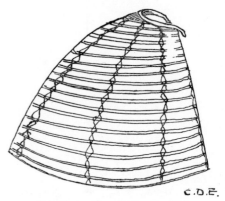

Crinoline or Cage Petticoat, 1860's

56

projected, merging by '68 into the Crinolette. Named varieties: CAGE AMÉRICAINE, CAGE EMPIRE, ONDINA, PANNIER, SANSFLECTUM, *q.v.*

CRISP

16th c. (F.) A veil. 17th c. A curl of hair.

CRISPIN

(1) 1839. MALE. A cloak for evening dress; with very large floating sleeves and lined with silk, wadded and quilted.

(2) 1842. FEMALE. A short mantle, occasionally sleeved, fitting close round the neck, with a small pélerine-cape. Cut on the cross, made of cashmere, satin or velvet, and often wadded.

CRISPIN CLOCHE

1842. (F.) A bell-shaped crispin, knee-length.

CROCHET

14th c. on. A hook. In the 15th c. used for fastening a shoe; in the 16th and 17th c's. attached at the waist of a woman's dress for suspending a pomander. The crochet was often an article of jewellery.

CROMWELL COLLAR

1880's. (F.) A deep turnover collar, the front nearly meeting edge to edge. Worn with morning dress.

CROMWELL SHOES

1868. (F.) Of leather with large buckle and tongue covering the instep. 'The favourite for croquet parties.' Revived in 1888 as a day shoe with high-cut front and a large bow.

CROP

Term denoting 'short', as in 'crop-doublet' (1640) and 'Crop-scratch wig' (1806). 'The Bedford Crop' or style of short hair favoured by the Duke of Bedford and his political friends (1790's) as a protest against the tax on hair powder.

CROP-DOUBLET

C. 1610. (M.) A short-waisted Doublet.

CROQUET BOOTS

1865. (F.) Of morocco leather often with fancy toe-caps and 'side springs' and described as 'rising to a point in front and back with tassels, and laced with coloured ribbons'.

CROSSCLOTH, FOREHEAD CLOTH

16th and 17th c's. (F.) (1) A triangular piece of material worn with a coif or caul; its straight border over the forehead, the point behind; tied on under the chin or at the back of the head. Often embroidered to match the coif with which it was worn.

(2) (M. and F.) 16th to 18th c. Plain crosscloths worn in illness or in bed to prevent wrinkles. 'Many weare such cross-clothes or forehead cloathes as our women use when they are sicke.' (1617, Fynes Moryson.) *See* also FRONTLET.

CROSS-GARTERING

2nd half 16th and early 17th c's. (M.) A mode of wearing a sash garter placed below the knee in front, the ends crossed behind the knee and brought forward to be tied in a bow above the knee, either centrally or on the outer side. Common with stockings worn over canions.

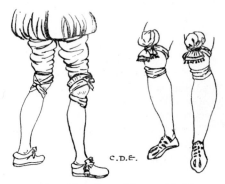

Cross-Gartering, 16th c. 2nd half

CROSS POCKET

18th and 19th c's. term. A pocket with a horizontal opening.

CRUCHES

Late 17th c. (F.) Small forehead curls.

CUE
18th c. Fr. Queue. The pendant tail of a wig. First appearing as a civilian mode *c.* 1720.

CUE-PERUKE
18th c. A wig with a cue.

CUFF, M.E. COFFE, CUFFE
15th c. on. (M. and F.) The turned-back part, actual or sham, of the sleeve of a garment so as to give an extra cover to the wrist, either for warmth or ornament. Originally it could be turned down over the hand, for warmth. A fur cuff was frequently added to women's gowns in 15th c. Men's cuffs have more

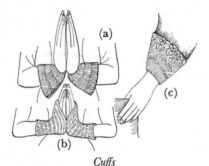

Cuffs
(a) *Early 15th c.* (b) *Late 15th c.* (c) C. *1628*

usually been a feature of display, such as the detachable lace cuff in the form of a reversed funnel-shape commonly worn with a falling-band (mid 16th to mid 17th c.) or a ruff. 'Holland to make yor Lordship Cuffes . . . 1 laced ruff and 2 payer of Cuffes.' (1632, Viscount Scudamore Accts. at Holme Lacy.) Replaced later by the ruffled end of the shirt or chemise sleeve.

The cuff of the coat sleeve (M.) became a striking feature in 18th c. until *c.* 1770, the cuff being either open behind (to *c.* 1750) or closed and known as Closed Cuff. *See* BOOT CUFF, MARINER'S CUFF.

The Closed Cuff, wide and winged (1750's), i.e. falling away from the sleeve on the outer side, gradually diminished, becoming small and close by *c.* 1770.

In 19th c. *see* FRENCH CUFF (M.) and AMADIS SLEEVE (F.).

CUFF-BUTTON, SLEEVE BUTTON, CUFF LINK
Late 17th c. on. Two discs, usually of metal, connected by a link, used to close the vent in the wristband of a shirt; replacing the earlier Cuff strings. 'A Cuff Button with a Diamond . . .' (1684, *London Gazette.*) 'Four Turkey Stone Sleeve Buttons set in Gold and Enamell'd.' (1686, *London Gazette.*)

The term 'Links' mentioned in Aris' *Birmingham Gazette,* 1788. Cuff strings, however, remained in general use until the 19th c. when a small mother-of-pearl button at the base of the cuff served to close it at that level.

Cuff-links, often jewelled, inserted close to the edge of the cuff, so as to be visible, became the general mode *c.* 1840.

CUFFIE, CUFF
14th c. A CAP or COIF, *q.v.* (Fr. Coiffe.)

CUFF STRING, SLEEVE STRING
17th c. (M.) The tie for the shirt sleeve at the wrist. 'A pr. of cuffs strings.' (1688, James Masters' Expense Book.)

CUIRASSE BODICE
1874. (F.) A very long tight day bodice, boned, descending over the hips; often made of a different material from the dress, the sleeves matching the trimming. 'It moulds the figure to perfection.'

CUIRASSE TUNIC
1874. (F.) A plain tight tunic worn with a cuirasse bodice.

CUKER
15th c. (F.) Part of the horned head-dress.
'She is hornyd like a kowe . . . for syn
The cukar hynges so side now,
Furrid with a cat skyn.'
(*c.* 1460, *The Towneley Mysteries* Surtees Soc.)

Cuirasse Bodice, 1878

CUMBERLAND CORSET

1815–20's. (M.) Corset worn by the Dandies of the period. 'Ordered a pair of Cumberland corsets with whalebone back.' (1818, *Diary of a Dandy*.)

CUMBERLAND HAT, HAT A LA WILLIAM TELL

1830's. (M.) A tall hat with an 8″ crown tapering upwards and a narrow brim turned up at the sides.

CUMMERBUND

1893 on. (M.) A wide sash of coloured silk or drill wound twice round the body in lieu of a waistcoat, and fastened on one side sometimes by ornamental buttons, or tucked in. Worn at first as a black waistband with evening dress; later, as coloured sash by day. For summer wear.

CUPEE

17th c. (F.) 'A pinner that hangs close to the head.' (1690, Evelyn, *Mundus Muliebris.*)

CUPOLA COAT

C. 1710 to 1780. (F.) Contemporary name for a Bell Hoop or Petticoat. A domed hooped petticoat distended with whalebone or cane hoops to the fashionable size. 'The cupola-coat allows all the freedom of motion . . . the compass of the coat serves to keep the men at a decent distance and appropriates to every lady a spacious verge sacred to herself.' (1747, *Whitehall Evening Post.*)

CURRICLE CLOAK

1801 to 1806. (F.) A ½- or ¾-length cloak shaped in at the waist, the front borders curving away from midline. Edged with lace or fur.

CURRICLE COAT

(1) 1808. (F.) A long coat with lapels, fastened at the bosom only, then sloping away towards the back. Very long sleeves. Sometimes called 'Gig coat' (1820's).

(2) 1840's. (M.) New name for the Box or Driving Coat, with one or more capes, *q.v.*

CURRICLE DRESS

1794 to 1803. (F.) A round gown worn with an over-tunic or half-robe usually of net. The tunic short-sleeved, open in front and thigh-length; the low neck sometimes filled in with a habit shirt.

CURRICLE PELISSE

1820's. (F.) A Pelisse with three capes.

CUSHIONET, QUISSIONET

1560 to 1630's. (F.) A form of bustle worn with a farthingale to give it a tilt up behind. 'A varingale and quissionet of fustian in Apres.' (1566, Will of Wm. Claxton of Burnehall.)

CUSHION HEAD-DRESS

A 19th-c. term for the circular padded roll worn by women in the first half of 15th c. *See* CHAPLET.

CUTAWAY COAT

See NEWMARKET. 'Formerly called the Newmarket.' (1876.)

CUT-FINGERED GLOVES

End of 16th and 1st half 18th c.'s. (M. and F.) In the former period the fingers were slashed to reveal the underlying rings:

'But he must cut his glove to show his pride
That his trim jewel might be better spy'd.'

(1597, Hall's *Satire*, IV.)

In the 18th c. the tips of the fingers were cut open, a fashion confined to women. 'Half a dozen of cut-fingered gloves.' (1719, Earl of Thanet Accounts, Kent Record Office.) '2 pair of fine white thread gloves that are open-fingered.' (1740, Purefoy Accounts.)

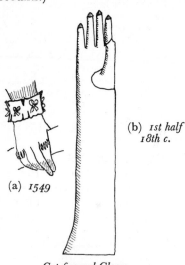

(b) *1st half 18th c.*

(a) *1549*

Cut-fingered Gloves

CUT-FINGERED PUMPS

16th c. (M.) Pumps slashed over the toes. ''Tis as good to goe in cut-finger'd pumps as corke shoes, if one wear Cornish diamonds on his toes.' (1591, T. Nashe, Introduction to Sidney's *Astrophel and Stella*.)

Cut-fingered Pumps
(a) *1539*   (b) *2nd half 16th c.*

CUT-IN or CHECK

19th c. (M.) The more or less horizontal cut-back of the material of a dress coat at the level of the waist.

CUT STEEL BUTTONS

Fashionable from 1770. (M.) Buttons of steel, the face chased and polished.

CUT-WIG

18th c. (M.) A small plain wig without a queue.

CUT-WORK, DAGGING

(1) The ornamental cutting in fantastic shapes, such as flames, leaves, etc., of edges of fashionable garments. Introduced, according to the Chronicle of St. Albans, *c.* 1346. Popular period 1380 to 1440.

(2) 16th and 17th c.'s. Decoration made by cutting out portions of the material and crossing the spaces with geometrical designs in needlework. 'White woorkes, alias cutwoorkes made beyond the seas.' Chiefly in Italy (1579) but by 1620 also in England.

CYCLAS, CICLATON, CINGLATON

13th c. (M. and F.) A rich gown worn on ceremonial occasions, e.g. at the coronation of Henry III and his Queen. *See* also GLOSSARY OF MATERIALS.

D

DAG, DAGGES, DAGGING, JAGS, JAGGING
14th to end of 15th c. (M. and F.) Dagging introduced *c.* 1346; also called CUT-WORK, *q.v.* The term applied to the slashing of any border of a garment into tongues, scallops, leaves, vandykes, called 'dagges', as a form of decoration.

DALK
From A.D. 1000 to end of 15th c. Usually a pin but also a brooch, clasp or buckle.

DANDIZETTE
1816 to 1820. The female Dandy conspicuous for her 'Grecian Bend'; the name did not survive more than a few years.

DANDY
C. 1816 on. (M.) A 'post-war' name for the Exquisite as represented by Lord Petersham. 'The made up male doll who, when wig, dyed whiskers, stiff cravat, padded breast, paint and perfume are taken away, sinks into nothing.' (*The Hermit in London,* ed. 1822.) By 1829 'Dandy has been voted vulgar and Beau is now all the word'. (Disraeli, *The Young Duke.*) Count D'Orsay was described as 'The last of the Dandies' whose logical heirs were The Heavy Swell, 1860's, and The Masher, 1880's, 1890's.

DANISH or OPEN BOTTOM TROUSERS
1870's. (M.) For boys; the legs reaching just below the knees and the bottoms open. Worn with a jacket.

Danish Trousers, 1870

DANNOCK
19th c. (M.) 'Dannocks, Darnocks, hedgers' gloves.' (Forby, *Vocabulary of East Anglia. C.* 1825.)

DART
A narrow dart-shaped piece cut out and the edges sewn together to improve the fit of a garment. *See* FISH, the corresponding term applied to male garments until mid 19th c.

D-B
Tailor's term for 'double-breasted'.

DEATH'S HEAD BUTTON
18th c. (M.) A domed button covered with a thread of metal twist or mohair, forming a pattern of four quarters.

DÉCOLLETAGE
(F.) The low neckline of a woman's dress.

DEER STALKER
1860's on. (M.) A tweed cap with ear-flaps worn tied together over the crown. For country wear.

Deerstalker, 1890

DEMI-CASTOR
17th and early 18th c's. (M. and F.) A beaver hat made partly of coney and therefore considered inferior to the CASTOR, *q.v.*

DEMICEINT, DEMYSENT, DYMY-SON GIRDLE, DEMI-GIRDLE, DEMISON
2nd half 15th c. to mid 16th c. (F.) A girdle with front ornamentation only. 'A half girdle or one whose forepart is of gold or silver and hinder of silk.' (1611, Cotgrave.)

DEMI-CORONAL
16th c. A tiara, i.e. half a coronet.

DEMI-GIGOT SLEEVE
1825 to 1830, also in 1891. (F.) A sleeve full at the shoulder, narrowing to the elbow, thence tight to the wrist.

DEMI-GOWN
Late 15th and 16th c's. (M.) A short gown, popular from 1500 to 1560; often worn on horseback. 'My short rydinge gown of worsett.' (1548, *Wills and Inventories of Northern Counties.*)

DEMI-HABILLEMENT, HALF-ROBE, HALF-GOWN
1794 to *c.* 1800. (F.) A low-necked, thigh-length tunic with short sleeves, worn over a round gown and pulled in at the waist by a narrow ribbon belt.

DEMI-RIDING COAT
See JUST-AU-CORPS.

DEMI-SLEEVE, DEMI-MAUNCH
16th c. (M.) A wide sleeve ending at the elbow.

DEMI-SURTOUT
1818. (M.) A light, fitting overcoat with a low collar.

DEMYSENT
See DEMICEINT.

DENMARK COCK
2nd half 18th c. (M.) A tricorne hat with its brim 'cocked', i.e. turned up high at the back and lower in front.

DERBY
(1) 1890's. (M.) A necktie usually called a 'Four-in-hand'; the tie was straight-sided with a slightly narrower centre and one end longer than the other. Tied in a knot presenting a free edge above and below.
(2) 1860's on. (M.) American name for the Bowler hat.

DETACHABLE SLEEVES
15th and 16th c's. (M. and F.) (1) MALE. Doublet sleeves might be tied to the arm-hole by 'points' (ties) and were removable at will.
(2) FEMALE. Separate sleeves were made for partlets.

DETTINGEN COCK
18th c. (M.) A tricorne hat with high equal cocks, front and back.

DIADEM BONNET
1869. (F.) Of lace and velvet forming an upright diadem above the forehead; tied on by a ribbon passing under the chignon and ruched strings loosely knotted under the chin.

DIADEM COMB
1830's. (F.) A wide curved comb with a high ornamental gallery in the shape of a diadem; worn as a head decoration with evening dress.

DIADEM FANCHON BONNET
1869. (F.) A mere border 1″ wide covered with tulle or ruching, trimmed with an aigrette of feathers or flowers. Short ruched lappets fastened in front under a satin bow beneath the chin.

DIANA VERNON BONNET
1879. (F.) A large bonnet with low crown and wide brim.

DIANA VERNON HAT

(F.) A straw hat with shallow crown, the brim wide in front and curved up on one side; rosette and broad ribbon strings placed under the brim. For country wear.

DICKEY, DICKY

(1) Late 18th and early 19th c's. (F.) A woman's under-petticoat.

(2) 19th c. (M.) A shirt-front with attached collar, of starched linen, worn over a flannel shirt. Known at end of 18th c. as a 'Tommy'. 'Never worn by a gentleman' (1840) but only by 'a Two-shirts-and-a-dicky sort of man'. (Surtees.)

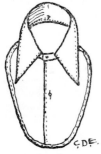

Dickey, 1890

DILDO

Late 17th and 18th c's. (M.) A sausage-shaped curl of a wig.

DINNER JACKET, DRESS LOUNGE, TUXEDO (American)

(M.) Introduced as 'Dress Lounge' in 1888, the term 'Dinner Jacket' used from 1898 on. A jacket for informal evening wear; at first with a continuous roll collar and lapels turning low to waist-level; faced to the edge with silk or satin. One or two buttons, but always worn open. From 1898 1 button only. The back cut whole, sleeves finished with cuffs. Materials: cheviot, corkscrew or velvet.

DIRECTOIRE BONNET

1878–80. (F.) A square, moderately high crown, the brim fitting over the ears, spreading out above the forehead.

Dress Lounge, 1889–90

DIRECTOIRE COAT

1888. (F.) The bodice of a day dress in the form of a D-B or S-B coat cut across horizontally above the waist-line in front, falling vertically at the sides and from a gathering at the back of the waist, to the ankles. Tight sleeves with cuffs. Worn with a wide folded sash round the waist. If D-B, worn with a habit shirt; if S-B, worn open with a shirt blouse. The revival of Directoire styles was inspired by Sardou's drama *La Tosca*, as played by Sarah Bernhardt (1887).

DIRECTOIRE HAT

1888. (F.) Similar to the bonnet but larger.

DIRECTOIRE JACKET

1888. (F.) A similar bodice of a day dress but without the skirt portion of the Directoire coat.

DIRECTOIRE SKIRT

1895. (F.) A day skirt made of 7 gores, the 4 at the back being fluted. Lined and stiffened with horsehair.

Thirteen to eighteen feet round the hem.

DIRECTOIRE SWALLOW-TAIL COAT
1888. (F.) The back of a Directoire coat, cut into tails with a deep central vent between. Afternoon dress style.

DISHABILLE
1713 on. 'We have a kind of sketch of dress, if I may so call it, among us, which as the invention was foreign, is call'd a Dishabille. Everything is thrown on with a loose careless air'. (Sept. 1713, *The Guardian*.) In late 19th c. an 'undress' style, i.e. for wearing on informal occasions.

DITTOS
From mid 18th c. on. (M.) Term denoting a suit of one material throughout.

DIVIDED SKIRT
1882. (F.) Introduced by Lady Harberton; a short kilted skirt cut so that when the wearer was standing still the division of the two legs was concealed. Worn for bicycling.

DIVORCE CORSET
1816. (F.) A padded metal triangle the point of which projected up between the breasts to thrust them apart.

DOG COLLAR
1860's. (M.) A plain shallow stand collar encircling the neck and overlapping in front. A successor to the All-rounder. Later, the name commonly given to the clerical collar buttoning behind.

DOLLY VARDEN BONNET
1881 on. (F.) A wide brim with wide ribbons crossing it to be tied under the chin. The name derived from the heroine of Dickens's novel, *Barnaby Rudge*.

DOLLY VARDEN CAP
1888. (F.) 'A little bit of gathered lace with puckered crown and a few short ribbons.' Worn with a tea-gown.

DOLLY VARDEN HAT
1871 to c. 1875. (F.) A straw hat with small low crown and very wide brim; slight trimming of flowers or ribbon. Worn at a forward tilt and tied on by ribbon under the chignon.

DOLLY VARDEN POLONAISE
1871. (F.) A Polonaise dress based on the Polonaise gown of c. 1780 but made of chintz or cretonne. Worn with a bright silk petticoat (skirt) plain, flowered or quilted. In winter the Dolly Varden might be of flannel or cashmere printed with a chintz pattern. A fashion favoured mainly by the Middle and lower Middle Classes.

Dolly Varden Dress and Hat, 1871

DOLMAN
1870's and 1880's. (F.) A mantle with a sleeve cut all in one with the side piece and hanging loose; sometimes made in the form of a sling. In the Bustle period the front had hanging mantlet ends and the back a full

basque tied to form a puff over the bustle. A cape was sometimes added.

Dolman, 1888

DOLMANETTE
1890's. (F.) A crocheted Dolman tied at the neck with a large ribbon bow; also 'if liked, sew a ribbon at the back to tie round the waist'.

DOMINO
(1) 17th c. (F.) 'A veil used by some women that mourn.' (1611, Cotgrave.)

(2) Early 18th c. (M. and F.) A cloak, usually black, worn with a mask at masquerades.

DONARIÈRE
1869. (F.) A round hood with attached pèlerine and sleeves; of quilted satin.

DONCASTER RIDING COAT
1850's. (M.) A loose form of Newmarket Coat, *q.v.*

DONNA MARIA SLEEVE
1830's. (F.) A day sleeve, immensely full from shoulder to wrist but caught in by a loop, along the inner side of the forearm from elbow to wrist.

DORELET, DORLET
Med. (F.) A hair-net embroidered with jewels.

DORMEUSE, DORMOUSE, FRENCH NIGHT-CAP
2nd half 18th c. (F.) An indoor undress white day cap with a puffed-up crown and edged on each side with deep falling flaps trimmed with lace and called 'wings'; popularly known as 'cheek wrappers'. These wings curved back from the temples, leaving the forehead and front hair exposed. The crown was trimmed round with ribbon. The Dormeuse was sometimes tied under the chin. In the 1770's the size greatly increased and the gable-shape was produced.

Dormeuse, 2nd half 18th c.

D'ORSAY COAT
1838. (M.) An overcoat in the form of a Pilot Coat (*q.v.*) but made to fit in at the waist by having a long 'fish' (dart) taken out below the arm-hole. Shallow collar. Slashed or flapped pockets in the skirts. No pleats, folds or hip buttons. Skirts cut to hang over the knees. Plain sleeves with 3 or 4 buttons of horn or gambroon.

DORSET THREAD BUTTON
18th c. to *c.* 1830. A button made on a brass wire ring covered with white

cotton threads radiating from the centre and kept flat. Used on underclothes from *c.* 1700.

DOUBLE
16th c. A term often denoting 'lined', e.g. 'double gloves' meant lined gloves.

DOUBLE BOUFFANT SLEEVE
1832–6. (F.) A short puffed evening dress sleeve, the puffing divided into two by a transverse band. Revived in 1855 for day, the sleeve to the wrist and the puffs being unequal; the division made just above the wrist. A lace ruffle added.

DOUBLE RUFF
1st half 17th c. (M. and F.) A ruff with a double row of flattened convolutions.

DOUBLE SLEEVE
1854; revived 1891. (F.) A loose oversleeve reaching half-way down the upper arm over a long tight sleeve to the wrist. Both made of the same material as the dress. For day wear, chiefly in summer.

DOUBLET, GIPON, POURPOINT
(1) 14th c. to *c.* 1670. (M.) The term Doublet, though used in France in 14th c., was not general in England for civilian wear until 15th c. It was a padded jacket worn next to the shirt; close-fitting and waisted but not usually belted unless worn without an over-garment.

Doublet skirts varied from nil or very narrow to covering the hips, according to the fashion of the day. In the 17th c. the skirts consisted of a series of tabs of varying depth. In the late 15th and early 16th c's. the front was widely open, requiring a stomacher or partlet fill-in.

The Dancing Doublet of 14th c. was often heavily embroidered.

(2) 1650 to 1670. (F.) Female doublets following the male style were sometimes worn by women on horseback.

'Doublets like to men they weare
As if they meant to flout us,
Thrust round with poynts and ribbons fayre. . . .'
(Will Bagnall's Ballet, *Musarum Delicoe.*)

Doublet, c. 1577

DOUILLETTE, DONNILETTE
1818 to 1830's. (F.) At first a quilted Pelisse for winter wear; in the 1830's it was winter dress in the form of a Redingote, made up of a caped pèlerine of merino, cashmere or stamped satin; with wide sleeves. To be worn over a cambric or silk walking-dress. 'She was wrapped up in a . . . figured satin douillette or wadded pelisse.' (1825, Harriette Wilson, *Paris Lions and London Tigers.*)

DOWNY CALVES
18th c. (M.) False calves woven into the appropriate part of the stockings to produce manly-looking calves. Patented 1788. *See* FALSE CALVES.

DRAGON'S BLOOD CANE
Early 18th c. (M.) A fashionable cane made from the frond stems of the Dragon Palm, a ratan palm from Malay.

DRAWERS
From 16th c. on. (M. and F.) (1) MALE. Essentially an under-garment

66

and until the 19th c. usually of linen.

(*a*) Short; knee-length or trunks cut full and square, tied in front with ribbon and pulled in behind by tapes over a short vent. Worn to end of 19th c.

(*b*) Long; ankle-length; some footed or with stirrup-band passing under the instep.

In the 1st half of the 19th c. the waistband had holes through which the tongues of the braces passed; from *c.* 1845 loops of tape were substituted for these holes. The vent at the back was filled in with a puff which could be reduced by tightening the lacing across it. From late 18th c. male drawers were made of cotton flannel or wool stockinette.

Long drawers in 19th c. were known as 'trousers' or 'long pants'.

(a) c. *1660*   (b) *1805*

Drawers (*Male*)

(2) FEMALE. From *c.* 1806; at first similar in cut to the male garment, but each leg separate or merely attached to the waistband. In 1806 'muslin drawers' spoken of and in 1807 'patent elastic woollen drawers of stockinette' for riding. In 1813 drawers with attached feet, for cold weather. While silk drawers were worn by the fashionables, the usual materials through the first half of 19th c. were long-cloth, cotton or merino, the garment very full, and reaching below the knee. In the 1840's broderie anglaise trimming might be added.

In the Crinoline period drawers of scarlet flannel were fashionable and often exposed to view. Sometimes

replaced by knickerbockers of that material, or in the 1890's of grey flannel. From 1870 on the garment became elaborately trimmed with lace, embroidery, tucks and frills, the legs much widened. *See* also COMBINATIONS.

Drawers (*F.*), *1895*

(3) The term 'drawers' was occasionally loosely applied, in 17th and 18th c's., to any garment—such as breeches—which could be drawn on.

DRAWN-WORK

16th and 17th c's. A form of decoration produced in a textile by drawing out some of the threads of the weft and warp to form a pattern, with the addition of needlework.

DRESS CLIP or PAGE

1840's. (F.) A metal hook, often in the shape of a negro's head, attached at the waist; from this was suspended a chain with a clip at the end; used for clipping the hitched-up skirt when walking.

DRESS CLOTHES

19th c. (M.) A term applied in the first half of the century to the costume for formal social functions in the day as well as in the evening. For both the essential feature was a tail-coat with foreparts cut in, the day dress coat closely resembling that of the evening except that the former was often cut so that the foreparts could be buttoned together (never possible

67

in the latter) and made S-B or D-B. The evening dress coat was always S-B. The waistcoat opening was always deeper in the latter than in the former.

While the day dress clothes might present a mixture of colours and materials—e.g. a brown cloth coat, blue silk waistcoat and lavender moleskin trousers (1829), the evening dress clothes—the coat black or dark blue, waistcoat tending to become white or black, with black trousers, pantaloons or breeches—by *c.* 1840. Breeches and pantaloons ceased to be part of evening dress after *c.* 1850. By that date the term 'Dress clothes' became gradually applied only to the evening costume; the day 'dress coat'—known for a few years as 'half dress'—soon became relegated to the costume of the indoor upper servant. By 1860 'The Walking Dress Coat is much adopted in France, there called the "Habit frac", synonymous with our "half dress", a style not in general wear in England'. (*The Gentleman's Herald of Fashion.*)

DRESS FROCK COAT

1870's and 1880's. (M.) A D-B Frock coat opening low with long narrow lapels faced with silk to the edge.

Often a narrow velvet collar. Worn with two pairs of its buttons fastened. The opening exposed more of the shirt-front than did the ordinary Frock coat.

Gradually in the 1880's replaced by the Morning Frock.

DRESS HOLDER

1870's. (F.) An elaborate form of Dress Clip with two pendant chains and clips.

DRESS IMPROVER

A term used in 1849 and for a few years from 1883 to '89 as a refined name for a bustle.

DRESSING-GOWN

1770's to end of 19th c. (1) MALE. The term rare in 18th c. A loose-sleeved wrap reaching the ground, often of elaborately patterned silk. In the 1850's and 1860's having a broad rolling collar and tied round the waist with sash or girdle. Generally worn with a tasselled skull cap. Until *c.* 1850 worn informally indoors as for breakfast. Subsequently becoming a bedroom garment, and as a wrap in which to visit the bathroom.

(a) *Evening*   (b) *Day*
Dress Clothes, 1849

Dressing-Gown, 1850

(2) FEMALE. Late 18th c. on. In first half of 19th c. usually of white cotton or cambric or wool, and very voluminous. After 1857 coloured and patterned dressing-gowns of a closer shape were worn. Always a bedroom garment.

DRESS LOUNGE
From 1888. (M.) A jacket for informal evening wear; at first only in the absence of ladies. The early name for DINNER JACKET, *q.v.*

DRESS PROTECTOR
1840's on. (F.) A crescentic piece of material sewn into the arm-holes of a dress to prevent staining from sweat. At first made of chamois leather; in 1848 of talc; in 1881 Canfield's 'Arm - pit shields of Indiarubber' patented.

DRESS WELLINGTON
1830 to 1850. (M.) An evening dress boot made to resemble an evening slipper and stocking, reaching to below the knee; made in one and worn within the dress trousers or pantaloons.

DU BARRY CORSAGE
1850. (F.) An evening dress style 'en chemisette' with ruching from the shoulders curving down to form an under-stomacher.

DU BARRY SLEEVE
1835. (F.) A large day sleeve with two bouffants, one to just above the elbow, the second to just above the wrist.

DUCHESS, DUTCHESS
Late 17th c. (F.) A ribbon bow, worn high, with the fontange hair style.

DUCHESSE PLEAT
1875. (F.) A pleating at the back of a skirt, consisting of four box-pleats on each side of the midline or placket opening.

DUCKBILLS
A modern term for the broad-toed shoes worn from *c.* 1490 to 1540.

DUCK-HUNTER
C. 1840's. (M.) 'A striped linen jacket of that species sometimes denominated a "duck-hunter".' (1841, *Heads of the People.*) Worn by waiters.

DUCKS
19th c. (M.) Trousers of duck. *See* GLOSSARY

DUDES
16th c. Slang term for clothes.

DUNCE'S CAP
(M.) A cone-shaped cap worn by a dunce at school. The name is derived from Duns Scotus, 'the Subtle Doctor' (d. 1308).

DUSTER
(1) 1870's. (M.) A short summer overcoat of melton or cheviot.
(2) 1880's. (F.) A summer overcoat or dust cloak, sometimes caped and belted like an ulster, and long to the skirt hem. Made of alpaca or silk. The 'Sling Duster' was a light, loose-fitting DOLMAN, *q.v.*

DUST GOWN
18th c. (F.) Contemporary term for a SAFEGUARD, *q.v.* 'A kind of Dust Gown or upper garment worn by women, commonly called a Safeguard.' (1706, Phillips, ed. Kersey.)
The Safeguard of the 16th and early 17th c's. was a protective overskirt worn when riding, *q.v.*

DUTCH CLOAK
Late 16th and early 17th c's. (M.) A short cloak with wide sleeves generally lavishly guarded (i.e. trimmed with bands).

DUTCH COAT
Late 14th and 15th c's. (M.) A short jacket, later called a Jerkin.
N.B.—From 14th to early 16th c. 'Dutch' meant German. In the 16th c. the word 'Dutch' was generally replaced by 'Almain'.

DUTCHESS
See KNOT.

DUTCH WAIST

C. 1580 to 1620. (F.) The square-cut waist of a woman's bodice, worn with a wheel-farthingale, the usual deep point being unsuitable. 'A short Dutch waist with a round Catherine wheel Fardingale.' (1607, Dekker and Webster, *Northward Hoe.*)

DUVILLIER WIG

C. 1700. (M.) A very long and high dress-wig named after a famous French perruquier of the period; also known as a 'Long Duvillier', and a 'Falbala' or 'Furbelow' wig. 'A long Duvillier full of powder' . . .

'Huge Falbala periwigs'. (1709, R. Steele, *The Tatler.*)

DUX COLLAR

1860's on. (M.) A shallow stand collar with the corners turned down in front.

DYES

All were of vegetable origin until the aniline dyes were introduced in 1859; the two first used in textiles for women's dresses were Magenta (1859), nearly resembling the modern Raspberry, and Solferino (1860), resembling the modern Fuchsia. Named after the two battles in the Franco-Austrian war (1859).

E

EAR-RING
(M., but mainly F.) A ring worn in the lobe of the ear as an ornament. Worn by early Saxons, then completely abandoned until the late 16th c. In the second half of 14th c. rings of gold for ladies' ears, mentioned in *The Romaunt of the Rose*, were a foreign fashion very uncommon in England owing to the shape of the headdresses of that period.

From late 16th c. rings were worn by women in both ears, while by men (late 16th c. to *c.* 1660) in one ear only.

EAR-STRING
Late 16th c. to *c.* 1620. (M. and F.) A short length of ribbon or a few strands of black silk, worn as an ear-ring, tied and allowed to dangle from one ear only, usually the left.

'What! Meanst thou him that walks all open-breasted,
Drawn through the eare with ribands.'
(1598, Marston, *Satires.*)

EARTHQUAKE GOWN
1750. (F.) Following two nocturnal earthquakes in London in March 1750 a third was foretold causing many to flee to the countryside against the predicted night of disaster. 'This frantic terror prevails so much that within these three days 730 coaches have been counted . . . with whole parties removing into the country. . . . Several women have made earthquake gowns; that is, warm gowns to sit out of doors all night. . . .' (April 4, 1750, Horace Walpole.) A precursor of the Siren-suit of two centuries later.

ECHELLES
End of 17th to near end of 18th c. (F.) A stomacher trimmed down the front with ribbon bows arranged like the rungs of a ladder.

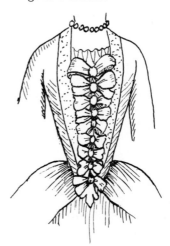

Echelles, 1698

ÉCOSSAISE HAT
1865. (F.) A Glengarry.

EDGE, NEYGE, AGE, OEGGE, EGGE
Late 15th and 16th c's. A term then used for a border or edging of goldsmithry trimming for a head-dress.

EELSKIN MASHER TROUSERS
C. 1884–5. (M.) Excessively tight trousers favoured by Mashers and considered as 'utterly mashy'.

EELSKIN SLEEVE
From 17th c. (F.) A tight-fitting sleeve. 'An eeleskin sleeve lasht here and there with lace.' (1602, Middleton Blurt, *Master Constable,* ii.) 'Jersey jackets and eel-skin dresses.' (1881, Miss Braddon, *Asphodel.*)

EEL SKIRT
1899. (F.) A day skirt very tight over the hips and slightly flared from below the knees, touching the ground

all round. Material cut on the cross and gored, having a front panel, two side and two back panels, all except the front piece having circular hems; fastened in front or at the side or, rarely, behind. No placket hole for inside pocket.

EGHAM, STAINES AND WINDSOR
Early 19th c. (M.) Nickname for a tricorne hat 'from the triangular situation of those towns'. (1824, *Spirit of the Public Journals*.)

ELASTIC ROUND HAT
1812. (M.) Patented that year. The crown was fitted inside with a steel spring by which it could be flattened at will and carried under the arm. The forerunner of the Gibus.

ELASTIC-SIDED BOOTS
1837. (M. and F.) Boots with gussets of indiarubber material inserted into each side. Patented 1837 by James Dowie.

ELBOW CLOAK
Late 16th and early 17th c's. An alternative name for the short cloak of those years.

ELBOW CUFF
1st half 18th c. (F.) The turned-back cuff of the elbow-length sleeve of a woman's gown. It spread round the point of the elbow but was very narrow at the bend.

ELEPHANT SLEEVE
C. 1830. (F.) A very large sleeve of a day dress in light materials; the bulk of the fullness hanging down from the shoulder to the closed wrist 'in the shape of an elephant's ear'. The name was also given in 1854 to the pendulous cape of the MOLDAVIAN MANTLE, *q.v.*

ELEVEN-GORE RIPPLE SKIRT
1895. (F.) A day skirt of 11 gores very narrow above and hanging in flutes; hem 20 feet round; lined and stiffened at the bottom with horsehair.

ELLIPTIC COLLAR
1853. (M.) A patent collar made with the fronts cut higher than the back; to be fastened in front or behind and detachable from the shirt.

EMPEROR SHIRT
1850–1860's. (M.) Of red flannel; worn by gentlemen in the country.

EMPIRE BODICE
1889. (F.) An evening bodice attempting to revive the 'Empire style' and made to appear short-waisted by an arrangement of silk scarves variously draped across the front and tied behind or on one side.

EMPIRE BONNET or CAP
1860's. (F.) A small close-fitting outdoor bonnet in the shape of a baby's bonnet.

Empire Cap, 1865

EMPIRE JUPON
1867. (F.) A wide-gored petticoat with 2 or 3 steels round the bottom, replacing the cage-crinoline. Worn with the so-called 'Empire style' dress of that date.

EMPIRE PETTICOAT
Another name for Empire Jupon.

EMPIRE SKIRT
1888 into the 1890's. (F.) A day skirt gathered at the waist, with a full-gathered flounce above the hem. (No 'steels'—i.e. half hoops—at the

back in the lining, as was usual at this date.) The evening dress version, ruched at the hem and embroidered with flowers, was slightly trained. In 1892 the Empire skirt (day) had 2 straight panels front and back and 2 triangular gores each side; slightly trained.

EMPRESS PETTICOAT
1866. (F.) An evening dress petticoat closely gored at the waist, spreading out to a circumference of 8 yards at the hem with a train 'nearly a yard on the ground'. Trimmed with a deep flounce from above the knee. Worn as a substitute for the cage-crinoline.

ENAMELLED BUTTON
18th and 19th c's. Very fashionable for men's coats in 1770's, and sometimes for men's waistcoats in 2nd half of 19th c. Also for women's dresses in the 1860's.

ENBRAUDE
Med. Embroider.

ENGAGEANTES
End of 17th to c. mid 19th c. (F.) In 17th and 18th c's. this French term indicated ruffles. 'Engageantes, double ruffles that fall over the wrist.' (1690, The Ladies' Dictionary.) From c. 1840 they were detachable white under sleeves edged with lace or embroidery. They ceased to be worn c. 1865.

ENGLISH CHAIN.
Early 19th c. (F.) An early form of chatelaine. 'Chain also denotes a kind of string or twisted wire; serving to hang watches, tweezer-cases, and other valuable toys upon. The invention of this piece of curious work was owing to the English; whence in foreign countries it is denominated the English chain.' (1819, Abraham Rees, Cyclopaedia.)

ENGLISH FARTHINGALE
1580's to 1620's. (F.) A roll farthingale, producing a tub-shaped hang of the skirt without any flattening in front. See FRENCH FARTHINGALE.

ENGLISH HOOD
C. 1500 to 1540's. (F.) Also described by 19th-c. writers as the 'Gable' or 'Pediment' head-dress. A hood wired up to form a pointed arch above the forehead. The early form hung in thick folds to the shoulders behind, with the facial borders continued into long lappets, called 'Chaffers', in front. An under cap was worn, but the smooth parted hair was visible under the gable until c. 1525. After that date the back drapery was replaced by two long pendant flaps sometimes pinned up, and the front lappets were shortened, turned up and pinned in place. The front hair was concealed in silk sheaths often striped, and crossed over under the gable point.

English Hood, 1527

ENGLISH NIGHTGOWN
18th c. (F.) An unboned loose dress worn for comfort and usually informally. See NIGHTGOWN. 'It was four o'clock . . . Mrs Damer . . . in an English nightgown.' (1769, Letters of Lady Mary Coke.)

ENGLISH WORK, ANGLICUM OPUS
Med. Very fine Anglo-Saxon embroidery worked by ladies 7th to 10th c. The work was so excellent that it was not only prized in England but celebrated abroad.

ENGLISH WRAP
1840's. (M.) A D-B Paletot-Sac resembling a loose Chesterfield. See TWINE.

ENGREYNEN
Med. To dye in the grain, i.e. dyed in the thread before weaving.

EPAULETTES
19th c. (F.) Ornamental shoulder pieces, very popular in the 1860's.

EQUIPAGE
18th c. (F.) An etui or ornamental metal case slung by a chain from the waist and containing knife, scissors, tweezer, thimble, etc.

ESCLAVAGE
Mid 18th c. (F.) Necklace composed of several rows of gold chains falling in festoons over the bosom.

ESTACHES
2nd half 14th c. (M.) French term for strings for attaching the hose (i.e. stockings) to the gipon. *See* POINTS.

ETON JACKET
1892 on. (F.) A day bodice cut like the boy's jacket of that name and worn open over a waistcoat; the fronts sometimes rounded in 1898, braided and frogged.

ETON JACKET BODICE
1889. (F.) A fitting jacket with large revers and flap pockets on each side; worn with a D-B fancy waistcoat with revers and a large cravat.

ETON SUIT
C. 1798 on. (M.) Worn by junior schoolboys; comprising a short jacket, the fronts cut square or slightly pointed with a shallow turned-down collar and wide lapels turning nearly to the bottom. The back with a slight point in the centre. Sleeves without cuffs. The foreparts cut back so that the jacket cannot be buttoned up. Worn with a S-B waistcoat having a narrow turned-over collar and buttoned high. Trousers of a lighter colour, commonly grey.

Originally the jacket was blue or red, becoming black in 1820 in mourning for George III.

Originally white ducks or nankin pantaloons were worn; at Eton College the Oppidans took to trousers in 1814 but the Collegers continued to wear knee breeches until *c.* 1820. An essential feature of the costume was the starched white 'Eton collar' turned down over the coat collar; worn with a white shirt and a black tie.

In the correct 'Eton suit' the bottom button of the waistcoat was left unfastened and the bottoms of the trousers turned up. 'Harrow Eton jackets have no point.' (1898, *The London Tailor.*)

Eton Suit, 1880's

ETUI
Term first used in 1610. *See* EQUIPAGE.

EYELETS, OILETS
18th and 19th c's. (Oilets was the earlier term.) Lacing holes for the passage of a lace, cord or tape, to join garments or parts of garments. Until *c.* 1828 these holes were bound with silk or thread; from 1828 they might be strengthened by a metal ring, as used in corsets by *c.* 1830 but not in the back-lacing of waistcoats until 1839.

74

F

FABALA, FALBALA
See FURBELOW.

FALDETTA
1850. (F.) A short waist-length mantle of coloured taffeta edged with deep lace round the hem, and wide sleeves.

FALL, FALLING BAND
(1) 1540's to 1670's. (M.) A turned-down collar at first attached to the shirt but from *c.* 1585 a separate item, the size and shape varying with the fashion; generally lace-edged. Worn as an alternative to the ruff and some-times worn with a ruff, between 1580 and 1615, and entirely replacing the ruff from *c.* 1640.

Falling Band, 1637

Falling bands were occasionally worn by women but very uncommon before 17th c.

(2) End of 17th c. (F.) A wrist ruffle but rarely used in this sense. 'Falls or long Cuffes to hang over the Hands.' (1688, R. Holme, *Armourie*.)

FAL-LALS
17th c. on. Any trifling decoration to costume. 'His dress, his bows, and fine fal-lals.' (1690, J. Evelyn.)

FALLING RUFF
See RUFF.

Falling Ruff, 1628

FALLS
1730 on. (M.) A buttoned flap to the front of breeches and, later, of pantaloons and trousers. 'Whole Falls' was the name given to a flap extending from one side seam to the other; 'Small' or 'Split Falls' was a narrow central flap. In each style the flap buttoned up to the front of the waistband. *See* SPAIR.

FALSE CALVES
See CALVES.

FALSE HIPS
1740's to 1760's. (F.) A pair of side hoops producing the excessive widen-ing of the skirt on each side over the hips. *See* OBLONG HOOP. 'I furnish'd her . . . with three pairs of hips.' (1705, Sir J. Vanbrugh, *The Con-federacy*.)

FALSE SLEEVES
See HANGING SLEEVES.

75

FAN

In common use by women from the 2nd half of 16th c. on. Until *c.* 1580 fans were rigid and made of feathers, silk or straw fixed to a decorative handle and variously shaped. From *c.* 1580 the *folding fan* came into use and both styles were popular until the 18th c. when folding fans became the rule.

The size varied greatly from time to time. In the 18th c. the fan was an essential to a fine lady's toilet.

'It's shake triumphant, it's victorious clap,
It's angry flutter and it's wanton tap. . . .'

(1730, Soame Jenyns,
The Art of Dancing.)

19th c. Fans of ivory were common in the early decades; painted fans in mid century, and in the 1880's fans decorated with animals—such as cats' heads the size of furry toy cats—were fashionable. In the 1890's large folding ostrich-feather fans with frames of ivory, mother-of-pearl or tortoiseshell.

Fans were carried by foppish men in the late 16th c. 'When a plum'd fan may shade thy chalked face.' (1597, Hall's *Satire*, addressed to the fops of the day.) And also carried by some of the fops of the late 18th c.

FANCHON

1830's on. (F.) A small kerchief for the head, the term being chiefly used for lace trimming falling about the ears of a day cap or outdoor bonnet.

FANCHON CAP

1840's to 1860's. (F.) A lace **or** tulle cap with side pieces covering the ears, or sloping down to them.

FANCIES

1650's to 1670's. (M.) Ribbon trimming for suits worn with open-legged breeches and also petticoat breeches. 'I've a new suite and Ribbons fashionable yclept Fancies.' (*C.* 1652, Richard Brome, *Mad Couple*, Prologue.) The amount of ribbon used was commonly 72 yards; but up to 250 yards was not unknown.

Fanchon Cap, 1865

FANFRELUCHE BODICE

1888. (F.) A day bodice with gathers from neck and shoulders sloping to a point just above the top of the corset.

FAN HOOP

1st half 18th c. (F.) Mentioned as early as 1713 but fashionable in 1740's and 1750's. A hooped petticoat, pyramidal in shape, but compressed front and back to form a fan-shaped structure over which the skirt fell with a curve up on each side.

FAN PARASOL

1790's to 1850. (F.) A small parasol with a hinge in the stick near the cover by which it could be tilted upright and then used as a fan.

FANTAIL HAT

1775 to end of 18th c. (M. and F.) A tricorne hat, the front cocks sloping down towards the back. The brim behind semicircular in shape and vertically cocked resembling an open fan. Fashionable for riding and sometimes worn by women on horseback.

FANTAIL WIG

Early 18th c. (M.) The queue of a wig hanging loose in a number of small curls.

Fantail Hat, 1786

FARTHINGALE, VARDINGALE, VERDYNGALE

C. 1545 to 1620's. (F.) A structure variously shaped (using hoops of rushes, wood, wire or whalebone) for expanding the skirt of a gown under which it was worn. Named styles were: English, French, Italian, Scotch, Spanish, also the Roll, Pocket and demi- or semi-circular Farthingale and Wheel Farthingale.

FARTHINGALE SLEEVES

End of 16th and early 17th c's. (M. and F.) Trunk sleeves or Bishop sleeves distended by wire, reeds or whalebone.

FASHION WAIST

19th c. (M.) A tailoring term indicating the length from the base of a coat collar to the waist seam.

FAUSSE MONTRE

End of 18th c. (M.) When it was fashionable for a man to wear two watches, often one of them was a sham, being perhaps a snuffbox disguised as a watch.

FAVOURITES

(1) 1690 to *c.* 1720. (F.) 'Locks dangling on the temples.' (1690, *The Fop-Dictionary.*)

(2) 1820 to 1840. (M.) 'Favourite' was a small tuft of hair worn under the chin.

FAX, FACTS, FEAX

Med. to *c.* 1610. The hair of the head.

FEARNOTHING, FEARNOTHING JACKET

18th and early 19th c's. (M.) A jacket resembling a sleeved waistcoat made of a thick woollen cloth called Fearnothing, Fearnought or Dreadnought. Worn by seafaring men, sportsmen, labourers and apprentices. '. . . that J. Tospill have cloaths with a fearnothing and stockings.' (1725, Stoke-by-Nayland Records.)

FEATHERBRUSH SKIRT

1898. (F.) A day skirt of light material having a series of overlapping flounces below the knees.

FEATHER PELTS

14th to mid 17th c. Skins of various birds with the feathers attached, used for trimming garments in place of furs. Especially those of the swan, ostrich, drake, crane, and vulture. 'A furre of drakes' necks for facing and furring his Lordship's gown.' (1550, Revels Accounts.)

FEATHERS

(1) MALE. Worn as ornaments, mainly on hats, from mid 15th c. (abroad, from mid 14th c.) off and on until end of 18th c. Chiefly feathers of ostrich; sometimes in 15th c. peacock, and end of 16th c. pyed feathers, 'figaro feathers'. In early 17th c. spangled feathers were fashionable.

Feathers, 1796. Worn at a Rout

77

(2) FEMALE. Worn from end of 16th c. when hats came into fashion, to end of 19th c. Usually attached to hat or bonnet but also, from end of 18th c., plumes worn ceremonially in the hair. Feathers, ostrich, grebe and others used in 18th and 19th c's. for dress trimmings, boas, mantles, pèlerines, muffs and fans.

FEATHER-TOP WIG
2nd half 18th c. (M.) A wig with a toupee made of feathers, usually drake's or mallard's. Worn by parsons and also sportsmen. 'Gentlemens' perukes for sporting made of drakes' tails.' (1761, *Ipswich Journal*.)

FELT
Mid 15th c. on. (M.) This term when used alone indicated a felt hat. 'And on his heade a felt.' (*C.* 1450, Merlin.) In the 17th c. the word was often loosely used for any kind of hat whether felt or not.

FENT
15th c. Meaning and corrupted to Vent, both being used in 15th c. but subsequently Fent became discarded for Vent, a functional slit in a garment. 'Fente of a clothe, fibulatorium.' (*C.* 1440, *Promptorium Parvulorum*.)

FERMAIL, FERMAYLL
15th c. A buckle or brooch. Later uses, heraldic.

FERRONIÈRE
1830's. (F.) A narrow gold or jewelled band worn low round the head and crossing the forehead. Worn with day or evening dress.

FICHU
1816 on. (F.) A term replacing the Handkerchief or Neckerchief, being a length of usually flimsy material worn round the neck and shoulders.

FICHU ANTOINETTE
1857. (F.) For summer wear, a morning fichu of fine muslin trimmed with black lace and narrow velvet ribbon, fastening with a small bow behind, the long ends floating at the

Fichu, 1864

back. It covered the shoulders like a shawl and crossed in front at the waist.

FICHU-CANEZOU
1820's. (F.) A form of deep collar, sometimes made with a small ruff and falling over the front and back of the dress bodice, but not covering the arms or sides.

FICHU CORDAY
1837. (F.) Of grenadine gauze with a broad hem run through with a ribbon; crossing over the bosom, it was tied behind. Day wear.

FICHU LA VALIÈRE
1868. (F.) The fronts not crossed but meeting edge to edge and fastened by a button.

FICHU-PÈLERINE
1826 on. (F.) A large covering for the shoulders, generally of white material, and often having a double cape and turned-down collar. The front having fichu ends carried down beneath the belt to knee-level.

FICHU RAPHAEL
1867. (F.) Of white tulle or lace, cut square over the shoulders and

upper part of the bodice. Worn with a high-necked bodice to 'give a dressy effect'.

FICHU-ROBINGS
1820's. (F.) A flat trimming from the shoulders to the waist to give the effect of a fichu.

FIGARO JACKET or SIGNORITA
1860's. Revived 1892. (F.) Figure fitting, curving away from the mid-line at the sides; tight sleeves with epaulettes. Worn over a waistcoat. A variation of the ZOUAVE JACKET, *q.v.*

FIG LEAF
1860's and 1870's. (F.) A small ornamental apron of black silk, without a bib. 'Known by the ladies as their fig-leaves.'

FILLET (M.E. FILET, FELET)
13th to 19th c. (F.) (1) A narrow band to tie about the hair of the head. In the 13th and 14th c's. the fillet was a stiffened circlet of linen worn with a barbette or frett or both.

*Fillet and Barbette
13th and early 14th c's.*

(2) In 18th c. the term was sometimes used to mean a hair-net covering the whole head; worn at night. '. . . take a very large fillet which must be big enough to cover the head. . . .' (1782, Stewart, *Plocacosmos.*)

(3) Early 19th c. A fillet of satin and pearls spirally twisted round the head was sometimes worn with evening coiffure.

FILLETING
17th c. A narrow tape.

FISH
1st half 19th c. (M.) A tailoring term for a 'dart', a narrow dart-shaped piece of material cut out and the edges then joined together to improve the fit of a garment. The dictum 'Where there is a crease there take out a fish' is attributed to George IV.

FITCHET
13th to mid 16th c. (F.) A French term for a vertical placket hole in the skirt of a gown.

FITZHERBERT HAT
1786. (F.) A modified form of the balloon hat, the wide brim oval in shape, the crown of puffed material slightly raised.

Fitzherbert Hat, c. 1786

FLANDAN
Late 17th c. (F.) 'A Flandan is a kind of Pinner (lappet) join'd with a Cornet (day cap).' (1694, *The Ladies' Dictionary.*)

FLANNELS
(1) 18th and early 19th c's. (F.) The large flannel gown or wrap worn by bathers at the seaside and at spas such as Bath.
'Oh! 'Twas pretty to see them all
  put on their flannels
And then take the waters like so
  many spaniels.'
(1766, C. Anstey, *The New Bath Guide.*)
(2) 2nd half of 19th c. (M.) Cricketing or boating costume. 'Beautifully dressed in white flannels.' (1895, E. F. Benson, *The Babe, B.A.*)

FLAT CAP

16th c. and unfashionably into 17th c. (M., sometimes F.) A cap with a flat crown spreading over a flat narrow brim. By 1570 it was being worn only by citizens and apprentices and known as the 'City Flat Cap'.

Such caps continued to be worn by young men and sometimes young women when at work.

Flat Cap, 1527

FLEA-FUR

16th c. (F.) Popular name for a fur stole of marten or sable.

FLIPE, FLEPE

16th c. A fold or flap, as in the flexible brim of a hat or cap. 'I tourne up the flepe of a cap.' (1530, Palsgrave.)

FLOCKARD, FLOCKET

15th and 16th c's. (F.) This article, unidentified, was generally listed in pairs. 'Item . . . for a pair of flokkardes for my Lady . . .' (1481, Howard Household Expenses.)
'In her furred flocket
And gray russet rocket.'
(1529, Skelton, *Elynour Rummyng.*)

FLORENTINE BUTTON

A 19th-c. name for a covered button.

FLOUNCE

Early 18th c. on. (F.) A deep gathered or pleated frill used as a trimming to women's garments.

FLOUNCE À DISPOSITION

1852 on. (F.) A flounce woven with the same border pattern as the dress material.

FLOURISH

16th c. To ornament profusely. A garment 'flourished with pearls' meant one lavishly decorated with them.

FLOWER BOTTLE

1865. (M.) A small glass bottle for flowers, worn in the button-hole which at that date was sometimes worked in the left-hand lapel of a morning coat for that purpose. A piece of broad ribbon was put under the turn to hold the flower bottle in place.

FLOWER HOLE

1840's on. (M.) A slit hole in the left lapel of a coat through which a flower stem could be inserted.

FLOWER-POT HAT or THE TURF HAT

1830's. (M.) 'Of grey felt, low crown like a flower-pot upside-down, the very large brim looped all round.' (i.e. rolled over.) (1830, *The Gentleman's Magazine of Fashion.*)

FLOW-FLOW

1885. (F.) The name given to a graduated cascade of coloured ribbon loops decorating the front of a bodice of an afternoon or evening dress 'to brighten it up'.

FLY CAP

See BUTTERFLY CAP.

FLY-FRINGE

18th c. (F.) A fringe of cord with knots and bunches of floss silk attached. Used to decorate gowns.

FLY-FRONT FASTENING

Rare before 19th c. A device for concealing a row of button fastenings by extending an overlap of the material over them. Very rarely used in 18th c. for waistcoats; introduced for trousers *c.* 1823; for breeches *c.* 1840. Also often used for overcoats (e.g. Chesterfields, M. or F.).

FLY SUIT. FLY-AWAY SUIT

18th c. (F.) A loose negligee dress. 'Apparell for my Daughters. Two flye Sutes. . . .' (1723, *Diary of Nicholas Blundell*, Univ. Press, Liverpool, 1952.)

FOB POCKET

17th c. on. (M.) A horizontal pocket in the front of the waistband of breeches or pantaloons, usually one on each side.

FOB RIBBON

C. 1740's to 1840's. (M.) A short ribbon attached to the watch in the fob pocket and dangling outside, suspending seals and watch-key. Worn with breeches or pantaloons only.

FOGLE

19th c. Slang for a silk handkerchief.

FOIL BUTTON

Patented 1774. Silk pasted on paper and applied to the under side of a glass button, as a foil.

FOLLY BELLS

15th c. (M.) A form of decoration composed of small bells suspended by chains from the girdle, the shoulder belt or a neckband.

FONTANGE

(1) *c.* 1690 to 1710. (F.) An indoor linen cap with a small flat crown behind and a tall erection of lace or lace and linen frills in front, kept erect by the commode (a wire frame). Two long lace or linen streamers called 'lappets' hung down at the back or were sometimes pinned up to the crown. The front hair was arranged in curls mounting up from the forehead in front of the fontange elevation.

Fontange—Back and Front, 1699

(2) In 1850 term used for ribbon gathered along the centre as ruching and used to edge a day corsage.

FOOTBALL SHIRT

1895. (M.) A cotton shirt with attached Shakespeare collar, superseding the earlier knitted football jersey.

FOOT-MANTLE, FOTE-MANTEL

14th c. (F.) Probably a petticoat worn by countrywomen on horseback, to keep their gowns from becoming soiled. *See* SAFEGUARD. 'A foot mantel aboute hir hippes large.' (*C.* 1386, Chaucer, *Prologue, Canterbury Tales.*)

FORAGE CAP

1st half 19th c. (M.) A cap adapted from the military and worn by small boys; it comprised a circular flat crown, its border stiffened with cane; a tassel hanging from the centre; a vizor in front, and sometimes held in place by a japanned leather strap passing under the chin.

Forage Caps (Boys), 1852

FOREBODY

17th and 18th c.'s. (M. and F.) The front part of the garment covering the chest (doublet or bodice). 'A doublet whose forebodie is fine stuff and the backe course.' (1611, Cotgrave, *Armourie.*)

FOREHEAD CLOTH

See CROSSCLOTH.

FOREPART

(1) 16th c. to *c.* 1630. (F.) Term applied to the decorative panel, often

mounted on a coarse underskirt, which filled in the front gap of some of the open farthingale skirts.

(2) 19th c. (M.) The fronts of a coat or waistcoat covering the chest.

Forepart (Embroidered), c. 1597

FORE SLEEVES, HALF SLEEVES

Late 14th to mid 17th c. (M. and F.) 'A foresleeve of a garmente which Kevereth the arme from the elbow downwarde.' (1538, Elyot, *Dictionarie.*) The sleeve covering the forearm was often of richer material, the upper arm portion being hidden by an over-garment. Fore sleeves were sometimes separate items. 'A doublet of yellow satin and the foresleeves of it of cloth of gold.' (1523, Invent. Dame Agnes Hungerford's husband.)

FORE-STOCKS

1st half 16th c. only. A term meaning fore sleeves and listed with a plackard. These matching the plackard were separate items. 'Item. Pd. for makyng of a payer of forestockes

and placard.' (1525, Lestrange Household Accounts.)

FORETOP

From 13th to end of 18th c. (M. and F.) The hair of the head or of a wig immediately above the forehead. In 18th c. called 'Toupee' or merely 'TOP', *q.v.*

FORKED BEARD

Mainly 14th c. but mentioned in 17th c. (M.) A beard trimmed in two peaks. 'A marchant was there with a forked beard.' (*C.* 1386, Chaucer, Prol., *Canterbury Tales.*)

FOUNDATION

1885 to end of c. (F.) An underskirt forming a foundation and giving substance to the overskirt, both being joined together at the waist to form one garment, worn with day dresses.

FOUNDLING BONNET

1880's. (F.) Small stiff brim, soft crown, usually of plush, and tied under the chin 'like the Quaker headgear'.

FOURIAUX

1st half 12th c. (F.) Silk sheaths enclosing the two long pendant plaits of hair worn by ladies of high rank. These sheaths were usually depicted white with red circular stripes.

Fouriaux, 1130–50

82

FOUR-IN-HAND

1890 on. (M. and F.) Also known as a 'Derby'. A necktie knotted in front, the knot presenting a free edge above and below, thus differing from the Sailor's Knot with its free edges on each side. Also worn by women with a morning blouse.

Four-in-Hand, 1894

FOURREAU DRESS

1864. (F.) A Princess style (i.e. with no seam at the waist) 'now beginning to be called by an old name "four-reau"'. It was buttoned all down the front and frequently worn with a Peplum fastened round the waist.

FOURREAU SKIRT

1864. (F.) A skirt sufficiently gored to fit the figure, and spread over the crinoline, without pleats at the waist. Morning dress style.

FOURREAU TUNIC

1865. (F.) The upper skirt (i.e. tunic) cut in one with the bodice and measuring about 6 yards round the hem. A double skirt for evening dress.

FRAISE

1836. (F.) A piece of embroidered muslin edged with ruching, folded across the bosom and secured by an ornamental pin; worn instead of a cravat with 'carriage dress'.

FRELAN, FRELAND, FRELANGE

Late 17th c. (F.) 'Frelan . . . Bonnet and Pinner together.' (1690, *The Fop-Dictionary*.)

FRENCH BEARER

19th c. (M.) The BEARER BAND (*q.v.*) of breeches or pantaloons made with falls and cut very narrow.

FRENCH BOA

1829 on. (F.) Long round tippet of swansdown, fur or feathers; very fashionable again in the 1890's.

FRENCH BOTTOMS

19th c. (M.) Trouser legs cut somewhat wider at the bottom of the leg than above.

FRENCH CLOAK

16th and 17th c's. (M.) Long, circular or semicircular in cut and described as 'compass' or 'half-compass'. Generally having a square flat collar or a shoulder cape; sometimes plain.

French Cloak, 1610

FRENCH CUFF

19th c. (M.) (1) A coat cuff with a side slit which was closed by buttons.

83

(2) From 1850's on, the name was also applied to a wide shirt cuff fastened by a link near the lower margin and by a button higher up at the wrist.

FRENCH FARTHINGALE
1580's to 1620's. (F.) This gave the same outline as the Wheel Farthingale (*q.v.*) producing a tub-shaped hang of the skirt, but with wider curves at the sides and a flattening in front. 'My wife . . . is underlayed not with a Frenche fardingale, whiche strottethe out by the sydes, But withe an English bumbaste wiche beareth out before.' (1588, Letter from John Adams, Lord Middleton's MSS.)

FRENCH FROCK
1770's to 1800. (M.) Worn for full dress and 'full trimmed' with gold embroidered buttons. *See* Frock.

FRENCH GIGOT SLEEVE
1890–7. (F.) The cuff prolonged over the back of the hand; a fashion introduced by Sarah Bernhardt.

FRENCH GORES
1807. (F.) Gores introduced into the skirt of a day dress to eliminate gathers at the waist.

FRENCH HEEL, POMPADOUR HEEL
1750's to 1780's. (F.) A high heel curving into a narrow base.
'. . . Her tott'ring form
Ill propp'd upon French Heels.'
(1784, Cowper, *The Task*.)

FRENCH HOOD
1521 to 1590; unfashionably to *c.* 1630. (F.) A small bonnet made on a stiff frame, worn far back on the head, the front border curving forward on each side to cover the ears. This border was usually trimmed with a ruched edging behind which was the nether billiment of goldsmithry; further back, arched over the crown, was the upper Billiment (*q.v.*). Behind this, falling down the back of the neck, was a curtain in formal pleats or, more often, a stiff-

ened flap which could be turned up and worn flat on the crown, the straight edge projecting over the forehead and known as a Cornet or Bongrace (*q.v.*). The English variation of the French hood (1525–58), and associated with Q. Mary, was flattened across the head, projecting wide of the temples, then turned in at an angle to cover the ears, otherwise the same. The hood was secured by a band under the chin.

French Hood, 1539

FRENCH HOSE
C. 1550 to 1610. (M.) Round or oval Trunk-Hose usually paned and with canions after 1570. Synonymous with Bullion Hose (Boulogne Hose), *q.v.*

FRENCH JACKET
See Petenlair.

FRENCH LOCK
See Love Lock.

FRENCH NIGHT-CAP
See Dormeuse.

FRENCH OPENING VEST
1840's on. (M.) The fronts cut low to expose much of the shirt-front.

FRENCH POCKET
17th c. (M.) The early form of horizontal slit pocket with the opening covered by a flap. 'A straight bodied Coat with French pockets.' (1675, *London Gazette*.)

84

FRENCH RUFF
1580 to *c.* 1610. (M.) The very large 'cartwheel' ruff, as stated by Stowe.

FRENCH SKIRT
See CORNET SKIRT.

FRENCH SLEEVES
2nd half 16th c. (M.) Sleeves possibly detachable and pinked or paned. 'A pair of French sleeves of green velvet.' (1547, Inventory of Wardrobe of Henry VIII.) 'Sleeves of cambric and calico for plucking out of French sleeves.' (1553, Inventory of the Palace of Westminster, Hatfield Papers.)

FRENCH VEST
1860's. (M.) A waistcoat with short lapels cut on and not turned; buttoned high.

FRENCH WORK
Early 19th c. (F.) Insertions of embroidery let into the front of a bodice.

FRET, FRETTE
O.F. Frete: trellis work. 13th to early 16th c. (F., rarely M.) (1) A trellis-work coif or skull cap made either of goldsmithry or material. 'A frett of goold sche hadde next hyre her.' (*C.* 1385, Chaucer, *Legend of Good Women*, Prologue.)
(2) In 16th c. sometimes meaning trellis-work ornamentation of a garment.

Frett, 13th c.

FRILEUSE
1847. (F.) A pelerine wrap of quilted satin or velvet, fitting into the waist behind, and having long loose sleeves. For wearing over the shoulders 'by the fireside or at the theatre'.

FRILL
16th c. on. An edging gathered to produce a rippled surface. 'Their flaunting ruffes . . . their borowed frilles and such like vanities.' (1591, R. Turnbull.)

FRILLING
2nd half 19th c. (F.) A gathered edging of stiff white muslin, worn at the wrists and neck especially of the widow's dress (1870's and 1880's).

FRINGE
Med. on. An ornamental border of pendant threads of various makes. In mediaeval period used largely for ecclesiastical garments but rare for lay dress before 15th c. 'Fringe of silke, yelowe, grene, rede, white, and blue.' (1480, Wardrobe Expenses, Edward IV.)
Fringed waistcoats, with fringe along the bottom of the foreparts, were fashionable between *c.* 1710 and *c.* 1730.

FRISETTE
19th c. (F.) (1) A crimped fringe of hair over the forehead, sometimes artificial.
(2) 1860's. A pad over which the back hair was rolled.
(3) 1869. Padding used in underskirts.

FRISK
1815–18. (F.) A bustle worn outside helping to produce the 'Grecian Bend'.

FRIZZE
17th c. on. (F.) Closely curled or crimped hair. 'Her hair brown of a natural Frizze or curl about the forehead.' (1685, *London Gazette.*)

FRIZZLE
(1) A Frizz-wig.
(2) 17th c. A small ruff.

FRIZZ-WIG
17th to mid 19th c. (M.) A wig closely crimped all over.

FROCK

(1) MALE. In mediaeval period the term was first used for monastic habit. (*a*) From that time on the term denoted a loose, sleeved outer garment of coarse material worn by farm-workers, carters and drovers, and later called a Slop-frock; in 19th c. becoming a Smock-frock.

(*b*) 16th c. A loose jerkin or jacket made to be comfortable; sometimes called a 'frocked jacket'.

(*c*) 18th c. From *c*. 1730. An 'undress' coat (except for the French Frock) following the changing styles of the body coat but always with a turned-down collar.

(*d*) 19th c. *See* FROCK COAT.

(2) FEMALE. (*a*) 16th and 17th c's. The term occasionally used for an informal gown.

(*b*) From 17th c. on. Term used for children's dresses. 'Instead of green sey that was wont to be used for children's frocks, is now used painted and India stained and striped calicoes.' (1678, *The Ancient Trades etc. by a Country Tradesman*.)

(*c*) End of 18th and during the 19th c's. The word 'Frock' was used for a back-fastening dress of thin material.

C.D.E.

Frock, 1790

Frock, 1777

FROCK COAT

End of 18th to end of 19th c. (M.) (1) End of 18th c. to *c*. 1815. The term 'Frock coat' was seldom used in 18th c. During this period it was a coat with tails and a turned-down collar.

(2) From *c*. 1816 on. It then became a formal waisted and close-fitting coat, at first S-B with roll or Prussian collar and no lapels; buttoned to the waist-level. Having a full skirt hanging vertically in front, the back with a vent, side pleats and hip-buttons.

By 1823 a seam at the waist, collar and lapels. Pockets on the hips under flaps. With minor variations this remained the basic style for the rest of the century; often called a 'Morning Frock coat' in 1870's and 1880's to distinguish it from the 'DRESS FROCK COAT (*q.v.*).

86

Frock Coat, 1853

(a) *Undress*   (b) *Dress*
Frock Coats, 1878

FROCK GREAT COAT, TOP FROCK

C. 1830 on. (M.) Cut like a frock coat but often longer and usually D-B. Intended for outdoor wear when it could be worn without an under-coat.

FROCK JACKET

1840's. (M.) A very short S-B frock coat just covering the seat. By 1860's the name was applied to a jacket without a seam at the waist or a back seam; collar, and lapels small and cut in one with the forepart.

FROG

18th c. on. An ornamental loop-fastening for a coat, used with a frog-button; associated with BRANDEN-BURGS, *q.v.*

FROG-BUTTON or OLIVETTE

A spindle-shaped braided button to pass through frogs for fastening a coat. *See* BRANDENBURGS.

FROG POCKET

19th c. (M.) A pocket in front of the side seam of breeches, and cut with a rectangular flap, the point secured by a button.

FRONT

17th c. on. A term applied to a forehead fringe of false hair.

FRONTLET, FRONTEL, FRONTAYL

15th, 16th and early 17th c's. (F.) (1) A decorative band worn across the forehead; in mediaeval period usually under a veil, i.e. coverchief. In 16th and early 17th c's. with a bonnet, caul or coif.

'Frontayle for a woman's head,
Some call it a fruntlet.'

(1552, Hulock.)

(2) 18th c. A frontlet was synony-mous with Forehead Cloth or Cross-cloth, a band smeared with cream and bound round the forehead to remove wrinkles.

'In vain, poor nymph, to please our
   youthful sight
You sleep in cream and frontlets all
   the night.'
                    (1722, T. Parnell,
                 Elegy to an Old Beauty.)

FROSE PASTE, FROWS PASTE, FROES PASTE

16th c. Earliest ref. 1527; mentioned until 1560's. Not identified
but probably the quilled or crimped
border to the front of a French hood
with which pastes were so constantly
associated in wardrobe accounts of
the period. When French hoods
went out of fashion references to
pastes vanished. The paste was 'fine
pasted paper such as paste-wives
made womens paste of'. (1570, Bil-
lingsley, *Euclid.*) This was the foundation for the border of velvet, lawn
or other rich material, sometimes
decorated with gold or jewels.

FROU-FROU DRESS

1870. (F.) A day dress with a low
corsage covered with a short muslin
tunic, the skirts rounded off in front
and worn over a light silk underskirt
trimmed with innumerable small
pinked flounces. Named from the
comedy by Meilhac and Ludovic
Halévy (1869).

FROUNCE

Mid 14th to end of 16th c. (F.) A
pleated or gathered frill, a flounce.
(Adapted from its meaning a wrinkle
of the brow, a frown.) The skirt over
the wheel farthingale was often
frounced to avoid the hard line produced by the understructure.

FROUTING

17th c. Rubbing perfumed oil into
a garment to sweeten it.

FROUZE, FRUZ

Late 17th and early 18th c's. A term
implying crimped false hair or a wig
worn to cover up baldness. 'This
woman . . . has adorned her baldness

Frounced Skirt over Wheel Farthingale, 1595

with a large white fruz.' (1678, Sir
G. Etherege, *The Man of Mode.*)

FULL BOTTOM, FULL-BOT-TOMED WIG, FRENCH WIG

1660 to early 18th c. (M.) Subse-

Full-Bottom Wig, c. 1700

88

quently worn on formal occasions and by the learned professions only. A massive wig with a centre parting and close curls framing the face, and extending all round on to the shoulders.

FUNNEL SLEEVE
See PAGODA SLEEVE.

FURBELOW, rarely BELOW, Fr. FALBALA

18th c. (F.) 'Plaited or ruffled trimming for women's petticoats (i.e. skirts) and scarves.' (1730, Bailey, *Dictionary*.) Furbelows were usually flounces of the same material as the garment or of lace; and were also used for whole gowns and aprons.

G

GABARDINE
Early 16th to early 17th c. (M., and in 17th c. occasionally F.) A long loose overcoat with wide sleeves and worn with or without a girdle at the waist. After 1560's it ceased to be a fashionable garment but remained popular among the poor and was defined as 'a cloake of felt for raynie weather'; and also as 'a horseman's cloak or coat'. See also GLOSSARY OF MATERIALS.

GABLE BONNET or HAT
1884. (F.) Its front brim rose 'like the angle of a thatched roof forming a point over the face'.

GABLE HEAD-DRESS
See ENGLISH HOOD.

GABRIELLE DRESS
1865. (F.) A day dress of which the bodice and front breadth of the skirt were cut in one; 3 large box-pleats at the back or one each side and one behind; all widths gored.

GABRIELLE SLEEVE
19th c. (F.) Very full to the elbow, thence narrowing to mid-forearm and finished at the wrist with a deep cuff. Used for spencers in 1820, for day dresses in 1830–5. From 1859 to 1869 the term was applied to a sleeve made up of a series of puffs from shoulder to wrist.

GADROON
19th c. (F.) An inverted pleat or fluting used as a trimming on caps and cuffs, and popular for skirts of dresses in the 1870's.

GAINSBOROUGH BONNET
1877. (F.) Close fitting with a high front brim and a broad crown sloping off abruptly behind. Generally of velvet trimmed with roses.

GAITER
End of 18th c. on. (M., and in 19th c. F. also.) A covering for the ankle or with it the small of the leg, and spreading out over the upper of the shoe or boot, with a strap passing under the instep. Generally buttoned up on the outer side. Fashionable for women from 1820's to 1840's and also in 1890's. Of silk, cashmere or elastic material.

GAITER BOTTOMS
1840's and 1850's. (M.) Term indicating the cut of the bottom of the trouser legs; 'Whole gaiter-bottoms' had the side seams brought forward 4″ from the heel, the fronts being 5″ wide and the backs 12½″; 'Half gaiter-bottoms' had the seams brought forward 1½″ making the fronts 8″ and the backs 11″ at the ankles.

GALATEA COMB
1890's. (F.) A decorative hair-comb with a few long prongs set in a curve with an ornamental looped handle.

GALATEA HAT
1890's. (M. and F.) Of Chinese or Japanese plait, made with a sailor crown and turned-up brim; worn by small children in summer.

GALLIGASKINS, GALLY-GAS-COYNES, GASKINS
C. 1570 to end of 17th c. but rare after 1620. (M.) (1) Knee-breeches, either wide and bombasted round the buttocks, or 'sometimes close to the buttocke like the Venetian galli-cascoyne'. (1610, S. Rowlands, *Martin Mark-all*.)

(2) In 19th c. the term was applied to leather gaiters worn by sportsmen.

GALLISLOPS, GALLYSLOPS, GALLY HOSE, GALLY BREECHES
(the last a rare term)
17th c. (M.) The same as wide GALLIGASKINS, *q.v.*

GALLO-GREEK BODICE
1820's. (F.) A bodice with narrow flat trimming descending from the shoulders, without quite meeting at the waist.

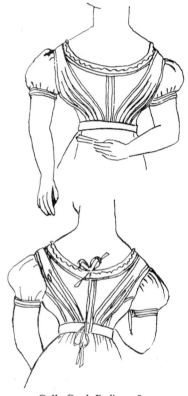

Gallo-Greek Bodice, 1820

GALLOWSES
18th and 19th c's. (M.) Braces, unfashionable before 1780's. 'Contrivances made of cloth, and hooks and eyes, worn over the shoulders by men to keep their breeches up.' (1730–6, Bailey, *Dictionary*.)

GALOCHE, GALAGE, GALOSS, GALOSSIAN, GALLOSES, GALLOSHOES, GALOSHES, GALLOTIVES
From 14th c. on. (M. and F.) A generic term for a protective overshoe though the nature varied. In the 14th c. they were buckled overshoes. In the 15th and 16th c's. they were the same as pattens, i.e. wooden soles secured by lachets. In the late 16th c. and early 17th they were wooden-soled low over-boots, buckled and worn by all classes. In 1607 Prince Henry had 16 gold buckles, 'with pendants and tongues to buckle a pair of galosses'. (Wardrobe Accounts.) In 17th c. 'galloshoes are false shooes or covers for shooes'. (1688, R. Holme, *Armourie*.)
In 18th c. they were usually called 'clogs'.
Rubber galoshes were introduced and patented in 1842.

GAMASHES
1590's to end of 17th c. (M.) Loose, long, cloth leggings often buttoned. 'Gamashes or upper stockings'. (1598, Florio.) In 17th c. they acquired soles. 'Gamashes, high boots, buskins or start-ups.' (1688, R. Holme, *Armourie*.) They were worn on horseback or by pedestrians as a protection against the dirt.

GAMBADO, GAMBADA, GAMBAGE
2nd half 17th and 1st half 18th c's. (M.) 'A kind of leather instrument attached to the saddle in place of stirrups.' (1656, Blount, *Glossographia*.) The gambado resembled a large boot open on the outer side.

GAMP
19th c. Popular name for an umbrella; so-called from Dickens's character of 'Mrs. Gamp'. (1843).

GARDE-CORPS
13th and early 14th c's. (M. and F.) A voluminous super-tunic with hood and long wide sleeves, often worn as hanging sleeves, the arm passing through a vertical slit in the upper half. No belt worn. A garment for winter wear. *See* HERIGAUT

GARIBALDI BLOUSE or SHIRT
1860's. (F.) Worn in place of a bodice, with any skirt (day). The

blouse was of scarlet merino trimmed with black braid; full sleeves or plain 'coat sleeves' gathered into a wristband and having small epaulettes. Small collar and black cravat. Generally worn with a Zouave jacket. The blouse usually overhanging the skirt and worn with a waist-belt.

Garibaldi Shirt (Female), 1864

GARIBALDI BODICE
1860's. (F.) A day bodice made loose and falling over the waistband or confined with narrow tucks from neck to waist; worn with or without a jacket. Also known as 'Russian Vest'. Garibaldi's visit to England in 1863 gave enormous popularity to anything named after him, from a blouse to a biscuit.

GARIBALDI JACKET
1860's. (F.) An outdoor jacket, short and square cut, without basques; made of scarlet cashmere with military braiding.

GARIBALDI SLEEVE
1860's. (F.) Full and gathered into a wristband. Worn with morning or afternoon dresses of thin materials.

GARIBALDI VEST
Same as GARIBALDI BODICE, *q.v.*

GARMENT
Any clothing for the body.

GARNACHE
13th to mid 14th c. (M.) A long loose super-tunic with short cape-like sleeves cut in one with the body

and falling over the shoulders. The side seams were sometimes left open or joined at the waist-level or from waist to hem.

In 14th c. a characteristic feature was two tongue-shaped lapels at the front of the neck; these were paler than the garment itself and often faced with fur. This garment was also called a TABARD, *q.v.*

Garnache, mid 14th c.

GARNITURE
'The trimming of a suit with Ribbons, precious stones etc., as Garniture of Diamonds.' (1706, Phillips, edit. Kersey.)

GARTER
Med. on. (M. and F.) A tie or band to keep the stocking in place on the leg, and placed above or below the knee. For the significance of 'ungartered', *see* under LOVE.

MALE. Until the 2nd half of 16th c. usually ties; subsequently ties or buckled bands.

In 17th and 18th c's some were like small decorative scarves, with fringed ends and tied in a bow on the outer side of the knee. Others were decorative bands with ornamental buckles, always placed below the knee. Garters might be of wool, worsted, crewel, list, or ribbon, taffeta, cypress and net. '2 yards of ribband for garters.' (1522, Lestrange Accounts.) 'A pair of silver garters buckled below the knee.' (1711, *The Spectator*.)

FEMALE. At the end of the 17th and throughout the 18th c. garters, worn above or below the knee, were often very decorative and sometimes woven with mottoes addressed to young men who sought them as trophies. 'Great quantities of silk garters are bought by the ladies with the following motto NO SEARCH.' (1739, Pilborough's *Colchester Journal*.)

In 19th c. the garter was usually a long narrow strip of knitted wool wound round the leg above the knee, or more elegant forms were of silk enclosing fine brass springs and having metal clasps. From *c.* 1830 india-rubber woven 'elastic' began to appear, becoming general by *c.* 1850. From 1878 these were replaced by suspenders.

GASCON COAT, GASKYN COAT
See JUPE.

GASCON HOSE
Synonymous with GALLIGASKINS, *q.v.*

GAUGING, GAGING or SHIRRING
A term applied to a series of close parallel runnings so that the material in between is fixed in gathers. A form of decoration extremely popular in bonnets of the 1840's and in dresses of the late 1870's and 1880's.

GAUNTLET
From mid 15th to the abandonment of armour in 17th c. the term was applied to a glove-like defence of the hand ; subsequently to a glove with a cuff spreading up the wrist. *See* GLOVES.

GEMMEWS, JEMEWS
15th c. (M.) The jaws of a bag working on pins at the side, or a mere

strengthening of leather or velvet round the jaws.

GENEVA HAT
Late 16th and early 17th c's. (M.) A broad-brimmed, high-crowned hat, sometimes untrimmed, worn by Puritan ministers and others.

GENEVA PRINT RUFF, GENEVA-SET RUFF
17th c. (M. and F.) A small ruff of Puritanical design modelled on that of the Genevan Calvinists. 'In print as Puritan ruffes are set.' (1613, Mynshul, *Essays*.) 'A little Geneva-set (ruff).' (1633, T. Adams.)

GENOA CLOAK
See SPANISH CLOAK.

GERMAN GOWN
See BRUNSWICK GOWN.

GIBOUN
1844. (M.) A loose wrap in the form of a small shoulder cape with wide sleeves, resembling the Caban of the period, but the fronts falling straight like a cloak without fastenings.

GIBUS, GIBUS HAT
1840's on. (M.) A top hat with a collapsible crown, the sides containing concealed in the lining a metal 'lazy tongs' ; when flat the hat could be carried under the arm. Worn with evening dress and replacing the earlier 'Elastic Hat'. Named after its inventor.

GIG COAT
1820's. (F.) *See* CURRICLE COAT.

GIGOT SLEEVE, LEG-OF-MUTTON SLEEVE
1824 to '36, 1862 and 1890-6. (F. and to a slight degree M. in 1820's and 1860's.) A day sleeve, very full at the shoulder, diminishing in size towards the elbow and gradually becoming tight at the wrist. In 1827 the upper portion was sometimes distended with whalebone hoops. In 1862 used only for summer dresses. In 1895 the gigot was 'monstrous',

requiring 2½ yards of material. It collapsed abruptly in 1896.

Gigot Sleeves, 1894

GILLS, SHIRT-GILLS
19th c. (M.) Colloquial name for the upstanding points of the shirt-collar.

GIMP, GUIMPLE
See WIMPLE.

GINGHAM
19th c. Colloquial name for Umbrella, the cheaper kinds being made of that material. *See* GAMP.

GINGLERS
Late 16th and early 17th c's. (M.) Spurs with one or two metal drops hung in an eye on the rowel-pin which rattled against the rowel when the wearer walked. Very fashionable at the period indicated. 'I had spurs of mine own before but they were not ginglers.' (1599, B. Jonson, *Every Man out of his Humour*.) 'You that weare Bootes and Ginglers at your heels.' (1604, S. Rowlands, *Swaggering Ruffian*.)

GIPON, Fr. JUPON
14th c. (M.) A military term adapted for civilian use. The Gipon was a close-fitting, waisted and padded garment worn next to the shirt. It ended near the knees at first but was much shortened in the 2nd half of the century. Buttoned or laced down the front, the sleeves long and tight with buttons up to the elbows on the outer side. No belt unless worn without an over-garment. The Gipon was the fore-runner of the Doublet and was so-called towards the close of that century.

GIPSER, GIPCIÈRE
14th and 15th c's. term. A purse or pouch.
'A gipser al of silk
Heng at his girdle . . .'
(*C.* 1381, Chaucer, *Canterbury Tales*, Prologue.)

GIPSER-RINGS
POUCH RINGS, *q.v.*

GIPSY BONNET
1871. (F.) A small flat bonnet only covering the crown of the head; trimmed with lace and feather.

GIPSY HAT
1800 to 1830's. (F.) A straw or chip hat with wide brim, always with ribbons passing from the crown over the brim and tied in a bow under the chin.

GIRAFFE COMB
1874. (F.) A very high ornamental hair-comb of tortoiseshell, worn in the day as well as with evening dress.

GIRDLE
Med. on. (M. and F.) A cord or band, tied or buckled, encircling the waist or hips. In Mediaeval period primarily to confine the flowing garments at the waist, or for suspending various objects or sometimes purely decorative. *See* KNIGHTLY GIRDLE.
'And by hire girdel heng a purs of lether
Tasseled with grene and perled with latoun.'
(*C.* 1381, Chaucer, *Miller's Tale*.)

94

GIRDLE GLASS
17th c. (F.) A hand mirror hanging from the waistband.

GIRDLESTEAD
Med. to 17th c. The waist-line.

GITE
14th and 15th c's. Later uses only poetical. A gown.

GLADSTONE OVERCOAT
1870's. (M.) A short D-B overcoat with a shoulder-cape and borders trimmed with astrakhan.

GLANDKIN, GLAWDKIN
Early 16th c. A rare term for the costly flowing gown of a royal wardrobe.

GLAUVINA PIN
1820's and 1830's. (F.) Ornamental pin with a large detachable head often tasselled; used to secure the elaborate coiffure.

GLENGARRY, GLENGARRY BONNET
1860's. (M. and F.) 'A Scotch bonnet higher in front than at the back.' (1858, *Simmonds's Dictionary*.) Generally decorated with a small feather and pendant ribbons behind; as worn in England.

GLOVES
From 12th c. but rare before 13th. (M. and F.) (1) MALE. Either covering the hand and ending at the wrist, or made with spreading cuffs as GAUNTLET GLOVES, *q.v.* Long gloves were rare for men but occasionally worn by fops in 17th c. when gloves were a feature and often elaborately decorated, fringed and scented. 'He is indeed a pattern of modern foppery. He was yesterday at the play, with a pair of gloves up to his elbows.' (1676, Etherege, *The Man of Mode*.)
In 18th c. 'Gants à l'anglaise' ended at the wrist, having a short slit on the back or a narrow turned-back cuff sometimes embroidered.
Materials: 16th c. leather (stag, sheep, horse, kid, suède, doe) also satin, velvet, knitted silk and worsted, variously coloured.
Some were slashed to show a finger ring.
In 17th and 18th c's. the same; also cordovan (Spanish leather) being soft and very fashionable.
In 19th c. always short and until *c.* 1870 often coloured for day, white for evening; lavender for weddings.
(2) FEMALE. As for men until *c.* 1640 when elbow-length gloves, close-fitting, of fine leather or silk, and generally white, sometimes embroidered, began to be fashionable and essential for full dress. In 18th c. elbow-length gloves were universal except with riding habits and, towards the end, with long-sleeved dresses.
In 19th c. either short to the wrist or long to the elbow; day, coloured; evening, white. A short evening glove was fashionable from 1830 to 1865; subsequently long, and by 1890's spreading up beyond the elbow.
See named varieties: BERLIN, LIMERICK, WOODSTOCK, YORK TAN, CHICKEN-SKIN, CUT-FINGERED.

Glove, 17th c.

GLOVE-BAND
From *c.* 1640 to *c.* 1700. (F.) A band of ribbon or plaited horsehair tied at the elbow over a long glove to keep it in place.

95

GLOVE-STRING

18th c. (F.) Similar to glove-band, made of ribbon or horsehair and tied or buckled at the elbow over a long glove. 'Diamond buckles to the glove-strings'—for full dress. (1783, *Lady's Magazine.*)

GODET PLEAT

1870's. (F.) A hollow tubular pleat, narrow above and expanding downwards to give a fluted effect to the skirt.

GODET SKIRT

1895. (F.) A day skirt with godet pleats at the back and sides often sustained by a fine steel in the hem and in the lining. 'A labyrinth of black elastic to keep the flutes in place'.

GOFFERED VEIL, NEBULA HEADDRESS

19th-c. terms for a head-dress worn by women from *c.* 1350 to 1420. The head-dress, made of linen, was draped over the head with a broad goffered frill surrounding the face and ending at the temples or chin. The back drapery fell to the shoulders, sometimes having a goffered border.

Goffered Veil, c. 1370

GOLE, GOLET

14th and 15th c's. (M.) (GOLET the 15th-c. name.) The cape portion of the hood or chaperon.

GOLF VEST

1894. (M.) Made S-B without a collar; having 2 side pockets and watch-pocket. Of scarlet knitted wool bound with braid.

GOLILLA

17th c. (M. and F.) A Spanish term sometimes used for the semicircular collar or 'band' curving round the back of the head with the straight border under the chin. Very fashionable from 1605 to 1630.

GONEL

14th c. A Gown.

GORED BELL SKIRT

1893. (F.) The front panel gored with 3 to 5 side gores; the back panel cut on the cross, keeping the fullness behind. Hem 10 to 16 feet round, lined with a footing of muslin or crinoline 9″ deep.

GORED SKIRT

(F.) A constructional method of cutting the material into pyramidal-shaped panels, narrow above, to produce a close fit at the waist, avoiding gathers or pleats; a method dating from the 14th c. Much used in the 19th c. (i.e. 1820's, late 1860's and mid 1890's, when it reached the highest degree of technical skill).

GORGET

(1) 14th and 15th c's. (M.) The cape portion of hood or chaperon. *See* GOLE.

(2) 1560's to 1620's. (M.) A military steel or plate armour collar spreading over the chest and worn as a mark of distinction by civilians.

GORGETTE, GORGET, WIMPLE

(1) 12th and 13th c's., rarely 14th and 15th to early 16th c. (F.) A neck covering. *See* WIMPLE, the more usual term.

(2) Late 16th c. (F.) The small ruff of a smock.

(3) 2nd half 17th c. (F.) A deep falling cape-like collar, generally called a 'whisk'.

GOTHIC CAP
1834. (F.) An indoor morning cap
with a very small crown, and trimmed
with ruching framing the face.

GOWCE
14th and 15th c.'s. Term meaning a
gusset.

GOWN
(1) MALE. Med. to *c*. 1600. A loose
long upper garment of a formal nature
varying in design over this period,
generally having wide and often hanging sleeves; after 1600 relegated to
the learned professions and officials.
Demi- or half-gown reached the
knees; side-gown or long gown
reached the ankles.
(2) FEMALE. Med. on. A term
indicating a woman's dress. In the
19th c. it implied a dress of uniform
material fastened in front, as opposed
to a frock fastened behind.

Gown (Male), 1510

Gipon and early Doublet; the sleeve
cut so as to form a circular plate-like
seam when inserted, thus overlapping
the front and back of the body.
Rare in England.

GRANNIE SKIRT, VICTORIA
    SKIRT
1893. (F.) Supposed to be a revival
of the skirt of 1830's; cut in a circular
shape from double-width material,
the hem 16 to 18 feet round; made
with flounces and tucks from knee
level, with a velvet band facing the
hem. Pocket, if present, behind in
the placket hole.

GRANNY BONNET
1893. (F.) A huge erection with
wide flaring brim and pot-like crown;
decorated with feathers.

GRAUNDICE
16th c. An ornament for the head;
a variant of CRAUNCE or CRANTS, *q.v.*

Gown (Male), 1532

c.D.F.

GRANDE-ASSIETTE SLEEVES
Mid 14th to mid 15th c. (M.) A
type of sleeve sometimes made for the

GREATCOAT
Term used from 18th c. on. (M. and
F.) An outdoor overcoat varying in

style according to the fashion of the day.

GREATCOAT DRESS
End of 18th c. (F.) A dress resembling a greatcoat. Worn by day.

GRECIAN BEND
1815–19 and again 1868–70. (F.) A fashion stance consisting of a forward stoop from the waist, the effect increased by a bustle and in the later period by a puffed-out overskirt.

Grecian Bend, 1868

Grecian Bend, 1818

GRECIAN SLEEVE
1852. (F.) An under-sleeve slit open at the side and closed with buttons.

GRECQUE
2nd half 18th c. (M.) A style of dressing the hair of the wig. 'Some people wear it cut short before and comed up en brosse very high upon the top of the head; it's called à la greque and is very pretty when well done.' (Jan. 1766, Lady Sarah Bunbury to Lady Susan O'Brien, *The Life and Letters of Lady Sarah Lennox*, J. Murray, 1902.)

By 1787: 'The hair is dressed in 2 long curls on each side and a Grecque

behind, divided like a horseshoe, inclining a little forward en coque'. (*Ipswich Journal.*)

1788: 'The hair is dressed in four curls on each side, three below and one above, and a grecque en dos d'âne turned off at top behind in the form of a horseshoe and tied behind in a long queue'. (*Ipswich Journal.*)

The side curls were arranged horizontally, ending at each side of the face.

GRECQUE CORSAGE
1850. (F.) An evening dress bodice, low off the shoulders, and square, with vertical pleats sloping down to a point in front.

GREGORIAN
Late 16th to mid 17th c. (M.) A wig so called after 'one Gregory a barber in the Strand'. (1670, Blount, *Glossographia.*)

GREGS
Galligaskins.

GRELOT
1860's. (F.) A ball-fringe, a fashionable trimming for dresses.

98

GUARD-CHAIN
C. 1825 on. (M.) A long chain of small links worn round the neck and attached to the watch, replacing the fob-chain.

GUARDS
16th c. and less fashionably to *c.* 1620's. (M. and F.) Decorative bands of rich material, plain or embroidered, used as borders to conceal seams on garments. 'A jacket guarded with velvet' meant one trimmed with guards.

GUIMPE
1890's. (F.) A chemisette worn with a low-necked dress, by girls (U.S.A.).

GWIMPLE
See WIMPLE.

H

HABIT
(1) Med. Originally the distinctive dress of a particular rank or profession, especially of religious orders.

(2) 18th and 19th c's. The dress or suit worn on horseback as Riding Habit. (F.)

HABIT BODICE
1877 on. (F.) A long cuirasse bodice with long basques or postillions behind. The bodice open in front and worn with a waistcoat.

HABIT D'ESCALIER
Late 18th and early 19th c. (F.) A full evening dress with HALF ROBE (q.v.) and short sleeves slit open from below and joined by ribbon ties resembling the rungs of a ladder.

HABIT GLOVE
18th c. (F.) A lady's riding glove; some of grey kid, some of York tan; usually short and resembling men's.

HABIT-REDINGOTE
1879. (F.) A Princess Polonaise, the overskirt as long as the underskirt behind and closed down to the knees in front.

HABIT SHIRT
18th and 19th c's. (F.) 18th c. Worn as part of a riding costume; it was a linen garment about 15″ deep in front and 11″ behind, and tied round with tape. A stand collar and ruffled shirt front, buttoned with 2 buttons; sleeves frilled at the wrist. Worn under a waistcoat.

19th c. Worn as a fill-in for a day dress. In 1815 a ruff was added to the neck; often of cambric or muslin. Habit shirt was often called a CHEMISETTE (q.v.).

HAIR BAND
15th to 17th c. (F.) A ribbon or fillet for binding the hair.

HAIR CAP
17th to 19th c's. (M. and F.) A travelling wig.

HAIR LACE
16th c. (1) Synonym for Hair-band.

(2) Synonym for CROSSCLOTH, q.v. Its purpose, 'to keep the wrinkles out of their foreheads'. (1698, Fryer, East India and Persia.)

HALF BOOTS
Late 18th and 19th c's. (M.) A name given to boots reaching to just below the calf of the leg.

HALF DRESS
Late 18th and 19th c's. A term then denoting the costume worn at day functions and at informal evening ones.

HALF-GAITERS
See SPATS.

HALF HANDKERCHIEF
18th and early 19th c's. (F.) Half of a square of material cut diagonally across; usually of decorative material. In the 18th c. worn usually on the head or round the neck.

From 1800 to 1830 an evening cap of triangular shape pinned to the crown with the point behind and the straight side curving round the head.

From 1830's generally known as a 'FANCHON', q.v.

HALF HOSE
19th c. (M.) A trade name for socks.

HALF KIRTLE
See KIRTLE.

HALF ROBE or HALF GOWN, or DEMI-HABILLEMENT
1794 to early 19th c. (F.) A low-necked, thigh-length tunic with short sleeves, worn over a round gown and pulled in at the waist with a narrow ribbon tie or belt. Many varieties.

HALF SHIRT
16th to 18th c's. (M.) A short shirt with decorative breast, intended to be worn over a full-length plain shirt or one that had become soiled.
18th c. Sometimes called 'SHAMS'. 'Half-shirts or shams of coarse linen.' (1772, Nugent, *History*.) Half shirts of a coarse material were occasionally worn by countrywomen.

'HALF-SKIRTS'
A 'ghost word' appearing only in the transcription of Pepys' Diary for 13 Oct. 1661, in the line 'left off half-skirts and put on a wastcoat'. The context clearly indicates that the phrase intended—and actually written—by Pepys should read 'half shirts'; the shorthand characters for 'sh' and 'sk' being very similar.

HALF SLEEVE
See FORE SLEEVE.

HAMMERCUT BEARD
C. 1618 to 1650; rarely to 1660. This combined beard and moustache, the small straight or—rarely—twisted tuft under the lower lip forming the handle of the hammer; the moustache, waxed horizontally, forming the cross-piece. 'Some with hammercut or Roman T.' (1621, J. Taylor, *Superbiae Flagellum*.)

HAND CLOTH
See HANDKERCHIEF.

HAND CUFF
See HAND FALL.

HAND FALL
17th c. (M. and F.) A turned-back, spreading cuff, sometimes double, trimmed with lace and starched. It might be worn with a standing or falling band, with a falling ruff and occasionally with a standing ruff. '12 rouffe bands and 8 payre of handefalles £1.10.' (1604, Inventory of Wm. Spicer, Exeter Records.)

HANDKERCHIEF
(1) Often distinguished as 'Pocket-handkerchief'. 16th c. on. (M. and F.) A square of linen or silk, often edged with lace, carried about the person and used for wiping the face or nose; the more elegant styles being used for display only, e.g. 'five handkercheves wrought with golde and red silke'. (1556, Nichols, *Gifts to Queen Mary*.) See BUTTONED HAND-KERCHIEF, TASSELLED HANDKERCHIEF.
(2) 16th c. on. (F.) A NECK-CLOTH or NECKERCHIEF (*q.v.*), the former term commonly used for the latter, in the 18th c. See HALF HANDKERCHIEF.
(3) 19th c. (M. and F.) Men's always larger than women's; often coloured for day use; even black for mourning (1804) or, later, with a black border up to an inch wide. 'Generally of silk, cotton not being known among the middling ranks since the duty has been taken off silk'. (1830.) India silk coloured, and foulard bordered with a white stripe (1830's). See also BANDANNA and BELCHER handkerchiefs. By 1840 a white silk handkerchief, often embroidered and edged with lace, was fashionable for evening wear. By c. 1870 the plain white cambric was correct for day and evening; in the former carried in the outside breast pocket, in the latter, in the tail-pocket. In the 1890's a fashion, borrowed from the military, of wearing the day handkerchief in the cuff of the left sleeve. At the close of the century a red silk handkerchief was often worn tucked into the opening of the evening dress waistcoat. Women's handkerchiefs, for day use, were of cambric, linen or cotton and white; for evening, often of lace or edged with lace or embroidery; about the middle of the 19th c. the corners of the handkerchief were rounded.

In addition to black-edged hand-kerchiefs worn by both sexes for mourning, the 19th c. also produced at the death of notable people huge 'mourning handkerchiefs' printed with the portrait of the deceased and details of his life.

HANDKERCHIEF DRESS

1880's. (F.) A dress composed of pieces of material resembling large bandanna handkerchiefs. 'Two compose the tunic, the point of the lower reaching nearly to the hem of the skirt which is plain in front, the back kilted. The point of the upper hand-kerchief shews beneath the deep basqued jacket-bodice, which is plain, coat-shaped with revers and worn with a waistcoat.'

HAND RUFF

C. 1560 to 1630's. (M. and F.) A small wrist-ruff. *See* RUFFLES. A 'pair of ruffs' meant hand ruffs only.

HAND SLEEVE

16th-c. term. The wrist portion of a sleeve and not a separate item.

HANGER

See SHOULDER BELT.

HANGING SLEEVES

C. 1400 to 1630. (M. and F. con-tinued academically.) Wide, long tubular sleeves with a slit in the upper half through which the arm could emerge, leaving the sleeve pen-dant. Some nearly reached the ground. Worn with gowns, houppe-landes, jackets and jerkins and some-times with women's dresses of the French farthingale style.

Sham or False Hanging Sleeves.

(1) *c.* 1560 to 1630's. (M.) Pen-dant streamers attached to the back of the arm-hole, being the remains of a true Hanging Sleeve had become merely ornamental. Worn some-times with jerkins.

(2) 1560's to 1630's. (F.) In 16th and 17th c's. women's sham hanging sleeves corresponded to those worn by men.

(3) 17th and 18th c's. (F.) These

represented 'leading strings' as worn by children, and remained, as a sign of youth, for girls and young women 'Carry my wedding suits to Mrs Arnold and tell her she has forgot the hanging sleeves to the gowns.' (1754 S. Richardson, *The History of Sir Ch Grandison.*)

Hanging Sleeves, c. 1500

HANSELINE, HANSLEIN, HEN SELYNS, HAUNSELEYNYS, HENSE LYNES

Late 14th and early 15th c's. (M.) The extremely short Doublet, also called Paltock, which came into fashion at this period.

HANSLET, ANSLET

A variation of Hanseline.

HARE POCKET

19th c. (M.) A large pocket inside the skirts of a shooting jacket or coat

HARLOT, HERLOT

Late 14th-c. expression. (M.) A garment for the lower limbs in which the hose legs (like stockings) and the breech were combined to form one resembling modern 'tights'. Pre viously separate hose legs had been worn and presumably the term 'harlot' was used for this new fashion which by many was considered in decent. (*See* Chaucer, *The Parson's Tale.*) The definition of harlot as 'ties or points securing the hose to the doublet', is incorrect, owing to a mis-translation of the original Latin text: 'Habent etiam caligas bipartitas et strangulatas quas cum corrigilis ligant ad suos "paltokkis", quae vocantur "harlottes", et sic unus "harlot" servit alteri, sine lumbare semper incedentes'. (*C.* 1362, *Eulogium Historicum*, III, 231, Rolls Series.) Which may be translated: 'They also have hose in two parts and tight, which they tie to their Paltocks and which are called Harlottes and so one serves the other always going without drawers'.

Herlots, late 14th c.

HARVEST GLOVES
15th to 18th c. (M.) *See* DANNOCK and HEDGER'S GLOVES.

HASP
17th and 18th c's. (M.) An ornamental 'hook and eye' fastening for coats instead of buttons. 'A set of gentlemen who take the liberty to appear in all public places without any buttons on their coats, which they supply with little silver hasps.' (1711, *The Spectator*.)

HAT
From 10th c. on. (M. and F.) A head covering generally consisting of a crown and brim; always designed to magnify the importance of the male head and to draw attention to it, emphasising the social class of the wearer; contrasting with the insignificant, close-fitting cap of the social inferior. Worn indoors as well as out, by men, until the Restoration of 1660, and in church until that time.

Hats were rarely worn by women until the late 16th c. except for travelling; and usually designed to attract male attention; hence in 19th c. hats were considered improper for women to wear on Sundays or in church, until *c.* 1875.

HAT A LA REINE
1863. (F.) A hat of Italian straw with shallow brim turned down all round a small flat crown with narrow ribbon hat-band, the fringed ends of which hung down behind.

HAT-BAND
14th c. on. (M. and F.) A length of gold, silver, coloured silk or ribbon bound about the base of the crown of a hat as an ornament. In late 16th c. very elaborate, often of goldsmith's work and enamelled, set with gems and pearls, or formed of a string threaded with buttons of precious metal. In late 16th c. the absence of a hat-band, together with a dishevelled appearance, was said to indicate that the wearer was in love. *See* LOVE.

The Cable Hat-Band (late 16th c. for a few years) was made in a twisted

Hat Band of Buttons, 1591

103

design resembling rope. 'I had a gold cable hat band, then new come up; it was a massie goldsmith's work.' (1599, Ben Jonson, *Every Man out of his Humour.*) *See* also MOURNING BAND.

HAT CAP
18th c. (F.) A term for a day cap worn under a hat. *See* UNDER CAP. (In 17th c. it was part of the military equipment for the English Foot sent to Ireland in 1601.)

HATIRE
Attire.

HAT-SCREW
Late 18th and early 19th c's. (M.) An implement, usually of boxwood, consisting of a screw-shaft with a curved horizontal piece at each end; used to stretch the cylindrically shaped crown of a beaver hat into an oval to fit the wearer's head. 'The natural shape of the common hat which, by its being made on a perfectly round block, requires to be brought to the oval shape by means of a screw . . . liable when exposed to rain to get soft . . . and return to its round form. . . .'
This inconvenience and the need for a hat-screw abolished in 1817 by the invention (of Messrs. Dando & Co.) of the 'Improved Oval-shape Beaver Hat, being finished upon an

Hat Screw, c. 1800

oval block, nothing can cause it to lose its shape . . .'. (Advert., 1817, *Ipswich Journal.*)

HAWK-GLOVE, later HAWKING GLOVE
13th c. on. (M.) A short glove worn on the left hand as a protection when the hawk was being carried on the wrist. In the 16th c. some of these gloves were lined with velvet and some embroidered.

HEAD
Late 17th and 18th c's. (F.) Often called a TETE. The shortened term for head-dress, generally indicating an indoor cap, but by the end of 17th c. it often included the whole arrangement of the coiffure. 'Lost, a Head with very fine looped lace.' (1700, *The Protestant Mercury.*) *See* QUADRILLE HEAD.

HEAD BAND
16th to early 18th c. Synonymous with cross-cloth although distinguished in technical documents. Like the cross-cloth, it was supposed, when medicated, to induce sleep. 'To promote sleep take common roses with the white of an egg well beaten . . . and make an Head band or fillet of it.' (1725, Bradley, *Family Dictionary.*)

HEAD CLOTH
Med. Synonymous with KERCHIEF.

HEAD-DRESS, HEAD-DRESSING
16th c. on. (F.) What was worn on the head.

HEADGEAR
16th c. on. (M. and F.) Any form of head covering.

HEAD KERCHIEF
Mainly 17th-c. term. A large handkerchief folded cornerwise and worn on the head.

HEAD RAIL
16th and 17th c's. (F.) A large form of kerchief or veil worn on the head and flowing down behind; generally edged with lace; sometimes starched and sometimes wired

up over the head (from 1590 to 1620). 'For mendinge, washinge and starchinge of a heade raille of fine sipers edged rounde aboute with white thred bone lace.' (1588, Egerton MS.)

HEAD SUIT
Synonymous with Head-dress.

HEART BREAKER
(1) (F.) *See* CREVE-CŒUR.
(2) (M.) *See* LOVE LOCK.

HEART-SHAPED HEAD-DRESS
C. 1420 to 1450. (F.) A descriptive term applied later to the templers covering the ears and extending upwards above the head, together forming a U-shaped dip above the forehead. These were secured by a decorative circlet and draped with a veil falling at the back.

Heart-shaped Head-dress, 1420–50

HEAVY SWELL
1860's. (M.) Term then applied to ultra-fashionably dressed gentleman. A 'rank Swell' was a flashily dressed person aping the appearance of his social betters.

HEDGER'S GLOVES, HEDGING GLOVES
16th to 19th c. (M.) A countryman's mittens. *See* DANNOCK.

HELMET CAP
1810. (F.) A day cap domed and shaped like a helmet, generally made up in stripes of lace and embroidery and tied under the chin with ribbons.

HELMET HAT
1870's. (M.) A hat with a helmet-shaped crown and narrow brim, made of cloth; chiefly worn at the seaside.

Helmet Hat, 1877

HEMISPHERICAL HAT
1850's and 1860's. (M.) A hard felt hat with bowl-shaped crown and narrow flat brim. By 1858 it had developed a knob on the crown, being then sometimes called a BOLLINGER (*q.v.*). Replaced by the BOWLER in 1860's.

HENLEY BOATER
1894 on. (M.) A blue or drab felt hat in the shape of a straw boater.

HENNIN
2nd half 15th c. (F.) French term for the steeple-shaped head-dress; very rare in England. Generally worn with 'loose kerchiefs atop hanging down sometimes as low as the ground'.

HENRI DEUX CAPE
1890's. (F.) A variation of the Tudor Cape but having a square yoke.

HENRIETTA JACKET

1890's. (F.) A ¾-length loose jacket with a deep collar falling over the chest in front; lined with quilted satin or merv.

HERIGAUT, HERIGALD, HERE-GAUD, GERYGOUD, HERI-GANS

2nd quarter 13th c. to early 14th c. (M., rarely F.) A gown-like garment of ¾ to full length with full, generally hanging, sleeves. *See* GARDE-CORPS.

HIGH-HEAD

18th c. (F.) Synonym for the Fontange.

HIGHLOWS

2nd half of 18th to near end of 19th c. (M.) 18th c. Boots reaching to the calf of the leg and laced up in front;

Herigaut (Male), mid 13th c.

Herigaut (Female), early 14th c.

HESSIANS

1790's to 1850's. (M.) Short riding boots, calf-length behind and generally curving up to a point in front to below the knee-cap and there decorated with a tassel. Made of black leather, sometimes bound round the top with a narrow border of coloured leather.

HEUSE, later HUSEAU, HOUSEL, HOUSEAU

1240's to near end of 15th c. A long riding boot reaching to mid-thigh and fitting the leg by means of buttons, buckles or straps on the outer side of the leg.

Hessians, 1824

106

made of stout leather. Worn in the country and by the unfashionables. 'Dressed in . . . a pair of Highlows.' (1757, *Norwich Mercury*.)
19th c. Boots reaching just above the ankle. 'A pair of polished highlows secured across the instep with a strap and buckle.' (1841, Arthur Armitage, *Heads of the People*.) Becoming more elegant, at length 'Highlows pass as patent-leathers'. (1878, W. S. Gilbert, *H.M.S. Pinafore*.)

HIGH-TOPS
See TOP BUTTON.

HIP BAGS
1883. (F.) A popular slang phrase for the pannier folds 'known in England as the Pompadour' and in America as the 'curtain drapery', which in the mode of that day draped the hip region.

HIP-BUTTONS
Late 17th to end of 19th c. (M.) The pair of buttons at the back of a skirted coat, heading the pleats on each side of the back vent; in the 19th c. generally at waist-level, and after 1823 on the seam at the waist. There is no evidence that these buttons were ever functional.

HIP-POCKET
1890's on. (M.) A cross pocket, with or without a flap, placed at the back of the hip of trousers. *See* CADDIE. To be distinguished from the tailoring phrase 'pockets on the hips', meaning outside pockets over the hip region in a skirted coat.

HISTORICAL SHIRT
17th c. (M.) A shirt embroidered in religious subjects.
'Sure you should not be
Without a neat historical shirt.'
(? 1619, J. Fletcher,
The Custom of the Country.)
See HOLY WORK.

HIVE
Term used from late 16th to mid 18th c. (F.) A high-crowned, hive-shaped hat of plaited straw with narrow or no brim. 'Upon her head a platted hive of straw.' (1597, W. Shakespeare, *Lover's Complaint*.) '. . . the hive, the milkmaid's chip hat, were rescued for atime from old women and servant girls to adorn heads of the first fashion.' (1754, *The Connoisseur*.)

HODTRENE
1st half 16th c. (F.) Probably the draped curtain or pendant lappets at the back of a hood, as in the ENGLISH or FRENCH HOOD, *q.v.*

HOGGER
See OKER.

HOLLOW LACE
16th c. A form of BRAID LACE used for edging.

HOLY WORK, HOLLIE WORK
Late 16th; mainly 17th c. Lace, cutwork and embroidery representing religious subjects, used in the ornamentation of shirts, smocks, bands and domestic linen. 'Collars of Hollie work' appear in an inventory of Mary Queen of Scots in 1578 but the fashion was spread by Puritan ladies towards 1620.
'She works religious petticoats; for flowers
She'll make church-histories. Her needle doth
So sanctify my cushionets! Besides
My smock sleeves have such holy embroideries
And are so learned, that I fear in time
All my apparel will be quoted by Some pure instructor.'
(1631, Jasper Mayne, *City Match*.)
See RELIGIOUS PETTICOAT, HISTORICAL SHIRT.

HOMBURG HAT
1870's on. (M.) A stiff felt with a dent running from front to back in the crown, the brim braided and slightly curved up at the sides. A style made fashionable by the Prince of Wales who frequented Homburg.

107

C.D.F.

Homburg, 1896

HOOD

Med. on. (M. and F.) A term usually indicating a loose soft covering shaped to fit over the head; worn as a separate garment or sometimes attached to an outdoor garment such as a cloak, etc.

The name often loosely applied to other kinds of women's head coverings such as the FRENCH HOOD, *q.v.*

For true hoods *see* CHAPERON (3), CAPUCHIN, LONG HOOD, PUG or SHORT HOOD.

Hood with Long Liripipe, 14th c. style

C.D.F.

Hood with Long Liripipe, 14th c. style

HOOKS AND EYES

Known in 14th c. as Crochets and Loops, but as hooks and eyes used from 1620 on. 'The needle lance Knights . . . put so many hookes and eyes to every hose and doublet.' (*C.* 1626, Egerton MS., Dick of Devonshire.) They were made of iron hammered flat; in 18th c. often of copper, sometimes tinned; early in 19th c. of brass; by 1840 of wire (brass or of japanned iron). *See* also HASP.

HOOP or HOOP PETTICOAT

C. 1710 to 1780 and to 1820 for Court wear. (F.) An under-petticoat variously distended with cane, wire or whalebone hoops. For the different shapes *see* BELL HOOP or CUPOLA COAT, FAN HOOP, OBLONG or SQUARE HOOP, POCKET HOOP.

The term 'hoop' was occasionally applied to the farthingale of the 16th c. 'The hoopes that hippes and haunch do hide.' (1596, Gosson, *Pleasant Quippes for Upstart Newfangled Gentlewomen.*)

HORN BUTTON

18th and 19th c's. A button of moulded horn.

HORNED HEAD-DRESS

C. 1410 to 1420; rarely to 1460. (F.) A head-dress worn with wide templers and wired up to resemble horns from which a pendant veil curtained the back of the head. 'She is hornyd

C.D.F.

Horned Headdress, 1416

like a kowe . . . for syn.' (*C.* 1460, *The Townley Mysteries*, 312, Surtees Soc.)

HORNS
14th c. (F.) Originally identical with BOSSES (*q.v.*) and so named

HORSE-SHOE CAP
Mid-18th c. (F.) A small day cap with long lappets.

HORTENSE MANTLE
1849. (F.) A ¾-length mantle with a falling collar and lapels, and a

Hooped Court Dress, 1799

because the spirally lapped bosses began to resemble rams' horns.

HORSEHAIR PETTICOAT, or CRINOLINE PETTICOAT
1840's to 1850's and again in 1868 to 1870. (F.) An under-petticoat made of crinoline, a material with a horse-hair warp and wool weft. The petticoat might be 6 feet round the hem which was often stiffened with lines of piping. Used to distend the skirt but replaced by the 'Cage Crinoline' and revived for a few years when the 'cage' was going out of fashion.

square-cut fringed cape descending to the waist. Named after Queen Hortense, the mother of Napoleon III.

HOSE
MALE. (1) Med. to 15th c. and again after 1660. The word then meant stockings.

(2) 1400 to *c.* 1620. The word then referred to leg-wear, the long tailored stockings being united at the fork and carried up over the buttocks forming 'tights'. These were known as 'long-stocked hose'. In the 16th c.

the upper portion was expanded and this was variously termed 'trunk hose', 'round hose', or 'upper stocks', the lower stocking portion called 'nether stocks'. From *c.* 1660 on hose meant stockings.

FEMALE. From Med. on, hose meant stockings.

'Her hosen weren of fine skarlet redde,
 Ful straite y-tyed.'
(*C.* 1387, Chaucer, *The Wife of Bath.*)

HOUNDS EARS
C. 1660's to 1680's. (M.) A popular name for the rounded corners of the large coat-cuffs with a deep turn-up and open behind.

HOUPPELANDE
End of 14th and throughout 15th c's., though after 1450 the term 'gown' was more usual. (M. and F.) A voluminous upper garment fitting the shoulders and generally falling in tubular folds. The length varied from reaching the thighs to trailing on the ground (in ceremonial costume). Earlier forms had high bottle-neck collars expanding round the head; in later forms the collar varied. Sleeves very wide, expanding to a funnel shape below; 'BAG-PIPE SLEEVES' (*q.v.*) were common in 15th

Houppelande, c. 1400

c. A belt usual but optional. The term 'Pellard' was applied to a houppelande, according to Ducange (late 16th c.).

Houppelande, c. 1415–20

HOUSE DRESS
1877 on. (F.) A plain princess robe, sometimes with a Watteau back, trained, worn without corsets informally at breakfast and indoors during the morning. By 1890 it had become a close-fitting TEA-GOWN, *q.v.*

HOUSEMAID SKIRT
1884. (F.) A plain skirt with 5 or 6 tucks round the lower part. Worn for homely occasions by young women.

HOUVETTE
See HOWVE.

HOWLING BAGS
Mid 19th c. (M.) Slang term for trousers with a loud pattern.

HOWVE, HOUVE
14th c. (M. and F.) A hood. 'Houvette' and 'Huvet' synonyms.

HOXTER
19th c. (M.) Slang term for an inside pocket of a coat.

HUKE, HEWKE, HEYKE, HUQUE, HEWK, HYKE, HEUQUE
(1) Mainly 1st half 15th c. Rare later; mentioned in French litera-

ture in 13th c. (M. and F.) A short over-garment of tabard design with front and back panels; occasionally with sleeves and generally belted.

(2) 16th and 17th c's. (F.) A large head-rail or veil enveloping the wearer to knees or ankles. It was known to English travellers from its use by women in the Low Countries although it originated in Spain, where it later became the Mantilla.

Doubtful if ever worn in England, though the expression 'to huke', meaning to veil, was used here.

HUNGARIAN CORD
1860's; most fashionable, 1867-8. (F.) A substantial silk cord used to border the hem of a trained skirt, in place of the conventional braid.

HUNGERLAND BAND
17th c. (F.) A kind of lace sometimes used for making bands i.e. collars; presumably 'point de Hongrye', a lace made at Halle of a style and pattern accepted as being Hungarian.

HUNTING BELT
1820's. (M.) A belt of whalebone worn by the dandy in the hunting field.

HUNTING NECKTIE
1818 to 1830's. (M.) Very broad and worn high round the neck with 3 creases each side verging towards the centre in front; the ends brought forward and crossed over and concealed under the coat; secured by a pin.

Hunting Tie, 1818–30

HUNTING STOCK
1890's. (M.) A large scarf of cellular cloth, folded and tied twice round the neck, concealing the absence of a collar. 'But few there are who can wear a hunting-stock and still look like a gentleman.' (1898, *The Tailor & Cutter*.)

HUNTLEY BONNET
1814. (F.) Resembling a Scotch bonnet, made in twilled plaid sarcenet and trimmed with a rosette and three feathers.

HURE
Term used from late 13th into 17th c. with 2 meanings. (M.) (1) The shaggy hair of a man's head. 'A staring, horrid, unkembed, or ill-kept pate of hair.' (1611, Cotgrave.)

(2) A cap of the skin of an animal with the hair on; later, possibly, a cap of piled felt or thrummed material; and still later, a round-topped felt cap.

HUSSAR BOOTS or BUSKINS
1800 to 1820's. (M.) Boots reaching the calf, rising to a slight point in front, occasionally having turnover tops and often shod with iron. Worn with pantaloons. A style borrowed by civilians from the military.

HUSSAR JACKET
1880's. (F.) A short jacket, braided and frogged; worn with a waistcoat to form the bodice portion of a day dress. From 1887 worn as an outdoor jacket.

HUSSAR POINT
1820's. (M.) A feature appearing in the cut of waistcoats, the bottoms of the fore-parts shaped to produce a beak-like point in the centre curving downwards when the garment was buttoned up. The sides of the fore-parts 'hollowed', i.e. cut with a slight curve over the hips.

HUVET
See HOWVE.

HYDROTOBOLIC HAT
1850's and 1860's. (M.) A hat with the crown ventilated by having a small hole in the centre protected by wire gauze. 'Becoming very general.' (1851, *Punch*.)

I

IMBECILE SLEEVE, SLEEVE A LA FOLLE

1829 to 1835. (F.) A day sleeve very full down to the wrist and there gathered into a narrow cuff. No stiffening but 'falls down in all its amplitude'. Named from the sleeve of 'straight-waistcoat' (for lunatics).

Imbecile Sleeves, 1834

IMPERIAL

1840's. (M.) (1) A loose fly-fronted Paletot overcoat.

(2) A narrow tuft of beard below the lower lip.

INCHERING

18th c. Measuring a person in inches for making a garment. 'Pd. for Inchoring the girls 2d.' (1729, Walthamstow Records.)

INCROYABLE BOWS

1889. (F.) Huge bows of lace and mousselaine de soie, worn at the throat with Directoire costumes (ot that date).

INCROYABLE COAT

1889. (F.) A coat with long coat-tails and wide lapels, worn with a lace jabot and waistcoat for afternoon dress; intended to resemble the swallow-tail coat of the Directoire period. A fashion inspired by Sardou's play *La Tosca* (1887).

INDIAN NECKTIE

From 1815 to 1830's. (M.) A muslin cravat, the ends brought round in front and secured by a sliding ring. In 1818 it was called a 'Maharatta'.

INDIAN NIGHTGOWN, INDIAN GOWN

17th and 18th c's. (M. and F.) (1) Synonym for BANYAN, *q.v.*

(2) Term occasionally used for a woman's négligée attire. 'Contented . . . instead of a variety of new gowns and rich petticoats, with her des-

Indian Nightgown, 1735

habillie or flame-colour gown called Indian.' (1673, Wycherley, *The Gentleman Dancing Master.*)

INDIA RUBBER
19th c. A patent for its use 1823. 'A recent discovery substituting India rubber for elastic wires.' (1831.) Previously brass wire springs covered with cloth had been used.

INDISPENSIBLE
1800 to *c.* 1820. (F.) A small handbag of soft material (silk or velvet) often square or lozenge-shaped, drawn in with a running string; suspended from the arm or hand by a length of ribbon. *See* RIDICULE.

INEFFIBLES
19th c. (M.) One of the many euphemisms for breeches or trousers. 'Our lower garments or Ineffibles sit but awkwardly.' (1823, *New Monthly Magazine.*)

INEXPRESSIBLES
Late 18th and early 19th c's. (M.) A euphemism for breeches or trousers. *See* UNMENTIONABLES.

INVERNESS
1859 on. (M.) 'The new name for the Cape Paletot.' A large loose overcoat, about knee-length, with a fitting collar and deep arm-length cape. In the 1870's the cape was usually incomplete behind, being sewn to the side seams.

In the 1880's the sleeves were often omitted, the cape being sufficient and then called 'Dolman cape sleeves'.

In the 1890's very large arm-holes under the cape were faced with a sling or 'arm-rest' to support the forearms.

IRISH MANTLE
15th c. (1) A cloak. *See* BRATT.
(2) A blanket.

IRISH POLONAISE
1770 to 1775. (F.) A day gown with a close-fitting, low, square-cut bodice fastened close down the front and fitting behind. The bodice had an overskirt pleated to it, this overskirt

Inverness, 1891

being bunched up behind and open in front. The underskirt, called a 'petticoat', was worn short. This style of polonaise was also called Italian, French or Turkish.

ISABEAU CORSAGE
1846. (F.) The bodice resembled a jacket descending to just below the hips where the edges were rounded off. The front, open at the bottom, was trimmed across with bands of galloon and silk buttons. The neck cut high with a falling collar. The sleeve nearly to the wrist with an open mancheron below each shoulder. A style of dress for morning wear.

ISABEAU SLEEVE
1860's. (F.) A triangular-shaped sleeve, the apex at the shoulder and widely open below; made with an inner and an outer seam. Used for dresses (with an under-sleeve or engageante); also for PARDESSUS and the MAINTENON CLOAK, *q.v.*

ISABEAU STYLE DRESS
1860's. (F.) A day dress, the bodice and skirt in one, shaped to the figure

heel forward under the shoe with wedge extension under the instep. The heel was made of wood covered with kid of a colour different from that of the shoe, generally white or cream.

Italian Heel, 1770-7

ITALIAN HOSE
C. 1600. Synonym 1or VENETIANS.

ITALIAN NIGHTGOWN, ITALIAN ROBE
1770's. (F.) A day dress of a semi-formal nature. (*See* NIGHTGOWN.) The bodice, with low neck and elbow sleeves, was boned and joined to a long overskirt open in front. The underskirt, called the 'Petticoat', was of a colour different from the rest of the gown. The overskirt could be hitched up like a polonaise by 'loops to two small buttons on the hips', or by running strings in the lining which were fixed to the hem, emerging at the waist with a large tassel at each hip, 'by which they draw up the robe to dance country dances'.

ITALIAN POLONAISE
1770's. (F.) Synonymous with ITALIAN NIGHTGOWN or Robe.

Isabeau Corsage, 1846

by goring, without a seam at the waist. A line of buttons or rosettes all down the front.

ITALIAN CLOAK
16th and 17th c's. (M.) A short hooded cloak; the same as the SPANISH CLOAK or GENOA CLOAK. 'He wears a short Italian hooded cloak.' (1590, Marlowe, *Edward II.*)

ITALIAN FARTHINGALE
The same as the WHEEL FARTHIN-GALE, *q.v.*

ITALIAN HEEL
1770's on. (F.) A small peg-top heel with slender waist placing the

J

JABOT
   19th c. (F.) A made-up cravat of lace or similar material, worn at the neck.

JACK
   Late 14th c. (M.) A short jacket; also a military garment.

JACK BOOT
   C. 1660 to 18th c. (M.) A boot made of hard leather and worn for riding.
   (1) Heavy Jack boots of 'bend leather', i.e. hardened by boiling or by applications of pitch paint, in the 17th c. had expanding bucket tops to enclose the knees and deep square heels and square toes. In the 18th c. the style was less cumbersome.
   (2) Light Jack boots were of softer leather and sometimes laced or buttoned on the outer side. In the 18th c. the front of the boot extended above the knee, the back being scooped out to allow for the bending of the knee.
   (3) Half Jack boots. See JOCKEY BOOTS.

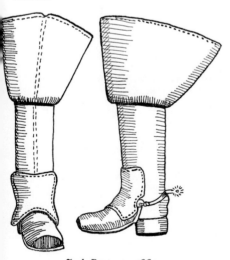

Jack Boots, c. 1660

JACK CHAIN
   17th c. (M.) A form of decoration; a chain made up of links each in the figure of eight and joined at right angles. Considered a trumpery ornament.

JACKET
   (1) MALE. 15th c. on. A short body garment. From 1450 to 1540 it was an upper garment worn over the doublet or occasionally alone with a plackard or stomacher; subsequently until *c.* 1630 it was worn over the doublet and often sleeveless, and usually called a 'JERKIN', *q.v.*
   Throughout the 18th c. the jacket was the main body garment 'in use among Country people' (1706, Phillips) and also worn by labourers, apprentices, seafarers, postillions and sportsmen; thus becoming a symbol of social inferiority; in the 18th c. the gentleman used it only when powdering. In the 19th c. it began to be acceptable *c.* 1840 as part of a gentleman's suit, replacing the coat, for informal occasions.
   (2) FEMALE. 16th c. on. The woman's jacket was an alternative kind of bodice, being then an essential part of the gown. In the 16th c. it was sometimes called a 'waistcoat' (i.e. short coat ending at waist level).
   In the 19th c. it was also worn as an upper garment, mainly for sports wear, or as a part of the 'tailormade' costume, especially in the 1890's.

JACK TAR SUIT
   1880's and 1890's. (M.) A sailor suit with 'Jack Tar' trousers; worn by small boys.

JACK TAR TROUSERS
   1880's. (M.) The legs cut without a side seam, close-fitting above,

115

Jack Tar Suit, 1890

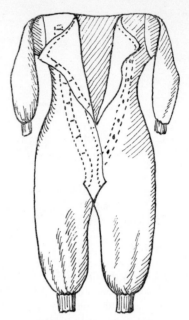

Jaeger Combinations, 1885

expanding below to 22″ round the ankles. Made with whole falls, and worn for yachting.

JAEGER UNDERCLOTHES
1880's. Introduced by a German Dr. Jaeger, for underclothing of natural wool, constructed on hygienic principles so as to envelop the whole trunk and limbs. Designed for both sexes.

JAGS, JAGGING
See DAGGES, DAGGING.

JAMBEE CANE
Early 18th c. (M.) A knotty bamboo walking-stick, then fashionable.

JAPANESE HAT
1867–9. (F.) A circular, plate-shaped hat without a crown, the straw brim sloping slightly downwards from a small central knob; trimmed with ribbon and tied on with ribbon passing under the chignon.

JASEY, JAZEY
Late 18th and 19th c. (M.) A wig made of Jersey yarn. 'Jasey, a contemptuous name for a wig or even a bushy head of hair, as if the one were actually as the other is apparently made of Jersey yarn.' (1825, Forley, *Vocabulary of East Anglia.*) Hence the slang name for a judge : 'the cove with the jazey'.

JEAN DE BRY
1799 to *c*. 1820. (M.) A D-B coat with high stand-fall collar and low-turning lapels. Sleeves greatly padded and gathered at the shoulders ; coat-tails short and scanty.

JEANETTE
1836. (F.) A necklace made up of a narrow tress of hair or velvet, suspending a small cross or heart.

JEANS
C. 1810. (M.) Trousers made of jean.

JELLYBAG
See NIGHTCAP.

JEMMY

19th c. (M.) A shooting coat, being a short frock coat with multiple pockets.

A Jemmy, 1830

JEMMY BOOTS

18th c. (M.) Light riding boots, a smart form of JOCKEY BOOTS, *q.v.*

JEMMY CANE

18th and early 19th c's. (M.) A little switch carried under the arm, most fashionable in the 1750's and 1760's.

JEMMY FROCK

18th c. (M.) A smart frock (*see* 18th-c. FROCK). 'The jemmy frock with plate buttons.' (1756, *The Connoisseur*.)

JERKIN, JERKING

C. 1450 to 1630. (M.) A jacket worn over the doublet and following the same pattern with slightly longer skirts; sometimes made with hanging sleeves. In 16th and 17th c's. jerkins were often sleeveless, having wings only.

JERSEY

1860's on. (M.) A knitted sleeved body garment generally made with horizontal stripes; worn for football

Jerkin (Sleeveless), 1568

in the 1870's on. Also worn by boys as a winter garment. 'Begin your jerseys.' (Nov. 1863, Mrs. Charles Darwin to her son.)

JERSEY COSTUME

1879. (F.) A blue or red knitted silk or wool jersey fitting the figure and reaching to thigh level; worn

Jersey Costume, 1879

117

above a serge or flannel kilted skirt. A style popularised by Mrs. Langtry, the 'Jersey Lily'.

JESSAMY GLOVES, JASMINE GLOVES
17th c. (M. and F.) Gloves heavily perfumed with jasmine but a variety of aphrodisiac scents were used. It was a custom to give a supply as a wedding present both to the bride and to the bridegroom. Thus a prospective mother-in-law wrote: 'I could not get so many woman's Jessamy gloves as she wrote for, they being a prohibited and scarce commodity; and at last I was fained to pick upon cordinent (i.e. the Spanish leather, cordovan) for men and perfumed kid for women; I had them perfumed better than ordinary that they might give content'. (1661, The Gurdon Papers, *East Anglian Notes & Queries*.)

JET BUTTONS
19th c. (F.) Worn in 1818 by women on half boots buttoned at the sides.

JIGGER BUTTON
19th c. (M.) A small concealed button (usually brass) fastening back the point of a wide lapel or the wrap-over of a D-B waistcoat. In washing waistcoats this button was of mother-of-pearl.

JIM CROW HAT
19th c. (M.) Of felt with very wide flapping brim; named from T. D. Rice's negro song and dance (1835).

JINGLE SPUR
See GINGLERS.

JOAN
C. 1755 to 1765. (F.) Sometimes called the 'Quaker Cap'; a close-fitting indoor cap shaped like a baby's bonnet, tied under the chin and trimmed round the face with a frill of muslin or lace.

JOAN-OF-ARC BODICE
1875. (F.) A tight day bodice, known as a 'Cuirasse bodice', shaped

like a pair of stays reaching to the hips, and covered with jet or steel beads; tight sleeves frilled at the wrists.

JOCELYN MANTLE
1852. (F.) A mantle, knee-length, double-skirted and with 3 capes each fringed; arm-holes but no sleeves.

JOCKEY
1820's on. (F.) A flat trimming applied over the outer part of the shoulder of a dress and having the lower border free.

JOCKEY BOOTS, HALF JACK BOOTS
C. 1680's to end of 18th c. (M.) A boot ending below the knee with turned-down top of a softer and lighter-coloured leather. Pulled on by leather or string loops on each side. After 1780's called 'Top Boots'.

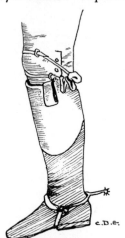

Jockey Boot, 18th c.

JOCKEY CAP
Late 17th c. on. (M.) A peaked cap of black velvet. In the 19th c. a light silk coloured Jockey cap came into favour for racing.

JOCKEY SLEEVE
Late 17th c. on. (M.) A close-fitting sleeve with small close cuff.

JOCKEY WAISTCOAT
1806 on. (M.) A straight waistcoat buttoned high with a low stand

collar cut off square in front leaving a deep gap under the chin. A fashion revived in 1884.

JOINVILLE
1844 to 1855. (M.) A necktie worn as a broad wide-spreading bow with square fringed ends. The name revived for an American scarf tie filling the space above the waistcoat opening. (1890's.)

Joinville Tie, c. 1850

JOSEPH
(F.) (1) mid 18th c. A green riding coat.
(2) 1800–10. An outdoor garment resembling a Jewish long tunic with loose sleeves.

JOSEPHINE BODICE
1879. (F.) An evening dress bodice with a very low round décolletage and a wide silk or satin belt draped round in folds.

JUBE
17th c. (M.) A short sleeveless coat or jacket.

JUIVE TUNIC
1875. (F.) A Princess style (i.e. without a seam at the waist) of over-bodice and skirt; the bodice with wide arm-holes, a V opening in front and behind; the skirt portion falling in a point to hip level and continued into a train behind. The

tunic worn over a dress constituted a 'costume' for outdoor wear without additional covering.

JUMP, JUMPE, JUMP-COAT
(1) 17th c. (M.) In early 17th c. a soldier's coat. 'A Colonel in beaten Buff with a scarlet Jump.' (1639–60.) Later, a civilian coat. 'Jumpe . . . extended to the Thighs, is open or buttoned down before, open or slit up behind half way; the sleeves reach to the wrist.' (1688, R. Holme, *Armourie.*)
(2) 18th c. (F.) Usually in the plural as 'Jumps'; a loose, unboned bodice worn instead of stays for comfort or during pregnancy. 'Bought my wife a new pair of jumps instead of stays.' (1716, *Marchant Diary.*)

JUMPER, OXONIAN JACKET
1861 to 1880. (M.) A S-B Tweedside jacket, the fronts cut straight; to button 3, but the fit improved by the introduction of 'SIDE-BODIES', *q.v.*

JUMPER COAT
See BEAUFORT COAT, 1880's. (M.)

JUPE, JUPON
(1) 1290 to 1400. (M.) *See* GIPON.
(2) 16th and early 17th c's. (F.) A riding coat generally worn with a safeguard (i.e. a protective over-skirt). 'A safeguard with jhup or gaskyn coat of faire cullored satten.' (1588, Nichols, *Progress of Q. Elizabeth.*)

JUPPO, JUPPA, JIPPO
Variants of male Jump, often implying one of meaner quality.

JUST-AU-CORPS, JUSTACORPS, JUSTICO, JUSTACOR, CHESTICORE, JUSTE
From mid 17th to early 18th c. (1) (M.) A close-fitting coat worn over a waistcoat. 'His justaucorps brac'd to his body tight.' (1705, Elsbob, *Hearne Collecteana.*)
(2) 2nd half 17th and late 18th c's. (F.) A riding coat; in the 17th c. shaped like a man's coat; in the 18th c. made with short basques and often called a 'Demi-riding coat'.

K

KALL, KELLE
A woman's CAUL, *q.v.*

KAMPSKATCHA SLIPPER or CHINESE SLIPPER
1786 to 1788. (F.) Made with a pointed toe turned up at the tip; the vamp moderately high, and a low French heel. '. . . perfectly adapted to the winter season; they are made of fine black Spanish leather and turned up at the toes in the Chinese taste; and securely guard the feet of the wearer from cold by being lined with white or fox-coloured fur which is brought over the edge and forms the binding.' (1787, *Ipswich Journal.*)

Kampskatcha Slipper, 1786

KATE GREENAWAY COSTUME
1880's and 1890's. (F.) A style of dress for small girls made popular by the artist of that name in her illustrations of children's books. A frock in the mode of the 'Empire' dress with high waist and puffed shoulder-sleeves, the skirt trimmed with a narrow flounce; made of light material patterned with flowers.

KEMES, KEMISE, KEMSE
See CHEMISE.

KENNEL
1500 to 1540's. (F.) A 19th-c. term for the Gable-shaped head-dress or English Hood.

KERCHIEF, KERCHER, KER-CHEVE, KARCHER
From early Med. to end of 16th c. (F.) A draped covering for the head.

See COVERCHIEF. In the 16th c. 'kerchief' was often loosely used for neckerchief, a similar covering for the neck.

KERSCHE
Med. Kerchief.

KEVENHULLER COCK
See KEVENHULLER HAT.

KEVENHULLER HAT
1740's to 1760's. (M.) A large felt tricorne hat, the front brim cocked high, forming a peak. 'A laced hat pinched into what our Beaux have learnt to call the KEVENHULLER COCK.' (1746, *The British Magazine.*)

Kevenhuller Hat, 1747

KEY CHAIN
1890's. (M.) A chain attached to a bunch of keys in trouser pocket; the other end of the chain attached to a braces button on the trousers.

KICKSIES
See UNMENTIONABLES.

KIRTLE

(1) 9th to end of 14th c. (M.)
A sleeved knee-length body garment,
the same as the TUNIC, *q.v.* In the
13th and 14th c's. it was commonly
worn with a courtpye. 'A kertil and a
courtepy.' (1362, Langland, *Piers
Plowman.*)

(2) From 10th to 19th c's. (F.) (a)
10th to end of 15th c. A sleeved
ground-length body garment worn
next to the smock and under the
gown or upper garment. In 14th c.
often worn without an overgarment,
especially by unmarried women.
'Damoselles two right young and full
semelyhede
In kirtels and none other wede. . . .'
(Chaucer, *Romaunt of the Rose.*)

(b) In 16th c. the gown and kirtle
formed a complete dress, the kirtle
being worn under the gown. A 'full
kirtle' was bodice and skirt; a 'half
kirtle' was skirt only.

(c) From 1545 to mid 17th c. the
kirtle meant the skirt or petticoat (as
the skirt of a dress was then called);
and subsequently as the name 'kirtle'
was dropped, 'petticoat' replaced it.

(d) In 18th and 19th c's. (apart from
poetical use) 'kirtle' was applied to a
short jacket. 'Kirtle, a kind of short
jacket.' (1706, Phillips.) 'Kyrtle, a
kirtle or short coat without laps or
skirts.' (1828, Craven, *Dialect.*)

(e) A SAFEGUARD, *q.v.* 'Kirtle, an
outer petticoat to protect the other
garments from dust etc. in riding.'
(1825, Forby, *Vocabulary of East
Anglia.*)

KISSING-STRINGS, BRIDLES
1st half 18th c. (F.) Strings for
tying the mob cap under the chin.

Kissing-Strings of Mob, 1745

KISS-ME-QUICK
1867–9. (F.) Popular name for the
very small bonnet then fashionable.

KNEE-BAND
End of 17th c. on. (M.) The band
closing the knee breeches below the
knee.

KNEE BREECHES
Worn from 1570's on. (M.) Breeches
closed below the knee, the normal
legwear of the 18th c.

KNEE BUCKLES
End of 17th c. on. (M.) Buckles
securing the breeches knee-band
below the knee.

KNEE CUFF
Mid 17th c. (M.) Probably a syno-
nym for PORT-CANON or CANNON, *q.v.*
'One paire of scollopp lynnen knee
cuffs worth three pounds.' (1659,
Middlesex Session Rolls.)

Kirtle, c. 1380

KNEE-FRINGE
1670–5. (M.) The hanging fringe of ribbons about the bottom edge of the open breeches.

KNEE-PIECE
The top portion of BOOT HOSE, *q.v.*

KNEE-STRING
17th and 18th c.'s. (M.) The ties for drawing in of breeches below the knee.

KNICKERBOCKERS
1860 on. (M.) A loose form of breeches introduced at first for the Volunteers, and used by civilians for country wear; 'cut three inches wider in the leg and two inches longer than ordinary breeches'. (1871, *The Tailor & Cutter*.)

The name derived from the (fictional) Dutch founders of New York as depicted by Washington Irving in his *History of New York by Dietrick Knickerbocker*, 1808.

Knickerbockers, 1861

KNICKERS
1890's. (F.) An under-garment similar to knickerbockers but usually made of flannel or longcloth, and worn instead of drawers and often without a petticoat.

Knickers, 1890

KNIGHTLY GIRDLE
Mid 14th c. to *c.* 1420. (M. and F.) A decorative belt comprising metal clasps joined together and fastened in front by an ornamental buckle or clasp. Always worn encircling the hips (not the waist) over the gipon or cote-hardie and only by the nobility.

KNITTED SPENCER
See SPENCER.

KNITTED VEST
1880's. (M.) A home-made knitted waistcoat in fancy colours, often with a fly front, and worn with a velvet lounge jacket.

KNOP
Med. A button or tassel, generally decorative in character.

KNOT
17th to mid 18th c. (F.) (1) A ribbon bow for decorating the head or gown. Feather knots were also used.

The *Bosom Knot*, worn at the breast.

The *Duchess*, 'a knot to be put immediately above the tower'. (1694, *Ladies' Directory*.) I.e. above the raised curls of the fontange coiffure.

A *suit of knots* : a set of bows for the gown and sometimes also for the head.

Top Knot: a large bow or bunch of ribbon loops worn on the top of the head, usually known as a 'Pompon' in fashionable circles of 18th c.

(2) 19th c. (F.) Name given to the hair when it was twisted into a 'bun' at the back of the head.

L

LABEL
15th c. (M.) The turned-back tongue-shaped lapel of the TABARD, *q.v.*

LABEL
19th c. (M. and F.) The small strip of material attached on the inner surface of a garment bearing the name of the owner, or maker, or both.
(1) MALE. The earliest example of a label on a man's coat (1822) was concealed under the yoke lining and of parchment bearing the owner's name. Paper labels were occasionally used, on bespoke coats and waistcoats until *c.* 1870, sometimes with the owner's measurements as well as name; together with the tailor's name. This was placed under the yoke lining or within a back pleat; near the close of the century, on the lining of the inside breast pocket.
Labels of cotton or silk fabric with the tailor's name and address woven on them began to appear by 1850 but not common until *c.* 1880's.
From 1870 the tailor's name might be woven on to the coat-hanger loop.
On waistcoats the name was often attached to the lacing tabs at the back, from *c.* 1840.
(2) FEMALE. The dressmaker's name woven on a label attached to the inner surface of the bodice or waistband, became usual from *c.* 1870.

LACE
(1) A tie for fastening or pulling together opposite edges, as for boots, stays, etc.
(2) Braid used for trimming.
(3) An openwork trimming of many patterns; both hand-made and machine-made. *See* GLOSSARY.

LACED
(1) Tightened or closed with cord or tape, etc.
(2) Trimmed with braid or lace.
In the 19th c. the second meaning was discarded.

LACING STUDS
1897 on. (M.) Oval brass hooks for criss-cross lacing up of men's boots, to avoid having to thread through eyelet holes. *See* BUTTON-HOOKS (1860's).

LAMBALLE BONNET
1865. (F.) A very small saucer-shaped bonnet of straw, worn flat on the head curving down slightly on each side, and tied under the chin with a large ribbon bow. Some were made with a very small curtain behind; others with lace lappets on each side of the chignon.

LANGET
15th c. (1) A thong, lace or strap for securing any part of the dress.
(2) Langettes—pair of—meaning a string of beads. (16th c.)
(3) The plume of a knightly head-piece.

LANGTRY HOOD
1880's. (F.) A detachable hood to any outdoor garment; resembling an academic hood displaying a coloured lining and attached by hooks or short ends crossing in front.

LANGUETTE
C. 1818–22. (F.) A flat, tongue-shaped, applied trimming, a common decoration for skirts and pelisses.

LAPEL
The turned-back upper part of the front of a coat or waistcoat, known,

in 2nd half of 19th c., as 'the turn'. *See* LABEL. (Med.)

LAP-MANTLE
Late 16th and early 17th c's. A covering for the knees; a rug.

LAPPETS
18th and 19th c's. (F.) Pendants from an indoor head-dress, hanging at the sides or behind, and made either plain or trimmed with lace.

LASTING BOOTS
Late 19th c. Boots of which the uppers were made of black cashmere.

LATCHET
Med. on. A strap to fasten a shoe or clog.

LAVEUSE COSTUME
1876. (F.) A day dress with an overskirt (called a Tunic) turned up 'like a washerwoman's', and draped round the sides, gathered behind and there buttoned.

LEADING STRINGS
17th and 18th c's. (Children.) Long narrow strips of material forming sham 'hanging sleeves' attached to the back of the arm-holes and used to control the child's efforts to walk. 'Buy me a pair of leading strings for Jak (aged 4); there is stuff made on purpose that is very strong.' (1715, *Verney Letters.*)

LEAF
See STAND-FALL COLLAR.

LEEFEKYE
16th and early 17th c's. A bodice.

LEEK BUTTON
1842 patent. A button with a metal shell or mould of pasteboard with a metal edge applied to it, covered with silk or other fabric, and having a flexible shank made of 'woven wire cloth'. Made at Leek.

LEGGING, LEGGIN
19th c. (M.) An extra covering for the leg from ankle to knee and sometimes higher; the term 'leggings' was not used in earlier centuries.

LEG-OF-MUTTON SLEEVE
See GIGOT.

LEICESTER JACKET
1857. (M.) A lounge jacket with raglan sleeves.

LETTICE CAP or BONNET, ERMINE CAP, MINIVER CAP
(1) 16th c. (F.) An outdoor bonnet covering the ears; triangular-shaped

Leading Strings, early 18th c.

Lettice Cap, 1527-8

above the head; made of lettice (a fur resembling ermine) or of miniver.

(2) 16th and 17th c's. (M.) A night-cap or house-cap made of lettice fur; in the 17th c. it was supposed to induce sleep. 'Bring in the Lettice cap. You must be shaved, Sir, and then how suddenly we'el make you sleep.' (1619, John Fletcher, *Monsieur Thomas.*)

LETTICE RUFF
Early 17th c. (M.) An error in spelling for 'Lettuce'; a ruff with flattened convolutions resembling the crinkled leaves of a lettuce. Cf. CABBAGE RUFF.

LEVITE GOWN, LEVETES
1780's. (F.) An open robe, often of linen, in which the back of the bodice appeared pointed although continuous with the overskirt; the bodice front often closed by cross-straps. Long sleeves. Worn with or without an apron. Day wear.

Levite Gown, 1780

LILY BENJAMIN
19th c. (M.) Colloquial term for the white overcoat much worn in the first half of the century. *See* BENJAMIN.

LIMERICK GLOVES
2nd half 18th and 1st half 19th c. (F.) Long or short; made of very fine leather, said to be made from the skins of unborn lambs. 'Lymarick gloves 1 pr. 3/-.' (1789, Biddulph Accts., Hereford Records.)

LIMOUSINE
1889. (F.) A long circular evening cloak, gauged round the throat with the fullness to fall in folds over the arms, as sleeves.

LINECLOTHS, PAIR OF
15th c. (M.) Linen drawers. 'A payre of lynclothys.' (*C.* 1474, Paston Letters, Inventory of Servants' Clothes.)

LIRIPIPE, TIPPET
C. 1350 to end of 15th c. (M. and F.) The long pendant tail of a hood. In 15th c. it was suspended from the male chaperon or wound round it, turban-wise; also sometimes pendant from the female head-dress, added as an ornament.

Liripipe of Hood, 14th c.

LIST
18th and 19th c's. The border or selvage of cloth; strips of selvage, joined together were used to make slippers. 'Her quiet tread muffled in a list slipper'. (1847. Charlotte Brontë: Jane Eyre.)

Liripipe of Chaperon, 15th c.

LITTLE LORD FAUNTLEROY DRESS

1886 on. (M.) A style of dress for young boys, made fashionable by the hero of Mrs. Hodgson Burnett's novel of that name (1886). It comprised a velvet tunic and knickerbockers and a white lace collar falling over the shoulders, faintly reminiscent of the

Cavaliers; with a wide sash round the waist and a bow with hanging ends on one hip.

The author's own description: 'a black velvet suit with a lace collar and with lovelocks waving about . . . the face'. The author was American and Oscar Wilde on his visit to U.S.A. in 1882 had declared the Cavalier costume to have been the most artistic male dress ever known, and had recommended its revival. He may therefore be said to have been responsible for the Little Lord Fauntleroy style of dress for boys.

LOCK STITCH

From *c.* 1860. Sewing by the lock-stitch machine (as opposed to the chain-stitch machine). It began to be used by English dressmakers from *c.* 1860.

LONG-BELLIED DOUBLET

See PEASCOD-BELLIED DOUBLET.

LONG CLOTHES

From 2nd half 17th c. The conventional dress of the infant in arms, gradually replacing the former swaddling clothes. A long 'gown', some 3 feet or even more in length, fastening at the back, with short sleeves; the whole often richly ornamented with lace and insertion. The garment appears to have been adapted from the 'Christening Robe' formerly only used on that particular occasion.

Little Lord Fauntleroy Suit, 1890

Long Clothes (Baby's), 1657

Long Clothes, 1877

Long-Stocked Hose, 1479–87

LONG HOOD
18th c. (F.) A soft hood made like the 'PUG' or 'SHORT HOOD', *q.v.* But the portion surrounding the face was continued into 2 long strips for tying under the chin or for swathing round the neck.

LONG LOCK
See LOVE LOCK.

LONG POCKET
18th and 19th c's. (M.) A vertical pocket in coat or overcoat. '. . . the two sorts of pockets—the long pocket with a plain or indented flap—the cross pocket with the round or the trefoil or scallop flap.' (1715, John Harris, *Treatise upon the Modes*.)

LONG STOCK, LONG STOCKING
16th and early 17th c's. (M.) The long stocking portion of trunk-hose to which they were joined high up the thigh. 'All the swarming generation of long stocks, short pain'd hose and huge stuff'd doublets.' (1607, Beaumont and Fletcher, *Woman Hater*.)

LOO MASK
From mid-16th into 18th c. (F.) A half-mask covering the upper part of the face only. *See* MASK.

Loo-Mask, 17th c.

LORGNETTE
Late 19th c. (F.) A pair of eye-glasses in a tortoiseshell frame with a long handle; for examing objects at a distance. 'Nearly every smartly dressed woman wears a lorgnette.' (1893.)

LOUIS XIII CORSAGE
1850. (F.) Day corsage of a Pelisse-robe, closed at the neck and waist,

128

with the centre open displaying a chemisette or cambric pleats or embroidery.

LOUIS XIV SLEEVE
1850. (F.) Cut to widen from the shoulder downwards, and usually edged below with rows of fluted trimming. Worn with an under sleeve or engageante.

LOUNGE SUIT
From 1860 on. (M.) A suit made up of a 'lounging jacket', waistcoat and trousers, all of the same material; for informal wear.

Lounge Suit, 1894

LOUNGING JACKET
C. 1848 on. (M.) A short-skirted S-B coat just covering the seat, slightly waisted and with or without a seam at the waist. Flapped pockets on the hips or slit pockets in the side seams, and outside pocket on the left breast. Corners rounded. The style varied according to the fashions of the day. *See* also ALBERT JACKET and THREE-SEAMER.

LOVE, INDICATIONS OF,
   in DRESS
16th and 17th c's. (M.) It was correct to show by a nice disorder in his dress that a man was in love; e.g. to go without a hat-band and to appear unbuttoned (a symbolic gesture). 'He taught me how to know a man in love. Then your hose should be ungarter'd, your bonnet unbanded, your sleeve unbuttoned, your shoe untied, and everything about you demonstrating a careless desolation.' (W. Shakespeare, *As You Like It*, 1623.)
   Compare this symbolism with the tradition that a bride entering her new home must have first removed all pins from her clothing.

LOVE KNOTS
16th c. (F.) Ornamental ribbon bows tied across coloured puffs emerging from sleeves with a vertical slash down the front.

LOVE LOCK
C. 1590 to 1650's. (M., sometimes F.) A long lock of hair usually curled, turned forward from the nape of the neck so as to fall over the chest in front.

LUNARDI HAT
See BALLOON HAT.

LYONS LOOPS
1865. (F.) The name given to the velvet straps used to loop up the overskirt in 3 or 4 places, when double skirts were in fashion.

M

MACARONI CRAVAT

1770's. (M.) A muslin cravat edged with lace and tied in a bow under the chin.

MACARONI SUIT

1770's. (M.) Introduced by 'travelled young men' back from Italy who founded the Macaroni Club in 1764 but the special style of suit did not develop until the 1770's; comprising a coat somewhat short and tight; 'their coat sleeves are so tight they can with difficulty get their arms through their cuffs . . . their legs are covered with all the colours of the rainbow. Their shoes are scarce slippers and their buckles are within one inch of their toe'. (1772, *The Town & Country Magazine.*)

They favoured a very small tricorne hat and attached a very large nosegay of flowers to the left shoulder.

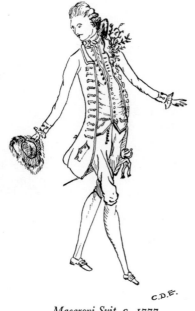

Macaroni Suit, c. 1777

c.D.F.

MACKINTOSH

1836 on. (M.) A short loose overcoat of Mackintosh's patent india-rubber cloth, with proof straps over the seams; colour, drab or dark green. The wearing of these garments met, at first, much opposition owing to 'the offensive stench which they emit'. (1839, *Gentleman's Magazine of Fashion.*)

MADRAS TURBAN

1819. (F.) A turban made of a blue and orange Indian handkerchief.

MAGENTA

1860. The first chemical dye to be used in dress materials. Hailed as 'the queen of colours'. Named after the battle in 1859. *See* SOLFERINO.

MAHARATTA TIE

See INDIAN TIE.

MAHOITRES, MAHEUTRES

Name used in France from 1394; in England from *c.* 1450 to 1480. (M.) Shoulder pads for broadening the shoulders of men's gowns and jackets.

MAIL COACH or WATERFALL NECKTIE

1818 to 1830's. (M.) A very large neckcloth sometimes composed of a cashmere shawl, folded loosely round the neck and tied once in front in a common knot over which the folds spread down 'like a waterfall'. Generally white and worn by 'professional swell drivers' and dandies.

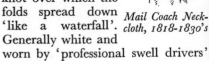

Mail Coach Neckcloth, 1818-1830's.

MAINTENON CLOAK

1860's. (F.) A very large black velvet cloak with wide sleeves;

trimmed with a deep pleated flounce covered with black guipure lace; sometimes embroidered.

MAINTENON CORSAGE
1839 and 1840's. (F.) A close-fitting evening bodice trimmed with ribbon knots down the centre front, with a fall of lace at the waist.

MAJOR WIG
2nd half 18th c. (M.) A military style of wig worn by civilians; a wig with a toupee and two corkscrew curls tied together at the nape of the neck to form a double queue behind. 'The two locks of my major perriwig.' (1753, J. Hawkesworth, *The Adventurer*.) 'His peruke which is naturally a kind of flowing Bob, but by the occasional addition of two tails it sometimes appears as a major.' (1754, *The Connoisseur*.) *See* BRIGADIER WIG.

Major Wig, 2nd half 18th c.

MALACCA CANE
18th c. A cane made from the 'clouded' or mottled stem of a Malacca palm; also called a 'Clouded cane'.

MAMELUKE SLEEVE
1828–30. (F.) A very full sleeve with a deep cuff; for day wear in thin materials.

MAMELUKE TURBAN
1804. (F.) A turban of white satin, the front rolled upwards like a hat-brim over a domed crown; trimmed with a large ostrich feather.

MANCHERON
19th c. (F.) A very short ungathered over sleeve in the nature of an epaulette, worn with day dresses or sleeved outdoor garments. The name gradually became replaced by 'epaulette' in the 1860's.

MANCHETTE
1830's to 1850's. (F.) A lace ruffle worn at the wrist for afternoon dress.

MANDARIN HAT
1861. (F.) A black velvet pork-pie hat trimmed with feathers over the back of the flat crown. (Recalling the Franco-British war with China ending Oct. 1860.)

MANDEVILLE
17th c. The name then given to the MANDILION, *q.v.*

MANDILION, MANDEVILLE
C. 1570's to 1620's, and subsequently for livery. (M.) A loose, hip-length jacket with close sleeves (later, sham) and open side seams. A garment often worn 'COLLEY-WESTONWARD', *q.v.*

Mandilion, c. 1577

MANON ROBE
1860's. (F.) A silk day dress, the fronts cut in one, the back with a broad double box-pleating flowing loosely down from under the collar

131

to the hem in the style of the 'WAT-
TEAU PLEAT' (*q.v.*). The hem trimmed
with a deep flounce.

MANT
17th and 18th c's. (F.) Short for
MANTO, MANTUA, *q.v.*

MANTEAU
(1) 16th c. (M.) A man's cloak.
'Manteau à la reître', or French
cloak, was either 'compass' (i.e.
circular) or 'half compass' (i.e. semicircular).
(2) A woman's Manteau. *See*
MANTUA.

MANTEEL
1730's to 1750's. (F.) A scarf-like
cape with long ends in front and
usually a falling hood behind.

MANTELLA, MANTILLA
1840's. (F.) A small mantle, deep
at the back, with long scarf ends in
front.

MANTELET, MANTLET
(1) Med. (M.) A short mantle or
cape. 'A Mantelet upon his shulder
hangynge, Bretful of Rubies reede.'
(*C.* 1386, Chaucer, *Knight's Tale.*)
(2) 18th c. (F.) 'Mantlet, a
small cloak worn by women.' (1730,
Bailey, *Dictionary.*)
(3) 19th c. (F.) A half-shawl,
rounded at the neck, some with a
falling hood or a small cape. Some
had short wide sleeves.
Worn as an outdoor cloak.

MANTLE, MANTIL, (O.E.)
MENTEL
The word reintroduced from France
in 12th c. and used since to end of
19th c. (M. and F.) (1) A long
voluminous cloak-like outer garment
reaching to the feet and made without a hood. An everyday garment
until 14th c. then generally ceremonial and for men usually fastened
on the right shoulder with 3 large
buttons, giving free play to the right
arm. Tied in front for women.
In 16th c. a 'double mantle' meant
a lined mantle.

In 19th c. the length varied and
some mantles had capes or a cape,
and some had sleeves.

Mantle (Female), c. 1470

(2) 17th and 18th c's. A large
wrap for infants in arms. 'The uppermost garment that nurses wrap

Mantle, late 14th c.

up young infants in before they coat them.' (1735, Dyche and Pardon, *Dictionary*.)

MANTUA, MANTEAU, MANTO, MANTON, MANTUA GOWN
Mid 17th to mid 18th c. (F.) A loose gown, the bodice unboned, joined to an overskirt which had a long train behind and was open in front exposing a decorative under-skirt called a petticoat. It was worn on all social or formal occasions. 'A long trailing mantua sweeps the ground.' (1712, J. Gay, *Trivia*.)

MANTUA HOSE
Knitted silk stockings made at Mantua.

MANTUA MAKER
17th and 18th c's. (M. and F.) A 'mantua tailor' or dressmaker.

MANTUA WOMAN
17th and 18th c's. (F.) A mantua dressmaker.

MARIE-ANTOINETTE SKIRT
1895 on. (F.) A day skirt with 7 gores, 1 in front, 2 on each side, and 2 behind, box-pleated; 12 to 18 feet round the hem.

MARIE-ANTOINETTE SLEEVE
See MARIE SLEEVE.

MARIE SLEEVE
1813–24 to 29, and 1872. (F.) A sleeve full to the wrist but tied into compartments by a series of ribbons. Revived in 1872 under the name 'Marie-Antoinette sleeve'.

MARIE STUART BODICE
1828. (F.) An evening bodice tight and boned down the front to a deep pointed waist.

MARIE STUART BONNET
1820's to c. 1870. (F.) A bonnet having the front brim evasé with a dip in the centre over the forehead. A style often worn by widows.

MARIE STUART HAT
1849. (F.) An evening dress-hat of tulle, having a stiff brim curled up with a central dip over the forehead.

MARIN ANGLAIS BONNET
1870's. (F.) Resembling a child's 'sailor hat', ornamented with flowers, feathers and ribbon; worn at the back of the head and tied under the chin with a ribbon bow.

MARINER'S CUFF
2nd half 18th c. (M.) A small round cuff crossed in front by a vertical flap often scalloped, with 3 or 4 buttons matching those on the coat.

Mariner's Cuff, c. 1760

MARINO FALIERO SLEEVE
1830–5. (F.) A large hanging sleeve caught in at the elbow by a ribbon band. Called after Byron's drama of that name.

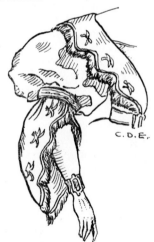

Marino Faliero Sleeve, 1830

MARLBOROUGH HAT
1882. (F.) A large flat hat of lace and Tuscan straw, trimmed with long shaded feathers and worn slightly on one side.

MARMOTTE BONNET
1832. (F.) A very small bonnet with narrow brim round the front like a small BIBI BONNET, q.v.

MARMOTTE CAP
1833. (F.) A half-handkerchief placed far back on the head and tied under the chin. Worn by day indoors.

MARQUISE BODICE
1874. (F.) An evening bodice with a frilled edge; the front shaped en cœur.

MARQUISE MANTLE
1846. (F.) A short taffeta mantlet with short sleeves and pulled in to fit the waist behind; trimmed with flounces and lace.

MARQUISETTO, MARQUISOTTED BEARD
2nd half 16th c. (M.) A close-cut beard.

MARY CAP, MARY QUEEN OF SCOTS CAP, MARIE STUART CAP
1750's and 1760's. (F.) An indoor cap curved up on each side above the forehead with a central V-shaped dip; made of black cypress or gauze and edged with French beads. 'As the cap was made of black gauze and saved washing; it had too much housewifery in it ever to be immense taste.' (1762, London Chronicle.)

MARY STUART CAP
See MARY CAP.

MASHER
1880's and 1890's. (M.) The elaborately dressed Dandy of the period; also known in the 1890's as a 'Piccadilly Johnny'.

MASHER COLLAR
1880's and 1890's. (M.) A very high all-round stand collar, worn by 'Mashers'.

MASHER DUST WRAP
1880's. (M.) A close-fitting Inverness with large arm-holes covered by the cape which was incomplete behind.

MASK, WHOLE MASK
C. 1550 to end of 18th c. (F., in 16th and 17th c's. occasionally by M.) A covering for the face to which it was shaped and pierced opposite the eyes, nose and mouth. The lighter masks had, at the mouth, a bead which was held by the wearer in the mouth. Masks were worn to conceal identity, to protect the skin from the sun, wind and rain when riding, and by ladies at the theatre. Vizard or Vizard mask was a whole mask; LOO-MASK was a half-mask, q.v. 'She's mask'd and in her riding suit.' (1611, Lord Barry, Ram-Alley.)

MATILDAS
19th c. (F.) (1) Velvet ornamentation round the hem of a dress.

(2) In 1840's a term applied to a bunch of flowers worn in the hair.

MATINEE
1851. (F.) A hooded pardessus made of jacconet or muslin and worn outdoors over a morning dress.

MAUD
1855. (F.) A plaid fringed wrapper, swathed round the shoulders and waist.

MAZARIN HOOD
C. 1675 to 1699. (F.) A chaperon of the 17th c. named after the niece of the Cardinal, Minister of Louis XIV.

M.B. WAISTCOAT
See CASSOCK VEST.

M-CUT COLLAR
19th c. (M.) A notch cut in the shape of an 'M', between the turned-over collar and the turned-back lapel of a coat; first appeared in 1800, ceasing for day coats c. 1850 but still used for many evening coats until c. 1870.

MECKLENBURG CAP
1760's. (F.) A 'turban roll' worn as an indoor cap, dating from the marriage of Charlotte of Mecklenburg to George III.

M-Cut Collar, c. 1825

MEDICI COLLAR, MEDICIS

18th and 19th c's. (F.) A collar, generally of net or lace, upstanding round the back of the neck, sloping down to nothing on the front of the bodice. 'A broad medicis of Dresden lace.' (1778, Sir N. Wraxall, *Memoirs of the Court of Berlin*.)

Medici Collar, 1782

MEDICI DRESS

1870's. (F.) A trained PRINCESS DRESS (*q.v.*) with short sleeves and tablier front.

MEDICI SLEEVE

1830's. (F.) A day sleeve puffed out to the elbow, thence tight to the wrist.

MEDUSA WIG

1800–2. (F.) A wig made up of 'a mass of snake-like curls hanging down'.

MELON SLEEVE

1809 to 1815. (F.) An evening dress sleeve distended and shaped like a melon, either round the shoulder or elbow length. Often worn with a transparent long sleeve as an extension to the wrist.

MELOTE

Med. Originally a sheepskin garment; later a cloak of any coarse fur, principally, if not solely, worn by monks or friars at their work.

MENTONNIÈRRES, CHIN STAYS

1820's and 1830's. (F.) Quillings of tulle or lace sewn to the insertion of bonnet strings and tied under the chin, forming a white frill round the lower part of the face.

MERMAID'S TAIL

1875 to 1882. (F.) Nickname given to the train of a tie-back skirt.

METAL EYELETS

Patented 1823. Eyelet holes with metal surround for use in stays, boots, etc., in place of the stitched lace holes.

MILAN BONNET

1st half 16th c. (M.) A cap with a soft beret-shaped crown and rolled-up brim often slit at the sides. The bonnet was sometimes slashed with decorative 'pullings out' or trimmed with aiglets. 'Myllaine bonetes of crimosyn sattin drawen through with cloth of golde.' (1542, Halle, *Chronicle*.) Black was the more usual colour.

MILAN COAT

Light armour.

MILITARY FOLDING HAT

See OPERA HAT.

MILITARY FROCK COAT

19th c. (M.) Worn by civilians from 1820. A Frock coat without flapped pockets, the fronts often braided. The early style made with a Prussian collar or roll collar but without lapels.

MILITARY STOCK

Mid 18th to mid 19th c. (M.) Worn by civilians. A made-up neckcloth stiffened with pasteboard (18th c.) or leather (19th c.) and tied or buckled behind. In 18th c. always black for military men, white for civilians; George IV abolished the white stock for civilians; William IV attempted unsuccessfully to restore it.

Military Stock, 19th Century Style

It was commonly made of corded silk edged with kid.

MILKMAID HAT

See BERGÈRE HAT.

MILKMAID SKIRT

1885. (F.) A plain skirt in striped material of two colours with an overskirt gathered at the waist, turned up on one side to show the lining and drawn through a loop of cord. Worn by day only.

MISTAKE HAT

1804. (F.) A hat of straw or chip with a tall flat-topped crown, the front brim, with a blunt point, turned sharply up, the back brim turned down. Worn on the back of the head.

Mistake Hat, 1804

MITRE HEAD-DRESS

C. 1420 to 1450. (F.) *See* Heart-shaped Head-dress. Both were descriptive terms applied by 19th-c. writers.

MITT

Mid 18th c. to *c.* 1870. (F.) An abbreviation of Mitten, a fingerless glove.

MITTEN, METTEYN, MYTAN, METING

14th c. on. (F., but the early style M.) (1) 14th to 16th c's. (M.) A glove with a single bag for fingers and one for the thumb. The palm was sometimes slit horizontally, to allow the fingers to protrude without having to remove the mitten. Usually worn by countrymen for warmth.

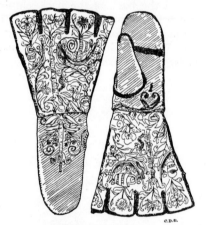

Mittens, late 16th c.

(2) Mid 17th c. on. (F.) Fingerless gloves with open thumb, usually decorative; of lace or net and often embroidered.

18th c. Mittens were usually elbow-length and the fingers emerged together through one opening covered along the back by a prolongation of the mitten into a pointed flap which usually had a decorative lining, visible when the flap was turned back. These mittens were made of kid, cotton, silk or—in plainer styles—worsted.

19th c. Mittens were long or short

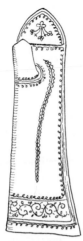

Mitten, 18th c.

and usually of net or openwork. In 1830's and 1840's short black mittens were worn with morning dress and long mittens with evening. These were revived for evening in 1870's.

Mitten, c. 1835–40

MITTEN SLEEVE

1891. (F.) 'The new mitten sleeve of lace etc. fitting the arm closely and reaching the knuckles; for dinner and theatre dresses.'

MOAB

1865–70. (F.) A turban hat with a bowl-shaped crown; nicknamed from the phrase: 'Moab is my washpot'.

MOABITE TURBAN

1832. (F.) A turban of crêpe arranged in multiple folds with an aigrette on one side. Worn tilted up off the face.

MOB CAP

18th and 19th c.'s. (F.) A white indoor cap of cambric or muslin with puffed caul and frilled border. Until

1750 bonnet-shaped with side lappets hanging loose or tied under the chin and called 'KISSING - STRINGS' or 'BRIDLES', *q.v.*

After 1750 usually not tied and fitting loosely over the head, the frilled border surmounted by a ribbon band. The size varied, being very large in the 1780's, subsequently smaller.

Plain mob caps of the 18th c. were worn in bed and called 'night-caps'.

The 'RANELAGH MOB' was quite different, *q.v.*

Mob Cap, 1805

MOCKADOR, MOKADOUR, MOC-TOUR, MOKETER

15th c. A handkerchief for the nose or a child's bib. 'For eyen and nose the nedethe a mokadour.' (Early 15th c., Lydgate, *Minor Poems*. 'Advice to an Old Gentleman.')

MOCKET, MOCHETER

16th and 17th c.'s. A handkerchief or child's bib. *See* MUCKINDER.

MODESTY PIECE

18th c. (F.) A strip of lace or lace-edged linen pinned to the corset in front to cover the 'pit of the bosom' in a low decolletage.

MOLDAVIAN MANTLE

1854. (F.) A long mantle with a deep cape falling the full length and falling over the arms on each side to form what were known as 'elephant sleeves'.

MONKEY JACKET
1850's on. (M.) A short unwaisted Pilot Coat.

MONMOUTH CAP
1570's to 1625; commonest in 17th c. (M.) A knitted cap with a tall crown and no brim or turn-up. Worn by Welshmen, soldiers, sailors and others for comfort. Made at Monmouth and also at Bewdley, Worcs. *See* BEWDLEY CAP.

Monmouth Cap, 1580

MONMOUTH COCK
2nd half 17th c. (M.) The brim behind turned up, i.e. 'cocked'.

MONOGRAM BUTTONS
1870's. (M.) Buttons of composition with owner's monogram in colour on a black background; fashionable for coats and waistcoats.

MONTAGUE CURLS
1877. (F.) An evening dress coiffure, the front hair arranged in a crescent-shaped fringe of curls gummed to the forehead.

MONTERO, MOUNTERA, MOUN-TERE, MOUNTIE CAP
Early 17th c. on. (M.) A peaked cap with flaps which could be let down each side and tied or buttoned under the chin. '. . . a montero or close hood wherewith travellers preserve their face and heads from frost biting and weather heating in summer.' (1611, Cotgrave.)

MONTESPAN CORSAGE
1843. (F.) An evening dress bodice, tight-fitting, with a very low square-cut decolletage and deeply pointed waist, front and back.

MONTESPAN HAT
1843. (F.) A small round velvet hat, the front brim turned up and trimmed with a plume. Worn with evening dress.

MONTESPAN PLEATS
1859 and 1860's. (F.) Large flat double or treble box-pleats in series, sewn to the waistband of a skirt made of heavy material.

MONTESPAN SLEEVE
1830. (F.) A day sleeve, the upper half full, caught in to a band at the elbow, then falling in a vandyked ruffle over the upper forearm.

MONT-LA-HAUT
Same as the COMMODE, *q.v.* 'Mont-la-Haut, a certain wier that raises the head-dress by degrees or stories.' (1694, *The Ladies' Dictionary.*)

MONTPENSIER MANTLE
1847. (F.) A mantle falling low behind with the fronts descending to a point, but slit up each side towards the shoulders, leaving the arms free.

MOPPET
18th c. A doll dressed in the latest French fashion and sent over to England to serve as a dress model.

MORAVIAN WORK
Early 19th c. A kind of cotton embroidery known later (*c.* 1850) as 'Broderie anglaise'. Originating from Moravian refugees expelled from Bohemia near the end of 18th c.

MORNING COAT
19th c. (1) MALE. Originally a riding coat or 'NEWMARKET', *q.v.* The fronts sloped off from the bottom button near the waist, and the skirt at the back had a vent up to the waist-level with two hip-buttons. A turned-down collar and short lapels. Usually S-B. Pockets in skirt lining.
After 1850 pockets in pleats; also flapped hip-pockets and one outside left breast.

138

Morning Coat, 1894

Morning Coat (Female), 1895

From 1860 to 1880 commonly called a 'SHOOTING COAT', S-B or D-B, with a ticket pocket above the flapped pocket on the right.

In the second half of 19th c. the MORNING COAT tended to replace its rival the FROCK COAT, for formal wear, especially when the fashionable waist level was low.

(2) 1895. FEMALE. A tailor-made version of the male MORNING COAT adopted by women as a development of the day jacket; worn over a waist-coat with masculine collar and neck-tie.

MORNING GOWN
18th c. to *c.* 1830's. (M.) A long loose coat tied at the waist with a sash or girdle and worn indoors as a form of négligé. *See* NIGHTGOWN, DRESS-ING-GOWN and BANYAN, all function-ing similarly.

MORNING WALKING COAT
See RIDING COAT.

MORTAR
17th c. (M.) A cap resembling a mortar in shape. 'I'll go to him with a mortar.' (1623, Middleton and Rowley, *The Spanish Gipsy*.)

MOSCHETTOS
Early 19th c. (M.) Similar to the pantaloons of the period but made to fit over the boots like gaiters.

MOSCOW WRAPPER
1874. (M.) A loose overcoat hang-ing full, with Pagoda sleeves, fly front fastening up to the neck, with a narrow turned-down collar of astra-khan fur which also trimmed all the edges.

MOTHER HUBBARD CLOAK
1880's. (F.) A ¾-length cloak of plush, velvet, brocade, satin or cash-mere, lined and quilted; fitting round the neck with a high collar and there tied; gauging over the shoulders and loose sleeves. After 1882 the side seams had vents allowing the back to be gathered up with a ribbon bow, to be draped over the bustle.

MOTHER-OF-PEARL BUTTONS
(1) Large; used on surface garments of both sexes, 1770 to 1800.

(2) Small, on underclothes from *c.* 1800; on men's shirts *c.* 1820. Also decorative on accessories.

MOUCHE
C. 1595 to end of 18th c. (F., occasionally M.) A black patch worn as an ornament on the face. *See* PATCHES.

MOULDS, MOWLDS
2nd half 16th c. (M.) Drawers stuffed out with horsehair, etc., to produce the bombasted shape fashionable, over which the ballooned breeches were worn. 'For black cotton to make a pair of mowldes 2/. For heare for them 12d.' 'To lyne a pair of vellet breeches to draw upon mowldes. . . .' (1569, Petre Accounts, Essex Record Office.)

MOURNING ATTIRE
(M. and F.) 14th and 15th c's. Black correct for all classes. 'In clothes black dropped all with tears.' (*C.* 1386, Chaucer, *Knight's Tale.*)

16th c. Black usual, but in Court circles white was permissible and was commonly worn by Royal widows.

Later : Black was universal.

MOURNING BAND
17th c. (M.) A scarf-like hat-band of black cypress worn by those following the hearse. 'The other men that follow the Herse have . . . hatt bandes of black sipres hanging down behynde called Trawerbandes, that is, mourning bands.' (*C.* 1618, Fynes Moryson, *Itinerary.*) This custom survived until *c.* 1880, the trailing hat-bands of male mourners being white when the deceased was a virgin. The black hat-band of the top-hat was deepened during the period of mourning, sometimes covering the sides nearly to the top, the depth indicating the degree of mourning ; a mode surviving to the end of the 19th c.

The mourning arm-band, of black cloth worn round the left upper arm, originally a military mode, became adopted by civilian men *c.* 1820 and gradually became a 'correct' symbol of mourning, the width of the band regulated by the relationship to the deceased. 3″ to 4″ was not unusual. The custom survived throughout the 19th c.

MOURNING GARLAND
17th c. A garland of willow or a hat-band of willow worn by such 'who have lost their love' in death or desertion.

MOURNING GLOVES
18th and 19th c's. Black kid, worn by all at funerals and by the bereaved subsequently for varying periods.

MOURNING HANDKERCHIEF
18th and 19th c's. (M. and F.) *See* HANDKERCHIEF (3).

MOURNING KNOT
18th c. (M.) A bunch of black ribbon attached to an armlet worn on the left arm. 'Officers to wear . . . a mourning knot on the left arm.' (1708, *British Apollo.*)

MOURNING POSY
17th c. A bunch of rosemary carried by mourners and finally cast upon the coffin.

MOURNING RIBBONS
17th c. (M.) Black ribbon worn on the hat.

MOURNING SCARF
17th and 18th c's. Of armozeen or lawn, up to 3¼ yards long; given, with hat-bands, to the principal mourners at a funeral.

MOURNING TIRE
17th c. (F.) A mourning veil.

MOUSQUETAIRE CUFF
1873. (F.) A large turned-back cuff on a day sleeve.

MOUSQUETAIRE GLOVES
C. 1890. (F.) Gloves with gauntlets embroidered and scalloped.

MOUSQUETAIRE HAT
1857–60. (F.) A brown straw hat, mushroom-shaped, with a pendant

edging of black lace all round the brim.

MOUSQUETAIRE MANTLE
1847. (F.) A black velvet mantle edged with braid, short loose sleeves, outside pockets and quilted satin lining.

MOUSQUETAIRE SLEEVE
1853; revived 1873. (F.) A full sleeve with a turned-back cuff cut into deep points.

MOUSTACHE, MUSTACHE, MUS-TACHIO, MOUCHADO, MUS-TAGE
From 16th c. on. 'A mostache is the berde of the upper lyppe.' (1551, W. Thomas, trans. of Bar-bard's *Travels in Persia*.) Very seldom worn in 18th c., considered in 19th c. a military appendage until the Crimean War (1853–6) encouraged civilians to adopt it.

MUCKINDER, MUCKENDER, MUCKITER, MUCKINGER
Early 16th to early 19th c. (1) A child's bib.
(2) A handkerchief for wiping the nose and eyes. 'Wipe your nose . . . where's your muckinder your grand-mother gave you?' (1607, Marston,

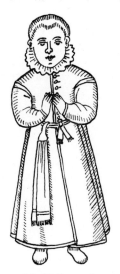

Muckinder, 1585

What you will.) 'Be of good comfort; take my muckinder and dry thine eyes.' (1633, B. Jonson, *Tale of a Tub*.)

MUFF
2nd half 16th c. on. (F., and c. 1600 to c. 1800 M., but uncommon.) A covering for both hands as a protec-tion against cold, though also used as an elegant accessory. Tubular or flat, varying greatly in size; made of fur, feathers, elegant materials, and padded within. 'Lost—a large sabble tip Man's Muff.' (1695, *London Gazette*.) In 18th c. women's muff and tippet were usually made to match. A pocket for card-case and purse was introduced in ladies' muffs of the 1880's.

Muff, 1821

MUFF BRACELET
2nd half of 17th c. (F.) A small muff worn round the wrist.

MUFFETEES
18th and 19th c's. (M. and F.). (1) Small wrist muffs made in pairs, worn for warmth or to protect the wrist ruffles when playing cards.

141

(2) Small muffs closed at one end and worn over the hands for warmth; some with a separate compartment for the thumb. 'Pray buy my mother a pair of black silk French muftees for the hands . . . they must be with thumbs to them.' (1748, *Purefoy Letters.*)

(3) 19th c. A coarse kind of mitten, 'either of leather or of knitted worsted, worn by old men'. (1808–1818, Jamieson.) Revived in 1877 as a wrist muff for women and called 'Muffatee'.

MUFFIN HAT
1860's. (M.) A round hat with a flat crown surrounded by a narrow upright brim; made of cloth, for country wear.

MUFFLER
(1) *See* CHIN CLOUT. 1530's to 1660's. (F.) A square of material folded diagonally and worn over the mouth and chin, sometimes including the nose. Worn apparently as a disguise.

(2) 19th c. A small woollen scarf worn round the neck for warmth.

MUFF'S CLOAK
Late 16th and early 17th c's. (M.) A sleeved German cloak, the same as the Dutch cloak; 'muff' being a depreciative term for German.

MUFF STRING
The ribbon suspending the muff from the neck; occasionally used.

MULES, MOILES, MOYLES, MOWLES
Term used in 16th c. and revived in 19th c. (M. and F.) 'A slipper without heel-piece or quarter.' Compare Pantofle.

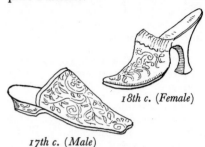

18th c. (Female)

17th c. (Male)

Mules

MULLER-CUT-DOWN
1870's. (M.) The popular name for a hat resembling a top-hat cut down to half its height; named after the murderer in 1864 whose cut-down hat led to his identification.

MUSHROOM HAT
1870's and 1880's. (F.) A mushroom-shaped straw hat plentifully trimmed over the small crown with ribbon, flowers or—in the 1880's—a bird.

MUSHROOM SLEEVE
1894. (F.) A short sleeve for evening dress; pleated round the armhole and edged with a lace frill.

N

NABCHET
16th c. Slang for hat or cap.

NAPKIN
16th to early 17th c. A handkerchief for wiping the nose.

NAPKIN-CAP
18th c. (M.) A plain night-cap or house-cap to cover the bald head when the wig was removed. 'He then took off his bag (i.e. wig), coat and waistcoat . . . and after some trouble put on a napkin-cap.' (1746, H. Walpole, *Letters.*)

NAPKIN HOOK
17th c. (F.) A hook for suspending the handkerchief from the waistband. A common form of gift or 'fairing' from young men to girls.

NAPOLEON NECKTIE
C. 1818. (M.) Said to have been worn by Napoleon on his return from Elba (1815). A somewhat narrow necktie surrounding the back of the neck, the ends brought forward and crossed in front without tying, and then fastened to the braces or carried under the arms and tied on the back. The colour was violet.
By *c.* 1830 this was becoming known as the CORSICAN TIE.

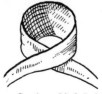

Napoleon or Corsican Neckcloth, 1818–30

NAPOLEONS
1850's. (M.) New name for long military boots reaching above the knee with a scoop out behind to allow

flexion. Worn by civilians on horseback. The name a compliment to the Prince, later Napoleon III.

NAPRON
Term used in 14th and 1st half 15th c's. From O.F. 'Naperon', diminutive of Nape or Nappe, a tablecloth. An Apron. From *c.* 1460 Appurn or Apron became the usual name.

NEAPOLITAN BONNET
1800. (F.) A bonnet of Leghorn trimmed with straw flowers and straw-coloured ribbons fastened to the crown and tied loosely on the bosom.

NEBULA HEAD-DRESS
C. 1350 to 1420. (F.) A descriptive term used by 19th-c. writers for a woman's head-dress described under GOFFERED VEIL, *q.v.*

NECKATEE
Mid 18th c. An unusual term for a neckerchief.

NECK BUTTON
Mid 17th c. (M.) An ornamental button worn at the neck of the short-style doublet of that period. This button, with a loop, closed the doublet at the top while below it was often left open to show a fine shirt.

NECK-CHAIN
Med. to mid 17th c. (M.) A gold or gilded brass chain worn as an adornment by men. Sometimes worn by mediaeval travellers as token money; a few links cut from it could serve as money. In the 17th c. it was usually called a JACK CHAIN, *q.v.*

NECKCLOTH
C. 1660 to mid 19th c. (M.) A general term for any kind of cravat or neckwear swathed round the neck as distinct from a collar. Prior to 1660

'Neckcloth' indicated a woman's neckerchief.

NECKED BONNET
1st half 16th c. (M.) Double or single (i.e. lined or unlined). A cap with a deep flap fitting round the neck at the back.

Necked Bonnet, c. 1505

NECKERCHIEF, NECKERCHER, NECK-KERCHIEF
Sometimes KERCHIEF, *q.v.* (1) Late 14th to early 19th c. (F.) ('Neckercher' in provincial use only in 18th c. and for children.) Any square or strip of linen or other material folded round the neck. 'On his (a child's) shoulder about his neck a kercheff fyne must be.' (*C.* 1460, Russell, *Boke of Nurture.*)
(2) In 19th c. both M. and F. The term occasionally applied to a large silk cravat.

NECK HANDKERCHIEF
18th and 19th c's. (M.) Synonym for Cravat or Necktie. 'To buy Cravats or Neck-Handkerchiefs.' (1712, Steele, *The Spectator.*)

NECKINGER
16th to 19th c. (F.) A corrupt form of NECKERCHER.

NECKTIE
19th c. (M.) A term coming into use about 1830 but not entirely displacing the earlier name 'Cravat'. A band of varying width and material

wound round the base of the shirt collar. For named varieties *see* separate headings.

NÉGLIGÉE, NÉGLIGÉ
18th and 19th c's. (1) A term used for both male and female informal attire.
(2) A mourning girdle of jet with a 9″ pendant end; worn by women as part of public mourning at the death of Princess Charlotte in 1818.

NELSON
1819–20. (F.) A bustle worn outside to enhance the effect of the Grecian bend. *See* FRISK.

NELSON HAT
1895. (F.) A straw hat, the brim sharply turned up, front and back, with a plume in front and ribbon bows at the peaks each side.

NETHER INTEGUMENTS
See UNMENTIONABLES.

NETHER STOCKS
C. 1515 to 1600. (M.) The lower or stocking portion of hose (resembling tights), the upper portion being variously called the 'breech', 'upper stocks' and, later, 'trunk hose'. *See* HOSE. The term was sometimes used for women's stockings at the end of the 16th c.

NEWGATE FRINGE
19th c. (M.) Colloquial term for a fringe of beard under the jaw.

NEWMARKET COAT
1838 on. (M.) Previously called a 'RIDING COAT' and from 1750 to 1800 called a 'NEWMARKET FROCK' which was a riding coat. *See* FROCK. The Newmarket Coat was a tail-coat, S-B or D-B, the fronts sloping away from above the waist level and often worn open.
The skirts were short with rounded corners; sleeves with cuffs; often with flapped 'hip-pockets'.
By 1850 it was generally called a 'CUTAWAY' and by 1870 it was merging into the MORNING COAT.

Newmarket Coat, Front and Back, 1849

NEWMARKET JACKET

1891. (F.) A close-fitting jacket, S-B or D-B, made hip-length; turn-over collar and silk-faced lapels cut

Newmarket (F.), 1890

on masculine lines. The characteristic 'Newmarket' feature of flapped pockets (real or sham) on the hips; close sleeves ending in a cuff or buttoned slit. Often part of a tailor-made costume of tweed. For day wear.

NEWMARKET OVERCOAT

(1) 1881. (M.) Resembling a S-B FROCK OVERCOAT cut short in the waist, very long in the skirts. Velvet collar and cuffs common. Usually made of homespun or shepherd's plaid.

(2) 1889. (F.) Tailor-made S-B or D-B and closed to the waist, the long skirts left open to reach nearly to the ground. Flapped pockets on the hips; close sleeves. Velvet collar, lapels and cuffs. Made of heavy cloth for winter wear.

NEWMARKET TOP FROCK

1895. (M.) An overcoat resembling a FROCK COAT with a broad velvet collar; pockets on the waist seam; skirts to 4″ below the knees. Made of a rough Cheviot, the body lined with silk or satin, the skirts with check material.

NEWMARKET VEST

1894. (M.) A waistcoat of a plaid or check pattern material and cut to button high. Made with or without flapped pockets. Worn especially by sportsmen.

NIFELS, NYEFLES

2nd half 15th c. (F.) A woman's veil.

NIGHT-CAP, SKULL CAP

14th to mid 19th c. (M. and F.) MALE. (1) A form of skull cap with close upturned brim, often decorative; a very common form from 16th c. and worn indoors for comfort, replacing the wig (when that was in fashion).

(2) A plain washable cap worn in bed from the earliest time. In 19th c. often called a 'jelly-bag' from its shape, usually of knitted silk with a tassel on the top. *See* also BIGGIN.

FEMALE. 18th and 19th c's. A mob cap tied under the chin and worn in bed.

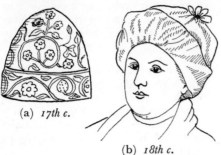

(a) *17th c.*

(b) *18th c.*

Night Caps (M.)

NIGHT-CAP WIG
Early 18th c. (M.) A bob wig with roll curls circling the back of the head from cheek to cheek.

NIGHT-CLOTHES
16th c. on. (M.) Until 16th c. men slept naked or in a day-shirt; subsequently a night-shirt varying in quality was worn in bed. Nobles in 16th c. wore embroidered shirts or 'wrought night-shirts'. By the 19th c. the night-shirt resembled a day-shirt with a loose turned-down collar, or a loose 'Nightgown', ankle length was worn.

NIGHT-CLOTHES
16th to end of 18th c. (F.) (1) Informal morning or evening attire. 'My lady Castlemaine who looked pretty in her night-clothes.' (1667, *Pepys' Diary*.)
(2) Until 16th c. women slept naked or in day-shifts. Subsequently in night-chemise. In 19th c. in long-sleeved, cotton, long-cloth or linen nightgowns.

NIGHT COIF
16th and 17th c. (F.) A woman's coif worn as négligée or in bed. The coif was often embroidered and generally worn with a forehead cloth. 'A night coyf of cameryck cutworke and spangils with a forehead cloth.' (1577–8, Nichols, *Progress of Q. Elizabeth*.)

NIGHTGOWN
16th to end of 18th c. (1) MALE. A loose gown or long coat cut to the contemporary fashion, worn as négligé indoors and informally out of doors for morning visits, in 17th and 18th c's. *See* MORNING GOWN and INDIAN GOWN or BANYAN.
(2) FEMALE. An unboned comfortable but often very elaborate dress worn indoors and out, and sometimes on formal occasions as at weddings. Also called a 'Morning Gown', although worn at any part of the day. Similar to MANTUA, *q.v.* In 19th c. a loose gown of cotton, linen or silk, worn in bed only.

Nightgown, 1870–80 (F.)

NIGHT-KERCHER
16th c. (F.) A neckerchief worn at night.

NIGHT-MASK
17th c. (F.)
'Here be fine night-masks, plaster'd well within,
To supple wrinkles and to smooth the skin.'
(1627, M. Drayton, *The Muses' Elysium*.)

NIGHT RAIL, NIGHT RAYLE
16th to early 18th c. (F.) A cape of lawn, holland, silk or satin falling to the waist or hips; worn in the bedroom or in bed.

146

NIGHT-SHIFT

Late 17th and 18th c. (F.) A chemise worn in bed only.

NIGHT-SHIRT

16th to end of 19th c. (M.) A shirt worn in bed only.

NIGHT SLIPPERS

Late 16th c. on. Slippers worn in the bedroom.

NITHSDALE

1715–20. (F.) A long hooded riding cloak. 'It is called a Nithsdale since Fame adorned a Countess with that name.' (1719, D'Urfey, *Pills to purge Melancholy*.)

The Countess had rescued her husband from the Tower by disguising him in her cloak and hood. (1715.)

NIVERNOIS HAT

1760's. (M.) A tricorne hat with broad spreading brim rolled over a flat crown; known as the 'Nivernois cock'. 'He wears this large umbrella-like hat. This is the Nivernois.' (1765, *London Magazine*.) Also called a 'Waterproof hat' because of its umbrella-like protection.

Norfolk Jacket, 1891

NORFOLK JACKET

1880 on. (M., sometimes F.) A modification of the NORFOLK SHIRT, *q.v.* A lounge jacket of mid-thigh length, made with a box-pleat to each forepart and a central box-pleat behind, large bellows pockets on the hips and a vertical slit pocket in the left breast; a belt of self-material. In 1894 a yoke was often added, the box-pleats starting from the yoke. Commonly made of Harris tweeds and homespuns.

NORFOLK SHIRT

1866 to 1880. (M.) The forerunner of the Norfolk Jacket. A short lounge jacket with box-pleat down the centre of the back and down each forepart; collar and wristbands made in the style of a shirt. Flap pockets in the front skirts; belt of same material. Always worn buttoned up. Of rough tweeds for country wear.

Norfolk Jacket, 1895

NORMA CORSAGE

1844. (F.) An evening bodice with a loose fold in the centre, caught in with a gold ornament.

NOSEGAY

Term used from 15th c. A small bunch of sweet-smelling flowers or herbs, the latter as an antidote to infectious diseases. In 16th and 17th c's. worn in the hat at weddings.

'A nosegay bound with laces in his hat,
Bridelaces, Sir, and his hat all green.'

(1599, Henry Porter,
The Two Angry Women of Abingdon.)

NOTCH

19th-c. term. (M.) The gap cut out between the collar of a coat—or waistcoat collar and the lapel. It varied in shape, a mere slit being called by tailors, a 'light'; the 'M-notch' was shaped like the letter M; a rectangular cut back was called a 'step'.

NOUCH

See OUCH.

NURSING DRESS

19th c. (F.) A dress constructed so that the wearer could suckle her infant without having to remove the bodice when this was fastened up the back by hooks and eyes; over each breast a small slit opening, closed by a button, was concealed under a robing or pleated folds of the bodice material. Such dresses were in use between *c.* 1820 and 1850.

NYCETTE, NICED

Late 15th and early 16th c's. (F.) A light wrapper for the neck.

O

OATLAND VILLAGE HAT

1800. (F.) A day hat, the brim curved up in front and behind, the crown dome-shaped with a ribbon round it. Of straw, twist or Leghorn. Named after the country house of the Duchess of York.

OBI HAT

1804. (F.) A straw or chip hat for walking; the high crown with flat top, a narrow brim rolled back in front; tied under the chin with ribbon strings passing over the brim from the crown which was also trimmed round with ribbon. Named after a character in a recent pantomime.

OBLONG HOOP, also called SQUARE HOOP

1740's to 1760's; and for Court wear, later modified, until 1820. (F.) An under-garment variously constructed, projecting out horizontally from the waist on each side, the front and back being flattened to give enormous breadth to the hips. Some were hinged allowing the wearer to fold the overskirt under the arms when passing through a too narrow doorway.

Oblong Hoops, 1740's–60's

OCTAGON TIE

1860's on. (M.) A made-up scarf, the front arranged in four tabs above the tie-pin with a neck-band fastened behind by a hook and eyelet hole.

Octagon Tie, 1890

OES, OWES

1570's into 17th c. (Generally F.) Small rings or eyelets sewn to the material of a garment to form decorative designs. 'Vaile of net lawne embroidered with Oes.' (1616, Chapman, *Masque of the Inns of Court.*)

Oblong Hoop Shape, 1743

149

OILETS
18th and early 19th c.'s. The early term for eyelets or lacing holes.

OKER, HOGGER, HOKER, COKER
16th c. (M.) 'Boots for ploughmen called Okers.' (1552, Hulcot.)

OLDENBURG BONNET
1814. (F.) A very large bonnet with wide projecting brim in front and a flat crown draped with ostrich feathers; ribbon ties under the chin. Named after the Duchess, a visitor to the Peace celebrations of 1814.

OLIVE BUTTON
Mid 18th c. on. A long oval button covered with silk.

OLIVETTE
Mid 18th c. on. An olive-shaped button of a BRANDENBURG, q.v. See also FROG BUTTON.

ONDINA CRINOLINE
1860's. (F.) A cage crinoline with the hoops arranged in 'wave-like bands'.

OPEN ROBE
19th c. (F.) A style of dress in which the skirt is open in front from the waist down so as to reveal an ornamental underskirt or 'petticoat'. Although this form of construction was used from the 16th c. on it does not appear to have been called 'open robe' until the 19th c.

It was chiefly fashionable, for day and evening, during the 1830's and 1840's.

OPERA HAT
Mid 18th c. on. (M.) 18th c. A small flat three-cornered hat made for carrying under the arm and also called a 'CHAPEAU BRAS', q.v.

19th c. to 1830. A crescent-shaped hat with a soft crown which could be compressed between the crescent-shaped side brims, and carried under the arm as the chapeau bras. Also called a 'MILITARY FOLDING HAT' or 'COCKED HAT'. After 1830, except for full dress: the Opera hat was the 'CIRCUMFOLDING HAT' and later the 'GIBUS', q.v.

Open Robe, 1846

ORANGE-BLOSSOM WREATH
See WEDDING VEIL.

ORPHREY, ORFREY, ORFRAY, ORFRIES, ORPHRIEIS
From 13th c. Embroidery with gold thread. From early 13th c. the term was applied to narrow bands of gold embroidery decorating the borders of garments, especially ecclesiastical vestments. Later it came to mean narrow strips of any kind of embroidery such as orphreys of blue, red and green, also plain velvet.

ORRELET, ORILYET, fr. OREIL-LETTE, OREILLET
2nd half 16th c. (F.) The side pieces of a woman's coif, covering the ears; also called 'cheeks and ears'. See COIF.

OSBALDISTON TIE, BARREL KNOT
1830's and 1840's. (M.) A necktie tied with the centre knot in the form of a barrel.

OUCH or NOUCH
13th to 15th c. A jewelled clasp or buckle, or a collection of jewels. See PONTIFICALS.

150

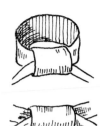

*Osbaldiston Neckcloth or Barrel
Knot, 1818–40*

OURLE, later ORLE
13th and 14th c's. A border of fur.

OUT-COAT
Late 17th and 18th c's. (M.) An overcoat for outdoor wear.

OVAL BEAVER HAT
1817. (M.) A hat made on an oval block, an improvement on the round block previously used, which required a 'hat screw' to stretch it to the shape of the head.

OVERALLS
19th c. (M.) Loose trousers of white cord or leather, worn for riding; adapted by civilians from those worn by the cavalry in early 19th c. 'To a Baragon Stable Jacket & overalls £1 : 13.' (1840, domestic bill.)

OVERCOAT
Term used from 18th c. on. (M., and from 1780 F. also.) A coat worn out of doors over an indoor suit. *See* GREATCOAT.

OVERSLOP
Term used from A.D. 950 to end of 14th c. A gown, stole, cassock or surplice.

OVERSTOCKS
See STOCKS.

OXFORD BUTTON-OVERS
1860's. (M.) 'Oxonian shoes which cover the instep and are closed by being buttoned instead of being stringed.' (1862, Mayhew Bros., *London Life and London Poor*.)

OXFORD GLOVES
Mid 16th to mid 17th c. Gloves often scented with the Earl of Oxford's perfume.

OXFORD TIE
1890's. (M. and F.) A narrow straight necktie having the same width from end to end. Worn by men with a lounge suit and by women with a morning blouse.

OXONIAN BOOTS, COLLEGIANS
C. 1830's and 1840's. (M.) A short boot, later black-japanned, having a wedge-shaped piece cut out from each side at the top to enable the boot to be pulled on easily.

OXONIAN JACKET or OXFORD
COATEE
1850's and 1860's. (M.) *See* also JUMPER. A 'real Oxford bang-tail coatee, bright blue with only two buttons and button-holes and all sorts of jolly pockets in original places.' (1855, F. Smedley, *Harry Coverdale's Courtship*.)

OXONIAN SHOE
1848. (M.) 'Laces up in front with 3 or 4 holes. The vamp comes well above the joint [i.e. ankle]. Seam across the instep.' (Sparkes-Hall.)

P

PADDOCK COAT
1892 on. (M.) A long overcoat without a seam at the waist, made D-B or S-B and fly front. A seam descended from the arm-hole to the top of the flapped pocket on the hip, to give better fit, in contrast to the old-style Paletot, otherwise resembling it in which there was a side-body. This was revived in 1893 and was then called by some the 'New Paletot'.

Both styles had deep side pleats concealing a back vent. Pockets were plentiful.

PAGE BONNET
1874. (F.) Identical with the CHARLOTTE CORDAY BONNET, *q.v.*

PAGES
See DRESS CLIPS.

PAGODA PARASOL
1790's to 1830's. The cover shaped in an ogee curve up the stick; when expanded it was said to resemble the roof of a pagoda.

PAGODA SLEEVE
1849 to 1860's. (F.) A sleeve with one seam on the inner side and cut so as to expand widely at the elbow where it was caught up at the bend, but falling on the outer side nearly to the wrist. Some were made with a slit up in front which by 1857 extended almost the whole length. By 1859 the name was being replaced by 'Funnel Sleeve'. Worn with engageantes.

PALATINE
1840's. (F.) A neck tippet with long flat ends reaching in front below the waist. *See* PALLATINE.

PALATINE ROYAL, or VICTORINE
1851. (F.) A fur tippet with a quilted hood and short ends in front.

PALE
Late 14th to early 16th c. A vertical stripe or one of a series of stripes of contrasting colours.
'But what art thou that sayest this tale
That warest on thy hose a pale.'
(*C.* 1384, Chaucer, *House of Fame.*)

PALETOT
A French term appearing in the 1830's, and rather loosely used to near the end of the century. (1) MALE. A short greatcoat made without a seam at the waist, and often

Paletot, 1850

152

having a whole back but always side seams. Often no side pleats. The back vent, if present, very short.

(2) FEMALE. 1839 to end of century. A ¾-length cloak hanging in stiff pleats from the shoulders and having a short stiff cape. Arm-holes, guarded with flaps. By 1843 it had 3 capes, a velvet collar and loose sleeves.

The Short Paletot, 1860's to 1880's, or YACHTING JACKET, q.v., was worn as an outdoor jacket.

The Long Paletot, 1865 to 1884, was usually a figure-fitting outdoor coat reaching below the knees, with tight sleeves and often trimmed with lace.

In 1870's some were sleeveless and made with a Watteau Pleat or in the casaque shape.

PALETOT-CLOAK

1850's. (M.) A short cloak scarcely covering the seat, fastened in front S-B or D-B with arm-hole slits; no sleeves.

Paletot-Cloak, 1852

PALETOT-MANTLE

1867. (F.) ¾-length cloak with a cape and hanging sleeves.

PALETOT-REDINGOTE

1867. (F.) An outdoor long coat cut to fit the figure without a seam at the waist; made with revers at the top and sometimes with circular capes. Buttoned all down the front.

PALETOT-SAC

1840's and 1850's. (M.) A short straight paletot, S-B or D-B, and often having a hood instead of a collar.

Paletot-Sac ("suited for end summer wear without an undercoat"), 1850

PALISADE

C. 1690 to 1710. (F.) A wire frame for supporting the high fontange coiffure. 'Palisade, a wire sustaining the Hair next the Dutchess or first knot.' (1690, J. Evelyn, *The Fop Dictionary*.) *See* also COMMODE and MONT-LA-HAUT (synonyms).

PALLATINE

C. 1680 to early 18th c. (F.) A sable shoulder wrap or tippet. 'That which used to be called a "sable tippet" but that name is changed to one that is supposed to be finer, because newer and à la mode de France.' (1694, *Ladies' Dictionary*.)

PALMERSTON WRAPPER

1853–5. (M.) A S-B Sac overcoat, the fronts hanging loose and wrapped across. Sleeves wide at the hands; no cuffs; wide collar and lapels, faced up to the edge of the button-stand and carrying 4 button-holes. Side flapped pockets. Named after the popular statesman of the day.

PALTOCK, PALTOK, PAULTOCK

14th to mid 15th c. (M.) A Gipon or doublet to which the hose of that period (tights and stockings all in one) were trussed (i.e. tied).

PAMELA BONNET

1845–55. (F.) A small straw bonnet, the narrow brim open round the face and sloping back to be continuous with the crown, flat behind and having a small curtain. Trimmed with ribbons and sometimes flowers. Named after the heroine of Richardson's novel.

Pamela Bonnet, 1846

PAMELA HAT

1845. (F.) A small gypsy hat of coarse straw.

PANEL SKIRT

1894. (F.) A day skirt consisting of an overskirt 2″ shorter than the underskirt and open on the left side to expose a decorative panel, e.g. of velvet.

PANES

1500 to 1650's. (M.) A decoration produced by slashing the material into long ribbon-like strips or by using ribbon lengths set close and parallel, joined above and below. Through the gaps part of the shirt (or sleeves) might be pulled out, or a contrasting coloured lining might be drawn out. E.g.: 'gown of crimson velvet with French sleeves lined with tynsell'. (1523, Inventory of Dame Agnes Hungerford.) The device was also common with trunk-hose.

Panes, 1625

PANIER

18th c. The French name of the side hoops or FALSE HIPS, *q.v.* The word was not used in England in the 18th c.

PANIER ANGLAIS

The French name for the Hoop petticoat; a term rarely used in England.

PANNIER CRINOLINE

1870's. (F.) Thomson's Pannier Crinoline combined a Cage Crinoline and a Bustle, the upper portion extending round the back and sides.

PANNIER DRESS

1868. (F.) A day dress with a double skirt, the upper bunched out round the back and sides by means of a draw-string below, the under-skirt trained, and trimmed with a flounce.

PANTALETTES

C. 1812 to 1840's. (F.) The feminine version of PANTALOONS, q.v. An under-garment like long straight-legged white drawers reaching to below the calf and there trimmed with lace or tucks. Visible below the skirt, with children, until c. 1850; a mode surviving into the 1840's for ladies' riding costume.

Pantalettes, 1823

PANTALOONS

(M.) (1) 1660's to 1670's. The same as PETTICOAT BREECHES, q.v. '... the pantaloons which are a kind of Hermaphrodite and of either sex.' (1661, J. Evelyn, *Tyrranus or the Mode.*) 'A paire of new fashion'd rideing pantaloons.' (1662, Sir Miles Stapleton, *Household Books.*)

(2) 1790 to c. 1850. Close-fitting tights shaped to the leg and ending just below the calf until 1817; then at the ankles, usually with short side

slits, strapped under the foot and known as 'tights', c. 1840.

Pantaloons, 1830

PANTALOONS

1812 to c. 1840's. (F.) An under-garment in the form of long, straight-legged drawers. *See* PANTALETTES, a term not often used before 1820. In the 1830's often called 'trousers'. 'With short dresses those who have not handsome legs generally wear pantaloons.' (1822.) But pantaloons appearing below the skirt went out of fashion before 1840 except for children.

PANTALOON-TROUSERS

C. 1815 to c. 1830. (M.) A hybrid, tight-fitting but moderately loose from the calf down, and without side slits. The bottoms were cut square or with the fronts hollowed out over the insteps.

PANTEEN COLLAR

1880's. (F.) (1) A high stand-fall collar, common with ladies' tailor-made jackets and coats.

(2) (M.) A white turned-down collar worn by the clergy until replaced by the stand collar, and the Prussian collar in 1860–70; the style favoured by Evangelicals and Nonconformist ministers.

PANTILE
1640's to 1665. (M. and F.) A popular name for the 'SUGAR-LOAF' hat, q.v. Similarly the 19th-c. slang term 'tile' for a hat.

PANTOFLES, PANTABLES, PANTACLES, PANTOBLES, PANTIBLES
End of 15th c. to mid 17th c. (M. and F.) Over-shoes in the form of mules. Very common from 1570.

PAPILLOTTE
18th c. (M. and F.) A screw of paper used to make a curl of hair.

PAPILLOTTE COMB
1828. (F.) A decorative comb of tortoiseshell 3″ or 4″ long, used to raise the hair at the sides.

PAQUEBOT CAPOTE
1830's. (F.) The same as the BIBI, q.v. The inside of the brim was trimmed with ribbon and blonde lace.

PARACHUTE HAT
See BALLOON HAT.

PARASOL
19th c. (F.) A light ornamental umbrella carried by ladies as a shield against the sun. From c. 1800 to c. 1840 the pagoda shape was usual; some, however, were small and hinged so that the cover could be turned upright to act as a fan ('Fan Parasol'). The telescopic stick of steel appeared by 1811; the small parasol with a folding stick for use in the carriage from c. 1838 on. From that time on the parasol became more elegant, with carved ivory handles (1830's and 1840's) and fringed borders, the covers of coloured silk and lace, black Maltese lace being fashionable (1860's).

By 1867 'the pagoda shape has entirely disappeared; handles are

longer; covers in stripes, brocade and satin'.

In the 1880's a domed shape was usual with linings in bright colours; handles with a large crystal or china knobs; 1886 introduced ribbon bows near the point and handle; 1888 sticks 'as long as alpenstocks' with knobs as large as billiard balls. 1890: covers of chiffon or crepe-de-chine with deep flounces or puffed all over; handles of Dresden china (1896) and in 1899 covers of fancy silk in broad coloured stripes.

PARCHMENT CALVES
2nd half 18th c. (M.) Parchment shapes worn inside the stockings to improve the shape of the legs. See CALVES.

PARDESSUS
1840's on. (F.) Generic name for any outdoor garment of half or ¾ length, with sleeves and shaped into the waist; often with rounded cape or pelerine; trimmed with lace or velvet.

Pardessus, 1849

PARDESSUS REDINGOTE
1850's on. (M.) The French name for the Frock Coat.

PARROCK
15th c. (M.) 'Parrock or Caban'. (C. 1440, *Promptorium Parvulorum*.) A loose cloak with arm-holes.

PARTI-COLOURED HOSE

Mid 14th c. to mid 15th c. (M.) Hose in the form of footed long stockings reaching above the fork as tights, the legs coloured differently or striped. 'Their hose are of two colours or pied with more' (*C.* 1413, 'Eulogium', anon.)

PARTLET, PATLET

(1) 1st half 16th c. (M.) A sleeveless jacket or merely a covering for the upper part of the chest and neck left exposed by a low-cut doublet, then fashionable. Partlets were often very decorative. 'A straight sleeveless jacket made like a partlett.' (1523, Letters and Papers, Henry VIII.)

(2) 16th and 17th c's. (F.) A fill-in (like a chemisette) for a low decolletage and made with a high collar from *c.* 1530's. 'He cannot make a standing collar for a partlet without the measurement for her neck.' (1533, Letters and Papers, Henry VIII.) *See* DETACHABLE SLEEVES.

PASS

17th c. (M. and F.) The front of a man's or woman's hat.

PASSE

1864. (F.) The bridge of flowers or trimming under the brim of a bonnet.

PASSEMENTERIE

19th c. Lace or gimp trimming used for dresses.

PATCHES

1590's to end of 18th c. (F., 17th and 18th c. M.) Small spots, variously shaped, of black velvet or silk, and applied with mastic as ornaments on the face. At various periods (e.g. early 18th c.) the arrangement of the patches on the face served to indicate the wearer's political party.

The wearing of patches by men was limited to Fops.

PATENT LACE

C. 1800 to *c.* 1820. A term commonly denoting machine-made lace. *See* GLOSSARY for Patent Thread and Loom Lace.

PATENT LEATHER BOOTS

1870's on. (M.) Ankle-length buttoned boots of patent leather uppers, worn for day and also evening dress.

PATROL JACKET

(1) 1878. (M.) A close-fitting hip-length jacket, S-B, closed by 5 buttons; Prussian collar; cross pocket on each hip and on left breast. Of military cut and worn with tight knee breeches for bicycling (on the high 'penny farthing' machine).

(2) 1889. (F.) A close-fitting hip-length jacket, the back without a centre seam, the front trimmed across with military braiding; tight sleeves with close cuffs. Stand collar. A military style inspired by the recent Egyptian campaign.

PATTENS

14th to mid 19th c. (M. and F.) Over-shoes consisting of wooden soles secured by leather straps and worn with boots or shoes to raise the wearer above the dirt when walking. The shape varied according to the period. Usually for country wear but very fashionable in the 15th c. and 18th c. Until the 17th c. the term was synonymous with CLOGS, *q.v.*

From *c.* 1630 pattens were raised on iron rings : 'The women leave in the passage their pattins, that is a kind of wooden shoes which stand on a high iron ring. Into these wooden shoes they thrust their ordinary leather or stuff shoes when they go out.' (1748, Pehr Kalm's Account of his Visit to England, Stockholm, 1753. Trans. J. Lucas, 1892.)

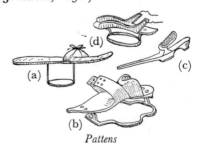

Pattens

(a) *1828* (b) *17th c.*
(c) *Late 15th c.* (d) *18th c.*

Countrywoman continued to use them until *c.* mid 19th c.

PATTI JETS
1869. (F.) Balls of polished jet hanging from a ribbon necklace, with similar earrings; for morning wear.

PAUTENER
Med. The bag hanging from the girdle.

PEA JACKET or PILOT COAT
1830's on. (M.) Worn either as an overcoat or as a short closed coat, and made of pilot cloth or mohair. D-B with wide lapels and velvet collar, the skirts closed behind. As an overcoat made loose and sack-like, the corners cut square, and ending above the knees.

In 1850's it was given huge buttons and often a short back vent.

From *c.* 1860 it became known as a REEFER, *q.v.*

Pea Jacket, 1868

PEAKED SHOE
See PIKED SHOE.

PEASANT SKIRT
1885. (F.) A full round tennis skirt made with 2 or 3 wide tucks and a fall of lace.

PEASCOD-BELLIED DOUBLET
C. 1570's to 1600. (M.) A term used by Bulwer in 1653 describing the fashion for padding the front of the doublet at the point of the waist to produce a bulge overhanging the girdle. Originally a Dutch mode. Also called LONG-BELLIED DOUBLET, KODPEASED DOUBLET.

Peascod-Belly of Doublet, 1583

PECTOLL
16th c. (M.) The breast of a shirt.

PEDIMENT HEAD-DRESS
A 19th-c. term for the 16th-c. ENGLISH HOOD, *q.v.*

PEEPER
18th c. 'Peeper, a spying glass.' (1785, F. Grose, *Dictionary of the Vulgar Tongue*.)

PEG-TOP SLEEVES
1857 to 1864. (M.) Sleeves cut wide above and narrowing towards the hand, a modified revival of the Gigot sleeve of the 1820's.

PEG-TOP TROUSERS, or ZOUAVE TROUSERS

1857 to 1865. (M.) The legs cut wide at the hips and sloping inwards to a close fit at the ankles. For day wear only and never a universal fashion. A modified revival occurred in 1892.

Peg-Top Trousers, 1863

PEIGNE GIRAFFE
See GIRAFFE COMB.

PEIGNE JOSEPHINE
1842. (F.) A high comb surmounted by small balls often gilt; worn at the back of the head with evening dress.

PEIGNOIR
Late 18th c. on. (F.) A loose wrapper of light material worn as a day négligée or informal morning wear. The corsage without bones, and in 1840 made with bishop sleeves. 'She . . . let down her peignoir from her shoulder'. (Gentleman's & London Mag. Sept. 1780).

PELERINE
1740 to end of 19th c. (F.) 18th c. A short cape with long pendant ends in front, often worn crossed over the bosom, passed round the waist, to be tied behind.

19th c. A cape-like collar, but from 1825 it reverted to the style of the 18th c. Commonly made of cambric or muslin, often embroidered or trimmed with lace.

PELISSE, PELLICE
18th c. to *c.* 1850's. Revived in a modified form in the 1880's. (F.) An outdoor garment with variations in shape and materials.

18th c. A ¾-length cloak with shoulder-cape or hood and arm-hole slits. Lined and trimmed with silk, satin or fur. 'A pellice of rich brocade lined with sables.' (1718, *Letters of Lady M. Wortley Montagu.*)

1800 to 1810. ¾-length with or without sleeves; subsequently ankle-length, sleeved and figure-fitting, often having one or more shoulder capes.

1880's. A long winter mantle, often of velvet, silk or satin, gathered on the shoulders and having large loose sleeves. Throughout the 19th c. a pelisse for infants in arms was a

1786   1816

Pellisses

159

long caped cloak, generally of cream-coloured cashmere, though bright colours (blue or scarlet) were also made.

PELISSE-MANTLE
1838 to 1845. (F.) A ¾- to full-length cloak with a cape reaching the waist and draped round the arms to form hanging sleeves. In the 1840's this mantle was pulled in at the waist behind.

PELISSE-ROBE
1817 to 1850. (F.) A day dress in the form of a pelisse fastened all down the front with ribbon bows or concealed hooks and eyes. After c. 1840 it became known as a 'REDINGOTE', q.v.

Pelisse-Robe, 1834

PELISSON
14th to early 16th c. (M. and F.) A furred over-gown or super-tunic; identical with PILCH, q.v.

PELLARD
See HOUPPELANDE.

PEMBROKE PALETOT
1853–5. (M.) A long-waisted D-B Overcoat reaching the calf; wide

lapels, two rows of 4 buttons, vertical breast pocket, 2 flapped side pockets; easy sleeves with turned-back cuffs.

PENANG LAWYER
19th c. (M.) Walking-stick with bulbous head, made from stem of a palm from Penang.

PENDICLE
17th c. (M.) A drop-earring, the style when only one was worn by men.

PENTES
1886. (F.) Pyramidal panels of silk or velvet in graduated stripes forming a full-length panel of an underskirt, with the overskirt or tunic draped so as to expose it.

PEPLUM
1866 revived in 1890's. (F.) A short tunic, i.e. overskirt, cut away front and back and hanging in points at the sides. For day dress.

PEPLUM BASQUE
1866. (F.) Peplum-shaped basque attached to a waistbelt and worn with a day or evening bodice.

Peplum Basque, 1866

PEPLUM BODICE
1879. (F.) An evening bodice with long side panels forming panniers.

PEPLUM DOLMAN
1872. (F.) A Dolman with long points on the sides.

PEPLUM JUPON
1866. (F.) A gored under-petticoat with 3 steels round the bottom and a deep pleated flounce, replacing the cage crinoline.

PEPLUM OVERSKIRT
1894. (F.) Drapery of fancy material, pleated into the waistband behind and there short but descending in ripples to the hem towards the front, and caught in along the whole length of the side seams of the front breadth, which is left uncovered.

PETENLAIR, PET-EN-L'AIR, FRENCH JACKET
C. 1745 to 1770's. (F.) (Somewhat earlier in France.) A thigh-length or sometimes knee-length jacket-bodice with sac-back, short elbow sleeves and often a stomacher front. Worn with a plain skirt (then called a Petticoat).
'Inspir'd by thee, the skilful engineer Lopp'd half the sack and form'd the pet-en-l'air.'
(1751, *The Gentleman's Magazine*, 'Hymn to Fashion'.)

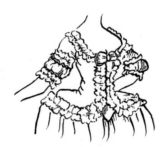

Petenlair, Front and Back, 1780

PEPLUM ROTONDE
1871. (F.) A waist-length circular Cloak with back vent and fringed borders.

PERDITA CHEMISE
1783. (F.) A day dress with a close-fitting bodice, a V-neck and a deep falling collar, single or double. The gown closed in front from bosom to hem by buttons or ribbon ties, and long tight sleeves buttoned at the wrist. A broad sash at the waist tied behind and flowing down the back of the skirt.

PERIWIG
See WIG.

PERUKE
See WIG.

PERUVIAN HAT
Early 19th c. (F.) Made of plaited strands of the leaves of the Cuban palm. 'Fraser's Patent Peruvian Hats . . . not injured by rain.' (1816.)

PETERSHAM COSSACKS or TROUSERS
1817–18. (M.) An excessively loose form of COSSACKS (*q.v.*) spreading out widely round the ankles and over the foot, or drawn in leaving a flounce round the ankle. Named after the Regency Buck, Charles, Viscount Petersham.

PETERSHAM FROCK COAT
1830's. (M.) Made D-B with broad velvet collar, lapels and cuffs, and large flapped pockets aslant on the hips. No side bodies.

PETERSHAM GREAT COAT
1830's. (M.) Made with a short shoulder-cape.

PETIT BORD
1835 to 1850. (F.) A form of headwear for evening dress; at first a small-crowned hat with a halo brim, trimmed with ribbon and aigrettes. In the 1840's it was much smaller becoming a toque hat usually of

velvet, with narrow upturned brim. The Petit Bord was always worn at the back of the head, often with a sideways tilt.

PETTICOAT

(1) *C.* 1450 to end of 16th c. but unusual after 1520. (M.) An under-doublet usually padded and worn for warmth; subsequently called a Waistcoat. 'In wynter next your shert use you to wear a pettycott of scarlet.' (1577, Andrew Borde, *Regyment.*)

(2) FEMALE. 16th c. on. An under-garment and as such often called an 'under-petticoat' until the 19th c. when the term always meant an under-garment. In the 16th c. usually of inferior material and tied to the body of the dress by laces ('points'). In the 17th c. often of white flannel. In the 18th of cambric or flannel and narrow, worn under the hoop and sometimes called a 'dickey'.

In the 19th c. the petticoat gradually became more elaborate and in 1840's several were worn, the undermost usually of flannel. In the 1860's white cotton petticoats were often bordered with broderie anglaise.

By the 1890's petticoats were often of silk or satin lavishly flounced, frilled, and bordered with ribbon and lace, producing a 'seductive froufrou' sound, in walking.

(3) The term 'Petticoat', before the 19th c., was also applied to the skirt of a dress, being part of the gown and not an under-garment.

PETTICOAT BODICE

1815 on. (F.) A petticoat with a sleeveless bodice to it, joined with a seam at the waist, by gores or gathers, thus contrasting with the 'PRINCESS PETTICOAT', *q.v.*

At first usually made with a low stomacher front; after 1825 buttoned up behind.

In 1890's the term was applied to a bodice covering the stays. *See* CAMISOLE.

PETTICOAT BREECHES, also called RHINEGRAVES and PANTALOONS

1660's to 1670's. (M.) Immensely wide in the leg and pleated or gathered on to a waistband, falling like a divided skirt to the knees or just above. Some had a lining forming baggy under-breeches gathered into a band above the knee. Always trimmed with ribbon loops at the waist and usually also down the outer side of the legs. *See* 'FANCIES'. Petticoat breeches continued to be worn as the livery of Running Footmen until mid 18th c.

Petticoat Breeches, c. 1660

PEWTER BUTTONS

Hollow pewter buttons were patented in 1683. A common kind of coat-button worn by the working classes in the 18th c.

PHRYGIAN CAP

9th to end of 12th c. (M.) A descriptive term used from the 18th c. as applied to a pointed cap with the apex turned over slightly towards the front. A common form of headgear in early mediaeval times.

PHYSICAL WIG

2nd half 18th c. (M.) Worn by the learned professions, replacing the full-bottomed wig. It resembled a large form of Long Bob swept back from the forehead with or without a centre parting, and standing out in a 'bush' round the back of the head, often hanging below the nape of the neck. 'What wags call a lion or a pompey.' (1761, *Gentleman's Magazine*.)

Physical Wig, 1787

PICARDS

17th c. (F.) 'New shoes of the French fashion.' (J. Evelyn, *Ladies' Dictionary*.)

PICCADILLY COLLAR

1860's on. (M.) A shallow stand collar separate from the shirt, fastened to it by a button at the back of the neck and a stud in front. But in 1895 'a deep stand-fall collar cut so as to leave free passage for the band of the scarf'.

PICCADILLY WEEPERS

1870's and 1880's. (M.) Long combed-out whiskers fashionable in those decades.

PICKADIL, PICKARDIL, PICCA-DILLY

(1) 16th c. (M.) A tabbed or scalloped border, as a form of decoration;

commonly used for doublet skirts, said to be 'wrought in pickadils'.

(2) Late 16th c. to *c.* 1630. (M. and F.) The term was now transferred to a tabbed and stiffened support for the back of a ruff or collar ('band'). 'How his band jumpeth with his pecadilly.' (1617, Henry Fitzgeffery, *Notes from Blackfryers*.)

PICTURE HAT

1890's. (F.) A large wide-brimmed hat of straw or light material, brightly coloured and trimmed with strongly contrasting colours. Named from Gainsborough's portrait of the Duchess of Devonshire.

PIEDMONT GOWN, ROBE A LA PIÉMONTÈSE

C. 1775. (F.) A variation of the Sack-back gown, in which the box-pleats were detached from the back of the bodice so as to form a bridge from the shoulders to the hips where the pleats again merged into the overskirt.

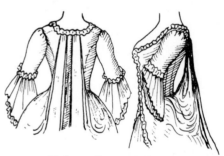

Piedmont Gown or Robe à la Piémontese, 1778

PIERROT

1780's to 1790's. (F.) A close-fitting, low-necked jacket-bodice with short basques. Generally worn with a flounced matching skirt ('petticoat'); for day wear.

PIERROT CAPE

1892. (F.) A ¾-length cloak with shoulder-cape and satin 'Pierrot' ruff.

PIERROT RUFF

1892. (F.) A ruff bordered with fur, on capes for outdoor wear.

PIFFERARO BONNET
1877. (F.) A felt bonnet with a blunt-pointed crown and narrow brim slightly turned up; feather trimming.

PIFFERARO HAT
1877. (F.) A hat with a short chimney-pot crown trimmed with an aigrette in front.

PIGEON-WINGED TOUPEE
1750's and 1760's. (M.) A toupee with one or two stiff horizontal roll curls projecting above the ears, with the foretop and sides smooth and plain. Worn with various queues. *See* AILE DE PIGEON.

Pigtail Wig, 1779

Piked Shoe, c. 1410

Pigeon-Winged Toupée or Aile de Pigeon, 1756

PIGTAIL WIG
18th c. (M.) A wig with a long queue spirally bound or interwoven with black ribbon and generally tied above and below with black ribbon bows.

PIKED SHOE, PEAKED SHOE
14th and 15th c's., mainly *c.* 1370 to 1410 and revived 1460 to 1480. (M. and F.) Shoes with long spear-like points extending beyond the toes; the same shape applied to pattens of the period. *See* also COPPED SHOES and CRACOWES.

Piked Shoes, c. 1470

PILCH, PILCHE
14th to early 16th c. (M. and F.) (1) A close-fitting over-gown lined with

Piked Shoes Early 15th c.

fur and worn by both sexes in winter and by the clergy for warmth in cold churches.

(2) From end of 17th c. on: 'now used for flannel cloth to wrap about the lower part of young children'. (1694, *Ladies' Dictionary*.)

PILLION
14th c. A hat or cap, mainly worn by ecclesiastics.

PILOT COAT
See PEA JACKET.

PINAFORE
19th c. A child's washable covering of the front of the frock to protect it from becoming soiled; similar to an apron.

PINAFORE COSTUME
1879. (F.) A tennis dress with a tunic having a bib-pinafore front and waistband, worn over a princess dress with a kilted skirt. The tunic made of fancy material such as Pompadour sateen.

PINCHBECK BUTTON
Used from 1770. The material an alloy of copper and zinc, invented by Christopher Pinchbeck *c.* 1700. Much used to simulate the more expensive gilt buttons.

PINKING, POUNCING
Late 15th to 17th c. (1) A form of decoration consisting of small holes or very short slits cut in the material or in the finished garment or shoes, and arranged so as to form a pattern. 'For one thousand and a halfe pynkes for a kyrtell . . .' (1580, Egerton MS.) 'This pair of shooes . . . pinckt, with letters for thy name.' (1600, Dekker, *The Gentle Craft*.)

(2) From mid 17th c. on. Pinking used in the modern sense of the word, an unhemmed border (i.e. with a raw edge) being cut in minute scallops or angles.

PINNER
(1) 17th to mid-18th c. (F.) The lappet of an indoor cap, the lappets being often pinned up.

(2) From *c.* 1680's. The term transferred to the indoor cap itself. 'A lady's headdress with long flaps hanging down the sides of the cheeks. . . . Some term this sort of long-eared Quoif by the name of a Pinner.' (1688, R. Holme, *Armourie*.) In the 18th c. the lappets were often omitted, the pinner being a flat circular cap with a frill.

(3) In the 17th c. the term was sometimes used for a TUCKER, *q.v.*

PINS
With the heads hammered on round the end of the shank; these were used until *c.* 1830 when replaced by the pin with head and shank in one.

PINSNET, PINSONET
16th c. Synonymous with PINSON.

PINSON
14th to end of 16th c. (M. and F.) A light indoor shoe, the earlier ones often furred. In 16th c. often worn with a protective overshoe. 'A pumpe or pinson to weare in pantofles'. (1599, Minsheu.) In 17th c. the term was being replaced by PUMP.

165

PIPED SEAMS

1820's on. (F.) A construction occurring first c. 1822 in muslin dresses and becoming a very general fashion in the 1840's; imitated in men's coats and waistcoats by narrow edging of cord (not true piping).

PIPES

17th and 18th c's. (M.) Small rolls of pipeclay used, when heated, for tightening the curls of wigs. *See* ROULETTES.

PIPING

Ornamentation by means of narrow cord enclosed in pipe-like folds along the seams of a garment.

PIPKIN, TAFFETA PIPKIN

C. 1565 to 1600. (F.) A small hat with a flat crown drawn in and pleated into a narrow flat brim; usually having a narrow jewelled hat-band and feather trimming.

PIQUE DEVANT, PICKDEVANT

1570's to 1600. A short pointed beard usually worn with a brushed-up moustache.

PIQUETS

1878. (F.) Ornamental sprays decorating evening lace caps worn by matrons.

PLACKARD, PLACART, PLAC-CARD, PLACCATE

Late 15th to mid 16th c. (1) MALE. A stomacher or chest-piece covering the V- or U-shaped gap of the low-fronted doublet or jacket.
(2) FEMALE. Mid-14th c. to *c.* 1520. The front panel or stomacher portion of a sideless surcoat, often embroidered or trimmed with fur.

PLACKET

16th c. on. (F.) A short opening or slit near the top of a woman's skirt or petticoat. In the 19th c. 'the opening at the back of a skirt or petticoat extending from the waist downwards, designed to enlarge the aperture made at the waistband to allow for passing the skirt over the head and shoulders'. (1882, *Dictionary of Needlework*.)

PLAIN BOW STOCK

1830's. (M.) A straight-sided stock of black silk with a bow in front.

PLASTRON

19th c. (F.) (Plastron, Fr. a Breast-plate.) The front panel of a bodice of a different colour and material from the rest of the bodice.

PLATED BUTTONS

18th c. (M.) The term usually denoted silver-plated as distinct from gold-plated, known as 'gilt'. Until *c.* 1750 the surface of silver was obtained by 'French plating'; later by 'Sheffield plating'. Very fashionable for men's coats.

PLATOFF CAP

1814. (F.) An evening cap of pale pink satin, the front scalloped; trimmed with a row of pearls and a pearl tassel from the crown. Named after the Cossack General attending the Peace celebrations in London in 1814.

PLEATED SHIRT, PLAITED SHIRT

1806 to 1870's. (M.) At first a day shirt with narrow vertical pleats down the bosom and no frill, the front closed by 3 buttons. From 1840 also worn with evening dress, the front being closed by ornamental studs.

PLEATED TROUSERS

See COSSACKS.

PLUDERHOSE

2nd half 16th c. (M.) A German and Swiss form of trunk-hose characterised by broad panes and wide gaps bulging with silk linings often overhanging the panes below.

PLUG HAT

C. 1830's on. (M.) American synonym for TOP HAT, *q.v.*

PLUMMET

17th c. A drop ear-ring. *See* PENDICLE. 'To clog the ear with plummets.' (1617, H. Fitzgeffery, *Satyres*.)

PLUMPERS

Late 17th to early 19th c. (F.) 'Certain very thin, round and light balls (of cork) to plump out and fill up the cavities of the cheeks.' (1690, J. Evelyn, *The Fop's Dictionary*.) 'Mrs. Button who wears cork plumpers in each cheek and never hazards more than six words for fear of shewing them.' (1780, Mrs. Cowley, *The Belle's Stratagem*.) 'Having been upset (carriage accident) Rosabella lost her plumpers.' (1825, Harriette Wilson, *Paris Lions and London Tigers*.)

PLYMOUTH CLOAK
17th c. (M.) A slang term for a cudgel or cane. 'With Plymouth cloaks in our hands.' (1677, Aphra Behn, *The Rover*.)

POCKET
From 15th c. on. (M. and F.) (1) MALE. Until mid 16th c. a small pouch independent of the garment and used for carrying money, etc.

From mid 16th c. A small pouch built into (*a*) trunk-hose from mid-16th c. (*b*) Into breeches from the end of 16th c. (*c*) Into coats from early 17th c., e.g.: 'The keys of my counting-house are in the left pocket of my coat'. (1633, W. Rowley, *A Match at Midnight*, Act 3.) Pockets becoming protected by flaps from *c.* 1690. (*d*) Into waistcoats 18th c. on.

See named varieties: BELLOWS, BREAST, CADDIE, CROSS, FOB, HIP, LONG, SALT-BOX.

A 'HIP-POCKET' (*q.v.*) has to be distinguished from a 'pocket on the hips', the former being in the back of the trousers, the latter being on the outside of a skirted coat over the hip region.

A 'pocket in the pleats'—i.e. at the back of the skirt of a coat with opening under a pleat—has to be distinguished from a 'pocket in the skirt', with its opening in the lining of the skirt.

A 'slash pocket' had a slit opening on the surface of a coat, the edges of the slit usually strengthened by welting.

A 'pocket in the seam' of a skirted coat meant a horizontal slit (not welted) in the waist seam, placed at the side; a common form of ticket pocket.

Pocket in the Pleats, 1806

(2) FEMALE. A separate article in the form of a small flat bag or a pair of such bags attached together by a tape. (18th c.) 'I keep in my pocket, ty'ed about my middle next to my smock.' (1701, J. Swift, *Mrs. Harris' Petition*.) These pockets, tied on round the waist under the dress, were reached through the placket hole. Those of the 18th c. were frequently ornamented with coloured needlework patterns. For the first twenty years of the 19th c. these tied-on pockets ceased to be worn, being replaced by the 'INDISPENSIBLE' (*q.v.*) carried in the hand.

A built-in pocket in the skirt, accessible through a pocket hole at the back, became usual *c.* 1840, when also a watch pocket was added, hidden in the folds of the bodice in front of the waist; a few years later this watch-pocket was transferred to the waistband.

The tied-on pair of pockets continued to be used when travelling and became known as 'railway pockets'.

A patch-pocket placed low down on the back of the skirt of Princess and Polonaise dresses in 1876 was a fashion welcomed by pick-pockets.

A novelty of 1899 was a pocket for the handkerchief placed in the lining of the skirt or in the border of the petticoat just above the hem.

POCKET HANDKERCHIEF
16th c. on. (M. and F.) *See* HANDKERCHIEF, and MOCKINDER. Elegant handkerchiefs were often carried in the hand for display, to mid 19th c. by women.

Men's handkerchiefs were always larger than women's, and in 19th c. often coloured (day only).

Mourning handkerchiefs: these in the Regency period might be entirely black; later white with a black border, its depth depending on the degree of mourning.

Materials: silk, linen, cotton; for display, lace.

POCKET HOOP
C. 1720's. (F.) Revived in 1770's. 'Hoops of the smallest size, commonly called Pocket-Hoops', were mentioned in the regulations at Bath Assembly Rooms, and again when the size of hoops was beginning to be reduced. E.g. Undress Fashions for July 1774: 'Light brown night gowns and coats (i.e. petticoats) with small pocket hoops . . .' (*The Lady's Magazine.*)

POINTED SLEEVES
See RAGLAN SLEEVES.

POINTS
15th to mid 17th c. (M.) Ties tipped with aglets and either functional or decorative. (1) Functional: for attaching hose, trunk-hose or breeches to the doublet; until 1630 for attaching detachable sleeves to the doublet, and for fastening the front of the doublet or jerkin.

(2) Decorative: used in bunches or separate bows to adorn male or female garments in 16th and early 17th c's.

Points with Aglets, c. 1650

POKE
A pouch or large bag. In the late 16th and early 17th c's. the term was synonymous with Pocket.

POKE BONNET, POKING BONNET
1799 to end of 19th c. (F.) A bonnet with an open brim projecting forward over the face. The term was applied to a large variety of styles, the 'poke' often very slight.

POKING STICKS
16th c. Sticks of wood or bone, heated, for setting the pleats of a ruff. By 1574 some were made of steel.

POKYS SLEEVES
See BAGPIPE SLEEVES.

POLICEMAN'S CAPE
1895. (F.) A cape cut in one piece from a circle.

POLISH BOOTS
1860's. (F.) Tall boots with pendant tassels and high coloured heels.

POLISH GREATCOAT
1810. (M.) A long, close-fitting coat, the collar, cuffs and lapels of Russian lambskin; closed by loops and frogs. Worn with evening dress.

POLISH JACKET
1846. (F.) A waist-length jacket with masculine revers and collar. Sleeves square and slit open to the

elbow along the inner side. Made of cashmere, lined with quilted satin and worn at the seaside or in the country.

POLISH MANTLE
1835. (F.) A knee-length mantle with pelerine-cape; of satin edged with fur.

POLKA
1844. (F.) A short shaped mantle or jacket with loose sleeves; made of cashmere or velvet lined with silk. An outdoor garment, a variety of the Casaweck.

POLO COLLAR
C. 1899. A starched white stand-fall collar, the fronts sloping apart.

POLONAISE, POLONESE
1770's to 1870's. (F.) (1) A dress with an overskirt bunched up behind and completely uncovering the under-skirt which was usually ankle-length or sometimes trained.

Polonaise, 1872

(2) In the 1750's the term was applied to a small hooded cloak.
(3) (M.) In 1773 a 'Polonese Frock' worn by gentlemen. In the 1830's the name 'Polonaise' was com-

monly used for a military Redingote, usually of blue cloth, as worn by civilians.

POLONAISE PARDESSUS
1840's. (F.) A short half-length Pardessus buttoned down the chest and then sloping away from the mid-line to reveal the dress. Some with a short, square pelerine-cape.

POLONIA, POLONY HEEL
17th c. (M. and F.) The high heel of boot or shoe which became fashionable in that century, causing the wearer to stagger in walking. 'Mounted Polonially till he reels. . . .' (1617, H. Fitzgeffery, *Notes from Black Fryers.*)

POLVERINO
1846. (F.) A large wrapping silk cloak, unlined, with or without a hood.

POMANDER
C. 1500 to 1690's. (F.) A receptacle of goldsmithry, containing perfume or ingredients thought to protect against infection. The form was usually a circular flat box or ball-shaped, with perforations. The pomander was suspended from the girdle in front. A variety of recipes for the contents were in use and these were loosely known as 'pomanders', e.g. 'make a pomander under this maner . . .' (1542, A. Boorde, *Dyetary of Helth.*) Pomanders were occasionally carried by Fops.

POMPADOUR
See POMPON.

POMPADOUR BODICE
1870's. (F.) A day bodice with a square opening over the bosom, tight elbow sleeves finished with deep frills. Common with polonaises.

POMPADOUR HEEL, FRENCH HEEL
1750's–1760's. (F.) A high slender heel, waisted and curving to a small base.

Pompadour Heel, 1750–60

POMPADOUR PARDESSUS
1850's. (F.) Of coloured silk, fringed, with demi-long sleeves; often hanging loose and fastened at the neck only. For summer wear.

POMPADOUR POLONAISE
1872. (F.) A polonaise of black foulard figured with large, brightly coloured flowers; worn with a plain skirt.

POMPEIAN SILK SASH
1860's. (F.) A wide black silk sash woven with mythological subjects; worn with a summer dress, generally a white jacket, bodice and coloured skirt.

POMPEY
See PHYSICAL WIG.

POMPON
1740's to 1760's. (F.) An ornament for the hair or cap. 'The ornament worn by ladies in the middle of the forepart of their headdress. Their figures, size and composition are

Pompon, 1741

various such as butterflies, feathers, tinsel, cockscomb, lace, etc.' (1748, *The London Magazine.*) Also ribbon. The word was short for 'Pompadour', which was sometimes used.

PONCHO
1850's. (M.) A D-B cape-like over-coat with very wide pagoda sleeves; also called a 'Talma'. (Not to be confused with 'Talma Cloak or Mantle'.)
1860's. (F.) A loose cloak ¾-length, buttoned from neck to hem; with small stand collar; full sleeves contracted at the wrist. The sleeves covered by a cape.

PONTIFICAL
See OUCH. 'A peyre of ouches other-wise call'd pontificalles of silver and gilt.' (1508, Will of Joan Hampton, Somerset Wills.)

PONYET, POYNET
(1) 14th to 16th c's. (M.) The fore-sleeve of a doublet and made of a different material. 'Doublet... with foresleeves of velvet called in those days poynettings of a doublet.' (1555, T. Marshe, *Institucion of a Gentleman.*)
(2) 17th c. (M.) 'Little bodkins' (1611, T. Cotgrave), worn with decorative points, *q.v.*

PORCELAIN BUTTONS
Patented 1785. A fashionable orna-ment on gentlemen's coats and waist-coats.

PORK-PIE HAT
1860's. (F.) A hat with a low flat crown of straw or velvet, with a narrow brim turned up close all round.

PORT CANNONS
See CANNONS.

PORTE-JUPE POMPADOUR
1860's. (F.) A belt with 8 suspen-ders, worn under the dress and used for hitching up the skirt when walk-ing.

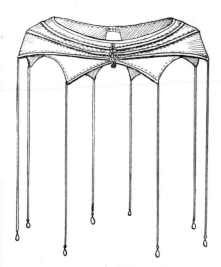

Porte-Jupe Pompadour, 1864

Porte-Jupe Pompadour in Action, 1864

PORTMANTUA
See CLOAK BAG.

PORTUGUESE FARTHINGALE
C. 1662 for a few years. (F.) A farthingale flattened front and back with great lateral expansion; a fashion brought over by Catherine of Braganza on her marriage to Charles II, but not adopted in England, the farthingale having ceased to be fashionable from c. 1630.

POSTBOY HAT
1885. (F.) A small straw hat with a high flat crown and a narrow brim sloping down all round. A plume of feathers in front. Worn perched on the top of the head.

POT HAT
See TOP HAT.

POUCH
12th to early 16th c. A bag or wallet slung from the girdle or attached to the belt of a gentleman, and generally worn with a knife or dagger stuck through the supporting strap.

POULAIN, POULAINE, PULLAYNE
1395 to 1410 and 1460 to 1480. A French term for piked shoes; term rarely used in England. See CRAKOWS.

POUNCING
See PINKING.

POURPOINT
See GIPON.

POWDERING JACKET, GOWN, or DRESS
18th c. (M.) A loose wrap-over coat, ankle length, or shorter when the term 'jacket' was used, worn to protect the clothes while the wig was being powdered.

PREGNANT STAY
1811. (F.) A corset enveloping the body from the shoulders to below the hips and elaborately boned, 'so as to compress and reduce to the shape desired the natural prominence of the female figure in a state of fruitfulness'.

PRINCE OF WALES' JACKET
1868. (M.) A loose version of the Reefer, with 3 pairs of buttons instead of 4.

PRINCE RUPERT
1896. (F.) A long figure-fitting coat of velvet or plush, worn with a blouse and skirt.

PRINCE'S SLEEVE

1830's. (M.) A sleeve with a pointed gore inserted into the seam at the wrist.

PRINCESS DRESS

1840's on. (F.) Also known as 'Agnes Sorel', 'Fourreau' and 'Gabrielle' dress. A dress made without a seam at the waist, the bodice and skirt being cut in one and the skirt gored. A style popularly associated with the Princess of Wales when *c.* 1878–80 it was very fashionable.

PRINCESS PETTICOAT or SLIP

1840's on. (F.) A petticoat (undergarment) with a bodice made in one with the skirt, without a seam at the waist. Popular in the 1870's and buttoned down the back. In 1882 it was buttoned down the front with box-pleats behind which were made to stand out like a bustle by means of tapes attached to side seams underneath and tied together.

PRINCESS POLONAISE or Fr. PETIT CASAQUE

1870's. (F.) A Polonaise dress made in the Princess style.

PRINCESS ROBE

1848. (F.) A day dress made in the Princess style without a seam at the waist, the skirt very gored. Trimmed all down the front with buttons and descending lines of ribbon on each side. Sleeves to below the elbows, open and worn with engageantes. A style rare at that date.

PRUDENT

End of 18th c. (M.) Thought to have been a winter wrap. 'Gentlemen begin to throw off their furs and prudents.' (1774, *Westminster Magazine.*)

PRUSSIAN COLLAR

19th c. (M.) A stand-fall coat collar, usually rather shallow, and the ends nearly meeting in front.

PUDDING SLEEVE, PUDDLE SLEEEVE

18th c. (M.) A large loose sleeve, especially of a clergyman's gown.

Princess Polonaise, 1876

'About each arm a pudding sleeve.' (J. Swift, *'Baucis and Philemon'*.) 'Recd. for altering a puddle sleve gown into a master sleve...' (1755. Domestic bills, Suffolk Record Office.)

PUFF

19th c. (M.) A gore of thin material filling in a V-shaped gap made in back of the waistband of breeches or trousers; the sides of the gap having lacing holes and a lace so that they can be drawn in to fit, producing a 'puff' between.

PUFFS or PULLINGS OUT

C. 1500 to 1650's. The pouches or bulges produced by the drawing out of material whether shirt or bright-coloured lining, through slashes or panes; a purely decorative device. *See* PANES.

PUG HOOD

18th c. (F.) The same as 'Short Hood', a soft limp hood made with pleats radiating from a central point at the back of the head. With or without a cape. Usually black with a coloured lining turned back to frame the face; tied under the chin with ribbon matching the lining when present. *See* LONG HOOD.

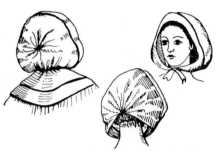

Pug Hood, early 18th c.

PULLINGS OUT
See PUFFS.

PULTNEY CAP
Mainly 1760's. (F.) A day indoor cap wired up in 2 curves with a dip in the centre over the forehead. 2 short lappets behind (optional).

PUMPS
2nd half of 16th c. on. (M. and F.) Shoes with thin soles and soft uppers (generally of Spanish leather) and flat heels. 'Pumps are shooes with single soles and no heels.' (1688, R. Holme, *Armourie*.) Dancing pumps were worn by children.
    19th c. Pumps with short quarters and low sides, trimmed with a ribbon bow until *c.* 1890; subsequently the tie was omitted. Worn with full evening dress.

PUNGE
Med. A purse.

PURFLE
16th c. 'The hemme of a gowne.' (1530, Palsgrave.) Also, a border of trimming.

PURFLED
16th c. Edged or bordered with trimming.

PURITAN BONNET
1893. (F.) A small flat bonnet without a crown, being oval or triangular with the point in front; trimmed with lace or an aigrette.

PURL
16th and 17th c's. (1) A pleat or fold of a ruff. 'I have seen him sit discontented a whole play, because one of the purls of his band was fallen out of his reach to order again.' (1618, N. Field, *Amends for Ladies*.)
    (2) A kind of silk, gold, silver or metal lace for edging neckwear.

PURSE
Med. on. At first a pouch, but from 14th c. a small bag without metal attachments, for carrying money, and capable of being cut. (Cutting of

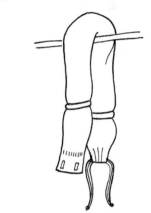

Purse, early 13th c.

Purse, early 17th c.

173

purses by thieves first mentioned 1362.) Throughout the centuries the shape changed and in 18th c. the knitted 'stocking purse' was popular. In the 19th c. metal fastenings became general, and from the middle of that century the 'sovereign purse', a metal tubular container with internal springs, holding sovereigns at one end and half-sovereigns at the other.

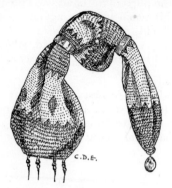

Purse called Stocking Purse, 18th c.

PUSSY-CAT BONNET
1814–18. (F.) A bonnet made of catskin, fashionable in those years.

PYGOSTOLE
1860's and 1870's. (M.) 'The least irreverent of names for the peculiar

M.B. coats worn by Tractarian curates.' A long form of surtout, worn with the M.B. WAISTCOAT, *q.v.*

PYJAMAS
1880's on. (M.) A sleeping suit, originating from India, a jacket and trousers of wool or silk in various colours and often striped; displacing the night-shirt. 'The doom of the sleeping shirt is written. Those possessed of any ought to preserve them carefully so that they can show to succeeding generations the wonderfully and fearfully made garments their forefathers slept in. . . . The pyjama sleeping suit is to take its place . . . of oriental origin, of silks, etc., generally striped.' (1897, *Tailor & Cutter.*)

PYRAMID STYLE
1845. (F.) A day skirt trimming of a series of horizontal bands—e.g. velvet—diminishing in width from below upwards.

PYRAMIDS
1858. (F.) Day skirt trimmings of triangular panels, the base below; the panels were of different colour and material from the dress and were sometimes alternating in two colours.

Q

QUADRILLE HEAD
Late 18th c. (F.) 'The ladies now wear the lappets to their gauze heads (i.e. caps) worked with aces of spades, hearts, diamonds and clubs, and call them Quadrille Heads.' (1792, *Northampton Mercury*.)

QUAIL-PIPE BOOT
Late 16th and early 17th c's. (M.) A high boot of soft leather which when worn fell into wrinkles in the leg portion and was considered very fashionable. 'A gallant that hides his small-timbered legs with a quail-pipe boot.' (1602, T. Middleton, *Blurt, Master-Constable*.) Compare: 'High shoes that are wrinkled like a quail-pipe'. (*C.* 1400, Chaucer, *Romaunt of the Rose*.)

QUAKER CAP
See JOAN.

QUAKER HAT
18th c. (M.) A three-cornered ('tricorne') hat with a fairly tall crown and an open cock. In the 19th c. this was replaced by a wide-brimmed round hat with a low flat crown.

Quaker Hat, 1858

crown, the material divided into segments; on a stiff head-band with or without a small vizor. 'Boys Satin Quarter'd Caps.' (Advert. 1757, *Norwich Mercury*.)

QUERPO, CUERPO
17th c. (M.) The term, from the Spanish word for 'body', used to denote a man without a cloak or upper garment; i.e. in body clothing only. (*See* UPPER GARMENT.) 'By my cloak and rapier, it fits not a

Quaker Hat, 1776   *Quartered Caps, 1830's*

QUARTERED CAP
Mid 18th to mid 19th c. (M.) Worn by boys, a cap with flat circular

gentleman of my rank to walk the streets in querpo.' (1647, Beaumont and Fletcher, *Love's Curl*.)

QUERPO HOOD
17th c. (F.) A plain soft hood.

QUEUE
Late 17th c. on. (M.) The pendant tail of a wig.

QUILLING
19th c. Small round pleats made in lace, tulle or ribbon lightly sewn down, the edge of the trimming remaining in open flute-like folds. Used for trimming dresses.

QUILTED PETTICOAT
(F.) (1) C. 1710 to 1750. Rare before or after. Worn as the skirt of a gown having an overskirt when the petticoat was exposed in front, but essentially part of the dress and not an under-garment.
(2) Early 18th c. and again from 1850. An under-garment, used in the 18th c., to distend the skirt and in the 19th c. mainly for warmth; made of satin or alpaca lined with wadding or eiderdown.

QUILTING
Runnings made in any material threefold in thickness, i.e. the outer or right side of good material, the under often of wadding, and the third a lining. The runnings made diagonally to form diamonds or a fanciful design, very common in the 18th c.

QUIZZING GLASS
18th and early 19th c's. (M. and F.) A monocle dangling from a neck-chain, a very fashionable accessory; in the 1820's the dandies often had the glass fixed in the head of their canes.

QUOIF, QUAFE
See COIF.

R

RABAGAS BONNET
1872. (F.) A small high-crowned bonnet with small brim turned up all round; the crown trimmed with feathers, flowers or ribbon drooping down behind. Tied under the chin with a large ribbon bow. Named from Sardou's political satire of that name (1871).

RAGLAN BOOT
Late 1850's. (M.) A boot of soft black leather reaching to mid-thigh and worn when hunting. Named after the Crimean general.

RAGLAN CAPE
1857 on. (M.) A loose sac-like overcoat, S-B, often fly-fronted; no vents. Distinguished by the cut of the sleeves at their insertion, first called POINTED SLEEVES, *q.v.*, and later, RAGLAN SLEEVES (a compliment to Lord Raglan of the Crimea). The sleeves of the Raglan cape were very wide at the hand; pockets without flaps. Commonly made of waterproof material.

RAGLAN COVERT COAT
1897. (M.) A Covert coat with Raglan sleeves.

RAGLAN OVERCOAT
1898. (M.) A revival of the Poncho (1850's) but with Raglan sleeves; full and long; side vents with 2 buttons and holes. Fly front fastening; generally of waterproof material, replacing the Mackintosh.

RAGLAN SLEEVE
1857 on. Instead of being inserted into a round arm-hole the sleeve was carried up into a point on the outer seam which ran up to join the collar seam, thus eliminating a separate

Raglan Overcoat, 1898

shoulder seam, through which rain was liable to percolate. *See* POINTED SLEEVE.

RAIL, RAYLE
Late 15th to late 17th c. (F.) A neckerchief folded and worn shawl-wise round the neck. *See* HEAD RAIL and NIGHT RAIL. 'The gathered piece of cloth which women throw about their necks when they dress them, is called a Rail.' (1678, *Phillips Dictionary.*)

RAILWAY POCKETS
1857 on. (F.) Flat bags with a side opening worn under the dress and tied on with tapes round the waist. With the crinoline dress this was designed to protect valuables from pickpockets.

RAILROAD TROUSERS
C. 1837 to 1850. (M.) The name given to trousers with vertical stripes, and soon applied also to trousers with horizontal and vertical stripes.

RAMILLIES WIG

18th c. (M.) Worn by officers of the Guards and those civilians affecting a military air. A wig with a long queue diminishing in size, of plaited hair tied with black ribbon bows above and below or sometimes only below. From 1780 the plait was sometimes turned up and bound by a ribbon tie at the nape of the neck or looped up high and secured by a comb to the back of the wig.

Ramillies Wig,
1733

RAMPOOR-CHUDDAR

19th c. (F.) A fine twilled woollen shawl from India; in various colours especially red and white. Fashionable in the second half of the century.

RANELAGH MOB

1760's. (F.) A gauze or mignionet handkerchief folded diagonally, worn over the head, the point behind; tied under the chin, the two ends then turned back and pinned behind and allowed to hang down the neck.

Copied from the silk handkerchiefs which market-women tied over their ears. A fashionable form of 'undress'.

RANELAGH or RATTLESNAKE TIPPET

C. 1775. (F.) Made 'of fine blond stuck with flowers'. (1775, *Lady's Magazine.*)

RATIONALS

1890's on. (F.) A popular name for the knickerbockers worn by the 'New Woman' when bicycling. *See* BLOOMERS.

RATTAN

17th and 18th c's. A cane made from an East Indian palm.

READY-MADE CLOTHES

18th c. on. (M.) Suits, ready-made, for the working classes were being advertised by the middle of the 18th

c., e.g.: 'Mens and Boys ready made broad and narrow Cloth Cloathes, Ratteen and Frieze Suits . . . Fustian Cloaths of all Sorts, Everlasting Waistcoats and Breeches, Velvet and Shag Waistcoats and Breeches, Russia Drab Frocks of all sizes, Fearnought and Duffle Coats and Waistcoats. . . .' (Advert., *Norwich Mercury*, May 13, 1758.)

READY-MADE DRESSES

18th and 19th c's. (F.) Ready-made dresses for the working classes were being advertised in muslin, calico and gingham, when those materials were popular at the close of the 18th c.

For the middle classes the custom began, in the 1840's, of buying the skirt ready-made with material sufficient for making the close-fitting bodice. By 1865 some ready-made morning dresses of materials, such as gingham or mohair, were being advertised but so long as the tight-fitting bodice remained the mode it was impossible to be 'in the fashion' without personal fittings by a dressmaker. However, by 1872 the ready-made dress (gallicé 'Confection') had become very popular.

REBATO

C. 1580 to 1635. (F.) (1) A white collar wired to stand up round the neck of a low-necked bodice to which it was pinned. 'Three rebateres of whight loome worke. Rebating wiers.' (1589, Essex Record Office.)

(2) In the 17th c. the term was transferred to the wired support of a collar or ruff. 'These great ruffes which are borne up with supporters and rebatoes.' (1631, Dent, *The Plaine Man's Pathway to Heaven.*)

REDINGOTE (1)

1830. (M.) Also called a POLONAISE, a greatcoat in military style, of blue cloth buttoned across with silk frogs. Sloping flapped pockets on the hips. Fur collar.

REDINGOTE (2)

(F.) (*a*) From *c.* 1790. A light overcoat fastening across the bosom.

178

(The bride) 'was all over Lace and then put on a plain gown and a silver Redingote for her journey'. (1799, *The Jerningham Letters*, ed. E. Castle, 1896.)

(*b*) From 1820; commonest from 1835 to 1860's. A variation of the Pelisse-robe, a gown derived from the pelisse; close-fitting and fastened down the front to the hem. In the 1840's the skirt was often *en tablier* and by 1848 the name had replaced 'Pelisse-robe'. By then the bodice and skirt were sometimes separate garments but previously the distinguishing features of the Redingote were that it should have the appearance of being a front-opening dress and be close fitting, with lapels.

(*c*) In 1890's the name was applied to an outdoor coat with fitting back and semi-fitting front.

Redingote, 1848

Redingote, 1821

REDINGOTE DRESS
1869. (F.) A day dress in the Princess style with a D-B bodice having

velvet revers or open over a waistcoat buttoned up to the neck.

REED HAT
1879. (F.) A hat of woven reeds capable of assuming any shape; worn for tennis or when bathing.

REEFER
1860 on. (M.) A very short D-B jacket with 3 or 4 pairs of buttons, low collar and short lapels; no back seam but short vents in the side seams; the fronts cut square. Sometimes worn as an overcoat. In 1890's it was unfashionable except when so worn. *See* PILOT COAT, PEA JACKET and YACHTING JACKET.

REEFER JACKET
1890's. (F.) An outdoor D-B jacket of blue serge, resembling the male garment.

REGATTA SHIRT
C. 1840. (M.) A striped shirt of cambric or 'Oxford shirting' for

Reefer, 1893

informal outdoor wear in the summer. The front without pleats or frill.

REGENCY HAT
C. 1810. (F.) A fur hat with turned-up brim and a gold hat-band.

REISTER CLOK, REITER CLOAK
1570's to 1670's. (M.) A full knee-length cloak sometimes with a flat square falling collar; sometimes caped. *See* FRENCH CLOAK.

RELIGIOUS PETTICOAT
17th c. (F.) Petticoats (i.e. skirts) embroidered with religious stories by Puritan women. 'She works religious petticoats....' (1631, Jasper Mayne, *The City Match.*)

RETICULE, RIDICULE
C. 1800 to 1820's. (F.) A lady's handbag, commonly lozenge-shaped or circular, of velvet, satin, silk, red morocco or made of coloured beads and drawn in with a running string. To contain handkerchief, purse, scent-bottle, etc., and much used in the absence of dress pockets in this period. *See* INDISPENSIBLE.

REVERS
14th c. on. In the 14th c. facings or borderings to a garment, generally of fur. Subsequently the term meant the turned-back edge of coat, waistcoat or bodice.

RHINEGRAVES
See PETTICOAT BREECHES.

RIBAND, RIBBON
(1) 14th to 15th c. The border of a garment.
(2) 16th c. on. A narrow band of silk or decorative material.

RIDICULE
See RETICULE.

RIDING BOOTS
Worn from mediaeval times on, but always long.

RIDING COAT
1825 to 1870's. (M.) A term applied to a short-skirted coat, the fronts slanting away from the waist level, with pockets in the pleats; later, flapped pockets on the hips were added. The corners of the skirts were rounded. The slope away

Riding Coat, 1853

from the midline in front steadily increased, starting above the waist level, producing a series having distinctive names:

1830's. Also called a MORNING WALKING COAT.

1838. Becoming called the NEW-MARKET COAT, *q.v.*

1850's. Becoming called a CUT-AWAY COAT.

1860's. Becoming the SHOOTING COAT, *q.v.*

1870's. Becoming 'the MORNING COAT—the latest adaptation of the old Newmarket Riding coat'. (*The Tailor & Cutter.*)

RIDING COAT DRESS

1785 to *c.* 1800. (F.) A dress resembling a greatcoat with deep collar and large lapels; buttoned all down the front and slightly trained; long tight sleeves. *See* GREATCOAT DRESS.

RIDING DRESS-COAT

1800's to 1860's. (M.) A coat with CUT-INS (*q.v.*) at the waist, resembling a shortened tail-coat with corners rounded. Worn for riding in town.

RIDING DRESS FROCK COAT

1820's. (M.) A frock coat with deep collar and large lapels; for wearing on horseback in town.

RIDING HABIT

18th and 19th c's. (F.) A costume specially designed for women riding (side-saddle) on horseback.

18th c. Consisted of coat and waistcoat modelled on the male garments, together with a skirt, called a 'petticoat', made without a train, until 1780 when a train was added. The RIDING COAT DRESS was also worn, *q.v.*

Riding Habit, 1715

19th c. At first a gown resembling the Riding Coat Dress and often trimmed with brandenburgs; subsequently the Redingote style, and by 1840 a jacket and long trained skirt became the usual mode.

1860. The skirt was now cut so as to fit over the pommel.

1870's. Trousers were worn under the habit skirt.

1890. Skirts began to be made without trains.

Riding Dress-Coat, 1852

181

Riding Habit, 1795

Riding Habits, 1894

RIDING HOOP

1720's. (F.) A small hoop sometimes worn on horseback. 'Riding habits £4:17:0. Riding Hoop-pettycoats, two, 17/-.' (1723, *Blundell's Diary and Letters.*)

RIGOLETTO MANTLE

1835. (F.) A knee-length mantle with pelerine cape; of satin edged with fur.

RIVELING, RILLING

12th to 14th c. (M. and F.) A shoe of raw hide with the hair on the outside. *See* BROGUES.

ROBE

(1) MALE. From the French meaning a gown; a term which came to be used for ceremonial wear. *See* GOWN.

(2) FEMALE. (*a*) A term rare in 18th c. unless for a French style of dress. 19th c. To signify a woman's dress consisting of an under-dress or skirt with an over-dress; the skirt being open in front and usually long behind, but the term was loosely used for a gown.

(*b*) A term sometimes used for an outdoor garment or pelisse which developed into the PELISSE-ROBE, *q.v.*

ROBE A L'ANGLAISE

1770's. (F.) A SACK-BACK GOWN (*q.v.*) with the pleats sewn down as far as the waist.

ROBE A LA PIÉMONTESE

See PIEDMONT GOWN.

ROBIN, ROBINGS

18th and 19th c's. (F.) Broad flat trimmings decorating a gown round the neck and down the front of the bodice, and sometimes continued down the borders of an open overskirt to the hem.

ROBIN FRONT

19th c. (F.) A bodice trimmed with robings descending from the shoulders to meet at the waist, forming a deep V-point.

ROCKET, ROCHET, ROKET, ROGET

(1) 14th and 15th c's. (F.) A woman's gown, usually of white linen. Also worn by the clergy.

(2) 16th and 17th c's. (M. and F.) A cloak of any colour. 'A scant cloak without a cape.' (1688, R. Holme, *Armourie*.)

ROGERIAN

16th c. (M.) A form of wig, not identified.

ROGUELO DRESS

1807. (F.) A bodice close fitting in front and trimmed with robings, but the back loose like a sack; a low collar with a triangular cape.

ROLL

15th c. (M.) The circular pad of the Chaperon (i.e. the hood converted into a cap or hat). The roll often of a different colour, e.g.: 'a hode of skarlet with a rolle of purpill felwet . . . item, I gret rollyd cappe of sangweyn greyred'. (1459, Fastolfe Inventory.)

ROLL, ROLLS, ROWLES

16th and 17th c's. (F.) Pads over which the front hair was turned to raise it from the forehead. 'The heare of a woman that is laied over her foreheade, gentyl women did lately calle them their rolles.' (1548, Elyot, *Dictionary*.)

ROLL COLLAR

19th c. The turn-over of a coat- or waistcoat-collar rolled in a curve, and without a notch between it and the lapel. After *c*. 1840 the name persisted for such a collar although laid flat.

ROLL FARTHINGALE

See Bum Roll.

ROLLIO

19th c. A trimming of material rolled into a very narrow tubular shape. *See* Rouleaux.

Roll Collar, 1829

Roll Collar, 1878

ROLL-UP BREECHES

Late 17th c. to mid 18th. (M.) Breeches worn with roll-up stockings and therefore buttoned and not buckled at the knee. 'Roule up breeches made buttoned downe the sides.' (1679, The Isham Accounts.)

ROLLUPS, ROLLERS, ROLL-UP STOCKINGS, ROLLING STOCKINGS or HOSE

Late 17th to mid-18th c. (M.) Long stockings drawn up over the knee of knee-breeches and then turned over in a broad flat roll. (Stolen) '½ doz.

pair of Roll stockins and 18 pair of short stockins'. (1697, *London Gazette*.)

ROMAN T BEARD

See HAMMERCUT BEARD.

ROQUELAURE, ROCULO, ROCCELO, ROCKLO

1st half 18th c. (M.) A knee-length cloak with a single or duoble cape-collar, and buttoned down the front ; a back vent for wearing on horseback. 'Lost, Blue Cloak or Roculo with brass buttons.' (1744, *Boston News Letter*.)

ROSEBERY COLLAR

1894. (M.) A white linen detachable collar, standing nearly 3″ high behind, the points in front rounded off. Named after the Prime Minister of the day, Lord Rosebery.

ROSES

C. 1610 to 1680. (M. and F.) Large decorative rosettes of ribbon or lace, often jewelled or spangled, mainly for shoes but also used on garters and hat-bands.

Shoe Rose, 1630

ROTONDE

1850's. (F.) A short circular mantle, generally of the same material as the dress. *See* TALMA MANTLE.

ROULEAUX

19th c. (F.) Lengths of material loosely puffed into a tubular shape, and used for trimmings of dresses, especially the bottom of skirts, in the 1820's.

ROULETTES

See PIPES and BILBOQUETS.

ROUND DRESS or GOWN

Late 18th to mid 19th c. (F.) A term indicating a dress with joined bodice and skirt, the latter closed all round (i.e. not open in front to expose an underskirt).

18th c. Occasionally made with a slight train.

19th c. No train, the term now meaning a dress without a train.

ROUND-EARED CAP

1730's to 1760's. (F.) Occasionally called a COIF. A white indoor cap curving round the face to the level of the ears or below. The front border with a single or double frill, generally with a small ruffle and 'pinch' in the centre. The back of the cap without a frill and drawn together by a running string. The back of the cap shallow, exposing much of the back-hair.

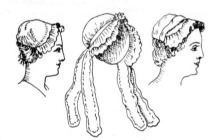

Round-Eared Caps, 1730–60

Side lappets, optional, and single or double, attached to the lower borders of the front frills. Single lappets were often pinned up to the crown or loosely tied under the chin, a style common with domestics.

From *c.* 1745 the frill at the sides widened and was starched, and later wired so as to stand out from the face as 'vast winkers'. At the same time the top of the cap narrowed with a small V-shaped pleat in the centre—'a pinched cap'. Lappets became less usual. Materials : cambric, lace, gauze, net, often with a bright silk lining. Trimming of ribbons, feathers or small artificial flowers.

184

ROUND HAT
Began to replace 'tricorne' in 1770's.

ROUND HOSE
See FRENCH HOSE and TRUNK-HOSE.
1550's to 1610. (M.) A form of trunk-hose padded and distended to resemble the shape of an onion.

ROUNDLET
A 17th-c. term for the ROLL (*q.v.*) of the Chaperon of the 15th c.

ROXALANE BODICE
1829 on. (F.) A low-necked bodice trimmed with broad bands of pleated folds across the top, sloping down to the centre and there meeting at an angle. The bodice always had a central bone down to the waist.

ROXALANE SLEEVE
1829 on. (F.) A bouffant sleeve for evening dress; i.e. puffed out above and below the elbow and there confined just above the bend by a fringed band. Worn with or without a manchette of white blonde lace.

ROXBURGH MUFF
1816. (F.) A swansdown muff caught in by a series of bands of white satin.

ROYAL GEORGE STOCK
1820's–30's. (M.) A stock of black Genoa velvet and satin, the satin sloping down across the velvet and tied in a bow in front.

Royal George Stock, 1830's

RUBENS BONNET
1872. (F.) A small bonnet with brim turned up on one side; trimmed above with a bow and a feather.

RUBENS HAT
1870's and 1880's. (F.) A hat with a high crown and brim turned up on one side; many variations worn.

RUFF
1560's to 1640's. (M. and F.) Revived on a small scale for women from 1740's to 1830, and again from 1874 to 1900. A circular collar of cambric, lawn or such-like material, in the form of a starched and goffered frill radiating from the neck; at first attached to the shirt collar band but by 1570 it had become a separate article.

It was usually closed all round for men, but also worn by both sexes with a gap under the chin.

The tubular folds were known as 'Sets' and formed by moulding them by means of 'Setting Sticks'.

C.D.F.

Ruff, 1586

The FALLING RUFF (*c.* 1615 to 1640. M. and F.). This was gathered without being 'set' into formal pleats, and was sewn to a high neckband from which it fell down to the shoulders.

The OVAL RUFF (*c.* 1625 to 1650. F.). A large closed Ruff set in formal tubular pleats spreading laterally over the shoulders. Generally worn with a large hat with spreading brim. This kind of ruff was never worn by men.

In the 17th c. women's ruffs sometimes had a small neck-frill of gauze or lace added to the inner border of the ruff.

185

Ruff, Oval, 1620

Ruffs were tied with tasselled BAND-STRINGS, *q.v.*

The SHORT RUFF was a small one favoured by PURITANS (M. and F.) in the 17th c.

RUFFLED SHIRT

18th to mid 19th c. (M.) A shirt with a goffered frill down the breast; worn for day and evening dress but from *c.* 1840 becoming gradually limited to evening only. The frill, which projected forward, varied in width up to 3".

RUFFLES

2nd half 16th c. to end of 18th c. (M. and F.) A somewhat rare term in the 16th c. (1) 16th and 17th c's. Synonymous with HAND RUFF, attached to the shirt sleeve. 'Very unseemly ruffles at their hands.' (1571, MS. Letter, Library of Corpus Christi College.)

(2) *C.* 1690 to end of 18th c. (F.) Deep flounces of lace or cambric, worn with elbow-length sleeves. Often multiple and scalloped.

(3) The term was also applied to the frilled front of men's shirts. 17th c. into 19th c.

RULLION

17th c. A shoe made of undressed hide.

RUMP, RUMP-FURBELOW, FALSE RUMP

1770's to 1800. (F.) A stuffed pad worn as a bustle, very prominent in 1770's and 1780's but later, if worn, very small. *See* CORK RUMP.

Rumps (Cork), 1787

RUNNING CLOTHES

Late 17th to mid 18th c. (M.) The clothing worn by a Running Footman. 'Francis Robinson, running footman . . . running clothes . . . drawers, stockings, pumps, cap, sash, and petticoat - breeches.' (1720, Wages, Duke of Somerset's Servants, *Gentleman's Mag.*, lxi.)

RUSSIAN BLOUSE

1890's. (F.) A loose tunic-bodice falling to the knees in front and a little longer behind, and confined at the waist by a belt.

RUSSIAN JACKET

1865. (F.) A short sleeveless jacket worn over a sleeved waistcoat.

RUSSIAN VEST

See GARIBALDI BODICE.

S

SABOT SLEEVE
19th c. (F.) A variation of the BOUFFANT, *q.v.* A single or double puffed - out expansion above the elbow, worn with evening dress from 1827 to 1836; and for day from 1836 to 1840, then becoming the VICTORIA SLEEVE, *q.v.*

SAC, SACK, SACQUE
16th, 17th and 18th c's. (F.) (1) 16th c. A loose gown, possibly for country wear. 'Frumpton's wench in the frieze sack . . . at the milking time.' (1599, George Peele, *Sir Clyomon.*)

(2) 17th c. Becoming now a more genteel garment. 'This strait-bodied city attire will stir the Courtiers' blood more than the finest loose sackes the Ladies use to be put in.' (1601, B. Jonson, *The Poetaster.*) 'My wife this day put on first her French gown call'd a Sac.' (1669, *Pepys' Diary.*) The exact nature of that garment is uncertain.

Sac-Back, c. 1745

(3) *C.* 1720 to 1780. Originating from France and there worn earlier. The essential feature of the Sack was the *Sack-back* consisting of two box-pleats, single, double or treble, stitched down on each side of the back seam from the neckband to the shoulders and thence left loose to merge into the fullness of the skirt below.

From 1720 to 1730 the gown fell loose all round, sometimes confined by a girdle.

From 1730 the bodice was shaped to the figure in front.

From 1750 the skirt was open in front revealing a decorative petticoat or underskirt, being part of the gown and not an under-garment. Stomachers with open bodices were common throughout.

From 1770's the box-pleats were sometimes sewn down to the waist as in the ROBE A L'ANGLAISE or cut loose as in the ROBE A LA PIÉMONTESE, *q.v.*

SACK-BACK JACKET
1896. (F.) A short loose jacket often edged with fur.

SAC OVERCOAT
1840's to *c.* 1875. (M.) A loose overcoat reaching nearly to the knees; 4 holes in front; cross-pockets with narrow welts at the front. Large sleeves wide at the bottom. Made with a whole back having a short slit at the bottom. The edges bound or double-stitched.

1860's. Buttoning high; very narrow collar and lapels; 3 or 4 holes in front; pockets optional. Some with velvet collar, lapels and cuffs.

SAFEGUARD
Late 16th to early 18th c. and in the West country in the form SEGGARD,

Sailor Blouse, 1894

Sac Overcoat, 1863

from 1745 to 1790. (F.) (1) An overskirt worn when travelling on horseback or riding, to protect from dirt or cold. Occasionally in the form of a large apron. Usually worn with a cloak or a jupe. *See* FOOT-MANTLE.

(2) (M.) A coloured stuff apron, also protective; worn by bakers, etc.

(3) 'A safe-guard, a sort of swathing band for a young child.' (1706, Phillip's *World of Words*, ed. J. Kersey.)

SAFETY PIN

The 'Danish Safety Pin' with wide protecting sheath covering the point came into use in 1878.

SAILOR BLOUSE

1890's. (F.) Worn by school-girls; a white linen blouse with blue cuffs and turned-over collar, imitating that worn in the Navy.

SAILOR HAT

1860 on. (1) (F.) 1860's. A crinoline hat with low flat crown and wide drooping brim; ribbon and feather trimming.

1880's: a Straw 'Boater' with slight variations in depth of crown and width of brim.

(2) (M.) 1880's. A popular form of headgear for small boys; a straw hat with wide évasé brim and ribbon round the base of the crown often embroidered with the fanciful name of a ship.

SAILOR SUIT

(M.) *C.* 1870. A popular style of dress for small boys, comprising at first a sailor's blouse worn with either a baggy pair of knickerbockers or DANISH TROUSERS (*q.v.*) with open bottoms and reaching just below the knees.

C. 1880 on. The suit had now developed a wide turnover white collar and the knickerbockers with legs closer-fitting. An alternative form was 'Jack Tar' trousers with bell-bottoms, ankle length. Usual accessories were a lanyard and 'boatswain's whistle'. Material: blue serge trimmed with braid. Worn with a Sailor hat.

188

Sailor Suit, 1890

SAILOR'S REEF KNOT TIE

1870's on. (M.) A popular form of tying the necktie, the central knot presenting vertical borders at the sides, the ends flowing loosely, often with a gap between. Most fashionable in the 1890's and rivalling the Four-in-Hand Tie *q.v.*

Sailor's Tie, 1890

SALT-BOX POCKET

C. 1790. (M.) A popular name for the rectangular flapped waistcoat pocket which had replaced the scalloped flap.

SANDAL

Med. to 16th c. (M.) A shoe consisting of a sole attached by straps variously arranged over the foot. Only worn by Monastic Orders and pilgrims; in the 17th c. also by Sovereigns at Coronations.

SANDAL-SHOES or SLIPPERS

1790 to end of 19th c. (F.) Thin-soled slippers cut low over the foot, with flat heels; tied on by criss-cross ribbons over the instep and round the ankle. For indoor and evening wear.

SANITARY BALL DRESS

1890. (F.) A ball dress with an under-bodice of cream or pink kid to protect the chest against the influenza epidemic of that year.

SANSFLECTUM CRINOLINE

1860. (F.) A washable cage-crinoline, the hoops covered with gutta-percha and others fitted with detachable flounce.

SANTON or SAUTOIR

1820's. (F.) A coloured silk cravat often worn with a small ruff which it served to support.

SARDINIAN SAC

1856. (M.) A loose S-B sac overcoat, the collar cut square, without lapels, full bell-shaped sleeves 'which are not used but allowed to fall loosely'. Fastened by cord and tassel in front.

SARPE, SERPE

15th c. (M.) A decorative collar worn round the neck and lying on the shoulders, as distinguished from a chain.

SASH

A term used from 16th c. on. (M. and and F.) A band or scarf of soft material, the ends tied but not buckled or otherwise fastened; worn round the waist or over the shoulder for ornamental purpose. Sashes were worn by men in 16th, 17th and 18th c's. with négligé. *See* Burdash. Worn by women in 16th and 17th

189

c's. with négligé but with dresses in 18th and 19th c's.

SASHUNES
Late 17th c. (M.) 'Stuffed or quilted leather to be bound about the small of the leg of such as have long heels, to thicken the leg, that the boot may sit straight and be without wrinkles.' (1688, R. Holme, *Armourie*.)

SAUCER-COLLAR
1898. (F.) The high, splayed-out collar of the day dress of that year.

SAUTOIR
See SANTON.

SAXON EMBROIDERY
See ENGLISH WORK.

S-B
19th c. (M.) Tailor's term for 'single-breasted', of a coat or waist-coat.

SCABILONIANS, SCAVILONES
2nd half 16th c. (M.) Apparently a new fashion of drawers, possibly of Muscovite origin. 'Nayler put off hys nether stockes and so bare foote and bare legged save his silke scavilones to the ankles—came in.' (1571, *Holinshed's Chronicle*.) See also BARREL HOSE.

SCALINGS, SCALING HOSE
2nd half 16th c. (M.) Apparently a new fashion in knee-breeches resembling Venetians. 'For a lace to drewe his skalinge hose together benethe the knee.' (1566, Sir P. Sidney's Accounts.)

SCALLOP
An ornamental border indented with segments of a circle so as to resemble the edge of a scallop shell.

SCALPETTE
1876. (F.) 'A false front of invisible net to which luxuriant tresses are attached.' Worn across the front of the crown of the head; an American invention.

SCARBOROUGH HAT
1862. (F.) A hat with a deep turned-up brim in front, sloping to a point behind; much worn at that time though considered by many to be 'rather vulgar'.

SCARBOROUGH ULSTER
1892. (M.) An Ulster with a cape and a hood but without sleeves.

SCARF
(1) Mid 16th c. on. (M. and F.) A narrow strip of material worn for warmth or show round the neck over the shoulders, or sometimes in 16th and 17th c's. worn by men baldrick-wise.
(2) 1830 on. (M.) A very large cravat spreading over the shirt front and usually held in place by a decorative tie-pin. By the end of 19th c. the term was being applied (by the trade) to any pendant necktie with ends much wider than the middle.

SCARF DRAPERY
1870's. (F.) Trimming consisting of material draped across the front of a skirt, the fold or 'scarf' trimmed with flounces, frills and ribbon variously arranged.

SCARF VEIL
See VEIL.

SCISSORING
See SLASHING.

SCOTCH FARTHINGALE
Late 16th and early 17th c's. (F.) Apparently of the wheel form. 'A Scottish farthingale . . . prithee fit, fit it. . . . Is this a right Scot? Does it clip close and bear up round?' (1605, Marston and Chapman, *Eastward Hoe*.)

SCRATCH BOB or SCRATCH WIG
1740 to end of 18th c. (M.) A bob wig, sometimes with one curl, covering only the back part of the head, the natural hair being brushed up over it in front. 'The one-curled Scratch.' (1764, *The Oxford Sausage*.)

Scratch Wig

SCRIP
Med. A pouch or wallet.

SCYE
19th c. (M.) Tailoring term for the curved lower segment of the arm-hole of a coat.

SEA CAP
Late 15th to early 17th c. (M.) Probably similar to a MONMOUTH CAP, *q.v.*

SEA COAT
Late 15th to end of 17th c. (M.) A lined and hooded coat mostly worn by seamen.

SEA-GOWN
Late 15th to early 17th c. A wrap worn at sea.

SEALSKIN COAT
1880's. (F.) Specially fashionable at that period, made full behind and from *c.* 1882 to 1888 trimmed with a broad flat bow over the bustle.

SEGGARD
See SAFEGUARD.

SEINT
Med. A girdle.

SELVAGE
Term used from 14th c. on. The edge of material so woven as to prevent unravelling.

SEMICIRCLED FARTHINGALE, or DEMI-CIRCLED
C. 1580 to 1620. (F.) *See* FRENCH FARTHINGALE.

SEMPSTRESS BONNET
1812. (F.) A bonnet tied on with very long broad ribbon strings crossed under the chin and then brought up to the summit of the crown and there tied in a bow.

SEÑORITA
1860's. (F.) A short muslin jacket shaped like a bolero, with elbow sleeves, worn over a dinner dress.

c.d.e.

Senorita, 1865

SERGE
19th-c. term. A kind of over-sewing often used on the raw edges of seams to prevent unravelling of the cloth. *See* also GLOSSARY.

SERPENT or DRAGON
18th c. (F.) A long hanging lock of hair rolled back upon itself. 'These serpents or dragons are seldom worn but at Court balls or by actresses on the stage.' (1768, G. Bickham, *The Ladies' Toilet.*)

Serpent, 1780

SETS
See RUFF.

SETTEE
Late 17th c. (F.) The double lappets of a lady's indoor cap.

SHADE
2nd half of 18th c. to early 19th c.; most fashionable in 1750's. (F.) A transparency of net or gauze or lace worn to 'shade' the bosom of a very low-necked gown. The shade sometimes had a small attached ruff at the neck.

SHADOW
C. 1580 to 1640. (F.) Similar to a BONGRACE (*q.v.*) but not part of a hood. Made of velvet, linen or lawn edged with lace. 'A French shadow of velvet to defend them from the sunne.' (1617, Fynes Moryson, *Itinerary*.)

SHAG-RUFF
17th c. (F.) A ruff with shagged or irregular outline.

SHAKESPERE COLLAR
1860's on. (M.) A shallow turn-over collar, the points projecting downwards onto the shirt-front.

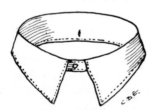

Shakespere Collar, 1890

SHAKESPERE VEST
1876–7. (M.) A waistcoat, S-B or D-B, of which the turn-over collar had wide points directed downwards, with a notch to a short narrow lapel.

SHAMEW
See CHAMMER.

SHAM HANGING SLEEVES
See HANGING SLEEVES.

SHAMS
See HALF-SHIRT.

SHAVING HAT
Early 18th c. (M.) A hat made of finely plaited wood-shavings instead of straw. ('Elizabeth Robinson, Shaving Hatmaker.' 1723, *London Gazette*.)

SHAWL
A term used from 2nd half of 18th c. (F., and also by M. in 1st half of 19th c.) A square or oblong wrap to cover the shoulders and upper part of the body, made in various sizes and materials. Used by women chiefly as an indoor accessory; by men as a protection in travelling by coach.

Made of wool, silk or cotton in mixtures or plain; the designs woven or printed or embroidered.

Varieties: (1) Cashmere. Originally made in Kashmir of the hair of the mountain goat. Made in England in 1818; in Edinburgh of Australian wool in 1826.

(2) French shawls imitating Kashmir patterns, in silk warp and woollen weft, from 1804. After 1815 of flowered silk with deep borders; up to 2½ yards square.

(3) Norwich shawls introduced in 1803 of silk warp and woollen weft in 'fill-over' patterns. Size a yard square.

(4) Paisley shawls from 1808, of silk or cotton warps and woollen or cotton wefts, or wholly of silk. By 1830 using 'Botany worsted' (i.e. Australian wool). Very fashionable in 1840's and 1850's, in 'pine pattern'. 'Reversible Paisley shawls', the pattern the same on both sides, introduced in 1860.

The size of the fashionable shawl increased with the expanding size of the skirt, reaching in the Crinoline period even to 12 feet long. *See* also RAMPOOR-CHUDDAR.

SHAWL COLLAR
1820's on. (M.) A term denoting a broad turn-over collar of a coat or waistcoat, continuous with the lapels, i.e. without a notch between. In the 2nd half of 19th c. the name was

gradually replaced by Roll Collar, *q.v.*

SHAWL WAISTCOAT
19th c. (M.) A term denoting (1) a waistcoat made with a shawl collar; (2) a waistcoat of material having a shawl design; (3) a waistcoat made from a shawl (rare).

SHELL
18th c. (F.) A loosely knotted curl of hair forming a bow.

SHIFT
18th c. (F.) The name in the 18th c. gradually replacing the older 'smock' for the under-garment known in the 19th c. as 'chemise'. Worn next the skin; of homespun, linen or cotton.

SHIP-TIRE
Late 16th and early 17th c's. Term denoting a high style of coiffure. 'Thou hast the right-arched beauty of the brow, that becomes the ship-tire.' (1598, W. Shakespeare, *The Merry Wives of Windsor*.)

SHIRT
Early Med. on. (M.) (1) Man's undermost garment worn next the skin until the introduction of the 'vest' *c.* 1840. A neckband appeared in the 14th c. and an upright collar in the 15th. Side vents added in the 16th and from then on such parts of the shirt as were exposed to view became variously decorated with embroidery, pleating, frills and lace. Coloured shirts for day wear, 19th c. *See* named varieties: Aquatic,

Shirt, 1795–1805

Corazza, Historical, Pleated, Ruffled, also Chitterlings, Half-Shirts.

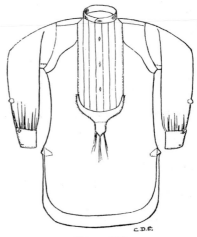

Shirt, 1866

(2) 1890's. (F.) A name applied to the summer blouse worn by women.

SHIRT-DRAWERS
1890. (M.) The shirt extended to reach the middle of the calf 'and the slits are in the centre of front and back instead of at the side; the shirt thus dresses the leg'. Thus drawers as a separate garment were not required.

SHIRT PIN
19th c. (M.) 'A shirt pin made of jeweller's gold wire.' (1825, T. Hook; *Sayings.*) Worn in the bosom of the shirt.

SHOE
Med. on. (M. and F.) A covering for the foot; usually a leather sole and leather or fabric upper, the shape varying greatly through the centuries according to function and fashion.

SHOE-BUCKLE
Mid 17th c. to *c.* 1790. (M. and F.) A Metal Buckle (*q.v.*), rectangular or oval in shape, attached to the front of the upper to hold the shoe in place; becoming highly ornamental and large *c.* 1770. 'Formerly, indeed,

the buckle was a sort of machine intended to keep on the shoe; but the case is now quite reversed, and the shoe is of no earthly use but to keep on the buckle.' (1777, R. B. Sheridan, *A Trip to Scarborough.*)

SHOE-HORN, SHOWING HORN
16th c. on. A semi-tubular implement with curved sides, of metal or horn, used to assist the foot to slip into a tight boot or shoe. 'A showing horn of iron.' (1576, City of Exeter Records.)

SHOE-LACES
19th-c. term. Laces for tying the sides of the uppers together; usually of braided mohair, but ribbons were used for women's shoes.

SHOE-ROSE
See ROSES.

SHOE-STRINGS
17th to mid-19th c. term. Ties for securing shoes; the strings commonly of ribbon. 'But he does not get his shoe-strings ironed.' (1825, Harriette Wilson, *Paris Lions and London Tigers.*)

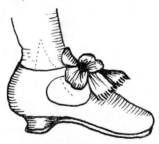

Shoe String, 1610

SHOE-TIE NECKTIE
1850's. (M.) A very narrow necktie 'not half so broad as a watch-ribbon', tied in a bow in front or passed through a ring, the ends dangling. See BYRON TIE.

SHOOTING COAT
1860's to 1880's. (M.) The name commonly given at that period to the Morning Coat.

SHORT HOOD
See PUG HOOD.

SHORTS
1820 to *c.* 1850. (M.) The name occasionally given to evening dress breeches.

SHORT SPATTERDASHES
18th c. These resembled Spats but were not then so called. They were chiefly worn by rustics.

SHOTTEN-BELLIED DOUBLET
1560's–1570's and 1600's. (M.) The short-fronted as opposed to the PEAS-COD-BELLIED doublet.

SHOULDER BELT
17th c. (M.) Previously the term used was BALDRICK, *q.v.* A diagonal belt passing across the body from the right shoulder to the left hip or lower, over the doublet, for suspending the sword or rapier. After 1680 it was gradually replaced by the waist belt and frog, worn under the coat and waistcoat; and in the latter part of 18th c. by the cut steel hanger with its chains.

SHOULDER HEADS, SHOULDER STRAPS
17th c. on. (F.) 'The straps passing over the shoulders and connecting the back to the front of a woman's dress.' (1682, R. Holme, *Armourie.*)

SHOULDER KNOT
C. 1660 to 1700. (M.) A bunch of ribbon loops, cord or lace sometimes bejewelled, worn as an ornament on the right shoulder. In 18th c. it became part of livery and 'a knight of the shoulder knot' meant a footman.

SICILIAN BODICE
1866. (F.) An evening dress bodice with a low square decolletage; attached to the bodice was a tunic in the form of 2 knee-length panels in front and 2 behind 'as four sash ends'.

SIDE
15th and 16th c's. The term then meaning 'long', e.g. 'side sleeves', 'side gown'.

SIDE BODY

1840's on. (M.) Tailoring term for a separate panel inserted into a coat from below the arm-hole down to the waist-seam, to give a closer fit.

Side Edge, 1861

Side Body, 1861

SIDE EDGE

19th c. (M.) A scalloped flap inserted into the back vent of a skirted coat and projecting from inside the pleat so as to resemble the flap of a narrow vertical pocket. This ornamental addition, unknown before 1810, first appeared then in some greatcoats; soon after 1820 frock coats and by 1829 day dress coats were often trimmed with side edges, which were revived in the 1840's and again in 1873 on some TOP FROCKS and OXONIANS. Side edges also survived in certain livery coats.

SIDELESS SURCOAT

C. 1360 to 1500; and as State apparel until c. 1525. (F.) A low-necked sleeveless and long over-gar-

ment, widely open at the sides from shoulders to hips, revealing the

Sideless Surcoat, 14th c.

195

sleeves and bodice of the kirtle. The front panel variously decorated was known as the PLACKARD, *q.v.*

SIDE PIECES
19th c. (F.) These in women's coats correspond to 'SIDE BODIES' in men's.

SILK HAT
1797 on. (M.) Invented by John Hetherington, a London haberdasher, and first worn by him on January 15, 1797, thereby provoking a riot; for which he was charged 'with a breach of the peace for having appeared on the Public Highway wearing upon his head a tall structure having a shining lustre and calculated to frighten timid people'. (*St. James' Gazette*, January 16, 1797.) This rival to the beaver hat became the top hat, the supreme headgear of the Gentleman from *c.* 1830 on; its surface of silk with a satin-like gloss on a felting of rabbit hair.

SIPHONIA
1850's and 1860's. (M.) A long weather-proof overcoat. The 'Pocket Siphonia' was a short thin variety capable of being rolled up and carried.

SKELETON SUIT
C. 1790 to *c.* 1830. (M.) A boy's suit consisting of a tight jacket having 2 rows of buttons on the front ascend-

Skeleton Suit, c. 1820

ing over the shoulders; ankle-length trousers buttoned to and over the jacket round the waist. Often of nankin. Trousers made with split falls.

SKIN-COAT
16th c. (M.) A leather jerkin worn by peasants and shepherds.

SKIRT
17th c. on. (1) MALE. That part of a man's coat below the waist; varying greatly in length according to the fashion of the day.
  (2) FEMALE. Very rarely applied before the 19th c. The lower part of a woman's dress hanging from the waist. Until the 19th c. the term used was 'PETTICOAT', (*q.v.*) For named varieties *see* under distinctive titles.

SKIRT RUFF
1880's. (F.) A thick ruching of material attached to the inside of the hem of a day skirt to make it stand out.

SKULL-CAP
From 17th c. on. (M.) A round-topped or flat cap fitting the head; worn as a NIGHT-CAP (*q.v.*) or in the 19th c. as a smoking-cap.

SLAMMERKIN, or TROLLOPEE
C. 1730 to 1770. (F.) A loose unboned morning gown with a trained sack-back and short petticoat (i.e. under-skirt). As négligée it could be worn without a hoop.

SLAP-SHOE
17th c. (F.) A mule, generally high-heeled. 'Slap shooes or Ladies shooes are shooes with a loose sole.' (1688, R. Holme, *Armourie*.)

SLASHING or SCISSORING
C. 1480's to 1650's. (M.) The making of slits of varying lengths in any part of a garment, as a form of decoration. The slashes were symmetrically arranged and the gaps filled in by pulling out puffs of a white under-garment, such as the

shirt; or, after 1515, of a bright lining
of a contrasting colour.

SLASH POCKET
19th c. (M.) A horizontally cut
pocket without a covering flap, in a
man's coat.

SLAVIN, SCLAVEYN, SCLAVIN
Late 13th to end of 15th c. A pil-
grim's mantle.

SLEEVED WAISTCOAT
C. 1660's to 1750's. (M.) *See*
WAISTCOAT.

SLEEVE HAND
17th-c. term. The open end of a
sleeve through which the hand is
thrust, whether the sleeve ends at the
wrist or higher up.

SLEEVELESS SPENCER
1800–1. *See* SPENCER.

SLEEVE STRING
See CUFF STRING.

SLEEVE TONGS
1890 on. (F.) Ornamental metal
tongs for drawing down the large
dress sleeves through the sleeves of
the jacket or overcoat.

SLING-DUSTER
1886. (F.) A Dust Cloak with sling
sleeves; often of silk in black and
white checks.

SLING SLEEVE
1885. (F.) A sleeve made from the
cape of a dust-cloak or mantle, the
cape being attached horizontally on
each side just above waist level with
an arm-hole above, supporting the
arm as if in a sling.

SLING-SLEEVE CLOAK
See BERNHARDT MANTLE.

SLIP
(1) 1888 on. (M.) A narrow under-
waistcoat of white piqué, fastened
inside the over-waistcoat with the
edge protruding as a white border;
correctly worn only with a MORNING
COAT. A fashion introduced by the
Prince of Wales.

Sling-Duster, 1889

(2) 17th c. on. (F.) An under-
garment serving as a foundation to a
dress especially when the latter is of
semi-transparent material. (To a
woman for) 'woorking slips for my
Lady 2/'. (1620, Lord William
Howard of Naworth, *Household Books*.)
In the 18th c. the term used for a
kind of corset-cover. 'Mrs. Lawson's
loose slip altered and made fit to the
new stays.' (1756, The Lawson
Family, *Domestic Accounts*.)

SLIPPER
16th c. on. (M. and F.) The word
'Slype-Shoe' used by Anglo-Saxons.
A generic name of a light form of low
shoe easily slipped on and off; generally with short uppers. But the word
'Shoe' was frequently used for slipper
thus defined, until the 19th c.

SLIP-SHOE
16th to mid-18th c. (M.) A mule
with a flat heel. 'They use a maner

197

of slippe-shoes that may be lightly putte of and on.' (1555, Watreman, *Fardle of Facions*.) The term 'slip-shod' when first coined *c.* 1570 meant the wearing of slip-shoes in which the wearer had to walk with a shuffling step.

SLIT
(1) 13th c. (F.) A pocket.
(2) 14th c. on. An opening in a garment.

SLIT POCKET
19th c. (M.) A vertically cut pocket in a coat or overcoat.

SLIVINGS, SLIVERS, SLIVES, SLEEVINGS
Late 16th c. and early 17th c. Wide breeches. *See* SLOP.

SLOP
(1) Late 14th and early 15th c. (M.) A short jacket worn over a doublet.
(2) Late 15th c. (M. and F.) A slipper.
(3) 1st half of 16th c. (M. and F.) A cloak or a nightgown. 'Sloppe—a nightgown.' (1530, Palsgrave.)
(4) Late 16th and early 17th c. (F.) A woman's cassock. 'A slope is a morning cassock for Ladyes and gentill Women, not open before.' (Late 16th c. Book of Precedence, Q. Elizabeth's Academie.)
(5) 2nd half of 16th and early 17th c's. (M.) This was the principal use of the word, namely to denote very wide knee-breeches, also called 'Slivings'. The term was also used occasionally for paned trunk-hose, especially the voluminous styles, e.g. PLUDERHOSE, *q.v.*
The official name—Great Sloppes —was used in various Sumptuary regulations forbidding tradesmen to wear such garments. Thus : 'Richard Bett, taylor, uses and has his calligas (i.e. footwear) with great sloppes contrary to the proclamation and form of the Statute. Fined 4d.' (October 1565, Essex Sessions Records.) 'A German from the

waist downwards, all Slopes.' (1599, W. Shakespeare, *Much Ado about Nothing*.) 'In a pair of pain'd (paned) slops.' (1600, B. Jonson, *Cynthia's Revels*.)
See also SMALL SLOPS for a similar restriction affecting University students, but the date of the latter— 1585—suggests a reference to knee-breeches while the date—1565—of the Essex Sessions Record suggests a reference to bombasted trunk-hose, not to breeches.
(6) Late 18th and early 19th c's. (M.) Name often used for the labourer's Smock. '. . . Wearing a light-coloured Coat, a Waistcoat and a Slop betwixt them and a pair of leather breeches.' (1774, *Norwich Mercury*.) 'A light half-straight coat over a brown slop and brown fustian breeches.' (1815, *Bury and Norwich Post*.)

SLOP-HOSE
15th to 18th c. (M.) Sailors' breeches. 'A sort of wide-kneed breeches worn by seamen.' (1736, *Bailey's Dictionary*.)

SLOPS
19th c. Old clothes.

SLOUCH HAT
18th and early 19th c's. (M. and F.) A hat with a flopping or uncocked brim.

Slouch Hat, 1805

SMALLCLOTHES
1770 to mid 19th c. (M.) A euphemism for breeches.

SMALL FALLS, SPLIT FALLS
See FALLS and SPAIR.

SMALL SLOPS
C. 1585 to c. 1610. (M.) Short breeches with open legs not covering the knees. '. . . Nor to weare anye Slop but the plaine small Slop, such as is not to be lett downe beneathe the knee. . . .' (Regulations for the apparel of University students at Cambridge in 1585.)

Small Slops, 1605

SMOCK
Anglo-Saxon term used to the end of 18th c. (F.) A woman's undermost garment worn next the skin. From late 13th to 17th c. fashionable smocks were often embroidered in gold or coloured silks.

17th c. With large balloon sleeves edged with ruffles, and in 18th c. slightly bell-shaped until c. 1740 when the ruffled border ceased to be visible.

At various times the materials used were: Linen, cambric, holland, occa-

sionally silk; for the poorer classes usually lockeram. *See* SHIFT.

SMOCK-FROCK
(19th-c. term) or merely SMOCK. (1) 18th and 19th c's. (M.) A loose gown of homespun or cotton, about knee-length; some with a 'sailor collar'; some made with a yoke. Generally smocked or gauged in front in various patterns associated with the locality. Worn by agricultural labourers.

Smock-Frock, 1868

(2) 1880's. (F.) An informal garment worn by women influenced by the Aesthetic Movement. 'No artistic dresser would be without a Smock cut exactly like a farm labourer's, with square turned-down collar, gatherings front and back, gathered full sleeves, worn over a habit shirt, and looped up over an under-skirt with a belt at the waist.' (1880.)

SMOCK PETTICOAT
17th c. (F.) An under-petticoat. '2 smock petticoats of worsted.' (1627, Lismore Papers.)

SMOCKING

1880's and 1890's. (F.) A form of needlework producing honeycomb ornamentation of which the basis is close gathers.

SMOKING JACKET

1850's on. (M.) A short round jacket, S-B or D-B, of velvet, cashmere, plush, merino or printed flannel, lined with brightly coloured material and commonly ornamented with brandenburgs, olives or large buttons.

SNAIL BUTTON

18th c. A covered button trimmed with French knots. Used on men's coats and waistcoats.

SNAKE

17th c. (M.) The name commonly given to Love Locks, (q.v.) 'The yard long snake he twirls behind.' (1676, J. Dryden's Epilogue to Etherege's *The Man of Mode*.)

SNOSKYN, SKIMSKIN, SNOW-SKIN, SNUFKIN, SNUFTKIN

Late 16th and early 17th c's. (F.) A small muff for the hands.

SOCKS

8th c. on. (M. and from 16th c. also F.) (1) From A.D. 725 to end of 16th c. the name was sometimes applied to a slipper.

(2) A short stocking. In mediaeval period it was worn with footless hose. In the 16th c. it was often worn with boot hose and stirrup hose.

From 1790 worn with pantaloons and in the 19th c. with trousers. Socks were kept up, from c. 1890, by elastic suspenders.

SOCK SUSPENDERS

See Suspender (2).

SOLED HOSE

Saxon and 13th c. to end of 15th c. (M.) Stockings of thick wool or thin leather, with leather sole attached, and worn without shoes.

In 15th c. Long-Stocked Hose (q.v.) joined above forming tights, might also be soled with leather.

SOLFERINO

1860. One of the two first aniline dyes used for dress material; corresponding to the modern 'Fuchsia' colour. Named after the battle (June 1859) in the Franco-Austrian War. *See* Magenta.

SOLITAIRE

(1) 1730's to 1770's. (M.) A black ribbon worn over a stock and usually with a bag-wig. A broad solitaire was draped round the neck and either tied in a bow under the chin or tucked into the shirt-front, or pinned into place, or loosely knotted and allowed to dangle. A narrow solitaire was worn close and tied in a stiff bow in front.

(2) 1835. (F.) A narrow coloured scarf worn round the neck, loosely knotted in front, with the ends hanging to the knees. Worn with a white day dress.

(3) 19th c. The name given to a single gem set in a brooch or tie-pin.

SORTI, SORTIE

Late 17th c. (F.) 'A little knot of small ribbon peeping out between the pinner and the bonnet.' (1690, J. Evelyn, *Mundus Muliebris*.)

SORTIE DE BAL

1850's to 1870's. (F.) An evening hooded cloak, generally of silk, satin or cashmere, with a quilted lining.

SOUFFLET SLEEVE

1832. (F.) An evening dress sleeve very short with full puffs vertically arranged.

SPAIER

Med. on. A term used for any vertical slit in a garment.

SPAIR

1840's on. (M.) A name sometimes given to the 'falls' of breeches. 'The Spair or Fall-down, called by some erroneously, the Fold.' (1843, J. Couts.) *See* Falls.

SPANGLES

Late 15th c. on. Small discs of shining metal, used as a trimming.

In 16th c. on the apparel of both sexes and on hats and stockings.

In 17th c. on garters, pantofles and shoe roses.

In 18th c. on men's coats and women's fans.

In late 19th c. occasionally on women's bonnets, and on evening dresses.

SPANISH BREECHES, SPANISH HOSE

1630 to 1645; revived 1663–70. (M.) High-waisted, long-legged breeches. Somewhat full in the seat with a few pleats into the waistband, the legs narrowed down the thighs to end below the knees, where they were either closed by ribbon rosettes or bows, or left open to overhang the stockings; the margins usually trimmed with ribbon bows. A trimming of braid or buttons down the outer side of the leg. The revived version, as described by R. Holme (1688, *Academie of Armourie*). '. . . are stret and close to the thigh and are buttoned up the sides from the knee with about 10 or 12 buttons, anciently called Trowsers.'

Spanish hose were hooked to the doublet lining and closed by buttons, not concealed by a fly.

SPANISH CLOAK

16th and 17th c.'s. (M.) (1) A short hooded cloak.

(2) 1836 on. (M.) A short round evening cloak shaped to the shoulders and lined with a bright-coloured silk.

SPANISH FARTHINGALE

C. 1545 to 1600. (F.) An underskirt distended by circular hoops of rushes, wood, wire or whalebone, and so disposed as to produce a funnel-shaped, domed or bell-shaped skirt. Some farthingales had a single hoop at the hem only. The under-skirt itself was made of mochado, fustian, buckram or woollen stuff; the more costly ones of silk or velvet.

SPANISH HAT

1804–12. (F.) A large hat of velvet, satin or sarcenet, the brim evasé, trimmed with feathers. For evening or promenade dress.

Spanish Hat, 1812

SPANISH JACKET

1862. (F.) A short outdoor jacket fastened down the chest in front and then sloping away to the back which ended at waist-level, with or without a small basque.

c.d.e.

Spanish Hose, 1635–40

SPANISH KETTLEDRUMS

1555 to 1570's. (M.) Colloquialism for TRUNK-HOSE, *q.v.*; in particular for the 'round hose' style.

SPANISH SLEEVE, or SLASHED SLEEVE

1807 to 1820. (F.) A short evening dress sleeve, puffed at the shoulder and slashed at the sides over a silk lining.

SPATS, or SPATTS

19th c. (M.) 'A small sort of spatterdashes that reach only a little above the ankle; called also half-gaiters.' (1802. *James' Military Dictionary.*)

Buttoned on the outer side. Not adapted for civilian use until mid 19th c. In 1860 Spats were worn with trousers and made of the same material. (Gaiters were similarly worn from *c.* 1805.) By 1878 they were fashionable with the Morning coat but incorrect with Frock coat until 1893, and made of box-cloth or canvas cloth (white, grey or fawn).

Spat, 1890

SPATTERDASHES

1670's on. (M.) Leggings of leather, canvas, cloth or cotton, generally reaching above the knee and laced, buckled or buttoned down the outer side. In the 18th c. there was sometimes an extension over the foot and a stirrup strap beneath. 'A sort of light boot without soles.' (1736, *Bailey's Dictionary.*)

SPENCER

(1) 1790 to *c.* 1850. (M.) A short waist-length jacket with a stand-fall collar or roll collar and cuffed sleeves; buttoning down the front, and worn out of doors as a protection for the chest, generally in the country or by sportsmen. 'Young Gentleman's Spencer or Tunic suit from £1:15:0.' (1838, *The Globe*, advert.)

Spencer, 1834-6

(2) 1790 to 1820's. (F.) A short jacket ending at the waist-level and worn as an outdoor garment or indoors for evening wear, and then very ornamental and often sleeveless.

The form followed the fashion of the dress-bodice with which it was worn. *See* CHINESE SPENCER and CANEZOU.

Spencers of 1815

(3) Late 19th c. (F.) A flannel or knitted sleeveless spencer was worn under the jacket for extra warmth by the elderly or infirm.

SPENCER CLOAK

1804. (F.) A cloak of worked net with short elbow sleeves.

SPENCERETTE
1814. (F.) A Spencer 'tight to the shape', closed over the bosom but the neck cut low and edged with a lace frill.

SPENCER WIG
18th c. (M.) A kind of wig worn in the first half of 18th c. Sometimes referred to simply as a 'Spencer'.

SPERE, SPEYER
Late 16th and 17th c's. The opening of a garment.

SPIKED SHOES
1861. (M.) Shoes with spikes permanently attached to the soles; for cricket. Patent, March 1861.

SPIT-BOOT
18th to mid 19th c. (M.) A boot combining shoe and gaiter, closed down the outer side by a series of interlocking fastenings, the last of which, at the ankle, was in the form of a sharp iron 'spit' or spike which was inserted into an iron socket. Mainly worn in the North. 'A pair of spit-boots.' (1707, N. Blundell's Diary.)

SPLIT FALLS, SMALL FALLS
See Falls.

SPLYTER-HAT, SPLINTER HAT
16th c. A straw hat made of braided strips of split straw called 'splints' as opposed to tubular whole straws.

SPOON BACK
1885. (F.) Name given to the circular folds of drapery at the back of the tunic (overskirt) of a woollen walking dress of the period.

SPOON BONNET
1860 to 1864. (F.) A bonnet with a narrow brim close to the ears, then rising up vertically above the forehead in a spoon-shaped curve, and sloping down behind to a small crown edged with a 'bavolet'.

SPRING BOOTS
1776. (M.) Made with a whalebone spring inside the back seam to check wrinkling.

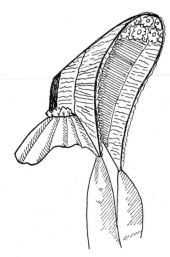

Spoon Bonnet, 1863–4

SQUARE
(1) 16th and 17th c's. (F.) A form of head-dressing. 'As women weare on their heads being sicke.' (1611, G. Florio, A Worlde of Wordes.)
(2) 16th to 18th c. (F.) The panel of embroidered linen or cambric forming the breast of the woman's shift.

SQUARE HOOP
See Oblong Hoop.

STALK BUTTON
1st half 18th c. A button with the shank made of catgut.

STAND COLLAR
19th-c. term. (M.) An upright collar of coat or waistcoat, made without a turn-down or 'leaf'.

STAND-FALL COLLAR
19th-c. term. (M.) A turned-over collar, the inner layer called the 'stand', the outer or turned-over part the 'leaf' or 'cape'.

STANDING BAND
See Band.

STARCH
First used in England c. 1560's, for stiffening ruffs, collars, etc. It was sometimes coloured yellow or blue; other colours were used abroad.

203

STARCHER

19th c.   (M.)   A starched CRAVAT, *q.v.*

STARTUP, STARTOP, STYRTOP, STERTOP

Earliest ref. 1517, but mainly late 16th and early 17th c's. (M. and sometimes F.) A high shoe reaching above the ankle, sometimes laced or buckled up, sometimes loose-fitting and then called a 'BAGGING SHOE', *q.v.* Worn by country folk and for sport; usually made of raw leather. A woman's startup might be more elegant. 'Her neat, fit startups of green velvet bee flouresht with silver.' (Late 16th c. Sylvester's trans. of Du Bartas.)

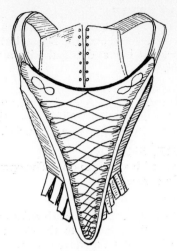

Stays, 18th c.

STATUTE CAP

1571 to 1597. (M.) A knitted woollen cap which the Statute of 1571 (repealed 1597) ordered all persons below a certain rank to wear on Sundays and Holy days on pain of a fine of 3/4. 'Better wits have worn plain statute caps.' (1588, W. Shakespeare, *Love's Labour's Lost.*)

STAY HOOK or CROCHET

18th c. (F.) A small hook attached to the front of the stays from which was hung the watch. They were often decorative. 'Silver stay hooks with fine stones.' (1743, *Boston Gazette.*) They were sometimes known as Breast Hooks. 'Gold and stone sett Breast Hooks. . . .' (1762, *Boston News Letter.*)

STAYS

The earlier name for CORSETS, *q.v.*

STEEPLE HEAD-DRESS

See HENNIN.

STEINKIRK

C. 1692 to 1730; unfashionably to c. 1770. (M. and F.) A long cravat generally edged with lace, loosely knotted under the chin and the ends either threaded through a buttonhole of the coat or pinned to one side, or sometimes left dangling. A fashion

Steeple Head-Dress, late 15th c.

and name derived from the battle of Steinkirk, August 1692.

Women wore the Steinkirk with a riding habit.

STICKING PLASTER DRESS

1893. (F.) A name given to a tight black satin evening dress of 1893.

STIFFENER

See CRAVAT.

STIRRUP HOSE, STIRRUP STOCKINGS

17th c. (M.) Long over-stockings with an under-instep strap instead of a sole; worn as a protection to finer stockings when riding; serving the same purpose as boot hose.

STOCK, STOCKS

(1) *C.* 1400 to 1610. (M.) The leg portion of hose (appearing as tights) and after 1550 the leg portion of TRUNK-HOSE (*q.v.*) and often called 'nether stocks', the seat part being known as 'upper' or 'overstocks' or 'the breech', before *c.* 1550.

From *c.* 1590 'stock' was occasionally used for STOCKING, *q.v.*

(2) *C.* 1735 to end of 19th c. (M.) A high made-up neckcloth often of

linen or cambric, stiffened with a frame of pasteboard and buckled or tied behind. The black military stock of the 18th c. was often adopted by foppish civilians and from 1820 was correct wear at Court by civilians.

A Hunting Stock of cellular cloth, tied twice round the neck and worn without a collar, became fashionable from *c.* 1890 for hunting and riding.

STOCK BUCKLE

18th to mid 19th c. (M.) The buckle fastening the stock at the back of the neck. In the 18th c. although often concealed by the wig the buckle was often ornamental, being plated, or of gold, silver or pinchbeck worked or plain, or set with jewels (real or sham).

STOCK-DRAWERS

17th c. A rare term meaning stockings.

STOCKINGS

2nd half 16th c. on. (M. and F.) A close-fitting covering for the foot and leg. Although worn from Saxon times they were called by other names (hose, nether stocks, stocks) until the above date. 'For two lambes skynes to make a paier of stockings 16d. For silke to stitche the clockes 2d. For cloth to sole them 2d.' (1570, Petre Accounts, Essex Record Office.)

'Stocking of hose' in the early 16th c. indicated the stocking portion of trunk-hose, being the leg portion of that garment and not a separate item.

'Stockings' for men and women might be knitted from 2nd half of 16th c. The materials and colours varied: wool, cotton, thread and silk, plain or embroidered.

From *c.* 1830 men took to wearing socks unless wearing breeches.

STOLE

A mediaeval ecclesiastical term borrowed, later, to designate a fur or warm shoulder-scarf as worn by women from 16th c. on.

STOMACHER

(1) Late 15th and early 16th c's. (M.) A chest piece often very ornamental, covering a V- or U-shaped gap of a doublet cut low in front.

(2) Late 16th c. to 1770's. (F.) A long ornate panel forming the front of an open low-necked bodice. The stomacher descended to a sharp or rounded point at the waist and the upper horizontal border formed the limit of the decolletage. For High Stomacher and Low Stomacher, *see* STOMACHER-FRONT DRESS.

Stomacher, late 17th c.

STOMACHER BODICE

1820's. (F.) A bodice with revers called 'Pelerine lapels', sloping down from the shoulders to a V at the waist, the enclosed space filled in with gauging or pleating, headed by a tucker.

STOMACHER-FRONT DRESS

A term used from 1800 to 1830 but the construction inherited from mid 18th c. (F.) A form of front fastening to a woman's dress; two types:

(a) High Stomacher. The upper third of the skirt is split down the sides forming a sort of tethered apron or inverted flap, to which is fastened the front of the bodice like an apron bib. This is pinned up at shoulder level. A draw-string at the waist tied behind secures the skirt flap and the join might be covered with a belt or sash.

(b) Low Stomacher. The skirt flap does not include the front of the bodice which is closed by a wrapping front with cross-over folds, or by a ROBIN FRONT, a COTTAGE FRONT or a WAISTCOAT BOSOM, *q.v.*

STOTE, STOAT

19th-c. term. A method of sewing two edges of material together so that there is no visible seam; used especially with thick materials.

STRAIGHT ENGLISH SKIRT

1890. (F.) A day skirt, ankle-length, the fullness at the back made by gathers or flat pleats, the front and sides shaped to the waist by darts. The front flat or slightly draped above. A stiff lining 12" up from the hem or a pleated muslin balayeuse.

STRAIGHT TROUSERS

19th c. (M.) Trousers in which the legs are cut the same width all the way down.

STRAIGHT WAISTCOAT

19th c. (M.) A tailoring term of that century, to denote a S-B waistcoat without lapels; with or without a stand collar.

STRAPPED PANTALOONS

C. 1819 to 1840's. (M.) Each leg was held down by a strap under the instep.

STRAPPED TROUSERS

1820's to 1850; unfashionably to 1860. (M.) Each leg was held down by a strap or a pair of straps under the instep.

STRING TIE

1896. (M.) A very narrow bow tie, then fashionable.

STRIPS

2nd half 17th c. (F.) Straight bands of material, plain or bordered with

Strapped Pantaloons, 1830

lace, worn crossing the shoulders to meet in a V in front and serving as an edging and fill-in to a low-necked bodice.

STROSSERS, STRASER
Late 16th and early 17th c's. (M.) Sometimes called 'trousers' but essentially an under-garment, knee or ankle-length; usually of linen cut on the cross to give a close fit.

STUD
C. mid 18th c. on. (M.) A button on a short neck with a broad base, used to fasten parts of a garment together by inserting it through complementary eyelet holes. In 18th c. its only use was occasionally to secure the shirt sleeve at the wrist. Studs were used to secure the front of the shirt from *c.* 1830 and in the 1840's three ornamental studs attached together by small chains (known as 'tethered studs') were commonly worn in evening dress. With the separate collar, coming into fashion for day wear *c.* 1860, a stud was

introduced in the back of the neckband of the shirt.

For evening wear studs with coloured stones, pearls, diamonds, etc. were fashionable until *c.* 1870 when they were gradually replaced by plain gold ones.

STYLE WIDTH
19th c. (M.) A tailoring term for the horizontal measurement from the midline seam on the back of a coat to the nearest margin of the arm-hole.

SUGARLOAF HAT
1640's. (M. and F.) *See* COPOTAIN. The brim, however, was usually broader than the earlier Copotain.

Sugarloaf Hat, 1659

SUIT, SUTE
Term used from 17th c. on. (M. and F.) Term generally denoting a complete costume made of one material throughout. (Wedding costume of the Princess of Wales, 1736): 'Dressed in a suit of rich silk.' (*Read's Weekly Journal.*)

SUIT OF APPAREL
16th and 17th c's. (M.) A suit of clothes consisting at least of doublet and hose, both being indispensable parts of such a 'suit'.

SUIT OF KNOTS
See KNOTS.

SUIT OF NIGHT-CLOTHES
18th c. (M.) A colloquial expression denoting the night-cap and night-shirt. 'Whip a suit of Night-Clothes into your pocket and let's

march off.' (1703, Colley Cibber,
She Wou'd and She Wou'd Not.)

SUIT OF RUFFS
C. 1560 to 1640. (M. and F.) A neck
ruff with matching hand ruffs.

SULTANA SCARF
1854. (F.) A loose scarf of oriental
colours, worn over a canezou, tied
below the waist with the ends left
dangling.

SULTANA SLEEVE
1859. (F.) A large hanging sleeve
slit open in front; the usual style of
sleeve with a casaque.

SULTANE
Late 17th c.; also 1730's and 1740's.
(F.) In 1690 described by Evelyn as
a gown trimmed with buttons and
loops. In 18th c. it was a dress with
short robings and a stomacher and a
plain back. Worn for travelling.
'My lady will travel in her sultane, I
suppose?' (1734, J. Gay, *The Dis-
tress'd Wife.*)

SULTANE DRESS
1877. (F.) A day dress in the Princess style, with a scarf elaborately
draped to fasten at one side.

SULTANE JACKET
1889. (F.) A sleeveless Zouave
'scarcely reaching below the shoulder
blades'.

SULTAN SLEEVE
1830's. (F.) A large hanging day
sleeve caught up in the middle of the
arm and forearm.

SUNRAY SKIRT
1897. (F.) A circular day skirt made
from 2 lengths of wide material joined
to form a square; the skirt then being
cut in a circle with a hole in the
centre for the waist.

SUPERTOTUS
Med. A sleeved and hooded cloak
worn by travellers.

SUPER TUNIC
9th to end of 14th c. (M. and F.)
Generally called 'Surcoat' or 'Sur-

cote' in 13th and 14th c's. (1)
MALE. A loose garment put on over
the head and worn over the tunic or
cote. The shape varied and by the
14th c. was closer fitting. Made long
if ceremonial; otherwise short to the
knees. Sleeves wide to the elbow or
wrist; less commonly close fitting and
long. For varieties *see* GARNASHE,
GARDE CORPS and TABARD.
  (2) FEMALE. A long loose garment
worn over the tunic or kirtle with long
loose sleeves, tubular or bell-shaped,
and in 12th c. sometimes with pendulous cuffs.

Super Tunic, 10th to 11th cs.

In 13th and 14th c's. generally
called a 'Surcoat'. Some were
sleeveless. (13th to mid 14th c.) *See*
SIDELESS SURCOAT.

SUPPORTASSE or UNDER-
  PROPPER
2nd half 16th and 1st half 17th c's.
(M. and F.) A framework of wire
generally whipped over with gold,
silver or silk thread, and fixed at the
back of the neck to support a large
starched ruff or band (collar). 'To
beare up the whole frame and body of
the ruff from falling.' (1583, Stubbes,

Anatomie of Abuses.) *See* Pickadil (2) and Rebato (2).

Supportasse, early 17th c.

SURCOAT, SURCOTE
See Super Tunic.

SURKNEY, SUCKENY
Med. (M.) A coarse loose frock or gabardine worn by carters and shepherds.

SURPLICE BODICE
1881. (F.) A day bodice made in full gathers from the neck over the shoulders and bust.

SURTOUT
(1) 1680 to 1840's. (M.) 17th c. Synonymous with the Brandenburg Overcoat, *q.v.*

18th c. mainly from *c.* 1730. A long loose overcoat with one or more spreading collars called 'capes'. Also called a Wrap-rascal.

19th c. from *c.* 1820's to 1840's, often called a 'Surtout Great-coat'; being an overcoat, S-B or D-B, made like a frock-coat and the forerunner of the Top Frock.

(2) Late 18th c. (F.) A caped overcoat. 'Mrs. Cholmeley's surtout lapelled, high stand-up velvet collar, and three scalloped capes, of fine mixt beaver, velvet sleeves.' (1785, Cholmeley Papers at Bransby.)

SUSPENDERS
19th c. (1) Another name for man's braces. '. . . A British sailor walking up the High Street with suspenders to his trousers . . . the suspenders crossed each other over his shoulders.' (1825, *Ackermann's Repository.*)

Surtout, 1853

It remained the accepted name for 'braces' in America and—in the trade—as an alternative in England.

(2) Sock Suspender, a device for preventing socks from slipping down; introduced in 1895 in the form of an elastic band round the calf with a pendant piece which clipped on to the top of the sock. This was obviously adapted from the female Suspenders (*q.v.*) and therefore considered for some years as 'effeminate'.

(3) In 1878 an elastic suspender, attached to the border of the corsets and clipping on to the top of the stocking, began to be used by women. In 1882 garters 'are almost things of the past, suspenders having superseded them; the suspender is made in satin and elastic with gilt mounts and clips, with a shaped belt fitting the corset'.

SWADDLING BANDS, SWEATH-BANDS
Med. to end of 18th c. Long bandages for wrapping round the body and limbs of an infant, giving it the appearance of a mummy. The infant usually remained thus swad-

dled until it was weaned. 'Bought a Blanket and Swadler for her child.' (1785, Essex Records.)

Among the upper classes swaddling was being replaced by 'Long Clothes' early in the 18th c.

Swaddling Clothes, 1587

SWALLOW-TAILS
C. 1850. (M.) A name beginning to be applied to the evening-dress coat.

SWANBILL CORSET
1876. (F.) A long back-lacing corset with a long metal busk in front shaped to curve over the lower abdomen.

SWATHE
19th c. A baby's binder.

SWEATER
C. 1890. (M.) A loosely knitted jersey reaching below the hips and worn outside the top of the knickerbockers. At first with a stand-up edge round the neck; for golf a polo collar was added in 1894. Cyclists continued to wear the earlier form but 'no man can wear it as it now stands without looking like a bounder'. (1900, *Tailor & Cutter.*)

SWIRE, SWORL, SWYRELL
Med. A twist or convolution used in embroidery or decoration of garments.

SWISS BELT
19th c. (F.) Fashionable 1815 and 1816; again in 1860's, 1880's and 1890's. A waistband broadening in front to a lozenge shape, pointed above and below. From 1860's on it might be laced across the front becoming a CORSELET.

SWISS BODICE
1867. (F.) A velvet bodice combining a Swiss belt, and worn with a sleeved chemisette.

SWORD
16th to end of 18th c. (M.) Part of a gentleman's outfit.

SYSTEM
See TOQUE.

T

TABARD
Late 13th and 14th c's. (M.) In late 13th c. it was a circular mantle of moderate length; in the 14th c. it was an over-garment, one form being the GARNASHE (*q.v.*). Also at this period it was a clerical-academic garment. Subsequently it became ceremonial and heraldic.

TABLET
16th c. (F.) Rare. An apron, anglicised from the French 'tablier'.

TABLIER SKIRT
Fashionable 1850's and 1870's. (F.) A skirt with the front breadth defined by descending trimmings on each side of it, suggesting a decorative apron.

TABLIER TUNIC
1875. (F.) An overskirt triangular in shape, one corner descending nearly to the hem of the skirt in front, the others fastened under the basque of the jacket-bodice.

TACHE
15th to 17th c. A brooch, clasp, buckle or hook.

TACKOVER
Term used from 18th c. (M.) The overlap of the pleat at the top of the back vent of a skirted coat.

TAFFETA-PIPKIN
See PIPKIN.

TAGLIONI
1839 to *c.* 1845. (M.) A greatcoat, usually D-B, with very large collar lying flat on the shoulders, very wide lapels reaching over the breast; collar, lapels and cuffs of quadrilled satin, velvet or 'a new silk material resembling fur'. The coat defining the waist, the skirts full and short without back or side pleats. A central back vent with a 3-cornered tackover at the top. Cross or slit pocket on each side. Sleeves with turned-back cuffs. The whole bound with a twilled binding. The waist seam through the foreparts only.

Named after the celebrated ballet-master Filippo Taglioni, the creator of the ballet *La Sylphide*.

Taglioni Overcoat, 1844

TAGLIONI FROCK COAT
C. 1838 to 1842. (M.) A S-B frock coat, the skirts short and full, often without hip-buttons. Made with a very broad collar and one large cape; slash or flapped pockets on the hips; back vent without pleats but a tackover.

TAIL
See TRAIN.

TAIL CLOUT
Late 16th to 17th c. A baby's napkin.

TAILOR-MADE

1877 on. (F.) A woman's costume for morning and country wear; usually of one material throughout and that a cloth; in the 1890's two materials were sometimes used.

The essential feature was that the costume was made by a tailor and not by a dressmaker, and that it was constructed on masculine lines, and often imitating the fashionable male cut of the day.

Although until late in the 18th c. women's ordinary dresses were man-made and the Riding Habit had always been made by tailors, it was a 'sign of the times' when Charles Worth set up as a dressmaker in Paris in 1858, and in 1867 'a London tailor has recently set up dress-making'.

Various outdoor garments for women—cloaks, ulsters, etc.—then began to be made by tailors but the complete costume becoming known as a 'tailor-made' dates from 1877.

TALLIEN REDINGOTE

1867. (F.) 'Worth has produced an extremely pretty covering for outdoor use called the "Polonaise" or "Tallien Redingote"' (1867). Made with a heart-shaped opening in front and a full back; trimmed with a sash and a large bow behind, and sash ends carried down each side terminating in bows. Made of the same material as the dress or of black silk.

By increased puffing at the back this garment developed into the ordinary 19th-c. POLONAISE, q.v.

TALMA

See PONCHO.

TALMA CLOAK

1850's. (M.) A knee-length cloak with a wide turn-over collar often quilted, and a silk lining. Worn with evening dress. Named after the famous French actor of the Consulate and Empire period. (Some writers at the end of 19th c. attributed the name to the English victory of the battle of the Alma in 1854; but the Talma cloak had appeared under that name in 1853.)

TALMA LOUNGE

1898. (M.) A lounge jacket made with Raglan sleeves, straight fronts and curved or slanting pockets.

TALMA MANTLE

1850's, 1870's, 1890's. (F.) 1850's: a long cloak with hood or tasselled falling collar, shortened in 1854 and called a ROTONDE, q.v.

1870's: made with sleeves.

1890's: a loose-sleeved overcoat of ground length, with a deep velvet collar or a lace cape.

TALMA OVERCOAT

1898. (M.) A Raglan overcoat with very wide arm-holes. 'It is fashionable to go about in a Talma with the hand thrust in the side in the trouser pocket.' (1899, The London Tailor.)

TAM-O'SHANTER

1880's. (F.) A soft round flat hat without a brim; having a bobble in the centre of the crown. Worn at this date of velvet, plush, cloth or crochet work. The name derived from the poem by Robert Burns.

TASSELLED HANDKERCHIEF

16th c. (M. and F.) A pocket hand-kerchief trimmed with tassels at the corners and often having a fringed border. See BUTTONED HANDKER-CHIEF.

TATER

15th c. (M.) Phonetic spelling for Tetour—a hood. 'With long taters down to the ars behynde' (i.e. hood or chaperon with long liripipes). (C. 1490, A Treatise of a Gallant.)

TATTERSALL VEST

1895 on. (M.) A sporting waistcoat in fancy materials with small checks; made S-B with 6 buttons, no collar, 4 flapped pockets.

TAURE

See BULL-HEAD.

TEAGOWN

From *c.* 1877 on. (F.) A loose dress worn without corsets and at first by married women only. 'The teagown arose from the habit of ladies having tea in the hostess's boudoir and donning smart dressing-gowns. Now that gentlemen are admitted to the function peignoirs have developed into elegant toilettes of satin, silk, etc.' (1877.) Its style followed contemporary fashions but from 1889 a high-waisted 'Empire' style was favoured, with long hanging sleeves and trimmings of yards of lace. A lace and muslin mob cap was worn with it.

Gradually in the 1880's this clinging style became 'permissible for young ladies'.

TEA JACKET

1887 on. (F.) Often replacing the Teagown. A jacket, close-fitting behind, loose in front, with tight sleeves; trimmed profusely with lace. It might be worn to replace the tailor-made bodice at afternoon tea.

TELESCOPE PARASOL

1811. The parasol stick was a steel tube which could be lengthened by being pulled out like a telescope.

TEMPLAR CLOAK

See CABAN.

TEMPLERS, TEMPLETTES, TEMPLES

1st half 15th c. (F.) Ornamental bosses of goldsmithry or fine needlework worn over the temples and enclosing the hair. They were supported by a connecting fillet crossing above the forehead, or by the rest of the head-dress. *See* BOSSES.

TENNIS SHOES

16th c. on. (M.) Shoes with soft soles. 'For sooling of syxe paire of shooys with feltys to playe in at tennys.' (1536, Wardrobe Accounts, Henry VIII.)

For lawn tennis, shoes with india-rubber soles appeared in 1878.

Templers, 1413

TERAI HAT

1880's on. (F., sometimes M.) A riding hat worn by Englishwomen in tropical countries. Made of fur or wool felt in the form of 2 hats sewn together at the edge of the brim. A red lining within and a metal vent fitted through the crown. The crown generally somewhat squat and the brim $3\frac{1}{2}''$ to $5''$ wide. 'She used to trot up and down Simla Mall . . . with a gray Terai hat well on the back of her head.' (1888, R. Kipling, *Plain Tales from the Hills.*)

Terai Hat, 1890

TERESA, THÉRÈSE

1770's and 1780's. (F.) A light gauze scarf worn on the head, sometimes tied over the indoor cap.

TERRIER OVERCOAT

1853. (M.) Resembled a Pilot coat. 'Black and tan colour with large china buttons.' (*Punch*).

TETE

See HEAD

TÊTE DE MOUTON
1730 to c. 1755. (F.) A head of false curls worn 'curled all over behind or tête de mouton'. (1782, *Plococosmos*.) 'We have imitations of it that will do as well; both sides of a fashionable head are now curled out to the best advantage.' (1731, *Weekly Register*.)

THEODORE HAT
1787. (F.) 'The crown exceedingly high with two rows of gauze and trimmed with fine blond net; bordered with blue satin. A large bouquet of poppy-coloured flowers in front, and behind deep lappets of gauze reaching to the waist.' (December 1787, *Ipswich Journal*.)

THREE-DECKER
1877 on. (M. and F.) An Ulster with 3 capes. *See* CARRICK.

THREE-FOLD LINEN BUTTON
1841 on. Introduced that year by John Aston; a button covered with 3 layers of linen.

THREE-SEAMER
1860 on. (M.) A round jacket with a central seam down the back and 2 side seams; as contrasted with the coat having side-bodies giving 5 seams.

THREE - STOREYS - AND - A - BASE-MENT
1886. (F.) The popular name given to the hats of that year which had very high crowns.

THRUM or THRUMMED HAT
16th c. (M. and F.) 'Felts are of two kinds—bare or thrummed.' (1547, Statutes at Large.) Thrummed hats, sometimes shortened to 'Thrums', were made of felt or sometimes of silk with a long pile or nap. These were mainly discarded for finer felts by the Upper Classes after 1560's.

TIBI
1840 on. (M.) A loop fastening button to button across the top of a coat, instead of button to button-hole.

TICKET POCKET
Appearing in some overcoats by 1859. (M.) A small pocket for a railway ticket, generally placed above the right-hand flapped pocket of the overcoat. In 1875 it was inserted just above the left cuff of the Inverness overcoat. In the 1890's a ticket pocket was added to the Lounge Jacket, above the right-hand pocket; and by 1895 a similar one was introduced in the Morning Coat.

TIE-BACK SKIRT
1874 to 1882. (F.) A day or evening skirt, trained, with a series of tapes sewn to the side seams within; by tying these tapes together the back of the skirt was bunched out and the front flattened. By this means was produced an extreme narrowing of the skirt in front of the tapes, thus creating a form of 'hobble skirt'.

TIGHTS
19th c. (M.) A term sometimes used for PANTALOONS (*q.v.*), especially those worn for evening dress.

TIGHT-SLACKS
1881. (M.) Trousers very tight at the knees and slack at the bottoms.

TILBURY HAT
1830's. (M.) A small hat with a high tapering crown, flat-topped and a narrow round brim.

TIPPET
(M. and F.) (1) Pendant streamers from the sleeves of the COTE-HARDIE, *q.v.*
(2) A LIRIPIPE, *q.v.*
(3) From 16th c. on. (F.) A short shoulder-cape.

TITUS HAIR or WIG, HAIR A LA TITUS
1790 to 1810. (M.) A cropped head of hair (or wig resembling it) intentionally dishevelled. *See* BRUTUS.

TOBY RUFF
1890. (F.) A neck-frill of chiffon or lisse gathered in 2 or 3 layers and tied at the throat with ribbon; for day wear.

Tippets of Cote-Hardie Sleeves, 1354

TOG
(1) Med. A coat, from the Latin 'Toga'.

(2) 16th c. Becoming a popular word for 'clothes'. 'I cut the Child's strings (leading strings) off from her coats and made her use togs alone.' (1617, *Diary of Lady Anne Clifford*.)

(3) Slang term for finery. 'Togged out' for dressed in finery.

TOILET, TWILLET
17th c. on. (M.) A loose linen (Fr. Toile) wrapper worn about the shoulders of a man while being shaved. 'The barber, after he had cast the linen toilet about his shoulders (asked) how shall I trim your majesty.' (1684, J. Phillips, transl. of Plutarch.)

Term also used in 18th c. for the loose wrapper worn by ladies while having their hair dressed.

TOILET CAP
17th c. (M.) A plain night-cap worn by men while being barbered.

TOP
See TOUPEE.

TOP BOOTS,
1780's on. (M.) Previously called JOCKEY BOOTS, *q.v.* Boots reaching to just below the knees with turn-over

tops of a lighter or different colour, e.g. brown over black. Loops for pulling on and also boot garters or strings. In the 19th c. button and strap for keeping in position.

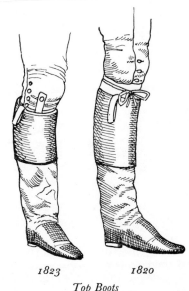

1823   *1820*

Top Boots

TOP BUTTON
A button of which the face alone was gilded. When the under-surface was also gilded it was known as an ALL-OVER. By mid 19th c. this type of button was known as a HIGH-TOP.

TOP COAT, OVERCOAT, GREAT-COAT
(M.) Terms which have tended to be used for any form of coat worn over the suit when out of doors. TOP COAT and GREATCOAT were names in use in the 18th c. while OVERCOAT came into use by middle of the 19th c. GREATCOAT implied a garment of heavy material suitable for travelling; TOP COAT indicated a fitting garment of lighter material, suitable for walking; OVERCOAT a similar garment but suitable for travelling by train.

TOP FROCK
1830 on. (M.) An overcoat cut like a Frock coat but usually somewhat longer and generally double-breasted. It was intended to be worn without

an under-coat while looking like an overcoat. *See* UPPER GARMENT.

TOP HAT, TOPPER
19th-c. term. (M.) *See* also CHIMNEY-POT HAT; POT HAT; SILK HAT; PLUG HAT. A tall high-crowned hat (resembling a chimney-pot) with a narrow brim usually slightly rolled up at the sides but at some dates (e.g. *c.* 1840) with a brim almost flat.

The shape appeared at the end of the 18th c. but not the name. Until *c.* 1830 it was a high-crowned Beaver but this was subsequently replaced entirely by the 'SILK HAT', *q.v.* This reached its extreme height *c.* 1850, with a crown some 8″ high. By the end of the century this was reduced to 5″.

The Top Hat was usually black but sporting varieties might be grey or brown; white was the fashionable colour for sportsmen from *c.* 1820 and was the colour generally worn by all gentlemen in the 1830's and 1840's.

Top hats might be worn by women riders from 1830's.

1830   1854   1867   1895

Top Hats

TOP KNOT
See KNOT.

TOPPER
See TOP HAT. 'His white topper.' (1820, *Sporting Magazine.*)

TOQUE, TOOCKE, TOCK, TUCK
(F.) (1) 16th and early 17th c's. A woman's head-kerchief or coif.

(2) *C.* 1815–20. 'A sort of triangular cushion or edifice of horse-hair called, I believe, a toque or a system, was fastened on the female head . . . and upon and over this

system the hair was erected and crisped and frizzed.' (1817, Maria Edgeworth, *Harrington.*)

(3) 19th c. A close-fitting turban-like hat without a brim, worn by day out of doors and sometimes also with evening dress. Made of a variety of materials (silk, satin, straw) and fashionable from 1817 to the end of the century except in the 1850's.

TOQUE-TURBAN
1840's. (F.) A turban in the form of a toque; for evening wear.

TOQUET
1840's. (F.) A small toque of satin or velvet with a shallow turned-up brim in front and trimmed with an ostrich feather. Placed far back on the head and worn with evening dress. In 1867 the term was used as 'a more elegant phrasing for the pork pie hat'.

TOREADOR HAT
1890's. (F.) A circular hat with a flat shallow circular crown; made of felt or straw and worn aslant. A fashion inspired by the opera *Carmen* and Emma Calvé's acting in the name part.

TORSADE
1864. (F.) A twisted or plaited coronet of velvet or tulle with long lappets; worn with evening dress.

TOUPEE, TOUPET, FORETOP, TOP
(1) 1730 to end of 18th c. (M.) The roll back from the forehead of the hair of a wig; previous to 1730 the wig had a centre parting.

(2) Late 19th c. (F.) A fringe or forehead frizz of false hair.

TOURNURE
1882 to 1889. (F.) The polite name for a bustle.

TOWER, TOUR
1670's to 1710. (F.) False curls added to the front hair up above the forehead; a coiffure generally worn with the FONTANGE, *q.v.*

TRAFALGAR TURBAN
1806. (F.) An evening dress Turban embroidered with the name of Nelson.

TRAIN or 'TAIL'
Med. on. (M. and F.) An elongation of the bottom of a gown at the back so that it trailed over the ground. A 'demi-train' was a short train produced by having the back of a gown made somewhat longer than the front.

A common feature of the ceremonial gown worn by men, e.g. at coronations, the length of the train depending on the rank of the wearer, such as high judicial and similar functionaries. Trains were worn by women of social rank, from the earliest times, the most singular being a train *in front* as well as behind, as indicated in a Book of Precedence of 1440: 'A surcoat is a morning garment made like a close or straight-bodied gowne, which is worn under the mantell; the same for a countess must have a trayne before, another behind. For a baroness no train. The trayne before to be narrow, not exceeding the breadth of 8 inches and must be trussed up under the girdle or borne upon the left arm.' (Harl. MS. 6064.)

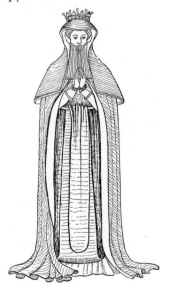

Train in Front

TRAWERBANDES
17th c. Mourning bands.

TRENCHER HAT
1806. (F.) A silk hat with a triangular brim rising to a point above the forehead.

TRESSOUR
14th c. A chaplet of goldsmithry or material worn on the head.

TRICORN, TRICORNE HAT
1690 to end of 18th c. (M.: and F. on horseback.) The 19th c. name for a three-cornered cocked hat.

1773   *1745*

Tricorne Hats

TRILBY HAT
1895 on. (M.) A soft-framed black felt hat, named from the play in which Beerbohm Tree played 'Svengali' in a hat of that description.

TROLLOPEE
See SLAMMERKIN. 'I did not wear one of their trolloping sacks.' (1733, Duchess of Queensberry.)

TROLLY CAP
2nd half 18th c. (F.) An indoor cap trimmed with trolly lace.

TROUSERS, TROWSERS
18th and 19th c's. (M. and F.) A garment enclosing the legs and extending from the waist to the ankles. Its 'legs' not shaped but varying in the degree of looseness. (1) 1730 to end of 18th c. (M.) Trowsers wide-legged, ending just below the calf, made with a narrow belt buttoned in front; a front opening buttoned but without a fly covering.

Worn by the lower orders in town

217

or country and by sailors and soldiers. 'A sea-faring man in . . . long trowsers.' (1771, *Salisbury Journal*.) 'A regiment of cavalry who on foot wear trowsers.' (1782, *The Torrington Diaries*.)

Also occasionally, though rarely, worn by the country Squire: 'In his best trowsers he appears, And clean white drawers.' (*C.* 1730, Wm. Somerville, *The Officious Messenger*.) Breeches, however, was the general rule for all classes.

(2) 1807 on. (M.) From that date trousers began to become fashionable for day wear and from *c.* 1817 for evening though not entirely replacing evening dress breeches until 1850.

The closure was by small falls; from 1823 occasionally by fly front closure which became general after *c.* 1840. Many named varieties, *q.v.*: AMERICAN TROUSERS, COSSACKS, EELSKIN MASHER TROUSERS, FRENCH BOTTOMS, GAITER BOTTOMS, PLEATED, RAILROAD, STRAIGHT, ZOUAVE TROUSERS and TIGHT-SLACKS.

(3) 19th c. (F.) Worn by women on horseback, under the voluminous skirt of the Riding Habit.

1st half 19th c. In the form of strapped pantaloons of coutil of cloth or, in the 1830's, of white florentine. In 1850's sometimes of chamois leather with black feet.

From 1860 on, of black or dark cloth (e.g. broadcloth or superfine) with strap and buckle at the back of the waist and an opening down the left hip; the seat lined with chamois leather or cotton.

The name 'trousers' was also applied to the long drawers with frilled ends to the legs visible below the hem of the skirts as worn by young girls *c.* 1830 to 1860.

TROUSER PRESS

C. 1890. (M.) An appliance consisting of two flat boards between which a pair of trousers was laid and the boards then tightened together by means of thumb-screws; by this means the fashionable crease down the front of the trouser leg could be maintained.

TROUSER STRETCHER

C. 1880. (M.) An appliance for stretching the legs of trousers to remove 'bagginess'. Two types were in general use: (1) A long steel loop bent into an H shape; inserted into the legs of a pair of trousers when not in use, thus preserving their shape by stretching the cloth.

(2) A wooden frame gripping each end of the garment and extending it by means of a screw action. Often combined with the boards of a Trouser Press.

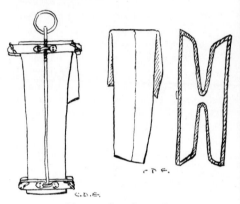

Trousers Stretchers, 1890

TROUSES, TROWSES

16th and 17th c.'s. (M.) The name commonly given to the under-garment (drawers) worn by men beneath the trunk-hose. 'Walks up and down in his gown, waistcoat, and trowses.' (1625, B. Jonson, *Staple of News*. Stage direction: the young man awaits his tailor to bring his suit of clothes.)

TRUNK-HOSE, TRUNK SLOPS, TRUNK BREECHES, TRUNKS, ROUND HOSE, FRENCH HOSE

C. 1550 to 1610. With canions to 1620. (M.) The upper portion of the male leg-wear, from the waist round the seat; this trunk part was variously distended, generally paned and joined to the stocking portion near the fork, or half-way down the thigh.

TRUNK SLEEVES
See CANNON SLEEVES.

TRUSS
(1) (verb) To tie up. A word used from late 14th c. to *c.* 1630. The expression 'to truss the points' meant to fasten with points (i.e. ties) long tailored stockings and, later, trunk-hose to the doublet.

(2) (noun) 17th c. (M.) A form of corset or waistcoat. 'A truss with satin sleeves.' (1606, Surrey Wills. The clothes of Mary Parkyn's husband.)

TRUSSES
1570's to 1590's. (M.) A name sometimes used for tight Venetians (knee breeches). '. . . others straight trusses and devil's breeches.' (1592, Nashe, *Pierce Penilesse.*)

TUBULAR NECKTIE
Patented 1852. (M.) A necktie of various materials woven in the form of a tube, eliminating a seam.

TUCKED SKIRT
1895. (F.) A day skirt with a broad box-pleat in front and pleats behind stiffened at the waist with horsehair; and side fullness given by a series of vertical tucks down the hips.

TUCKER
(1) 17th c. (F.) 'A Pinner or Tucker is a narrow piece of cloth, plain or laced, which compasseth the top of a woman's gown about the neck part.' (1688, R. Holme, *Academie of Armourie.*)

(2) 18th and 19th c's. term. (F.) A white edging, usually frilled, of lace, lawn, muslin or soft material, to a low-necked bodice. In 19th c. an accessory to evening dress. When it was turned over to hang down over the front of the bodice it was called a 'Falling Tucker'.

TUDOR CAPE
1890's. (F.) A circular cape with a pointed yoke front and back and a velvet Medici collar. Usually in embroidered cloth.

TUFT
15th c. A tassel. In 18th c. the name was applied to the tassel pendant from the centre of mortar-boards worn at the Universities.

TUNIC or COTE
(1) 9th to early 14th c. (M., and more rarely F.) A loose body garment of varying length, equivalent to the KIRTLE, *q.v.*

Tunic, c. 1165

(2) 1660's to 1670's. (M.) Tunic or Surcoat, a loose coat hanging to just above the knees, buttoned down the front and having 'commodious sleeves'. Always worn with a 'vest' (i.e. a loose UNDERCOAT, *q.v.*) The tunic and vest were introduced by Charles II from France.

(3) 1840's and 1850's. The costume of small boys; a form of jacket, close-fitting to just below the waist, with a gathered or pleated

Tunic, 13th c., with characteristic 13th c. sleeves

skirt to just above the knees; sleeves long or ending well above the wrists to shew white shirt sleeves. Fastened down the front. Worn with trousers to the ankles or to just below the knees.

C.D.E.

Tunic of Boy, 1853

TUNIC DRESS

19th c. (F.) A dress with an over-skirt, this being the tunic. It varied

in length and design but was usually closed all round.

TUNIC SHIRT

Patented 1855. (M.) A shirt open all down the front, so that it did not require to be put on over the head.

TUNIC SKIRT

1856 on. (F.) A double skirt. In 1850's a popular form for ball dresses, the upper skirt or tunic trimmed with lace, the underskirt with a deep flounce. In 1897 day skirts were sometimes double, and known by this name.

TURBAN

1760's to 1850's. (F.) A head-dress of material folded round the head or made up into that design. Worn for dress or undress until the 19th c., when it became mainly a form of evening attire.

TURF, TYRF, TARF

(1) 15th c. The turn-up or facing of a hood or sleeve.

(2) 16th c. on. (M.) The turn-up of a cap, usually at this date called a bonnet. 'A black Milan bonnet, double turfed.' (1526, Papers etc. Henry VIII.)

TURF HAT

C. 1830. (M.) A hat with a tall, slightly tapering crown, flat-topped and a broad brim turned up on each side.

TURKEY BONNET or HAT

15th and 16th c's. (M.) Any tall cylindrical brimless hat. 'To weare Powle's steeple for a Turkey hat.' (1566, John Heywood, *The Spider and the Flie.*)

One of the instances of foreign fashions then in demand: 'We Englishe men can mocke and scoffe at all countreyes for theyre defectes but before they have many times mustred before us we can learne by lytle and lytle to exceede and passe them al, in al that which at first sight we accompted both vyle and vyllanous. The Spanish cod-peece on the bellye; the Itallyan waste under the hanch bones; the Dutch Jerkin and the Turkie Bonnet; all these at the first we despised and had in derision. But immediately we do not onlye reteyne them but we do so farre exceede them that of a Spanish cod-peece we make an Englishe footeball . . . and of a Turkie bonnet a Copentank for Caiphas.' (1576, George Gascoigne, *Delicate Diet for Droonkardes.*)

Turkey Bonnets, late 15th c.

TURKEY GOWN

2nd quarter 16th c. on. (M.) Supposed to be of Turkish origin and probably identical with the long Hungarian coat with long narrow sleeves; the gown loose, or fastened down the front with loops or buckles and straps. This was regarded as the principal *lay* gown and later adopted by Puritan ministers who regarded the voluminous gown-sleeves worn by the established clergy as savouring of Popery. 'Do not somme wear side gownes having large sleeves with tippets, whiche is not well liked of your secte; some of more perfection (i.e. the Puritans), Turkey gownes, gaberdines, frockes or nightgownes of the most laye fashion for avoiding of superstition.' (1570 . . . Harding, *Computation.*)

A Turkey Gown of black velvet, bordered with silver and furred with lynx, having '77 round gold buttons, black enamelled' is described as made for Henry VIII.

Turkey Gown, 1538

TURNOVER

17th c. (F.) A woman's headkerchief.

TURRET BODICE

1883. (F.) A bodice with a basque cut into tabs.

TUXEDO

1898. (M.) The American term for a DINNER JACKET (*q.v.*) closed with one button only.

TWEEDSIDE

1858 on. (M.) A loose lounge jacket, S-B, buttoned high, often only the top button used. Length to mid-thigh; small collar and sometimes short lapels; patch or slit pockets. 'One of the most ugly but fashionable garments it has ever been our duty to describe.' (1859, *Gentleman's Herald of Fashion.*)

TWEEDSIDE OVERCOAT

1850's. (M.) A knee-length form of the Tweedside jacket.

Tweedside, 1864

TWINE
1840's. (M.) 'As the French call it', an ENGLISH WRAP, *q.v.* A D-B paletot-sac resembling a loose CHESTERFIELD, *q.v.*

TWIST BUTTON
1860's. A button covered with strong cotton twist.

TYE
18th c. (M.) A wig with a tied-back queue.

TYES
Late 19th c. (F.) An American name for girls' aprons.

TYROLESE CLOAK
1809. (F.) A shoulder cape sloping down to the knee-level in front with rounded ends. Made of sarcenet edged with lace.

TYROLESE HAT
1869. (F.) A felt hat with a small flat-topped tapering crown and a narrow brim turned up slightly at the sides. Trimmed with a feather cockade on one side.

U

UGLY

1848 to 1864. (F.) The popular name for an extra brim, resembling the front of a calash, worn round the front of a bonnet as a protection against the sun. Made of half-hoops of cane covered with silk, and when not in use could be folded flat.

C.D.E.

Ugly, 1862

complete or as a strap across the back. At first it had a detachable hood but in the 1870's a detachable

Ugly, 1848

Ugly, 1854

ULSTER

1869 on. (M. and F.) (1) MALE. An overcoat with a waistbelt either

Ulster, 1876

cape was more usual; by 1875 a ticket pocket was inserted in the left sleeve just above the cuff.

Made S-B or D-B buttoned front; in 1890's a fly front was common. Length varied; in the 1870's the garment reached to the ankles.

(2) FEMALE. From 1877 on. A long overcoat sometimes trained; otherwise similar to the male garment except for the 'Three Decker' or CARRICK variety, *q.v.*, in which there were 2 or 3 capes. Made of cloth or waterproof material.

UMBRELLA

(1) 17th c. on. (M. and F.) At first used chiefly as a sunshade by women, the shape being nearly flat. 'There she lay flat spread as an umbrella.' (1616, Ben Jonson, *The Devil is an Ass.*)

18th c. Of oiled silk or linen, the ribs of whalebone or cane, the shape of the cover being pagoda-shaped or domed. Regarded as essentially an article for women only, its use by men being considered as effeminate. Colonel Wolfe in Paris observed in 1752: 'The people here use umbrellas . . . I wonder that a practice so useful is not introduced into England'. Actually Jonas Hanway had ventured to do so *c.* 1750.

By 1800 the pagoda shape was general, the frame of whalebone with metal stretchers. Patent tubular metal frames *c.* 1835.

1848 alpaca covers introduced. 1852 S. Fox patented metal ribs U-shaped on cross section.

Cheaper forms were covered with gingham which then became a popular name for the article itself.

By the middle of the century it had become fashionable for gentlemen to carry umbrellas, 'the great point seems to be to get one as long and light as a sunbeam'. (1858, *Punch.*)

For the rest of the century it remained correct to carry one provided it was always rolled up. By 1895 'closely rolled umbrellas will be seen more frequently than ever before.

Fashionable men are already wedded to them.' (*Tailor & Cutter.*) Ladies' umbrellas of variously coloured silks preserved something of the elegance of the Parasol though larger.

(2) 1800 to *c.* 1810. (M.) Slang name for a very broad-brimmed hat of that date. 'A large slouched beaver umbrella that wanted only a crape hatband to sanctify it for funeral.' (1800, C. L. Lewes, *Memoirs.*)

UMBRELLA ROBE

18th c. A long over-garment. 'Paid for an Umbrella robe to be used in wet weather at funerals.' (1768, Essex Records.)

UMBRELLA SKIRT

1891. (F.) A skirt of double width material cut on the cross with only one seam down the back, concealed under box-pleats. Shaped to the hips by darts and slightly trained. Lined throughout and tied back inside.

UNDER CAP

(1) 16th c. (M.) An indoor cap, usually in the form of a coif, sometimes like a skull-cap and worn under a hat, cap, or bonnet ('bonnet' being then a term denoting a kind of cap.) Usually limited to old men. The under cap was sometimes called a Night-cap and then worn alone.

Under-cap, 1587

(2) 16th to mid 19th c. (F.) An indoor cap worn under an outdoor hat or bonnet. The shape varied throughout the centuries but many approximated to the coif form.

UNDER PROPPER
See SUPPORTASSE.

UNDER SLEEVES
See ENGAGEANTES.

UNDERVEST, VEST
C. 1840's on. (M. and F.) This under-garment, on the hygienic principle of 'wool next the skin', was usually of merino, thigh-length and sleeved; buttoned with a short vent at the neck. It replaced a flannel under-waistcoat. Inferior qualities were of flannel; from 1875 ladies adopted coloured vests of washable silk and gussets shaped for the breasts were then introduced.

In the 1890's vests of natural wool and lambs' wool, with ventilating perforations in the armpits, appeared; these, for men, were then called 'undershirts'.

UNDER-WAISTCOAT
From c. 1790. (M.) A sleeveless waistcoat, shorter than the over-waistcoat but somewhat protruding above its upper margin; the visible portion of rich material contrasting in colour with that of the over-garment. Most fashionable c. 1825 to 1840 when several under-waistcoats might be worn, one above the other; in the 1840's its use was becoming restricted to evening wear, ceasing to be fashionable after c. 1850. Revived in 1888 in the form of a white SLIP, q.v.

UNDRESS or COMMON DRESS
18th and early 19th c's. (M. and F.) A term indicating unceremonial attire such as worn for everyday purposes, especially morning dress.

UNIVERSITY ATHLETIC COSTUME
1886. (M.) A vest with half sleeves; knickerbockers to below the knees;

a sash round the waist; ankle socks and laced shoes.

UNIVERSITY COAT
See ANGLE-FRONTED COAT.

UNIVERSITY VEST
1872. (M.) A D-B waistcoat with 2 pairs of buttons, the front corners sloping away from the bottom button; worn with a UNIVERSITY COAT, q.v.

UNMENTIONABLES
19th c. (M.) One of the many euphemisms for a man's trousers or breeches; the expressions, ranging from the sublime to the ridiculous, began c. 1800 with 'Inexpressibles'; later, 'Unwhisperables', 'Nether Integuments', 'Don't Mentions', 'Bags' and 'Kicksies'.

UNWHISPERABLES
See UNMENTIONABLES.

UPPER GARMENT
17th c. on. (M.) The extra outer garment which distinguished the gentleman from his inferiors.
'Because we walke in jerkins and in hose,
Without an upper garment, cloake or gowne,
We must be tapsters, running up and down.'
(1613, S. Rowlands, *Knave of Hearts*.)
No gentleman would consider himself properly dressed, out of doors, unless he was wearing either an 'upper garment'—cloak, cassock or gown—or was carrying a sword. Without such a garment he was 'in querpo', q.v.

(Significantly the Garter Star was worn on an 'upper garment' whereas the Lesser George was worn in querpo.)

When Pepys visited the Tower of London, which ranked as a Royal Palace, he had to remove his sword at the gate whereupon he realised he was 'improperly dressed' and had to retire to a tavern while he sent for his cloak. (October 30, 1662.)

Traces of this symbolism survived to the end of the 19th c. The Victorian gentleman in Town had to carry a stick (representing his weapon) unless he was wearing an overcoat. The Lower Orders were assumed to have neither.

UPPER STOCKS

See STOCKS.

V

VAMP, VAMPEY
15th c. on. From O.F. Avantpied. The upper front part of a boot or shoe.

VANDYKE
1750's on. (F.) (1) A term denoting a dentate border, either in lace or material, edging a garment, or an actual ruff itself.
'Circling round her ivory neck
  Frizzle out the smart Vandyke;
Like the ruff that heretofore
Good Queen Bess's maidens wore.'
        (1755, Francis Fawkes, *Odes*.)
  (2) A lace-bordered handkerchief. 'This article has been lately revived and called a vandyck.' (1769, *London Magazine*.)

VANDYKE DRESS
18th c. (M.) A fashion for being painted in a costume resembling that of the Vandyke period. 'I am drawn in the Vandyke dress . . . sleeves and breast slashed.' (1770, Diary of Silas Neville.)

VARENS
1847. (F.) An outdoor jacket; short with loose sleeves, made of cashmere or velvet lined with silk. A variation of the CASAWECK and POLKA, *q.v.*

VEGETABLE IVORY BUTTONS
1862. Made in the shape of balls, from the seed of the S. American palm tree.

VEIL
(1) Med. (F.) A COVERCHIEF, *q.v.*
  (2) Late 18th to end of 19th c's. (F.) A piece of transparent material such as net, lace or gauze worn with outdoor bonnet or hat and arranged to cover part or the whole of the face, or sometimes draped behind as a form of trimming; and then often large and white or black, as in the 1820's and 1830's.

In 1860's half veils were fashionable.

The Scarf veil (1870's) entirely covered the face and was 'long enough to be thrown round the neck as a scarf'; worn at the seaside.

In 1889 and '90's large spotted veils were worn, pulled in under the chin by a string 'rather like a nose-bag'. *See* VOILETTE and WEDDING VEIL.

Veil, c. 1375

VENETIAN BONNET
1800. (F.) A small straw bonnet trimmed with straw wreaths or flowers, the strings emerging from a bow at the back and tied loosely on the bosom.

VENETIAN CLOAK
1829. (F.) A black satin cloak with a collar and cape and wide hanging sleeves.

VENETIANS
C. 1570 to 1620; most fashionable in 1580's. (M.) Knee breeches. 'Venetian hosen, they reach beneath the

227

knee to the gartering place of the legge, where they are tied finely with silke points or some such like.' (1583, Philip Stubbes, *Anatomie of Abuses*.)

Venetians were usually pear-shaped, wide and often bombasted round the hips and narrowing towards the knees (*c.* 1570–95). Some, however, were voluminous throughout and were called Venetian slops. Others were 'close to the buttocke like the Venetian galligascoigne'. (1610, S. Rowlands, *Martin Mark-All*.) They were also called 'TRUSSES', *q.v.*

Venetians, 1574

VENETIAN SLEEVE

1858. (F.) A day sleeve fitting at the arm-hole, then expanding widely to mid-forearm and slit up the front nearly to the shoulder. Worn with a large puffed engageante having a close cuff.

VENETIAN SLOPS

See VENETIANS.

VENEZ-A-MOI, VENZE MOY

See ASSASIN.

VENT

A term used from 15th c. on, for a vertical slit up, usually from the hem of a garment, such as coat, shirt, etc., and made for convenience. 'Item, 1 jakket of red felwet, the vents bound with red lether.' (1422–83, Paston Letters.)

VENTOYE

17th c. A fan of the Italian type consisting of a short stem with a rectangular vane at the top.

VERONESE CUIRASSE

1880. (F.) A jersey bodice lacing up at the back.

VERONESE DRESS

1880's. (F.) A day dress with a long plain Princess tunic of woollen material, knee-length, with deep points extending to the hem of the silk under-skirt, made with deep box-pleats.

VEST

(1) 1660's to 1670's. (M.) A knee-length coat with elbow sleeves, generally confined at the waist by a sash or buckled girdle, and always worn under a TUNIC or SURCOAT, *q.v.* This tunic and vest, mainly a Court fashion, was the fore-runner of the 'coat and waistcoat' style and as such the beginning of 'modern dress'.

(2) 19th c. Synonymous with 'waistcoat'.

(3) 1794 into 19th c. (F.) A short sleeveless bodice of varying design, worn with full evening dress.

(4) From 17th c. on. (M. and F.) A term at first used for an under-waistcoat worn for warmth.

(5) An under-garment worn next to the skin. *See* UNDER-VEST.

(6) Early 19th c. An elegant term for the French long corset. 'New invented Parisian vests . . . made of rich French Twillet, with double cased bones that will never break. The form of them is particularly elegant, by a Reserve on the peak . . . (which) has the pleasant and very

essential effect of keeping the gores . . . in the proper position, and obviates that unpleasant rucking and chafing that is in all the long corsets that have been invented. . . .' (Advert. July 3, 1802, *Norfolk Chronicle*.)

VICTORIA BODICE
1899. (F.) A full evening-dress bodice with very low square or round decolletage secured by shoulder straps. Generally trimmed with frills and ruchings of tulle.

VICTORIA BONNET
1838. (F.) A bonnet of satin, the small crown without stiffening, the brim rather close and arching round the face to below the chin; there rounded and curving up towards the crown. The brides pass from this point, under the brim to be tied under the chin. Interior of the brim often trimmed with flowers. A long full bavolet at the back.

VICTORIA MANTLE
1850's. (F.) A knee-length mantle with shoulder-cape cut square and short in front, descending to below the waist behind or merely vandyked. Wide hanging sleeves.

VICTORIA PELISSE-MANTLE
1855. (F.) A D-B mantle buttoned down the front, knee-length, with flat collar and short wide sleeves having reversed cuffs; side pockets.

VICTORIA SKIRT
See GRANNIE SKIRT.

VICTORIA SLEEVE
1838 and 1840's. Revived in 1890's. (F.) A day sleeve with a large volan (flounce) at the elbow and two smaller ones above; the forearm tight with a closed cuff.

VICTORINE
(1) 1849 and 1850's. (F.) A narrow flat neck tippet with short ends in front, tied with ribbon at the throat and edged with fur.
(2) 1899. (F.) A waist-length or ankle-length cloak with a high fluted collar rising from a shaped fur flounce.

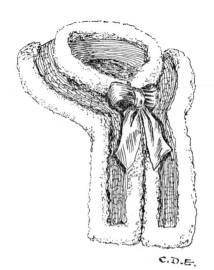

C.D.E.

Victorine, 1849

VIGONE
Mid 17th c. (M.) A hat made of vicuna wool instead of beaver fur.

VIOLIN BODICE
1874. (F.) A day bodice with a piece of dark material, in the shape of

C.D.E.

Violin Bodice, 1877

229

a violin body, inserted down the back. This was prolonged into the skirt when made with a princess dress.

VIRAGO SLEEVE
1st half 17th c. (F.) 'The heavily puffed and slashed sleeve of a woman's gown, then fashionable.' (1688, Randle Holme, *Armourie*.)

Virago Sleeves, 1630

VISITE
From 1845. (F.) A generic name for a loose outdoor covering ranging from a pelerine, mantle or cloak, to a caped overcoat in 1880's. In 1890's it was given a double cape and a high collar.

VIZARD
A whole mask. *See* MASK.

VOIDED SHOE
16th c. A shoe with short uppers, leaving only a toe-cap and instep strap. Very fashionable in 1st half

16th c. 'Crepida, a low voyded shooe, with a latchet.' (1565, Thomas Cooper, *Thesaurus*.)

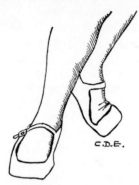

Voided Shoes, 1528–30

VOILETTE
1840's. (F.) A diminutive veil then very fashionable.

VOLAN
19th c. A small flounce commonly used as a trimming to a sleeve.

VOLUPERE
14th c. (M. and F.) A cap or head-dress. 16th c. (F.) A head-dress. Not identified.

VULCANISED RUBBER BANDS
1845 on. Patented that year, for garters and belts.

VULCANITE BUTTONS
1888. Also known as Ebonite, a hard form of vulcanised rubber, capable of being cut and polished.

W

WADDED HEM
1820–8. (F.) The hem of a skirt padded out with cotton wool.

WAISTBAND
(1) 18th-c. term on. (M.) The band of material attached to the top of breeches, trousers, etc. At the centre of the back was a short vent with lacing holes on each side for lacing across; this vent, after *c.* 1790, was generally closed by a 'puff' of chamois leather. The waistband, inherited from the trunk-hose, ceased to be fashionable after *c.* 1836 though continued in AMERICAN TROUSERS, *q.v.*

(2) 19th c. (M. and F.) Name given to a detachable belt.

WAISTCOAT
MALE. (1) 16th c. to 1668. A waist-length under-doublet (sometimes called a 'Petticoat', i.e. a short coat) usually quilted and worn with or without sleeves which were detachable. Worn for warmth or if for display then of rich materials.

(2) 1668 on. An under-coat, at first cut on similar lines to the coat, but without hip-buttons and pleats, the sleeves being discarded from *c.* 1750 though occasionally worn by the elderly until *c.* 1800.

Becoming shorter *c.* 1775 the front skirts were mere flaps which disappeared by 1790.

Constructed S-B until 1730's the D-B form becoming common in 1780's and usual in 1790's. Both forms fashionable at various times in the 19th c. for day wear, the D-B form becoming permissible for evening dress in the 1890's.

For named varieties: *see* JOCKEY W., STRAIGHT W., TATTERSALL W., SHAWL W., FRENCH W.

Waistcoat, Sleeved, 1720–25

Waistcoat, Sleeved, 1720–25

WAISTCOAT

FEMALE. (1) 17th c. A close fitting jacket-bodice worn with a skirt (called a 'petticoat') or with a bed-gown for extra warmth.

(2) 2nd half 18th c. on. Cut on the same lines as the male garment and worn with the riding habit, or as a fill-in for an open bodice, when the waistcoat was sometimes sham having sewn-in front panels only.

(3) 1st half 19th c. A flannel waistcoat sometimes worn as an under-garment for extra warmth; replaced by the introduction of the under-vest. (C. 1840.)

(4) 1851. A fashion for wearing elaborately embroidered waistcoats with carriage dresses; these were darted to fit the figure and were sometimes made from brocaded male waistcoats of the 18th c.

(5) 1880's and 1890's. Waistcoats, cut on mannish lines, were common in the tailor-made costumes of those decades.

WAISTCOAT-BOSOM DRESS

1800 to 1810. (F.) A dress made in the low-stomacher style (q.v.), the bodice buttoned down the front.

WAIST SEAM

From 1823 on. (M.) A horizontal seam uniting the body of a coat with its skirts.

WARDLE HAT

1809. (F.) A straw hat with a conical crown. The name recalling the notorious scandal of the Duke of York and Mary Ann Clarke, exposed by Colonel Wardle in 1809.

WARDROBE

(1) 15th c. A room in which clothes were kept.

(2) 16th c. on. The clothes belonging to a particular person.

(3) 19th c. A piece of furniture for containing clothes; the second meaning was also employed.

WATERFALL BACK

1883 to 1887. (F.) The skirt of a morning or walking dress made with a series of flounces down the back from waist to hem so that with a projecting bustle 'the skirt seems to pour itself over a precipice'.

WATERFALL NECKCLOTH

See MAIL-COACH NECKTIE.

WATERPROOF

1880's on. A name beginning to be applied to many forms of outdoor garments of which the threads composing the material used had been rendered waterproof before weaving; thus distinct from those textiles impregnated with solution of india-rubber. (See MACKINTOSH.) In 1893 Burberry's patent waterproof material was composed of an outer layer of gabardine with an inner of soft tweed; in 1896 Mandeburg's 'silk striped proofing' was similarly used.

WATERPROOF CLOAK

1867. (F.) A cloak with a small tasselled hood of waterproof material.

WATTEAU BODY

1853 to 1866. (F.) A day basquine bodice with low square neck, the fronts not meeting but filled in by a chemisette crossed by ribbon bows to the waist closing the bodice; elbow sleeves with deep lace ruffles.

WATTEAU COSTUME

1868. (F.) A bodice with a fichu front and round skirt edged with deep pleating; and an over-dress looped up at the sides of the skirt, with a WATTEAU PLEAT (q.v.) behind from neck to hem.

WATTEAU PLEAT

2nd half 19th c. (F.) A revival of the 18th c. SACK BACK, q.v. Employed occasionally, especially in the 1850's and 1860's for afternoon wear and in the 1880's and 1890's for Teagowns.

WATTEAU POLONAISE

1870's. (F.) A polonaise with a Watteau back, usually of white material strewn with flowers.

232

WATTEAU ROBE

1850's. (F.) A ball dress in the open-robe style and Watteau back with a lace inset.

WEARING SLEEVES

17th c. (F.) Sleeves worn on the arms as opposed to hanging sleeves usually sham. 'Three gownes with wearing slevis and long slevis for three other gownes.' (1612–13, Warrant to the Great Wardrobe on Princess Elizabeth's marriage.)

WEDDING DRESS

19th c. (F.) Previous to 19th c. there was no set formula for this dress except that it was usually white. From 1800 to 1840 it was a semi-decollete evening dress with short sleeves and long white gloves. From 1830 a wedding dress was usually white lace over silk or satin. From 1844 a white afternoon dress replaced the evening low-necked gown, and in 1867 white book muslin was often used instead of silk or satin.

From 1880's the dress was always high necked but by then 'a bride is often married in her going-away dress', a choice which was permissible throughout the century.

WEDDING GARTER

16th to 18th c. (F.) This was generally blue, the colour associated with the Virgin Mary, but sometimes white or red. The bride's garters were trophies eagerly sought for :

'. . . let the young Men and the Bride-
Maids share
Your garters; and their joynts
Encircle with the Bridegroom's
Points.'
(1648, Herrick, *Hesperides*.)

Fragments of them were then worn in the young men's hats.

WEDDING GLOVES

White gloves were distributed among the wedding guests. 'Five or six pair of the white innocent wedding gloves.' (1599, Dekker, *Untrussing of the Humorous Poet*.)

WEDDING KNIVES

15th, 16th and 17th c's. (F.) A pair of knives contained in one sheath were given to the bride and then worn as a symbol of her married status. 'See at my girdle hang my wedding knives.' (1609, Dekker, *Match Me in London*.)

WEDDING SUIT

19th c. (M.) Previously this had been merely a ceremonial 'full dress' suit, often with white waistcoat and stockings. By 1820 a blue dress coat with gilt buttons white waistcoat and black knee-breeches had become the convention; by c. 1830 the breeches were commonly replaced by white trousers or pantaloons. In the 1850's the frock coat was beginning to replace the (day) dress coat. 'Mr. P. consulted me about his wedding-coat whether it shall be a frock-coat, which I advised though I believe not quite correct with a bride's veil.' (1853, *Lady Elizabeth Spencer Stanhope's Letter-Bag*, ed. A. M. W. Stirling.)

By 1860 the costume had become a blue or claret-coloured frock coat, white waistcoat and lavender doeskin trousers. In the 1870's the frock coat was being replaced by the morning coat which by 1886 had become the rule, reverting in the 1890's to a black frock coat, light-coloured D-B waistcoat and grey striped cashmere trousers, with patent leather button boots A white button-hole flower was worn from c. 1850. A black silk top-hat, replacing the beaver, became general by 1840. Light - coloured gloves, becoming lavender-coloured from c. 1870.

WEDDING or BRIDAL VEIL

Always white lace, especially of Brussels or Honiton (c. 1840's). A fashion known in 17th c. but rare before c. 1800 when until c. 1860 the veil was attached to the head and hung down the back almost to the ground. From c. 1830 an orange-blossom wreath was added.

From 1860 the new fashion was for

the veil to hang over the face down to the waist or knee though the old style survived into the 1880's.

From 1892 a new mode was for one corner to hang over the face to knee level and 'the fullness drawn back on either side with jewelled pins'.

WEED, WEYD, WEDE
A mediaeval name for a garment, the word still being used in the 16th c.; surviving through the 19th c. in the term 'widow's weeds'.

WEEPERS
18th and 19th c's. (M.) 18th c. Muslin arm-bands. 'Mourners clap bits of muslin on their sleeves and these are called weepers.' (1762, O. Goldsmith, *The Citizen of the World.*)

19th c. Broad muslin hat-bands tied round a mourner's hat, the two ends hanging down behind to the waist; worn at a funeral. Black the general rule but white if the deceased was a maid. Becoming uncommon in the last quarter of the century.

WELCH WIG
1st half 19th c. (M.) A worsted cap with a fluffy surface, worn by travellers and others. 'The sexton's Welch wig which he wore at rainy funerals.' (1849, Albert Smith, *The Pottleton Legacy.*)

WELLESLEY WRAPPER
1853. (M.) A short sac-like wrapper made D-B and often bordered with fur. The front fastened with military brandenburgs.

WELLINGTON BOOT
1817 on. (M.) Similar to a Top Boot but without the turnover top.

WELLINGTON COAT
1820 to 1830. (M.) 'A kind of half-and-half greatcoat and under-coat (i.e. frock coat) meeting close and square below the knees.' (1828, *The Creevey Memoirs.*)

WELLINGTON FROCK
1816 to 1820's. (M.) The forerunner of the Victorian Frock coat; at first a S-B coat with roll or Prussian

Wellesley Wrapper, 1853

collar but no lapels; buttoned down to the waist; a full skirt to just above the knees. The fronts meeting without a cut-in; the back with a central vent, side pleats and hip-buttons. No waist seam.

In 1818 a horizontal 'fish' (i.e. dart) was added at the waist-level to improve the fit; this fish became in 1823 extended into a seam at the waist. Flapped pockets in the skirt at the sides of the waist were usual.

WELLINGTON HAT
1820's and 1830's. (M.) A tall beaver hat 'the crown 8 inches deep and over-spreading at the top'. (1830, *Dissertatio Castorum.*)

WELLINGTON PANTALOONS
1818 to 1820's. (M.) Pantaloons with side slits from the calf down, closed by loops and buttons.

Wellington Hat, 1820

WELT

Term used from 16th c. A strengthened border of a garment or part of one, and in 16th c. a decorative border synonymous with a 'GUARD' (*q.v.*) 'Gownes welted with velvet.' (1592, *Quips for an Upstart Courtier.*)

WHALEBONE

Med. on. (1) Med. The ivory of the walrus was often meant.

(2) The horny substance from the upper jaw of the whale. *See* GLOSSARY.

WHALEBONE BODICE or BODIES

16th and 17th c's. (F., and children.) A bodice of a gown stiffened with whalebone strips; sometimes an under-bodice as a pair of stays and sometimes combining both, the front being decorative and the back, if covered by an over-gown, plain like a corset. '. . . the first time the child (a girl aged three) put on a pair of whalebone bodies . . .' (1617, *Diary of Lady Anne Clifford.*)

WHEEL FARTHINGALE, CATHER-INE WHEEL FARTHINGALE, ITALIAN FARTHINGALE

1580 to 1620's. (F.) A wheel-shaped structure made of wire or whalebone and covered with material,

often silk. It was worn round the waist, with a slight tilt up behind. The skirt of the gown was carried out horizontally over this and then allowed to fall vertically to the ground from the circumference of the wheel. This was a variation of the FRENCH FARTHINGALE (*q.v.*) giving the same tub-like appearance.

WHISK

2nd quarter 17th c. on. (F.) A broad falling collar generally trimmed with broad lace. 'A woman's neck-whisk is used both plain and laced, and is called of most a gorget or falling whisk because it falleth about the shoulders.' (1688, R. Holme, *Armourie.*)

Whisk, 1625–30

WHITTLE

17th c. on. (F.) A large white shawl usually of Welsh flannel, worn by countrywomen, especially by a mother carrying a baby. 'My whittle that is fringed.' (1668, Will of Jane Humphrey, of Dorchester, Mass., U.S.A.)

'A lying-in's expensive too,
In cradles, whittles, . . .'
(*C.* 1730, W. Somerville,
The Yeomen of Kent.)

WHOLE BACKS

19th c. A term denoting coats made without a central back seam.

WHOLE FALLS

See FALLS.

WIDE-AWAKE
19th c. (M.) A broad-brimmed low-crowned hat of felt or stuff. For country wear.

WIG, PERIWIG, PERUKE
(M. and F.) An artificial covering of hair for the head; worn by men and women for decorative purposes; often in 16th, 17th c's., and by men almost universally during the 18th until c. 1790; and by women especially from c. 1795 to 1810. For named varieties see: ADONIS, BAG-WIG, BOB, BRIGADIER, CAMPAIGNE, CATO-GAN, CAULIFLOWER, CAXON, CLUB, CUE-PERUKE, CUT-WIG, DUVILLIER, MAJOR, PIGEON-WINGED, PIGTAIL, RAMILLIES, SCRATCH, TOUPEE, TYE.

WIMPLE
Late 12th to mid 14th, rare later, in 15th c. (F.) A long piece of white linen or silk draped over the front of the neck and swathed round the chin, the ends being pinned to the hair above the ears. It was worn with a veil or a fillet or both, or sometimes alone. (Not to be confused with the pleated barbe of the widow.)

In 1809 the name was used for a gauze covering of the head, worn with evening dress.

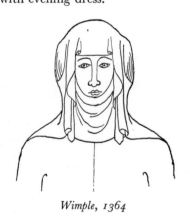

Wimple, 1364

WIMPLED
16th c. (1) Disguised.
(2) Arranged in folds, as with a muffler which was worn like a wimple. 'Why are they wimpled? Shall they not unmask them?' (1590, *Three Lords and Ladies of London.*)

WINGS
(1) c. 1545 to 1640's. (M. and F.) Stiffened and generally decorative bands, often crescentic, projecting over the shoulder seam of doublets and jerkins and also women's gowns. With detachable sleeves the wings hid the ties.
(2) 2nd half 18th c. (F.) The side flaps of an indoor cap thus constructed, such as the dormeuse cap.

WINKERS
C. 1816 to 1820. (M.) The very high points of the shirt collar which, as worn by the ultra-fashionables of the day, reached up to the corners of the eyes.

WITCHOURA MANTLE
1808 to 1818; and in 1830's. (F.) A mantle with a deep cape and fur trimming. In 1830's the name was revived for a mantle without a cape but with a high stand collar and very large sleeves. Trimmed or lined with fur; always a winter garment.

WITCH'S HAT
1800 on. (F.) Similar to a GYPSIE HAT (*q.v.*). The essential feature being that the brim was bent down by ribbon strings passing over it from the crown, to be tied under the chin.

WOODSTOCK GLOVES
18th c. (M. and F.) 'Riding gloves made of fawn skin; got them at Woodstock where they are famous for making them.' (1777, *Letters of Mrs. Graham.*)

WOOLWARD
16th c. Clothed wholly in woollen materials; i.e. without a linen shirt. 'I go woolward'. (1590, *Love's Labours Lost.*)

WRAPPER (1)
18th c. (F.) A term used for a woman's bedroom négligée which might also be worn in bed. 'My Lady generally was in Bed with nothing on but a loose Gown or Wrapper.'

(1744, Report of the Annesley Cause; evidence of the maid. *The London Magazine and Monthly Chronologer.*) 'Fine thick printed Cotton . . . to make two wrappers for my mother.' (1739, *Purefoy Letters.*)

WRAPPER (2)

1840's and 1850's. (M.) In 1840's a name applied to various forms of loose overcoat, both S-B and D-B and sometimes used for a CHESTERFIELD. In 1850's it was defined as a loose thigh-length overcoat cut to wrap over the front, sometimes buttoned

Wrapper, 1850

but more often held in place by the hand. The collar was a deep shawl type. Often worn with evening dress.

WRAPPING FRONT DRESS

1800 to *c.* 1830. (F.) The bodice of a low STOMACHER-FRONT DRESS (*q.v.*) made to fasten in a cross-over manner.

WRAPPING GOWN

1st half 18th c. (F.) A term applied to a dress having a bodice with a wrap-over front continuous with the upper part of the skirt.

Wrapping Gown, 1740–50

WRAP-RASCAL

C. 1738 to 1850. (M.) A loose form of overcoat; in the 19th c. usually applied to a countryman's or to the kind worn by those travelling on the outside of a coach. Generally made of heavy materials.

Y

YACHTING JACKET or SHORT
  PALETOT
1860's to 1880's. (F.) A short
square-cut outdoor coat reaching to
hip level. Made S-B or D-B, with
large buttons and loose sleeves.

YANKEE NECKCLOTH
1818 to 1830's. (M.) *See* AMERICAN
NECKCLOTH.

YEOMAN HAT
1806–12. (F.) Hat with a full deep
soft crown and close up-turned brim
or none, but the crown gathered into
a broad band. For morning or
walking dress.

Yeoman Hat

YOKE BODICE
1880's and 1890's. (F.) A bodice or
blouse made with a yoke. A similar
yoke was often added to the Norfolk
jacket from 1894.

YOKE SKIRT
1898 on. (F.) A day walking skirt
made with a pointed yoke joined to
the lower part which was cut from a
circle. Worn with a foundation or
under-lining attached at the waist
only. Some were made with a
flounce below the knees.

YORK TAN GLOVES
1780 to 1820's. (F., and sometimes
M.) Gloves, long or short, of fawn-
coloured soft leather. 'York tan
gloves . . . the smooth surface inside,
tied high above the elbows.' (1788,
Mrs. Papendiek's Memoirs.)

YORK WRAPPER
1813. (F.) A high-necked morning
dress, buttoned behind; made of
jacconet muslin, the front decorated
with alternate 'diamonds' of lace or
needlework.

ZONE

1770's and 1780's. (F.) A fill-in for an open bodice of a gown, the shape varying according to the shape of the exposed gap.

Zone, late 18th c.

Zone, late 18th c.

ZOUAVE COAT or ORIENTAL WRAPPER

1845. (M.) A cloak-like coat with velvet collar and cuffs, and lined and quilted throughout with silk. 'Has the advantage of a coat and a cloak, can be worn as a riding or walking coat or opera cloak.'

ZOUAVE JACKET

(1) Fashionable 1859 to 1870 and in 1890's. (F.) A jacket of silk, velvet or cloth, without a back seam, the front borders rounded off and fastened at the neck only. Many variations but all retaining the main features. The original design adopted from the Algerian Zouave troops in the Italian war of 1859.

(2) 1860's. (M.) A similar jacket, worn by little boys.

Zouave Jacket (Female), 1864

Zouave Jacket (Male), 1864

239

ZOUAVE PALETOT

1840's. (M.) A paletot of llama wool, waterproofed. 'May be worn with or without an under-coat. One of the most gentlemanly and unassuming garments offered to the public.'

ZOUAVE TROUSERS

See PEG-TOP TROUSERS.

GLOSSARY OF MATERIALS

ADRIANOPLE. 1878. An unglazed cotton lining; in 1880 a red calico printed with arabesques.

AEROPHANE. *C.* 1820. A fine crimped crepe.

ALAMODE. 17th c. 'A thin light glossy black silk.' (Chambers.) Often spoken of as 'Mode'.

ALBERT CRAPE. 1862. A superior quality of black silk crape for mourning. In 1880 of silk and cotton.

ALEPINE, ALAPEEN, ALLOPEEN. 18th c. A mixed stuff of silk and wool or of mohair and cotton.
In 1832 the name of a textile resembling Bombazine.

ALEXANDER. Med. A striped silk material.

ALGERINE. 1840. A twilled shot silk, green and poppy or blue and gold.

ALLEJAH, ALAJAH. Early 18th c. Any kind of corded stuff. A corded silk fabric from Turkestan.

ALLIBALLI. Early 19th c. An Indian muslin.

ALPACA. 1841. A springy shiny textile, of the wool of the Alpaca goat and silk; later, cotton. Invented by Sir Titus Salt in 1838.

ALPAGO. 1843. 'A stout satin delaine.'

AMEN. 19th c. Also called DRAFT. A fine quality of figured Lasting.

AMICE. 16th c. Some kind of grey fur, possibly squirrel.

AMY ROBSART SATIN. 1836. A satin 'with white ground with white flowers traced in gold thread, or pale-coloured ones in silver'.

ANABAS. Early 18th c. A cheap cotton material.

ANCOTE VALE VELVET. *C.* 1840. A cotton velvet.

ANDALUSIAN. 1825. A fine open washing silk with a broché pattern.

ANGLO-MERINO. *C.* 1809. A textile nearly as fine as muslin, manufactured at Norwich and made from George III's merino flock.

ANGOLA, ANGORA. 1815. 'The new lama cloth', made from the hair of the llama goat, from the neighbourhood of Angora. Originally imported as 'MOHAIR' (*q.v.*). Later (1850) woven with a warp of coloured silk under the name of 'Poil de chèvre'.

ANTERNE. Early 18th c. A stuff of wool and silk or of mohair and cotton.

ANTWERP LACE. 17th and 18th c's. Probably a bobbin-lace, with a vase as the chief motif.

APPLEBLOOM, APPLEBLUE. 14th c. A cloth resembling in colour, and perhaps in pattern, apple-blossom.

AQUERNE. *C.* 1200. Squirrel's fur.

ARIEL. 1837. A woollen gauze quadrilled in white on coloured ground.

ARMAZINE. 18th c. A strong corded silk used for ladies' gowns and gentlemen's waistcoats.

ARMINE. *See* ERMINE.

ARMOIRE. 1880. A very thick corded silk.

ARMOISE, ARMOISIN, ARMOZEEN. 16th c. A taffeta, generally black. 19th c. 'A stout silk almost invariably black, used for hatbands and scarves at funerals.' (1840, Perkins.)

ARMOZEAU. 1820's. 'A silk similar to lutestring but not so thick.'

ARMURE. 1850. A rich silk and wool textile with an almost invisible design such as a twill, a triangle or a chain, on the surface.

ARMURETTE. 1874. A fancy silk and wool textile.

ATLAS. 17th and 18th c's. A smooth silk cloth imported from India; term applied in England to tawdry silks woven with gold and silver threads. Also applied loosely to a gown of that material. 'Ladies with tawdry atlasses.' (1706.)

ATTABY. 14th c. A silk textile; the name becoming later TABBY (*q.v.*).

AUGUSTA. 17th c. A fustian made at Augsburg.

AVIGNON. 19th c. A silk taffeta used for coat linings.

AYLESHAM. 13th and 14th c's. Usually a linen but also a cloth made at Aylesham in Norfolk.

AZURE. 16th c. A blue cloth similar to PLUNKET (*q.v.*).

BADGER. Med. The fur of the animal, not used by the gentry.

BAFT. 16th c. A coarse cotton fabric, red, blue or undyed, or printed in checks.

BAGDAD. 1872. An Eastern silk fabric striped like Algerienne but with wider lines and of thicker substance.

BAG HOLLAND. 17th c. A fine quality of linen used for shirts.

BAISE, BAIZE, BAYS. 16th c. A woollen textile resembling a thin serge introduced by Walloon refugees in 1561. One of the many 'New Draperies' (*q.v.*).

BALDEKIN, BAUDEKIN. Med. A rich silk fabric with gold thread, of the nature of brocade.

BALEEN. 14th c. The horny substance in the upper jaw of the whale, used in armour; and in dress from the 16th c. when it became known as whalebone.

BALERNOS. 1874. A very soft and silky mohair.

BALZARINE. 1830's. A cotton and worsted textile similar to barege.

BALZERINE. 1889. A narrow striped grenadine with broad silk crepe stripes.

BAMBULO. 1885. A coarsely woven, slightly transparent shot canvas cloth.

BANGAL. 17th c. Various piece goods imported from Bengal.

BARATHEA. 1840's. A black silk and worsted mixture used for mourning. Later, a worsted fabric in twill hopsack weave.

BAREGE. 1819. A semi-transparent textile of silk and wool, the former thrown up on the surface; open mesh. Sometimes of all wool.

BAREGE DE PYRENEES. 1850. A barege printed with delicate foliage and brilliant flowers.

BAREGE-GRENADINE. 1877. A cotton and jute barege.

BARLEYCORNS. 18th c. A checked material, sometimes scarlet; exact nature unknown.

BARLINGHAM. 14th c. A taffeta woven at Burlingham, near Norwich.

BARMILLION. 17th c. A variety of fustian made in Manchester (1641).

BARPOUR. 1847. A twilled silk and wool mixture.

BARRACAN. End of 18th and 19th c's. A coarse thick corded stuff resembling camlet; the warp of silk and wool, the weft of Angora goat's hair. In 18th c. often watered.

BARRAGON. 18th c. Perhaps identical with Paragon.

BARRAS. 17th and 18th c's. A kind of canvas or linen imported from Holland and used for neck-cloths.

BARRATEE. 19th c. A silk stuff, a variety of Barathea.

BARRISTER'S PLAID. 1850's. A small check pattern cloth used for trouser material.

BASIN DE LAINE. 1855. A thick woollen dimity, the right side ribbed, the other with a long soft nap.

BATH COATING. 18th and 19th c's. A thick double-raised baize, used for overcoats.

BATISTE. 1820's. A dressed cotton muslin with a wiry finish.

BATISTE DE LAINE. 1835. 'A new material of the Chaley kind but mingled with silk. It is striped with satin stripes which form squares, and is always in two colours strongly contrasted.'

BAUDEKIN. Med. A very rich silk of the nature of brocade.

BAUSON SKIN. 16th c. The skin of the badger.

BAYADERE. 1840's. A striped silk and wool textile, the stripes being alternately plain and satiny.

BAZAN, BASEN. 13th c. Sheepskin tanned in oak or birch bark.

BEARSKIN. 17th c. As a dress fur, first mentioned in 1619.
18th c. A rough material used for men's frocks (working-class).

BEARSKIN CLOTH. 19th c. A thick coarse woollen textile with a shaggy nap; resembling Dreadnought.

BEAUDOY. 18th c. A worsted material used for stockings.

BEAUPERS. 16th and 17th c's. A linen similar to bunting.

BEAVER. (1) Med. The fur of that animal used for gloves.
(2) Late 18th c. A woollen overcoating with one face sheared, heavily

milled and nap-raised finished. Much used in the 19th c. when beaver leather was also used for Woodstock gloves.
(3) 19th c. A hat material of felted wool and rabbit's fur, with a nap of beaver hair, in the superior quality hat.

BEAVERTEEN. 19th c. A cotton twilled cloth in which the warp was drawn up into loops forming an uncut pile. Mentioned in 1827.

BECHE-CASHMERE. 1848. A woollen textile 'thicker than flannel and as soft as silk'.

BED. C. 1600. A coarse thin worsted similar to say.

BEDFORD CORD. 19th c. A combination of plain weave and whipcord, the cords running in the direction of the warp; of all wool or cotton and wool. Used specially for riding breeches.

BEGIN. 14th c. A rayed silk fabric.

BEIGE. 1874. A woollen vicuna, usually coffee-coloured; a firm thin worsted with a smooth twill.

BELGIAN LINEN. 1879. A thick damask-like linen with coloured pattern on a cream ground.

BELLADINE, BELLANDINE. 18th c. A fine white silk fabric from the Near East.

BEND-LEATHER. 17th and 18th c's. Leather from the back and flanks of an animal; used for the legs of jack-boots.

BENGAL. 17th c. A mixed fabric with cotton base from the East Indies. Mentioned in 1680. Defined by Johnson (1755) as 'a sort of thin slight stuff of silk and hair, for women's apparel'. Striped varieties in cotton having 'Bengal stripes' were popular.

BENGALINE. 19th c. (1) 1869. A very light mohair, self-coloured or brocaded with very small flowers.

(2) 1880. Similar to a silk barege.

(3) 1884. 'A new name for Sici-lienne ; a corded silk and wool textile, the weft of wool.'

BENGALINE POPLIN. 1865. A poplin with a thick cord.

BENGALINE RUSSE. 1892. A shot wool and silk, flecked in contrasting colours.

BERLIN CANVAS. C. 1820. Made of silk union yarns in various colours, the threads having a strong cotton core.

BESSHE, BISE, BICE, BISSHE. 13th c. The fur of an animal, possibly squirrel or similar creature.

BIRDSEYE. 16th c. A silk fabric with light spots on a dark ground ; popular for women's hoods.

BLACK-A-LYRE. 14th c. A black cloth from Lire in Brabant.

BLACK ELASTIC. 1884. A cloth resembling a melton 'but as soft as a vicuna'. (*Tailor & Cutter*.)

BLACKERYBOND. 16th c. Blackalyre in long narrow ribbons. 'Blackerybond for gyrdells.' (1550, Middleton MSS.)

BLACK LACE. 17th c. Probably Mechlin or Brussels lace ; this and 'black and white' lace were fashionable after the Restoration of 1660.

BLACKS. 17th c. A common name for any black material used in mourning attire.

BLACK WORK. 16th c. Embroidery in black silk, generally upon linen. Often worked in an all-over pattern in continuous scrolling. Popular for collars, smocks, wristbands and handkerchiefs. This and a similar embroidery in red, called 'Red Work', were classed as 'Spanish Work'.

BLANKET, BLANKET CLOTH. Med. to 17th c. A white woollen cloth used by the humbler classes.

BLANKET CLOTH. 19th c. A heavy, all-wool West of England cloth with a raised finish. Much used for overcoats. *See* WITNEY BLANKET.

BLAUNCHMER, BLAUNDEMER, BLAUN-DEVER, BLAUNER. 14th and 15th c's. A fur, the animal uncertain but presumably white and apparently costly.

BLONDE LACE. 18th and 19th c's. A silk lace of 2 threads twisted and formed in hexagonal meshes. Introduced c. 1730-40. Being produced from unbleached silk was known at first as 'Nankins' or 'Blondes' (Beck).

BLUE. (1) 15th c. Stafford Blue, a blue cloth woven in that county.

(2) 16th and 17th c's. Coventry Blue, a blue cloth woven at that town.

BLUEING. 18th c. A blue material. 'For 3 yards of Blewin.' (1715, Essex Records.)

BOBBIN LACE. 16th c. A lace composed of a coarse thread, made with bobbins (as distinguished from needle-lace).

BOCCASIN. 16th c. 'A kind of fine buckram that has a resemblance to taffeta.' (Cotgrave.)

BOKASYN. 15th c. A kind of fustian (Fairholt).

BOMBAZET. 18th and 19th c's. A slight twilled textile of cotton and worsted, usually black and used for mourning.

BOMBAZINE. 16th c. Introduced by Flemish weavers at Norwich in 1572. Of a silk warp and worsted weft ; at first the natural colour and classed as 'White Work' ; from 17th c. onwards usually black and used for mourning. Its surface had a twilled appearance.

BONEETTE. 1877. A wool and silk textile having a damask pattern over it.

BONE LACE. Late 16th c. Lace made on a pillow with bone bobbins.

BOOK MUSLIN. 19th c. A muslin with a hard finish, somewhat coarser than Swiss muslin.

BORATO, BORATON, BURATO. 16th c. A thin light stuff of silk and worsted resembling bombazine.

BORSLEY. 18th c. A stuff made of combing wool.

BOTANY. 19th c. A worsted at first made of merino wool grown near Botany Bay, Australia; imported from c. 1830. Later, a term denoting the finest grades of worsted. 'Shawls of Botany worsted.' (1830.)

BOUCLÉ CLOTH. 1886. A cloth having knots and curls on the surface.

BOURACAN. 1867. A kind of ribbed poplin.

BOURRETTE. 1877. A woollen cloth, twilled, having multi-coloured knots and threads of spun silk upon it.

BOXCLOTH. 19th c. A heavily milled woollen fabric with a dress face resembling felt. Used for driving coats.

BRAID. Med. on. A narrow band of various textile materials, woven by interlacing; used as an edging to garments.

BRANCHED VELVET. 15th and 16th c's. Figured velvet.

BRAWLS. 18th c. A blue and white cotton fabric from India.

BRAZILIAN CORDED SARCENET. 1820. A coloured sarcenet with a thick white satin cord running through it.

BRIDGWATER. 16th c. A broadcloth manufactured in that town.

BRIGHTON NAP. Early 19th c. A woollen cloth resembling baize but with knots on the surface; made in Norwich.

BRILLIANETTE. C. 1790. A glazed woollen textile, striped and flowered; made in Norwich.

BRILLIANTE. 1840's. A cotton textile with a small lustrous fleck.

BRILLIANTINE. 1836. A very light textile of silk and cashmere wool.

BRILLIANTS. 1863. A silk textile, the white ground having a small damask pattern.

BRISTOL RED. 16th c. A West of England cloth dyed red at Bristol.

BRITANNIA. 17th c. A linen imported from Brittany.

BRITISH CLOTH. 17th c. See BRITANNIA, the name by which it was often called.

BROADCLOTH. Med. A fine woollen cloth of plain weave.
19th c. A cloth made of fine merino yarns in plain twill weave, heavily milled with dress face finish.

BROCADE. Med. A fabric with a pattern of raised figures (Beck). A silk interwoven with threads of gold and silver (Strutt). In 18th c. the raised figures were in coloured silks, formed by extra weft.

BROCANTINE. 1898. A fine woollen textile brocaded with silk in monochrome pattern.

BROCATELLE. 19th c. A heavy corded silk with a raised arabesque pattern in self-colour.

BROCHÉ. 19th c. A velvet or silk with a satin figure on the face.

BROELLA. Med. A coarse cloth worn by countrymen and monks.

BROGETIE. 17th c. Probably a coarse form of brocade.

BROGLIO-BROGLIO. 18th c. A kind of camlet.

BRUNSWICK CLOTH. 15th c. A linen cloth woven at Brunswick.

BRUSSELS. 14th c. A cloth in various colours imported from Brussels.

BRUSSELS CAMLET. Mid 18th c. 'A stronger kind of Irish Poplin much worn for habits and coats.'

BRUSSELS LACE. 18th c. A point lace, the designs worked separately and applied to a net ground worked with bobbins.

BUCKRAM. 16th c. A material, probably of linen or cotton, similar to lockeram; used for hose and women's gowns.

BUCKRAM CANVAS. 16th c. Buckram stiffened with gum and used for linings.

BUCKSKIN. 15th c. Leather from the hide of the buck, used for gloves.
18th c. Used for making leather breeches.

BUCKSKIN CLOTH. 19th c. A closely woven twilled woollen cloth of a cream colour, replacing the leather of that name; used especially for riding breeches.

BUDGE, BOGE, BOGEY. Med. White or black lambskin, with the wool dressed outwards and used as a trimming.
17th c. Occasionally kidskin.

BUFFIN. 16th c. An inferior form of camlet, used for gowns, doublets, etc., of the poorer classes.

BUGLE. 16th c. on. A tubular bead, commonly black; a number threaded together used to decorate a dress.

BULGARIAN CLOTH. 1883. A cream-coloured cotton fabric, plain or striped, worked in tinsel and coloured silk.

BUNTING. 1881. A coarse kind of nun's cloth.

BURAIL. 17th c. A 'silk rash', a stuff half silk, half worsted.

BURDET. 18th c. A mixed fabric of silk and cotton. 'All sorts of half-silks such as English and Turkey burdets. . . .' (1740.)

BURE, BURET. 17th c. 'Stuff that's halfe silk and halfe worsted.' (Cotgrave.)
1874. A coarse woollen stuff with broad diagonal rib.

BUREL. C. 1300 and on. A coarse woollen cloth of a dark red colour.

BURIDAN. 1836. A wide horizontally striped silk of two tones of one colour.

BURLAP, BORELAP. 17th c. A coarse linen.

BURNET. 13th c. A cloth of a brown colour.

BURRACAN, BURRAGON. 16th and 17th c's. A coarse cloth.

BUSTIAN. A kind of fustian.

BYSSINE. 13th c. A fine cloth, the nature of it unknown.

BYZANTINE. 1881. A dull semi-transparent textile of silk and wool closely woven; used for mourning.

BYZANTINE GRANITE. 1869. A dark brown woollen textile enriched with scattered threads of gold.

CACHEMIRE. 1876. A textile of fine wool and silk, the patterns usually of Eastern shades.

CACHEMIRE ROYAL. 1889. Resembles a rich cashmere with a silk back.

CADDAS, CADDACE. C. 1400. A floss silk, wool or flock used for padding.

CADDIS. 16th c. A woven tape; also a coarse serge.

CADDIS LEATHER. 16th and 17th c's. Leather from Cadis.

CAFFA. 16th c. A kind of coarse taffeta (Cotgrave).

CAFFOY. 18th c. A textile imported from Abbeville, nature unknown; also made (1744) in Ireland, containing mohair.

CALABER. Med. The fur of the grey squirrel.

CALAMANCO, CALIMANCO. 16th c. A woollen textile, plain, striped or checked, and glazed.
18th c. Of single worsted, glazed.
19th c. A cotton and worsted textile, highly glazed, plain or twilled.

CALEDONIAN SILK. 1810–20. Similar to poplin but with a more silky surface and having a chequered pattern on white ground.

CALICO. From 16th c. Originally of Indian cotton but from *c.* 1600 to 1773 the weft of cotton with warp of linen; since then entirely of cotton. Named from the town of Calicut on the coast of Malabar; hence sometimes known as Calicut cloth.

CALICUT CLOTH. 16th c. *See* CALICO.

CALTON. 17th c. A coarse narrow cloth, made in the North of England, and similar to frieze.

CAMAYEUX SILK. 1850. Chiné silk fabric with colour on colour.

CAMBAYE. 18th and 19th c's. A cotton cloth from India. 'A coarse chequer cloth.' (1727, A. Hamilton.)

CAMBRESINE. 18th c. A fine linen from Cambray and also from the Near East.

CAMBRIC. 16th c. on. A very fine quality of linen.

CAMELEON. 1830. A silk figured in large bouquets on the outside and stripes on the reverse.
1840's. A silk shot in 3 colours.
1850's. A shot poplin.

CAMELINA. 19th c. A vicuna cloth with very small basket pattern and loose upstanding hairs on the face.

CAMELINE. Mentioned in 1284. Thought to be a textile of camel hair.

CAMLET, CHAMBLET. 15th c. Thought to have been at first a kind of mohair; later of various mixed materials. Home-woven camlets from *c.* 1600, and later often watered. Sometimes 'half silk, half hair' (1675). In 18th c. sometimes of wool or silk or hair or mixtures; in the 19th c. with cotton or linen added. Made plain or twilled.

CAMLETTO, CAMLETTEEN. 18th c. 'A stuff of combing wool' (1739). 'A sort of fine worsted camlets.' (1730, Bailey.)

CAMMAKA. 14th c. A costly material, probably of silk and camel hair, from the East, used for royal and ecclesiastical garments.

CAMOCHO. 16th and 17th c's. A silk fabric from Italy.

CAMPANE LACE. 17th c. 'A kind of narrow lace, picked or scalloped.' (1694, *Ladies' Dictionary.*) The scallops in the shape of little bells. ('Campane', a bell.)

CANDLEWICK. 14th c. A cloth worn by servants.

CANTALOON. *C.* 1600. A fancy name invented for a variety of worsted, a single camlet.
18th c. A West of England cloth (Defoe). A worsted woven of fine single yarns.

CANTOON. 19th c. A fustian with a fine cord on one side, and a satiny surface of yarns running at right angles to the cords on the other.

CANVAS. 16th c. A coarse linen, generally imported. A superior quality woven with lines of thread, silk or metallic thread, and decorated with tufts at intervals or stitched with quilting. Hence 'tufted canvas'.

CARACULE. 1892. Astrakhan with a wide curl in the hair.

CARACULE MATERIAL. 1894. A crocodile mohair surface over a sort of flannel lining giving the effect of black shot with colour.

CARDA. 14th c. A cloth used in the making of surcoats, probably for linings.

CARDINAL WHITE. Late 16th c. A white undyed woollen homespun.

CARMELINE. 1870. A fine cloth similar to vicuna.

CARMELITE. 1890's. An all-wool plain-weave textile similar to thin beige.

CARNAGAN. 1820's. A cloth used for trousers.

CARPMEAL. 15th c. to 18th c. A coarse cloth used chiefly for linings; made in the North of England.

CARPMEAL WHITE. 16th c. 'Commonly used for linings of hose.'

CARREL, CURRELLES. 16th c. A cloth of silk and worsted; probably identical with Coral cloth.

CARRODARY. 18th c. Original name of Cherryderry, an Indian cotton fabric.

CARY. 14th and 15th c's. A coarse cloth.

CASBANS. 19th c. A cotton similar to Jaconet but stouter; used for linings.

CASHMERE. 19th c. A fine soft woollen fabric first imported from Cashmere; imitated as 'Thibet cloth' in Yorkshire and at Paisley in 1824. These were twilled fabrics of fine worsted. The original material was the wool of the Thibet goat.

CASHMERE SYRIEN. 1840. A very fine twilled cashmere, more substantial than Mousselaine de Laine but very soft and without a wrong side.

CASHMERE TWILL. 1890. A cotton imitation of French cashmere.

CASHMERIENNE. 1880. A fine woollen textile with a twill on both sides.

CASIMIR. 1877. A thin twilled woollen textile of worsted warp and woollen weft in a diagonal twill weave.

CASIMIR DE SOIE. 1853. A silk and wool textile having the appearance of shot silk.

CASSENET. Early 19th c. A fancy dress fabric with a diagonal twill, the warp of cotton, the weft of fine wool or of wool and silk mixed; for summer wear.

CASSIMIR, CASSIMERE. 18th and 19th c's. A cloth patented by Francis Yerbury of Bradford-on-Avon in 1766. The name had appeared in Dyer's poem 'The Fleece' in 1757:

'The glossy fleeces, now of prime esteem,
  Soft Asia boasts, where lovely Cassimire
  Spreads her delicious store . . . a region term'd
  The Paradise of India. . . .'

Yerbury stated: 'There were two species of my thin cloth distinguished by the name CASSIMIRE; one is quilled in the weaving with a flat whale, the other with a round one . . . the woof must not be spun in the same manner as for common cloth but drawn out into a much finer thread. . . .' Mr. K. G. Ponting in his *The West of England Cloth Industry* (1957) comments: 'This is obscure. Is he referring to different types of twill? He may have used a weave—such as the Venetian or doeskin—which does not show a twill on the back.'

Until c. 1820 only imported Spanish merino wool was used for this material; then the German wools from Saxony and Silesia began to displace the Spanish, which had declined in quality. The German in turn were replaced c. 1850 by the Australian merino wools. Before then the names CASSIMERE and KERSEYMERE (*q.v.*) had become confused and used often indifferently by writers; by the introduction of Australian merino the two fabrics themselves ceased to be distinguishable.

The early Cassimir has been described (*The Trowbridge Woollen Industry* by R. P. Beckinsale) as cloth 'in which the woof and the warp were usually spun to much the same fineness and to which a diagonal ribbing was given in weaving', the cloth being heavily milled.

During the Napoleonic war years when Spanish wool was in short supply substitutes were used including cotton mixtures; in 1817 there was advertised 'Patent Mohair Cassimere for waistcoats and trowsers'.

CATALAPHA. 17th c. A silk stuff, the nature unknown.

CATALOWNE. 17th c. Said to be identical with Buffin; an inferior kind of Camlet.

CATGUT. Catgut, in the modern sense, a material made from the intestines of sheep, was used in the 18th c. to form the stalk of a certain kind of coat button.

CATGUT LACE. 17th and 18th c's. Trade name for a kind of lace, possibly of horsehair; certainly not of catgut. '5¾ (yards) of fine broad cattgutt border at 20/.' (1693, Bill for lace, for Queen Mary.)

CATLING. 17th c. A variety of Lutestring.

CATSKIN. Med. Only black or white skins were given this name; the tabby variety was classified as 'Wild cat'.

CAUNGEANTRIES. 16th c. A fabric of worsted warp and silk weft having a spot effect.

CAURIMAURI. 14th c. A coarse fabric probably identical with Cary.

CELESTRINE. Med. A light blue form of Plunket.

CENDAL. Med. A silk fabric resembling a coarse sarcenet.

CENDRYN. Med. A grey cloth of a good quality.

CHADOE. 17th c. A printed cotton or cotton and linen textile from the East Indies.

CHAIN LACE. 16th and 17th c's. A braid lace made of a single cord knotted upon itself.

CHAISEL, CHEISIL. Med. A fine linen used for shirts and smocks.

CHALLIS, CHALEY. 1831. A thin twilled textile of silk and worsted; originally of silk and camel hair. Printed in colours.

CHALLIS BAREGE. 19th c. A thin form of Challis, sometimes corded or striped.

CHALON. Med. A cloth friezed on both sides (Chaucer).

CHAMBERTINE. 1872. A textile of linen and wool; used for summer dresses.

CHAMBLETTE. 17th c. A fabric originally all silk; later, with worsted weft. Woven in plain weave.

CHAMBRAY. 1880's. A thick strong coarse zephyr.

CHAMLET. See CAMLET.

CHAMPEYN, CHAMPAIGNE CLOTH. 15th c. A fine linen cloth.

CHANGEABLE. Term used before the 19th c. to denote shot material.

CHANNON CLOTH. 15th c. A worsted cloth.

CHATOYANTE. 1847. A thin woollen of grey ground covered with broad satin checks.

CHECKERY, CHECKERS. 15th and 16th c's. A checkered cloth.

CHEKLATON, CICLATON. 13th and 14th c's. Originally a scarlet textile; later, cloth of gold.

CHELE. Med. Fur from the marten's throat.

CHENEY. 17th and 18th c's. A woollen or worsted stuff; probably a short name for PHILIP AND CHENEY (q.v.).

CHENILLE. 18th and 19th c's. A fine silk cord having a surface like plush; used as a trimming.

CHENILLE LACE. 18th c. A French lace, the ground silk honeycomb in geometrical designs, filled with thick stitches and outlined with white chenille.

CHERRYDERRY. 18th c. An Indian cotton fabric similar to gingham.

CHEVEUX DE FRIZE. 18th c. A narrow lace with a vandyke edge, used as a trimming. Often spoken of as 'frize'.

CHEVERIL. Med. Kid leather; used for gloves.

CHEVIOT. 19th c. A rough-finished fabric from strong coarse wool well milled. A form of Scotch tweed.
    1880. The name given to a soft woollen textile made in tiny hair stripes and checks; used for ladies' dresses.

CHEVRON DE LAINE. 1878. A fine diagonally woven cloth, of German make, each horizontal line being reversely twilled.

CHICORÉE. 19th c. Material cut with its edge left raw (unhemmed).

CHIFFON. 1890. A delicate silk barege or grenadine.

CHINA CREPE. 19th c. A crepe made of raw silk, gummed and twisted; thicker than ordinary crepe.

CHINA DAMASK. 1879. A cotton damask in two shades with palm pattern.

CHINA GAUZE. 1878. A gauze in light colours sprinkled with tufts of floss silk.

CHINA GRASS. 1870. A plain weave fabric spun from China grass; used for summer waistcoats.

CHINCHILLA. 19th c. The fur of a small S. American animal. Chinchilla muffs advert. 1823.

CHINÉ SILK. 1820's. A silk of which the pattern has the appearance of having 'run'.

CHINTZ. 17th and 18th c's. A glazed calico of cotton and linen, having printed patterns in colours. Originally imported from India.

CHISAMUS, CICIMUS, SISMUSILIS. Med. A variable fur 'probably of the Pontic mouse'.

CICLATON. See CHEKLATON.

CISELÉ VELVET. 1876. A fabric with satin ground having a raised pattern in velvet.

CIVET. 17th c. The fur of the Civet cat.

CLEMENTINE. 1834. A rich thick silk gauze used for bonnet-linings, etc.

CLOTH OF GOLD. Med. A very rich fabric woven of flat threads of gold.

CLOTIDIENNE. 1833. A ribbon-striped satin.

COBURG. 1840's. A wool and cotton twilled stuff resembling French merino.

COBWEB LAWN. C. 1600. A very fine transparent linen.

COGWARE. 14th c. A coarse common cloth resembling frieze; made in the North of England.

COLBERTEEN. 17th and 18th c's. 'A kind of open lace with a square grounding.' (Randle Holmes, 1688.) 'A lace resembling network.' (1694, *Ladies' Dictionary*.)

CONCERTINA CLOTH. 1892. A corded cloth with silk lines running through it.

CONEY. Med. The fur of the mature rabbit.

CONSTITUTION. 1800. 'A bold ribbed velvet cord', for riding breeches.

CORAH SILK. 19th c. A light white washing silk from India.

CORDED SHAG. 1807. A shag with a marked cord, resembling corduroy.

CORDELIÈRE. 1846. A silk and wool fabric.

CORDOVAN. Med. A fine Spanish leather.

CORDUASOY. ? 18th c. 'A thick silk woven over a coarse thread.' (Fairholt.)

CORDUROY. 18th c. A thick corded stuff of cotton, with a pile like velvet.

CORDUROY VELVETEEN. 1879. A corded velveteen, used for ladies' dresses.

CORDWAIN. Med. Cordovan or Spanish leather.

CORINNA. 1837. A richly flowered silk fabric resembling embroidery.

CORKSCREW. 1870's. A worsted cloth 'having the appearance of a rib running across at a very low angle.' (*Tailor & Cutter.*)

COTELÉ. 1865. A thick ribbed silk.

COTELETTE. 1881. A stocking-woven woollen which does not stretch.

COTELINE. 1892. A striped woollen corduroy.

COTOLINE. 1886. A black mixture of faille and wool, resembling Ottoman but softer.

COTSWOLD. 16th c. Wool of a very high quality from Cotswold sheep; much used for making caps.

COTTON CLOTH. 15th to 17th c's. Woollen cloth of which the nap has been 'cottoned' or raised. 'They rayse up the cotton of such Fustians.' (1495, Act II, of *Henry VII.*)

COTTON RUSSET. 16th c. Russet cloth with a long nap.

COUCHOUC. 19th c. Indiarubber which began to be used for such articles of dress as garters and stays in the 1820's, in the woven material known as 'elastic'.

COURTAULD'S NEW SILK CREPE. 1894 'Almost as thin and soft as chiffon.' ·

COUTIL. 1840's. A French species of jean but lighter in weight; a twilled cotton cloth.

COVERT. 19th c. An all-wool cloth with worsted warp in 2 colours twisted together.

CRAPE, CREPE. 17th c. on. A transparent crimped silk gauze; originally black and as such used for mourning, for which purpose and colour the

spelling 'Crape' remained in use; the later spelling 'Crepe' (19th c.) denoted a similar material but of various colours and worn for general use.

CRAVENETTE. 1899. Patented by Bradford Dyers Ltd. A process, applied to cloth, of rendering the fibres water-resistant; much used for covert coats.

CREMIL, CREMYLE. 14th c. A lawn of cotton used for kerchiefs.

CREPE DE CHINE. *C.* 1860. A very soft China crepe of fine silk warp and worsted weft.

CREPELINE. 1870's. A cheap substitute for crepe de Chine; made of mohair and worsted.

CREPE POPLIN. 1871. A silk and wool textile slightly repped but crinkly like crepe.

CREPE ROYAL. 1889. A transparent kind of crepe de Chine.

CREPON. 1866. A China crepe with a silky lustre and a soft feel.
  1882. A wool or silk or mixed fabric with a silky surface resembling crepe but thicker.
  1890's. A woollen textile creped to look puffed between stripes or squares of plain weave. Often with a slight admixture of silk in it.

CREST CLOTH, CRESS CLOTH. 15th and 16th c's. A species of linen often used for linings.

CRETONNE. 1867. A twilled unglazed cotton fabric printed in colours.

CREWEL. 16th c. 2-threaded worsted (Bailey). Used chiefly for garters, girdles and trimmings; especially the dresses of the lower classes (Fairholt).

CRINOLINE. 1829. 'A new material made of horsehair.' Soon after it became a material of horsehair and cotton, used to make stiff under-petticoats.
  1856. The name commonly applied to the 'Artificial crinoline' or

hoop at first of whalebone and then of wire or watch-spring, containing a large number of circular hoops held together by material or tapes.

CRISP. 14th and 15th c's. A lawn; the name then replaced by Cyprus or Pleasaunce but the original name revived *c.* 1600 for one of 'the New Draperies'.

CRISTYGREY. Med. A fur classed in 1393 as 'Wildware'. the fur being that taken from the animal's head or 'crest'.

CROCUS. 18th c. A linen dyed yellow with saffron.

CROPPES. 15th c. Fur made up of pieces cut from the rump part of an animal.

CROSS LACE. 16th c. A kind of braid lace.

CROWN LACE. 16th c. A lace 'the pattern worked on a succession of crowns with acorns and roses'.

CULGEE, CULGAR. 17th and 18th c's. An East Indian silk fabric richly coloured. 'There are two sorts, the one is Satten, the other is Taffety. Much used for Handkerchiefs and for Gowns.' (1696, *Merchants' Wharehouse Opened.*)

CUBICA. 19th c. A fine Shalloon, made of worsted; for linings.

CURLED CLOTH. 17th c. A woollen cloth with a long napped surface.

CUT-AND-SLASH LACE. 17th c. Cut-work lace. '... apron laced with cut and slash lace.' (1677, *London Gazette.*)

CUTTANEE, COTTONY. 17th and 18th c's. A fine East Indian linen used for shirts, cravats, etc. Also of silk or with metal stripes.

CYCLAS. Med. A rich stuff of purple colour, imported (Planché).

CYPRESS. 16th c. A light transparent material of silk and linen in plain or crepe weaves. Both white and black; the latter used for mourning.

CYPRUS. *See* CRISP.

DAGSWAIN. 15th and 16th c's. A very coarse cloth.
'Symple rayment doth serve us full well,
Wyth dagswaynes and rouges (rugs) we be content.'
(1547, Boorde, *Introduction to Knowledge.*)

DAMASIN, DAMASELLOURS. 17th and 18th c's. A silk brocaded with metal threads.

DAMASK. Med. on. A figured fabric of silk or linen of which the woven pattern appears reversed on the back.

DELAINE. 1830's. A soft all-wool fabric of plain weave, the warp of worsted, resembling but less 'musliny' than MOUSSELAINE DE LAINE (*q.v.*).

DENIM. 18th c. An imported serge; the name shortened from 'serge de Nîmes'. Later, the name of a coloured twilled cotton textile.

DENMARK SATIN. 19th c. A variety of LASTING, woven with a satin twill.

DERRY. 19th c. 'Brown derry as a strong wide-width linen is called.' 1872, *Cassell's Household Guide*, Part 2.

DESOY, SERGE DE SOY. 18th c. A stout twilled silk (Perkins); used for linings in the 19th c. under the name of 'SILK SERGE'.

DIAGONAL. 1870's. A worsted cloth with a multiple twill running diagonally in pronounced contrast. A fashionable coat material.

DIAMOND LACE. 16th c. A braid lace woven with a diamond pattern.

DIAPER. 16th c. A linen cloth patterned by opposite reflections from its surface.

DIEPPE SERGE. 1872. A serge with a coarse diagonal twill.

DIMITY. 17th c. 'A fine sort of fustian; a cotton stuff.' (Bailey.)

19th c. A stout cotton fabric, plain or twilled, with a raised pattern on one side, sometimes printed.

DIPHERA. 1842. A fine soft kid leather; used for ladies' bonnets.

DJEDDA. 1866. A poil de chèvre with silk spots.

DOESKIN. 19th c. A soft fine West of England cloth, the warp set very close so that the weave lines are invisible; the surface smooth and level. Designed to resemble soft doeskin leather. A fashionable material for trousers about the middle of the 19th c.

DOGSKIN. 17th c. on. Used as a leather for gloves.

DOILY. 17th c. A woollen stuff, used for petticoats. Named after the originator 'who kept a linnen-drapers shop in the Strand'. (Sir Hans Sloane.)

DOMETTE. 19th c. A loosely woven kind of flannel with cotton warp and woollen weft.

DONEGAL TWEED. 1890. 'A kind of homespun tweed, brown in colour.' Used for heavy overcoats. Made in plain or in 2 and 2 twill.

DORCAS. 18th c. An Indian cotton material.

DOREA. 17th and 18th c's. An Indian muslin with very broad stripes.

DORNECK. 16th c. A linen cloth made in Norfolk. Used for servants' clothes.

DORRETTEEN. 1792. A silk and wool twist in thin invisible stripes. Made in Norwich.

DORSETTEEN. 18th c. A fabric of worsted warp and silk weft.

DOWLAS. 16th to 19th c. A coarse linen used chiefly for shirts, smocks, etc., chiefly by the poorer classes.

DOZENS. 16th to 18th c. A kind of kersey or coarse woollen cloth. 'Northern Whites commonly called Dosins.' (1523.) Also made in the West of England and known as Western Dozens.

DRAB. 18th and 19th c's. A thick strong cloth, usually twilled, of a dull brown or grey colour.

DRAFT. *See* AMEN.

DRAP DE BERRY. 17th and 18th c's. A woollen cloth woven at Berry in France.

DRAP DE FRANCE. 1871. A double-twilled cashmere.

DRAP DE SOIE. 19th c. Synonymous with Poplin.

DRAP DE VELOURS. 1861. A thick soft velvety cloth.

DRAP DE VENISE. 1866. A ribbed poplin.

DRAP FOURREAU. 1867. A thick smooth cloth with a plush surface on the inner side.

DRAWBOYS. 18th c. A name given to figured materials which at first required the use of boys to regulate the treadles of the looms; superseded by the Jacquard loom. 'Fine figured Drawboys for Women's coats with Fringe.' (1750, *Boston Gazette*.)

DRAWN-WORK. 16th c. Drawn-thread work produced in a textile by drawing out some of the threads to produce a pattern.

DREADNOUGHT. 19th c. A coarse thick woollen cloth with a shaggy nap; used for overcoats by countrymen.

DRESDEN. 18th c. 2nd half. A point lace then in high fashion; a kind of drawn-work.

DRILL. 18th and 19th c's. A stout twilled linen, used for summer suits. 'Dressed in . . . a white drill Frock.' (1757, *Norwich Mercury*.)

DROGUET. 1860. A kind of cloth of mixed materials with brocaded figures in various colours upon it. A cheap imitation of brocaded silks.

DRUGGET. 18th c. A plain or corded woollen stuff 'very thin and narrow, usually all wool, and sometimes half wool and half silk; having sometimes a twill but more usually without'. (1741, Chambers.)

DUCAPE. 18th and 19th c's. A plain-wove stout silk fabric. 'Of softer texture than gros de Naples.' (Beck.) Often brocaded or glacé. (19th c.)

DUCK. 19th c. A coarse white linen made from double warp and weft; much used for trousers, in hot weather.

DUFFEL, DUFFLE. 18th c. 'A coarse woollen.' (Defoe.)
19th c. 'A stout milled flannel, often friezed.' (1835, Booth.) Later, cloth with a thick shaggy nap, used for overcoats; hence the nautical 'duffle coat'.

DUNGAREE. 17th and 18th c's. A coarse Indian calico.

DUNSTER. 14th to 16th c's. A woollen broadcloth made in Somerset.

DURANCE. 16th to 18th c's. A durable woollen cloth. A worsted made at Norwich.

DURANT. 18th and 19th c's. 'A glazed woollen stuff called by some "Ever-lasting".' (1828, *Webster's Dictionary*.)

DURETTO, DUROTTA, DURETTY. 17th c. A durable textile of mohair and woollen thread or silk. '6 yds durotta to line waistcoats 8/.' (1723.)

DUROY. 18th c. A coarse woollen West of England cloth not to be confused with corduroy but akin to tammy. 'Wearing a grey Duroy coat and wastcoat.' (1722, *London Gazette*.) *Also* a glazed cotton in damask weave. (1791, Norwich.)

DUTTY. 17th c. A kind of fine cloth or possibly a calico.

ECCELIDE. 1837. A cashmere and silk textile, chiné and striped.

EGYPTIAN CLOTH. 1866. A soft fabric of silk with some wool.

ELASTIC. 19th c. The first patent for applying caouchouc (indiarubber) to thread to form 'elastic' material was taken out by Hancock in 1820. The term 'elastic', however, had been applied in the 18th c. to stretchable textiles cut on the cross.
In 1884 the name was also applied to a new cloth 'resembling a melton but as soft as a vicuna'. (*Tailor & Cutter*.)

ELATCH, ELATCHA. 17th c. An Indian striped silk, not to be confused with allejah.

ELEPHANT CLOTH. 1869. Made of twisted flax-cord and having a basket-like mesh.

ELLEMENTES. 17th c. A worsted fabric.

ELMINETTA. 18th c. A thin cotton textile.

ELYSIAN. 19th c. A woollen overcoating cloth with a nap finish in diagonal lines or ripples.

EMBROIDERY. Med. on. The enriching a material by working needlework figures in silk upon its surface.

ENAMELLED. 18th c. A term denoting a stiffening of a textile with gum.

ENGLISH POINT LACE. C. 1670. A name applied to Brussels lace smuggled into this country; so called to avoid tax.

EPANGELINE. 1868. An all-wool rep-like material.

EPANGLINE. 1890's. A woollen sateen with a slight cord.

ERMINE. Med. The white winter fur of the Stoat. Powdering of ermine (the spots made from the animal's tail to distinguish royal from ordinary ermine) began in the second half of 14th c.

ERMINETTA. 18th c. A thin linen or cotton material.

ESMERALDA. 1831. A white crepe or gauze embroidered in black and gold.

ESTAMINE. 17th and 18th c's. An open woollen fabric.
19th c. A somewhat thick serge, firm in texture (1876). 'All-wool figured estamens.' (1890's.)

ESTRICH, ESTRIDGE. 16th c. A felted material made from the down of ostrich feathers; used for hats as a substitute for beaver.

ETRUSCAN CLOTH. 1873. A cloth with a rough surface like towelling.

EVERLASTING, LASTING. 18th c. and 19th c. to c. 1840. A stout worsted fabric with double warps and single weft. 'A cloth with a shining surface.' (1829.)

EXHIBITION CHECKS. 1851. Cloth with a large check pattern, used for trousers in the year of the Great Exhibition.

FAILLE. 1863. 'An unwatered moire silk', softer and brighter than grosgrain.

FAILLETTE. 1898. A soft woollen fabric, ribbed, with a gloss like silk.

FALDING. Med. A coarse cloth resembling frieze.

FARRENDEN, FARRENDER, FARENDINE. 17th c. A cloth of silk and wool.

FEARNOUGHT, FEARNOTHING, DREADNOUGHT. 18th c. A stout cloth almost impenetrable to wind and rain. A thick cloth with a long pile. 'A fear nothen Jacket and Wescot.' (1741, Essex Records.)

FEATHERS. 15th c. on. Especially those of the ostrich; worn by men as decorative additions to headgear until near the end of the 18th c. and by women from 16th c. onwards; in the 19th c. especially, feathers of every native and of many foreign birds used for headgear, muffs, mantles, etc.

FELT. Med. on. A solid composition of the fibres of wool and the hairs of fur; united without weaving but by matting together by heat, moisture and pressure. A material much used for making hats.

FELTED KNITTING. 16th c. A process whereby a knitted article, usually a cap, purposely knitted too large, is soaked, rubbed and pummelled to produce felting and shrinkage to the desired size.

FERRET. 17th c. A narrow ribbon of silk or cotton; a kind of tape.

FIGURED STUFFS. 18th c. 'Designs of flowers, figures, branches, etc., impressed by means of hot irons.' (1741, Chambers.)
19th c. The designs in coloured threads are woven on the material.

FIGURERO. 17th c. A woollen fabric.

FIGURETTO. 17th c. A costly flowered stuff; thought to have been woven with metallic threads.

FIGURY. 15th c. A satin and velvet woven with patterns.

FILLED MUSLIN. Mid 19th c. A fine muslin with 'lappet spots' produced by zigzagging extra warp ends over the top of associated warp threads.

FILOZELLA, FILOZETTA, PHILISELIE. 17th c. A double camlet. 'A kinde of coarse silke.' (1598.)

FINGROMS. 18th c. A coarse kind of serge principally made at Stirling (Defoe).

FITCHEWS, FITCHET, FILCHES. Med. The fur of the Polecat or Fitch, the under fur being yellow-buff, the upper fur a rich glossy brown approaching to black.

FLANDERS LACE. 17th c. A bone lace made at Brussels or Mechlin.

FLANDERS SERGE. 17th c. An English-made worsted fabric.

FLANNEL. Med. and on. Originally a Welsh-made woollen material though called in 16th c. 'Welsh cottons'. Made of woollen yarn slightly twisted, with open texture. Of plain or twill weave.

FLANNELETTE. 1876. Originally an American cloth, one side twilled, the other with a plush-like surface, and made mostly of wool; later, almost entirely of cotton, to imitate flannel.

FLORAMEDAS. 17th c. A flowered or figured stuff, the nature of which is unknown.

FLORENCE. 15th c. A woollen cloth originally imported from Italy.

FLORENCE. 19th c. 1840's. A corded barege or grenadine. Also a thin kind of taffeta used for linings.

FLORENTINA. 18th and 19th c's. A variety of prunella; a woollen material woven from combed wool.

FLORENTINE. 16th c. A silk or satin textile imported from Florence.
19th c. 'A silk stuff chiefly used for men's waistcoats; striped, figured, plain, or twilled. Two other stuffs are known under this name, one composed of worsted (the old Florence); the other of cotton resembling jean and generally striped; used for trousers.' (Beck.) The latter referred to in 1817 as 'the newly invented National Florentine'.
1882. 'A twilled silk thicker than florence.' (*Dictionary of Needlework.*)

FLORINELLE. Late 18th c. A glazed brocade striped and flowered; made at Norwich.

FLURT SILK. Med. Figured silk.

FLUSHINGS. 19th c. A heavy woollen fabric similar to duffels.

FOREST CLOTH. 16th to 18th c's. A woollen cloth of good quality originally from the Forest of Dean.

FOREST WHITE. 16th and 17th c's. A white homespun made at Peniston. When dyed red or blue it was known as a Penniston.

FOULARD. 1820's. Originally from India; later from France. A soft light washing silk, twilled.

FOULARD POILE DE CHEVRE. 1870. A foulard-like fabric of goat's hair 'with the brilliance of Jap silk'.

FOULE. 1882. 'A material resembling casimir with a silky look.' Soft and velvety. A twilled woollen.

FOX FUR. Med. Fur of the native fox was used from early Middle Ages. The fur of the Russian black fox, from *c.* 1600.

FOYNES. Med. The fur of the polecat.

FRENCH JET. 1893. A dress trimming composed of jet facets applied to metal discs.

FRIEZE. Med. A napped woollen cloth, originally Irish. 'A coarse kind of cloth manufactured in Wales.' (1662, *Fuller's 'Worthies'.*)

FRISE BROCADE. 1885. A brocade with the pattern upstanding like terry velvet.

FRIZADO. 16th and 17th c's. A heavy worsted cloth similar to baize.

FROU-FROU. 1870. A satin-like washing cloth.

FUSTIAN. Med. A coarse twilled textile with linen warp and cotton weft (Beck). The surface resembling velvet; hence the term 'Mock velvet'.
The name appears to have been also applied in the 14th c. to a woollen or worsted cloth made at Norwich.

FUSTIAN ANAPES. 17th c. A fustian from Naples; a kind of velveteen. 'Mock velvet or fustian anapes.' (Cotgrave.)

FYCHEUX. 15th c. Fur of the foumart, 'otherwise called the Polecat or Fichet'.

GABARDINE. 1879. A patent waterproof cloth of Egyptian cotton proofed before weaving.

GALATEA. 19th c. A strong firm striped cotton fabric woven in imitation of linen, with a marked twill.

GALLOON. 17th to 19th c. A woollen or thread kind of ferret used as an edging of garments.
1848. 'Galloons are now of pure silk.'

GAMBROON. 1817. A twilled cloth of worsted and cotton warp and a cotton weft, in plain weave; also of mohair. Used for waistcoats, breeches, and trousers.

GARLICKS. 17th c. A linen from Gorlitz, Prussian Silesia.

GASSED LACE. The thread first passed through a gas flame to scorch off superfluous fibres. 'British Gassed Lace commonly known by the name of Urling's Lace.' (1823.)

GAUZE. 13th c. on. A very thin silk textile, semi-transparent.
18th c. Made of silk and also of linen.
19th c. Also of cotton in many varieties.

GAUZE ILLUSION. 1831. A fine close gauze of silk resembling tulle.

GAUZE SYLPHIDE. 1832. A fabric of alternate stripes of gauze and satin ribbon, the latter brocaded with bouquets of flowers.

GAZELINE BAREGE. 1877. A semi-transparent textile of pure llama wool, resembling a barege.

GAZE PERLEE. 1833. Semi-transparent gauze with small silk squares figured on it.

GENAPPE CLOTH. 1863. A textile of wool and cotton, generally striped in 2 shades of the same colour.

GENET, JENNET. Med. The fur of a species of civet cat, grey or black.

GENOA PLUSH. 1887. A plush with a very short thick pile resembling velvet. A cotton velveteen.

GENOA VELVET. 18th and 19th c's. An all-silk brocaded velvet.
1876. 'A term now applied when the ground is satin and the arabesque figures are velvet.'

GENTISH. 18th c. A textile originating from Ghent.

GERMAN SERGE. 18th c. A serge made of worsted warp and woollen weft.

GIMP. 17th c. on. A coarse lace formed by twisting threads round a foundation of wire or twine. Made in various qualities of silk, wool or cotton. Used as a trimming.

GINGERLINE. 17th c. A cloth, formerly a reddish violet colour.

GINGHAM. 18th c. A cotton fabric made from dyed yarn; first made in Glasgow in 1786.
19th c. The name given to a stout chequered cloth originally of linen, later of cotton.

GLACÉ SILK. C. 1840. A plain taffeta with a peculiar lustrous surface.

GLAZED HOLLAND. 18th c. A Dutch chintz.

GOALY. 1874. A kind of ecru silk, the texture like fine canvas.

GODELMING. 14th c. Calfskin leather prepared at Godalming.

GOSSAMER. 19th c. A rich silk gauze used for veils.

GOURGOURANS. 1835. 'A dress material of a light-coloured ground with white satin stripes.'

GRANITE. 1820's. A stuff made of chenille and used for head-dresses.
1865. A sort of chiné woollen textile in 2 shades of one colour.

GRAZET. 18th c. A cheap woollen stuff of a grey colour.

GRENADINE. 19th c. An open silk or silk and wool gauze resembling barege but with a more open mesh. Many varieties both plain and figured; also an all-wool Grenadine. Often used for shawls.

GREY. Med. Thought to be the fur of the grey squirrel imported from Germany.

GRIS. Med. A grey fur, possibly squirrel.

GROGRAM. 17th and 18th c's. 'A taffeta, thicker and coarser than ordinary.' (Bailey.) Originally of silk and mohair and then known as Turkey Grogram. The material was apparently stiffened with gum.

GROS, GROSGRAIN. 19th c. A stout silk fabric of rich quality showing a cord, less perceptible than in poplin, running from selvedge to selvedge.

GROS DE LONDRES. 1883. Similar to Ottoman silk but with a much finer cord comprising 'two small grains between two large'.

GROS DE NAPLES. 18th and 19th c's. 18th c. Resembled taffeta, but stouter.
19th. A corded silk somewhat resembling Irish poplin. 'Lutestring now termed gros de Naples.' (1837, Mrs. Papendiek.)

GROS DE ROME. 1871. A crinkled silk, between a China crepe and a foulard.

GROS DE SUEZ. 1867. A silk textile with 'three small grains between two larger'.

GROS DE TOURS. 1833. A rich corded silk resembling terry velvet; almost identical with REP IMPERIAL (q.v.).

GROS DES INDES. 1827. A heavy silk with narrow transverse stripes.

GROS D'HIVER. 19th c. A silk between a tabby and a paduasoy.

GUIPURE LACE. 19th c. A lace of large pattern which is held together by connecting threads; without a net ground.

GULIK HOLLAND. 18th c. A very fine white linen, used for shirts.

HABIT CLOTH. 19th c. A smooth close form of Broadcloth, without a twill.

HAIRBINES. Late 18th c. A worsted in plain weave with rough surface, resembling mohair. Made at Norwich.

HAMBROW. 16th and 17th c's. A fine linen from Hamborough in Germany.

HAMILTON LACE. 18th c. A coarse lace of the diamond pattern, made at Hamilton from 1752. Named after the Duchess of Hamilton.

HANDEWARPES. 16th c. A white or coloured cloth made in East Anglia.

HARDEN. 16th and 17th c's. A common linen made from tow or the coarsest quality of hemp or flax (Beck).

HARE. Med. The fur of the legs of hares; the white winter fur of the Irish hare was most esteemed. Mentioned in A.D. 1278.

HARLEM STRIPES. 18th c. A linen from Holland.

HARRATEEN, HARRITEEN. 18th c. A woollen stuff made from combing wool.

HARRINGTON. C. 1835. A stout cloth, 'both sides smooth and napped', often with tufted surface. Used for winter overcoats.

HARRIS TWEED. 2nd half 19th c. A rough homespun tweed cloth, of a loose weave; hand made in the Outer Hebrides.

HARVARDS. 1890's. A cotton striped shirting in 2 and 2 twill or in plain weave.

HENRIETTA CLOTH. 1890's. A cloth resembling fine cashmere but with silk warp or weft.

HERCULES BRAID. C. 1850. A narrow braid in black or white, having a heavy ribbed weave.

HERRINGBONE LACE. 15th and 16th c's. Lace having a chevron pattern.

HESSIANS. 18th c. A coarse cloth of hemp or jute.

HOLLANDS. 17th and 18th c's. A fine linen first imported from Holland; later the name applied to any fine linen. 'That manufactured in Frizeland and called frize holland is the strongest and best coloured.' (1741, *Chambers's Encyclopædia*.) 'There are two sorts of yarn or thread in Dutch or Flemish linen ... the warp is made of Flanders yarn; the shute of Silesia. The Scotch hollands are made of the same yarn both in warp and shute, either from home flax or the best foreign.' (1742, *The Champion*.)

HOLLMES. 17th c. A sort of fustian.

HOLLOW LACE. 16th c. A braid lace used for edging.

HOPSACK. 1860's. A woollen in plain weave, the threads in weft and warp interlaced with 2 or more threads instead of one. Becoming a fashionable dress material in 1890's.

HOPSACK SERGE. 1891. A coarsely woven woollen serge-canvas.

HOUNSCOT SAY. 15th c. An English worsted material.

HOUSEWIFE'S CLOTH. From 15th c. 'A middle sort of linnen cloth between fine and coarse, for family uses.' (1727–41, *Chambers's Encyclopædia*.)

HUGUENOT LACE. Early 19th c. An imitation lace with a muslin net ground on which floral cut-out designs were sewn.

HUMMUMS. 18th c. A plain weave cotton cloth from East India.

HUNGERLAND LACE. 17th c. A lace made at Halle in the Hungarian style. 'Your Hungerland bands and Spanish quellio ruffs.' (*C.* 1630, Massinger: *The City Madam*.)

IMPERIAL, CLOTH IMPERIAL. Med. A silk fabric with figures in colours and gold thread. Originally made at Byzantium.

IMPERIAL GAUZE. 19th c. 'An open gauze having a white warp with a coloured weft.'

IMPERIAL VELVET. 1870. A fabric in alternate stripes of corded silk and velvet, the latter double the width of the former.

INDERLINS. 18th c. A coarse hempen cloth from Hamburg.

INDIAN. 18th c. Either drawn muslin lace ('Indian work') or muslin.

INDIAN DIMITY. 18th c. 'Now called twilled calico.' (1837, Mrs. Papendiek.)

INGRAIN. Med. Wool dyed before weaving, especially scarlets, crimsons and purples.

INKLE. 16th to 18th c's. A kind of linen tape sometimes white but usually coloured, used as a cheap binding by the lower classes.

IONETIS. Med. The genet, the fur of which resembles the marten's.

IPSIBOE. 1821. A yellow crepe. Named from the romance by Vicomte d'Arlincourt. 1821.

IRISH CLOTH. 13th to 15th c's. Of wool ('frieze') or linen.

ITALIAN CLOTH. Second half of 19th c. A cloth of botany weft and cotton warp, having a glossy face; used for coat linings.

JACCONET. Early 19th c. A thin cotton textile between a muslin and cambric. Similar to nainsook.

JANUS CORD. 1867. A black rep of wool and cotton, the fine cord showing equally on both sides. Much used for mourning.

JAPANESE PONGEE. 1870. A silk of the same texture as crepe but with a smooth surface.

JAPANESE SILK. 1867. A silk textile hard and springy, resembling alpaca.

JAPAN MUSLIN. 18th c. Muslin worked in a loom to produce an indistinct or 'japanned' figure.

JAPAN STUFF. 17th and 18th c's. Thought to be calico. 'Short under-petticoats, pure, fine, Some of Japan stuff, some of Chine.' (1661, J. Evelyn, *Tyrannus or the Mode.*)

JARDINIÈRE. 1841. A striped and gauffred crepe strewn with small flowers.

JEAN. 16th c. on. A twilled cotton cloth or fustian. 19th c. A twilled sateen.

JEANS FUSTIAN. 17th c. A jean containing wool.

JERSEY. 1879. An elastic woollen material resembling fine knitting. 18th c. The name applied to 'the finest of the wool separated from the rest by combing'. (Bailey.) The name originated from a worsted made of wool from that island, in the 16th c.

KARAMINI. 1878. A light woollen fabric with a slight fleecy surface.

KENDAL. 14th c. on. A coarse woollen cloth, usually green, originally made at Kendal.

KENTING. 18th c. A kind of fine linen from Holland ; imported into Ireland in mid 18th c. but later made there.

KERSEY, CARSIE. Med. on to early 19th c. A coarse woollen cloth but many varieties in quality and pattern. 'A double-twilled say.' (Booth.) The name attributed to the Suffolk village where it may have originated. Much used for making stockings before the introduction of knitting. One of the traditional 'narrow cloths' of Yorkshire, in 18th c. Also made in Devonshire in 17th and 18th c's.

KERSEYMERE. 18th and 19th c's. 'A fine twilled woollen cloth of a peculiar texture, one third of the warp being always above and two thirds below each shoot of the weft'—was a 19th-c. description. Its nature in 18th c. is uncertain. Apparently introduced as a rival to the patented Cassimir, and possibly very similar, the name first appears in an advertisement in the *Bath and Wilts Chronicle,* January 30, 1772, as 'KERZYMEAR'. Whether then made of English or Spanish wool is uncertain but after 1820 the Saxony merino wool was replacing the Spanish and at the same time the names Kerseymere and Cassimir were becoming used indifferently, at least in fashion journals.

By 1845 Perkins regarded them as merely a matter of spelling, an example followed by Beck in 1885, and by later writers. The confusion in the earlier records is increased by the habit, in inventories and tailors' bills, of abbreviating names of materials ; e.g. 'Saxon drab kersey' (1822) may have been short for 'kerseymere'.

KILMARNOCK. 18th c. A Scottish woollen serge made in that town.

KINCOB. 18th c. An Indian gauze generally embroidered with gold or silver.

KLUTEEN. 1815. A striped French figured silk, used for ladies' spencers and pelisses.

KNICKERBOCKER. 1867. A thick coarse woollen stuff, self-coloured or speckled. The date coincides with the introduction of the garment of that name and presumably the material was designed for its make.

KNITTING. A continuous web made by interlocking a series of loops in a single thread, using long metal needles.

It is agreed that knitting was practised in this country early in the 16th c. Some authorities, however, put the introduction much earlier. A kind of braiding technique, known in Danish archaeological literature as 'Sprang', of which specimens were found in Coptic graves in Egypt and also in Swedish graves of the 8th and 9th c's. is thought by some to have been a form of knitting, though this is in dispute.

Mr. James Norbury permits us to quote him as follows : 'You are perfectly safe in saying that "knit caps" were made in England during the 14th, 15th and 16th centuries. "Felted" caps were knitted first before being felted. . . . As early as 1320 in an Oxford Inventory (authority : Thorold Rogers. *History of Agricultural and Prices in England*) are listed two pairs of "Caligne de Wyrsted" —knitted gaiters.'

Under Edward IV 'certain Acts were passed to protect the British knitters from their Continental rivals. . . . Sleeves, caps, and some form of loose waistcoat were knitted in England at this time.'

Machine knitting by a stocking frame was invented in 1589 by the Rev. William Lee. (*See* STOCKINETTE ; STOCKING-KERSEY.)

KNOTTING. 17th and 18th c's. A fancy threadwork made by the knitting of knots in the thread ; similar to tatting. Used for bordering garments, and at the end of the 18th c. stockings were occasionally made of knotting.

LACE. A term used from the Middle Ages to denote a variety of articles of dress. (1) A cord, usually of closely-woven thread or silk and commonly with aiglets at the ends ; used for drawing together 2 edges ; e.g. shoe-lace, stay-lace.

(2) A narrow braid woven on the loom.

(3) Braid lace as an edging to a garment, not appearing until the second quarter of 15th c. Often of metal thread.

(4) An openwork fabric of linen, cotton, silk, woollen or metal threads, from 16th c. After 1660 a distinction was made between 'bobbin' or 'bone lace' made on a pillow by threads attached to bobbins, and needlework, known as 'point lace'.

(For machine-made lace, *see* LOOM LACE.) (For kinds of point lace, *see* under respective names : e.g. 'BRUSSELS LACE', 'CROWN LACE', 'ORRIS LACE', etc.)

LAID WORK. 16th c. A form of decoration corresponding to 'appliqué'.

LAINE FOULARD. 1861. A silk and wool washing silk fabric.

LAKE. Med. 'A kind of fine linen or perhaps lawn.' (Strutt.)

LAMBSKIN. 14th c. on. Black and white skins used for lining and facing garments.

LAPLAND BEAVER. 1859. A textile with 'a twill on the face and has the appearance of plush ; made in a variety of colours'. Used for capes and outdoor garments.

LASTING. *See* EVERLASTING.

LAWMPAS, LAMPAS, LAMPORS. 14th c. A kind of crepe.

LAWN. From 14th c. on. (1) A very fine semi-transparent linen cloth.

(2) Also a coarse country cloth, mentioned in Sumptuary Laws of 1363 : ploughmen, shepherds, carters, etc., forbidden to wear any sort of cloth but 'blanket and russet lawn'.

(3) 17th c. 'Lawns commonly called French lawns', being a very fine quality of cambric.

The name was originally derived from the French town of Laon where the fabric was said to have been first made (Skeat). Identical with Cloth of Rheims and similar to Cambric (first made at Cambray), 3 neighbouring cities famous for the quality of their linens.

LEMISTER, LEMSTER. 16th c. A fine woollen used for knitting caps ; the Herefordshire wool being much used for this purpose. *See* BEWDLEY CAPS and MONMOUTH CAPS.

LENO. Late 18th c. and early 19th c. A gauze-like linen fabric.

LEOPARDS. 15th c. Leopard's skin.

LERION. 12th c. on. Thought to be the fur of the dormouse.

LETTICE. Med. A white fur resembling miniver; possibly the fur of the ferret or polecat.

LEVANTINE. 1815. A twilled sarcenet.
1840's. A rich faced, stout twilled silk textile similar to the surah of the 1870's.

LEVANTINE FOLICÉ. 1837. A soft rich silk with arabesque patterns.

LIBERTY ART SILKS. 1870's on. Originally an East Indian tussore silk printed in Europe; becoming in the 1880's and 1890's a generic name for artistically designed silks usually of Indian weave, sold under that registered trade mark.

LIMOUSINE. 1874. A thick rough woollen, coarser than cheviot, and having a hairy surface.

LINCLOTH. 13th c. Linen cloth.

LINCOLN GREEN. 14th c. A green cloth used especially by huntsmen, verderers, etc.

LINEN. Med. on. A woven textile made of flax; made in this country from Roman times or before. Many varieties and qualities.

LINSEY-WOOLSEY. 16th c. A cloth of linen and wool, said to have originally been made at Linsey, Suffolk. The warp of thread, the weft of worsted.

LISSE. 19th c. An uncrimped silk gauze.
1894. 'The new name for improved uncrushable chiffon.'

LIVERY LACE. 18th and 19th c's. A worsted braid woven with a design peculiar to the household where it was to be worn.

LIZARD, LUZARD. 16th and 17th c's. The fur of the lynx.

LLAMA. 1889. 'An elastic make of cloth of the vicuna class.' Made from the hair of the S. American goat of that name.

LLAMA CLOTH. 19th c. A cloth with a llama wool face, and finished with a long nap. Used for overcoats.

LOCKERAM, LOCKRAM. 15th to 17th c. A coarse linen, used for shirts and smocks, worn by the poorer classes.

LOOKING-GLASS SILK. 1892. 'A glacé with a suspicion of moire on its shining surface.'

LOOM LACE. 16th c. on. Lace woven on a loom, imitating bobbin or point lace. 'For loome lace to make Mistris Margarett a payre of ruffez.' (1554–5, Willoughby Accts., Lord Middleton's MSS.)

LORETTO. 18th c. A fine silk fabric used for waistcoats.

LOUISINE. 1880's. A very thin kind of surah silk.

LOVE. 18th and 19th c's. A thin silk with narrow satin stripes in it; used for ribbons.

LUCERN. 16th c. on. The fur of the lynx.

LUISINE. 1834. A heavy rep silk.

LUMBARDINE. 16th c. A fine gauze identical with PLEASAUNCE.

LUSTRE. 19th c. A thin kind of poplin, of silk and worsted.
1890's. A variety of mohair with a shiny surface.

LUTESTRING, LUSTRING. Late 16th c. to 19th c. Originally a fine, somewhat lustrous taffeta. In the 19th c. a very fine corded silk with a glossy face.

LUTHERINE. 18th c. Listed under 'Mixed goods' and probably an early form of LUSTRE.

MACABRE. 1832. A light silk and wool textile figured in small designs and edged with a Gothic border.

MADONNA. 19th c. A fancy alpaca, plain weave with satin stripes.

MADRAS. 1825. A muslin with transparent ground having a pattern in thick soft thread apparently darned upon it.

MALINES. 1885. A fancy canvas closely woven, having the appearance of being interwoven.

MANCHESTER COTTONS. 16th c. 'Its woollen cloths which they call Manchester cottons. . . .' (1590, Camden.) The true cotton fabrics of that city date from *c.* 1640.
18th c. The name given to a textile with stripes of cotton and wool.

MANCHESTER VELVET. 18th c. A cotton velvet.

MANTLING. 18th c. Rough blue and white checked cotton cloth for aprons.

MANTUA SILK. 17th c. 'Those glorious Italian silks which our countrymen find more difficulty in imitating than any other.' (1758, *A New Geographical and Historical Grammar.*)

MARABOUT. 19th c. Feathers of a species of stork.
1877. A woollen soft to the touch but looking rough and mossy on the surface.

MARBLE. 13th to 18th c. A cloth woven or dyed in colours to resemble marble markings. A similar material was made in silk.

MARBRINUS. 14th c. A worsted fabric woven with pale-coloured warp and coloured wefts to imitate a marble appearance.

MARCELINE. 1833. 'A brilliant but slight kind of sarcenet.'

MARCELLA. 18th and 19th c's. A cotton quilting or coarse piqué with a diaper pattern in relief. Used for waistcoats.

MARGUERITE. 18th c. A dress fabric woven of silk, wool and linen.

MARIPOSA. 1872. A washing sateen with stripes alternately plain and dotted.

MARLI-MARLY. Late 18th c. A French light linen.

MARLY-LACE. 18th and 19th c's. A lace of a hexagonal mesh net powdered with small round rosettes. Originally of cotton; later of thread and of silk.

MARRY-MUFF, MARAMUFFE. 17th c. A cheap kind of cloth; also known as PIRAMID. Of woollen yarn, plain weave.

MARTINIQUES. Late 18th c. A woollen fabric made at Norwich.

MARTRONS, MARTERS. Med. The fur of the pine marten; a rich dark brown.

MASKEL LACE. 15th c. A spotted lace net.

MATELASSÉ. 1839. A firm substantial silk woven to resemble quilting.

MECCA. 1877. A gauze of the thinnest texture with dashes of silk in the wool.

MECHLIN LACE. 18th and 19th c's. A bobbin lace, the foundation a plain net, the pattern outlined by a flat cord or thread.

MECKLENBURGH. 18th c. A wool damask with stripes in coloured floral designs. Made at Norwich.

MEDLEY. 17th to 19th c. A cloth made of wools of different colours.

MELROSE. 18th c. A textile of silk warp and wool weft.

MELTON. 2nd half of 19th c. A heavily milled woollen cloth with a short dense nap; closely woven. Resembling beaver cloth.

MEMPHIS. 1836. A semi-transparent textile of very fine cashmere wool.

MERINO. 1826. A thin twilled woollen cloth, originally made of wool of the Spanish merino sheep. A worsted plainback very soft to the touch. 'French merino' indicated the better qualities, though made in England. Inferior qualities containing cotton appeared under many fancy names.

MERINO CREPE. 19th c. A mixture of silk and worsted having a shot effect.

MESSELAWNY. 17th c. 'A 17th century stuff.' (Beck.) Its nature unknown.

MEXICAN CLOTH. 1865. Of strong raw silk, washable.

MIGNONETTE. 18th c. A light fine pillow - lace, fashionable for head-dresses in the 2nd half of that century.

MIKADO. 1875. A silk alpaca imitating Jap silk; made by Lister of Bradford.

MILANESE TAFFETA. 1880. A semi-transparent silk textile woven on the cross.

MILK AND WATER. 16th c. A cloth probably so named from its colour; composition unknown.

MINIKIN. 17th c. A form of baize; a plain weave worsted made in Norwich.

MINIVER. Med. The fur of the white weazel (Topsell). But its nature is much disputed; its colour seems to have been pure white. It was first mentioned in 1278.

MINKS. 15th c. The black fur of the *Putorius lutreola*, resembling sable but shorter and more glossy.

MIRROR VELVET. 1890's. A watered velvet having the appearance of reflections in its surface.

MISTAKE. 1806. A shaded silk used for ribbons.

MOCKADO. 16th, 17th and 18th c's. An imitation of velvet, usually of wool.

MOCK VELVET. 17th c. Naples fustian; a twilled cotton fabric.

MOHAIR. 17th c. on. A closely woven stuff of the hair of the Angora goat; two varieties of the material, one plain, the other watered.

18th c. 'Of silk, both warp and woof, having its grain wove very close.' (1738, Chambers.)

19th c. Woven with silk, wool or cotton warps; and resembles alpaca.

MOIRE ANTIQUE. 19th c. A heavy stout watered grosgrain, the watering being in irregular waves.

MOIRETTE. 1896. A light worsted fabric with a watered surface and slightly stiffened. Used for 'rustling foundations' and petticoats.

MOIRE VELOURS. 1897. A silk and wool watered velvet with a large irregular design.

MOLESKIN. 19th c. A coarse fustian, strong and twilled; resembles barragon. Used for trousers by working-men.

MOLLETON. 1865. A sort of thick smooth flannel in plain weave or 2 and 2 twill; used for dressing-gowns. Later often of cotton.

MOMIE CLOTH. 1880's. Of cotton or silk warp and woollen weft, resembling a fine crepe; usually black and used for mourning.

MONKEY SKIN. 1858. A fashionable material for ladies' muffs.

MONKS' CLOTH. 15th c. A worsted material.

MONTPENSIER CLOTH. 1871. A smooth soft cloth twilled on the wrong side.

MORAVIAN WORK. Early 19th c. A revival of the 16th-c. cutwork with button-holing at the edges; a forerunner of broderie anglaise.

MOREEN, MOIREEN. 18th to 19th c. An all-worsted textile with a watered surface to imitate moire.

MORELLY. 17th c. A kind of Tabby. 'A morelly coate striped yellow and black.' (1681, *Verney Memoirs*.)

MORISCO WORK. 16th c. Couched embroidery in gold or silver in arabesque patterns. 'A pair of sleeves of Morisco work.' (1547, Inventory of the Wardrobe of Henry VIII.)

MOROCCO LEATHER. 17th c. on. Goatskin leather tanned with sumac and generally red.

MOSCOW BEAVER. 1868. A shaggy napped beaver cloth, for overcoats.

MOSS CLOTH. 1878. A soft rich textile of silk and wool; mossy texture.

MOTLEY. 14th c. on. 'A cloth which they (the Danish courtiers) call Kentish cloth, we c Motley.' (1617, Fynes Moryson.)

MOULTAN MUSLIN. 1840's. Muslin with a woven pattern 'worked with a lappet wheel, made exclusively at Glasgow'.

MOUNTAIN MOSS. 1859. 'Resembles fur beaver but is lighter and softer.' Used in mixed and plain colours; e.g. for loose capes.

MOUSSELAINE DE LAINE. 1833. A fine light woollen cloth of a muslin-like texture; often 'figured in gay patterns like a calico print'. Of cotton warp and worsted weft, if of English make; of all wool if French.

MOUSSELAINE DE LAINE CHINÉ. 1841. As above, with chiné patterns.

MOUSSELAINE DE SOIE. 19th c. A very fine soft silk textile with an open mesh; the early form of chiffon.

MOUSSELAINE THIBET. 1832. A silk and wool textile, semi-transparent, with a watered surface.

MOUSSELAINE VELOURS. 1832. Mousselaine de laine figured with cut velvet stripes.

MOZAMBIQUE. 1865. A silk broché wool grenadine.

MULL MUSLIN. 19th c. A soft thin muslin, not silky; finer than nainsook.

MUNGO. A cloth made from disintegrated woollen rags, especially those hard-twisted and felted. *See* SHODDY.

MUSCORD. 17th c. A woollen cloth.

MUSCOVITE. 1884. 'A handsome thick corded silk.'

MUSCOVITE VELVET. 1883. A velvet brocade on a ribbed silk ground.

MUSER. 16th c. A spangle hanging by a thread from the surface of a garmen instead of being stitched down.

MUSLIN. 17th c. A fine cotton fabric having a downy nap on its surface. 'The flimsy muslins from India' began to be imported c. 1670, displacing the flaxen linens and cambrics in the fashionable world. Manufactured in this country and Scotland c. 1780. The varieties used in the 19th c. may be classified: (1) Book muslin. Similar to Swiss but coarser; (2) Indian. Soft, thin, opaque, with a slight 'greasy' feel; (3) Leno. Very open and stiff; (4) Madras. Transparent ground with a pattern in thread darned upon it; (5) MULL (*q.v.*); (6) Organdy. Soft and opaque with a raised spot worked in it; (7) Swiss. With a hard finish and nearly transparent.

MUSTERDEVILLERS, MUSTERDEVELIN, MUST DEVILES, etc. 14th and 15th c's. A woollen cloth woven at Montivilliers in Normandy. No contemporary evidence that the name refers to 'mustard colour'.

MYLLION. 16th c. A fustian from Milan. 'A piece of millyan fustian. . . .' (1588, Essex County Sessions Rolls.)

NAINSOOK. 18th c. A somewhat heavy Indian muslin.

NAK, NAQUET. Med. A cloth of gold brocade imported from the Near East.

NANKEEN, NANKIN. 18th c. A cotton cloth of a yellowish-brown colour, originally from Nankin.

NAPLES LACE. 16th and 17th c's. A black silk lace made at Naples.

NAPS. 18th c. A term denoting cloths subjected to 'friezing' or twisting the nap into knots.

NATTE. 1874. A firm substantial silk woven to resemble cane-platting.

NEAT'S LEATHER. Med. Made from the hide of 'neat' cattle, i.e. oxen; used for footwear.

NEEDLEWORK LACE. End of 16th c. to c. 1660. The name then given to point lace.

NEIGEUSE. 1877. A soft twilled woollen with a surface speckled or 'clotted', and rough-faced.

NET. 16th c. on. A fabric of fine mesh, such as was used for veils, etc.

NETTLECLOTH. 17th c. Linen made from nettle fibres in place of hemp. Synonymous with Scotch cloth. 'Three linings for partlets, of nettle-cloth wrought with red silk.' (1553, Hatfield Papers.)

NETWORK. 16th and 17th c's. Lace consisting of a ground of net of square meshes on which is worked the pattern, sometimes cut out of linen and appliqué, but more usually darned with stitches like tapestry. 'A sute of blacke net worke.' (1574, Lord Middleton MSS.) 'A suit of network' appears to have been a set of matching bands, ruffs, ruffles, etc., sufficient to garnish a man's suit of clothes or a woman's dress.

NEW DRAPERY. 16th c. Refugee weavers (Walloons) in 1561 and Netherlanders in 1568 who settled in Colchester, Norwich, Maidstone, etc., introduced stuffs to which they gave new names; known as 'the New Drapery', to include 'Sarges, Perpetuanoes, Bayes', etc.
By the 'Old Draperies' were understood such textiles as broadcloth and the kersies. It appears that some of the so-called 'New Draperies' were but old ones under new names; and that 'a buffyn, a catalowne, and the pearl of beauty, are all one cloth; a peropus and paragon all one; a saye and pyramides all one; the same cloths bearing other names in times past'. (Complaint by the Worsted Weavers of Norwich, temp. James I.)

NONE-SO-PRETTYS. C. 1770. A linen tape on which were woven figures in colours.

NORWICH CREPE. 19th c. A textile with silk warp and worsted weft, of 2 shades of a colour; had the advantage of being reversible, and unlike bombazine had no twill.

NORWICH FUSTIAN. 16th c. A worsted material woven at Norwich in imitation of Naples fustian; the name legalised 1554.

NORWICH GROGRAINE. 16th c. A fine worsted fabric made at Norwich.

NORWICH SATIN. 16th c. A worsted fabric made at Norwich; the name by which Russel Satin and Satin Reverse were known.

NOVATO. 17th c. A fabric of wool or silk. 'A paire of ash couller novato hose.' (1614, Lismore Papers.)

NUN'S CLOTH. 1881. 'A fine thin un-twilled woollen fabric formerly called mousselaine de laine; it is a kind of bunting.'

NUN'S THREAD, SISTER'S THREAD. 16th c. A fine white thread made in the convents of Italy and Flanders and used for netting and lace.

NUN'S VEILING. 1879. A kind of thin woollen barege; synonymous with Voile. Later, used as a synonym for Nun's Cloth.

OLDHAM. Med. A coarse worsted textile made in Norfolk, the name probably a corruption of Aldham.

OILED LEATHER. 18th c. Leather dressed with fish oil, to imitate chamois leather; much used for labourers' breeches.

OLLYET. 17th c. A woollen textile made at Norwich. Similar to bombazine.

ONDINE. 1871. A very soft and brilliant silk and wool mixture.
1893. A corded silk crepon.

ONDULE. 1865. Cloth having a wavy appearance in the warp.

ORGAGIS. 18th c. A coarse Indian cotton cloth.

ORGANDY. 19th c. *See* MUSLIN.

ORIENTAL SATIN. 1869. A soft and thick all-wool or silk and wool textile, woven in 2 colours, one brilliant, the other dark.

ORLEANS CLOTH. 1837. Resembles an untwilled coburg, the warp of thin cotton, the weft of worsted.

ORPHREY. Med. Gold embroidery; later, a border of narrow strips of any kind of embroidery.

ORRIS LACE. 17th and 18th c's. A lace woven with designs in gold or silver threads.

OSBRO. 17th c. A worsted fustian often mixed with silk.

OSNABURG, OZENBRIG. 16th c. A German linen.

OTTER FUR. Med. The fur of that animal; mentioned *c.* A.D. 1200.

OTTOMAN PLUSH. 1882. A silk textile having a broad corded ground with plush figures of close thick pile.

OTTOMAN REP. 1882. A repped lustrous satin woven on both sides with flat cording.

OTTOMAN SATIN. 1832. A rich shaded satin brocaded with flowers.

OTTOMAN SILK. 1882. 'A term loosely applied to every kind of silk with a horizontal thick cord and two or three cords in between.'

OTTOMAN VELVET. 1869. A velvet with coloured patterns brocaded over it.
1879. A richly repped uncut velvet.

OUNCE. 16th c. Originally the fur of the lynx but later applied to that of other small feline animals.

OUTNAL THREAD, WOTENALL THREAD. 16th c. Thought to be 'the Flemish brown flaxen thread'.

OXFORD. Early 19th c. A corded cotton and wool textile.

OXFORD SHIRTING. 19th c. A cotton cloth, plain weave, with narrow coloured stripes.

PACKING WHITE. A woollen cloth mentioned in the Act of 1483.

PADOU. 18th c. A silk ribbon, imported from Padua.

PADUA SERGE. 1863. A silk serge used for linings.
18th c. A material for poor women's gowns.

PADUASOY, POODESOY, PATTISWAY. 17th and 18th c's. The name being a corruption of 'pou de soie' (17th-c. French). A strong corded or grosgrain silk, usually black; becoming obsolete by 1750 it was reintroduced a century later as 'Poult de soie'.

PALMYRENE. 1827. A textile between a poplin and a barege; embroidered in silks.

PALMYRIENNE. 1831. A shot wool-and-silk textile, resembling mousseline de soie.

PAMPILION. 16th c. A species of felt.
15th–16th c's. Black Budge fur from Navarre.

PANNE. 1899. A soft silk material between velvet and satin. A light velvet with a flattened pile.

PARAGON. 17th c. A kind of double Camlet similar to Peropus. 'The Paragon, Peropus, and Philiselles may be affirmed to be double Chamlet, the difference being only the one was double in the warp and the other

in the woof.' (*C.* 1605, 'Allegations on behalf of the Worsted Weavers'.)
18th c. A stuff made from combing wool.

PARAMATTA. 19th c. A textile at first made with silk warp and worsted weft, resembling coburg. Later, with cotton warp. Used chiefly for mourning.

PARAPES. 17th c. Resembled paragon.

PARCHMENTIER. 19th c. A thin stiff wool cloth made at Norwich.

PARCHMENT LACE. 16th and 17th c's. A lace usually of gold or silver but occasionally of coloured silks. A pillow lace.

PARIS CLOTH, TOILE DE PARIS. Med. and 17th c. Originally a fine white linen; later a woollen cloth.

PARISIAN CLOTH. 19th c. An English textile of cotton warp and worsted weft.

PARISIENNE. 19th c. A French material of merino wool with small brocaded designs; also an English of worsted (1842); a figured Orleans.

PASSEMENTERIE. 19th c. A trimming of braids and fringes ornamented with beads, silk and metallic threads.

PATENT THREAD, URLING'S PATENT. 1817. Cotton thread gassed to scorch off the finer fibres; from which Urling's Patent Lace, machine-made, was formed.

PEAK LACE. 16th and 17th c's. Lace with the outer edge margined by a series of angular indentations.

PEARL OF BEAUTY. 17th c. One of the many fancy names of 'the New Drapery', but 'a buffyn, a catalowne, and a pearl of beauty are all one cloth; may be affirmed single chamblettes, differing only in breadth'. (1604.) A striped worsted 'by colours in the warp and tufted in the stripes'.

PEAU DE SOIE. 1880's. A dull silk with a sateen finish.

PEELING or PEELON. 18th c. A kind of thin satin.

PEKIN. 1830's. A silk textile of the nature of taffeta, having fine stripes running through it; hence 'Pekin stripes'.
1879. A term also applied to any textile with alternate dull and lustrous stripes.

PEKIN LABRADOR. 1837. A Pekin silk flowered in wreaths.

PEKIN POINT. 1840. A very rich white silk painted with flowers or bouquets with foliage, with a light mixture of gold in the pattern.

PEKIN VICTORIA. 1842. A silk fabric with a satiné ground, shot in white and cherry or blue, with patterns in white.

PELLUCE. 16th c. The early form of the word plush.

PELLURE. Med. A generic name for furs.

PELURIN. Med. Purfled or edged with fur.

PENNISTON, PENNYSTONE. 16th to 18th c. A coarse frieze made originally at Peniston, Yorks. (*See* FOREST WHITE.)

PERCALE. Early 19th c. A fine calico slightly glazed and often having a small printed design.
1863. 'A fine glazed linen.'

PERCALINE. 1848. A cotton textile between a gingham and a muslin, striped or quadrilled, and printed in colours.

PEREALE TAFFETA. 1859. A cambric sarcenet.

PERKALE. 1818. French cambric muslin.

PEROPUS. 17th c. A double camlet, often watered. (*See* PARAGON.)

PERPETUANA, PERPETS. End of 16th c. One of the 'New Draperies', a glossy-surfaced woollen fabric, the warp of combing wool, the woof of carding wool. 'The sober perpetuana - suited Puritans.' (1606, Dekker, *The Seven Deadly Sins*.)

PERSE. 13th and 14th c's. A textile thought to be of the nature of serge of a bluish colour.

PERSIAN. 17th into 19th c. A thin soft silk, usually plain; much used for linings of coats, gowns, etc.

PERSIAN THIBET. 1832. A woollen textile with embroidered designs similar to those on shawls.

PETERSHAM CLOTH. Late 19th c. 'A heavy woollen cloth having a round nap surface.' (1904, *Tailor & Cutter*.)

PETERSHAM RIBBON, PETERSHAMS. *C.* 1840. Thick double ribbon, generally watered, plain, figured or striped.

PHILIP AND CHENEY, PHILIP AND CHINA. 17th and 18th c's. A woollen textile akin to camlet. But it was capable of being watered: '15 yeardes of water'd Philip and Cheney.' (1627.)

PHILOSELLE. 17th c. A variety of camlet. (*See* PARAGON.)

PILLOW. 18th c. A kind of plain fustian.

PILOT CLOTH. 19th c. A thick twilled cloth with a nap on one side; of indigo-blue colour. Used for greatcoats.

PINTADO. 17th c. An East Indian cotton fabric printed in colours.

PLAINBACK. *C.* 1813. At first an imitation of Cotton Jean in worsted; later there developed from it the single-twilled merinos.

PLEASAUNCE. 16th c. 'A fine species of gauze striped with gold.' (Strutt.) Used for head-coverings. See CRISP.

PLODAN. 16th c. A coarse woollen checked material. Worn by women for cloaks.

PLOMMETT, PLUMMET. 16th and 17th c's. A woollen or mixed cloth made at Norwich. Possibly a form of PLUNKET (*q.v.*).

PLOUGHMAN'S GAUZE. 1801. A fine gauze with satin spots; used for ladies' evening dresses.

PLUNKET, PLONKETE. Med. A woollen textile, usually of a blue colour.

PLUSH. 16th c. A long-napped velvet of cotton or wool or silk; usually of wool and hair (e.g. goat's) mixed.
    19th c. A shaggy hairy kind of cotton velvet with a long soft nap resembling fur.

POILE DE CHEVRE. 1861. A textile of goat's hair (weft) and silk (warp) in plain weave; having a shiny satin-like face.

POINT LACE, or POINT. Late 16th c. on. A thread lace made wholly with the needle on a parchment pattern. The term 'Needle - point' is modern. Known as 'Point lace' from 1660; previously as 'Needlework lace' to distinguish it from Bone-lace, Cutwork and Drawn-work.

POINT JEAN. From 1660 on. A bobbin lace not used in England earlier.

POINT DE VENISE. From 1660. 'I never saw anything prettier than this high-work on your point d'Espagne. . . . 'Tis not so rich as point de Venise.' (1676, Etherege, *Man of Mode*.)

POINT OF SPAIN. From 1660. Spanish Point lace.

POLAYN. Med. Fur of the black squirrel, believed to have come from Poland.

POLDAVIS. Late 16th c. A coarse linen.

POLONY WOOL. Late 17th c. Used in making imitation beaver hats.

POMET LACE. 16th c. A silk lace.

POMPADOUR. 18th c. A rich silk taffeta with satin stripes and floral sprigs in colours. 'Mr. Clarke was dressed in pompadour with gold buttons.' (1762, Smollett, *Launcelot Greaves*.)

POMPADOUR CHINÉ. 1840. A woollen twilled textile with a small chiné pattern and striped horizontally in minute thread-like stripes.

POMPADOUR DUCHESSE. 1850. A satin with broad stripes divided by other stripes sprinkled with tiny flowers.

POMPADOUR SHANTUNG. 1880. A thick washing silk like foulard, covered with Pompadour designs on a brilliant ground.

POMPADOUR SILK. 1832. A silk fabric with black ground and a highly raised pattern in detached sprigs, in lemon, rose and green.

PONGEE. 1870's. A tussore silk of an ecru colour.

POPEL, POPLE. 15th c. Squirrel fur, from the back of the animal.

POPES MINSTERS. 17th c. Nature unknown. Possibly a linen imported from Munster.

POPLIN. From 1685 on. Manufactured in Ireland from early 18th c. A kind of rep with silk warp and wool or worsted weft, having a fine cord on the surface. 3 classes, the single, the double, and the terry; the last being richly corded and—unlike terry velvet—is the same on both sides. Poplin may be plain, watered or brocaded.

POPLIN BROCHÉ. 1841. A poplin with broché patterning.

POPLINETTE. 1859. 'Sometimes known as Norwich Lustre and occasionally as Japanese silk.' Made with a glazed thread and silk.

POPLIN LACTEE. 1837. A poplin shot with white.

POPLIN LAMA. 1864. Similar to mousselaine de laine but softer and thicker.

PORRAYE. Med. A green cloth imported. The name used in 16th c. to denote the colour green.

POULT DE SOIE. 19th c. A pure corded silk of a rich quality.
1863. 'A mixture of silk and alpaca with a shiny surface.'

PRESIDENT. 1870's. A heavy union cloth woven on the doublecloth principle; the face cotton warp and wool weft.

PRINCE'S STUFF. 18th c. A black woollen material closely woven in plain weave, used for clerical and legal gowns and also for mourning.

PRINCESS STUFF. 17th and 18th c's. A dress fabric made of goat's hair warp and silk weft.

PRINCETTA. 1800 to 1840. A worsted of silk warp and worsted weft.

PRINTED FABRICS. 16th c. on. Earliest English reference: '1535-6. Wardrobe Warrant. For making of a shamewe of blacke printed satten.'
Printing of textiles was set up in London in 1676, at first for the printing of calico, using wood blocks. Printed materials for women's dresses very fashionable in the 1830's.

PRUNELLA, PRUNELLO. 17th and 18th c's. A coarse form of black shalloon, used especially for academic, legal and clerical gowns.

PUKE. 15th and 16th c's. An imported woollen cloth, usually nearly black in colour, dyed before weaving.

PULLICAT. 16th to 18th c's. From Pulicat near Madras. A cotton fabric much used at the close of the 18th c. for making coloured handkerchiefs.

PUNTENADO. 17th c. Italian needlepoint lace.

PURED. Med. A term denoting the white fur of the underside of an animal.

PURLE. 16th c. on. 'A kind of edging for Bone Lace.' (Bailey.) 'A narrow braid.' (Planché.)

PURLED VELVET. 16th c. Velvet enriched with patterns worked in loops of gold thread.

PURNELLOW. 18th c. A worsted textile.

PYRAMID. 17th c. A wide coarse and thin form of SAY (*q.v.*).

QUILTING. 18th and 19th c's. A ready-made padding usually of satin interlined with cotton; used for petticoats and linings of gentlemen's coats.

QUINTIN. 17th c. 'A sort of French linnen cloth that comes from St. Quentin in Picardy.' (1687, Miege.)

RADZIMIR. 1849. A black all-silk textile used for mourning.

RAGMAS, RAGMERSH. 14th to 16th c. An oriental fabric figured in gold.

RAPLOCH WHITE. 16th c. A coarse undyed woollen homespun.

RAS DU MORE. 18th c. From Ras de St. Maur, later becoming Radzimir, of a heavy black silk resembling Armozeen; used for mourning.

RASH. 16th c. A smooth textile, either of silk and then called SILK RASH, or of worsted, CLOTH RASH; later known as SHALLOON.

RATEEN. 17th c. A thick twilled cloth usually friezed.
18th. c. The generic name of a class of coarse woollens.

RATINET. 18th c. A thin form of Rateen.

RAY. 14th c. A word used to indicate that a material is striped but the name appears also to have been applied to a material that was not coloured.

RAYNES. Med. A fine quality of linen made at Rennes.

RED WORK. *See* BLACK WORK.

REGATTA SHIRTING. *C.* 1840. A cotton textile with narrow coloured stripes.

REGENCE. 1889. A rich silk textile with a ribbed satin face.

RENFORCÉE. End of 17th c. A strong silk fabric akin to Alamode, introduced by French refugees after the Revocation of the Edict of Nantes, 1685.

REP. 19th c. A cloth with heavily marked transverse ribs. Many varieties, not all of wool. Some of silk or silk and wool (such as poplin).

REP BLUET. 19th c. A dark-blue silk rep figured with cornflowers in black satin.

REP IMPERIAL. 1835. A rich silk imitating Terry velvet.

REP SARCENET. 19th c. A textile between gros de Naples and a fine cut French velvet.

RHADAMES. 1883. A soft satin with a diagonal grain.

ROANES. 15th c. on. A fine woollen cloth, usually tawny in colour; made at Rouen.
17th c. A linen cloth from Rouen.

ROSADIMOI. 1820. A corruption of the name 'Ras de St. Maur' and later called RADZIMIR (*q.v.*).

ROSETTA. 1st half 18th c. A striped or checked textile, probably silk.

ROSILLE DE SOIE. 1840. A dead silk with pattern in network strewn with flowers in monochrome.

ROSKYN, RUSKIN. Med. The summer fur of the squirrel; a red chestnut colour.

RUG. 16th to 18th c. A coarse kind of Frieze worn by the poorer classes.

RUM-SWIZZLE. 1850. An Irish frieze made of undyed wool.

RUSSALINE. 18th c. A woollen textile made at Norwich.

RUSSEL CORD. 1880's. Originally an all-worsted cloth but soon with cotton warp. Resembled a coarse corded alpaca; used for linings.

RUSSEL SATIN. 16th c. A Norwich fabric of worsted with a lustrous satin-like finish. (*See* NORWICH SATIN.)

RUSSELLS. 16th c. Revived in 18th c. A worsted with a lustrous surface like satin; made at Norwich. Synonymous with Russel Satin.

RUSSET. 15th and 16th c's. A coarse cloth or homespun (Bailey). Sometimes brown but sometimes grey. Worn by the poorer classes.

RUSSIAN CREPE. 1881. A species of mat cloth closely interwoven.

RUSSIAN DUCK. 19th c. A fine bleached linen canvas; used for summer wear.

RUSSIAN VELVET. 1892. A light woollen of even grain and checked, the stripes being small round raised twists of a different colour from the foundation.

RUSSIENNE. Early 19th c. A silk textile.

SABELLINE. 17th c. The skin of the zibelline marten.

SABLE. Med. The fur of an animal resembling the weazel and of a rich dark glossy brown. But some were black; hence the use of the word as a synonym for black.

SACKCLOTH. 16th and 17th c's. A hempen material coarser than canvas; of various colours and worn for outer garments chiefly by the lower classes.

SADDLE TWIST. 1865. A trousering 'with a narrow thread of a rib'.

SAGATHY. 18th c. A slight woollen stuff, a kind of serge; sometimes mixed with a little silk.

SAINT MARTIN'S LACE. 16th and 17th c's. A cheap copper braid lace made in the parish of St. Martin's, London.

SAINT OMER. 17th c. An English worsted textile.

SALISBURY FLANNEL. 18th c. 'The principal manufactures of this city are flannels, druggets, and the cloths called Salisbury Whites.' (1768.)

SAMITE. Med. A costly silk, frequently interwoven with threads of gold or silver.

SAMMERON. 16th c. A fine quality of linen. 'A cloth between flaxen and hempen, finer than the one and coarser than the other.' (Halliwell.)

SARATA SHIRTING. C. 1870. A linen shirting material.

SARCENET. Med. A thin soft silk textile having a slight sheen on the surface; of taffeta weave, variously coloured; sometimes 'shot'.

SARCIATUS, SARZIL. Med. A coarse woollen cloth, worn by the lowest classes (Strutt).

SARDINIAN. 1870. A heavy twilled woollen napped cloth, the nap slightly knopped. Used for overcoats.

SATARRA CLOTH. 1893. 'Like a hopsack in texture but the surface finished to look like a fancy worsted.'

SATEEN. 1838. A cotton textile with a shiny satin-like face.

SATIN. Med. on. A silk twilled textile which has been given a smooth glossy surface by the application of heat; the back is dull. The brilliancy of the surface was augmented by dressing.

SATIN ANTOINETTE. 1834. Satin with white ground and satin-shaded rays and small detached bouquets of flowers.

SATIN BLONDE. 1833. Satin flowered in white on coloured ground, resembling blonde lace on satin.

SATIN CASHMERE. 1893. An all-wool fabric with soft silky surface and uncrushable.

SATIN DE CHINE. 1850. A satin of silk and worsted.

SATIN DE LAINE or SATIN CLOTH. 1836. A woollen cloth with a smooth surface, used for gentlemen's pantaloons.

SATIN DU BARRY. 1832. A satin with alternate stripes of black and figuring.

SATIN DUCHESSE. 1870. A thick plain satin, very durable.

SATINÉ PLAYÉ. 1873. A striped cotton and wool mixture, the face very satiny and the stripes twilled.

SATINESCO. 17th c. An inferior kind of satin. One of the many 'New Draperies' originating from Norwich.

SATIN ESMERALDA. 1837. A rich satin of various colours with applications of velvet of a darker shade.

SATINET. 17th to 19th c. A thin slight satin usually striped; 'used by the ladies for summer Nightgowns'.
1816. A silk and wool fabric with a satin stripe.

SATIN FONTANGE. 1841. A satin with broad stripes alternately white and coloured.

SATIN FOULARD. 1848. A silk fabric satined either in stripes or spots.

SATIN JEAN. 1870. A finely twilled cotton fabric with a satin gloss.

SATIN MERINO. 1846. A textile of which the right side is finer and more silky than cashmere; the wrong side resembles plush.

SATIN MERV. 1886. A broad-ribbed satin.

SATIN MERVEILLEUX. 1881. A soft twilled satin resembling thick rich surah but with a brighter face and duller back.

SATIN MONTESPAN. 1833. A rich silk of a dead white ground, striped in large squares.

SATIN POMPADOUR. 1835. A satin with white ground embroidered in coloured flowers.

SATIN REVERSE. 16th c. Synonym of NORWICH SATIN.

SATIN TURC. 1868. A soft and very brilliant woollen textile.

SATIN VELOUTÉ. 1837. A satin 'as rich as velvet and as supple as muslin'.

SATIN VICTORIA. A woollen material resembling silk, with narrow stripes.

SATTINET. End of 18th c. A worsted in satin weave; made in Norwich.

SAXONY. End of 18th c. on. Originally the name given to a fabric made from the merino wool grown in Saxony. By c. 1820 the name in this country for a type of cloth of merino or botany quality, a group to which soft tweeds and fine whipcords belong. The material was noted for being smooth, soft and dense.

SAY. Med. 'A thin woollen serge.' (Bailey.) 'A soft light twilled fabric of wool and silk.' (Linthicum.)

SAYETTE. Late 16th c. One of 'the New Draperies', a textile of wool and silk.

SCARLET. Med. Originally a rich fabric; later, a colour.

SCOTIA SILK. 1809. A textile of cotton and silk resembling broché.

SCOTS CLOTH. 17th c. Linen woven of nettle fibres. (See NETTLECLOTH.)

SEAMING LACE. 17th c. A moderately wide net lace of cutwork, bonework or needlework without edges; used instead of a seam to unite the breadths of linen in a shirt or smock.

SEDAN LACE. 17th c. Cutwork lace made at Sedan.

SEERSUCKERS. 18th c. An Indian cotton textile. 'Canterbury Muslins and Seersuckers 13/- to 28/- per gown.' (1791, *Salisbury Journal*.)

SELISIE LAWN. 18th c. A cambric imported from Silesia.

SEMPITERNUM. 17th and 18th c's. A twilled woollen stuff resembling serge; named for its durability.

SEMPRINGHAM. 14th c. A Lincolnshire cloth.

SERCHE. C. 1600. Thought to be a kind of mohair.

SERGE. Med. to 1900. A loosely woven twilled worsted, becoming commonly used from 17th c. on. Many varieties were imported with names of origin distorted, e.g. Serge of Chalon (1649) became Shalloon; Serge de Nîmes became Denim.

17th c. on. A loosely woven twilled flannel, the warp of worsted, the weft of wool.

SERGE DUSOY. 18th c. 'A stout twilled silk, the twill curiously fine.' (Perkins.)

SERGENIM. 18th c. Serge de Nîmes. *See* DENIM.

SERGE ROYALE. 1871. A textile of flax and wool, with a bright silky appearance.

SHAG. 16th to 18th c. A shaggy cloth, generally of worsted. 'A thick-piled cloth with a nap of worsted or silk.' (Linthicum.) Often used for linings.

SHAGREEN. 18th and 19th c's. A silk fabric with a grained ground.

SHALLOON. 16th to 19th c. 'A slight woollen stuff' (Swift), originally made at Chalon; first known as Rash. Later, much used for linings of men's clothes. A loosely woven woollen stuff twilled on both sides.

SHAMOY. 18th c. Chamois leather.

SHANKS. 15th and 16th c's. Black fur from the legs of kids, goats and lambs. For lining and bordering garments.

SHANTUNG. 1870's. A thin soft textile of undyed China silk.

SHEEP'S GREY. 17th c. A homespun cloth of undyed black and white wool.

SHEEP'S RUSSET. 16th c. Probably identical with FEARNOUGHT. 'Sheep's russet cloth called friars' cloth or shepherd's clothing.' (1598, John Florio, *A Worlde of Wordes*.)

SHEPHERD'S CLOTH. 18th c. Identical with FEARNOUGHT.

SHODDY. A remade cloth similar to MUNGO, but composed of rags of worsted and other woollen materials loose in texture.

SICILIENNE. 1870. A fine quality of poplin, the warp of silk, the woof of cashmere wool.

SILESIA. 18th and 19th c's. A thin coarse linen with glazed surface.

18th c. Used for neckcloths and cravats.

19th c. Much used for linings; usually of a brownish colour.

SILISTRIENNE. 1868. A wool and silk textile of a firm texture.

SILK. Med. on. This product of the silkworm has always been imported, either in its raw state or as a silk fabric. The manufacture by weaving silk in this country was introduced by Flemish refugees in the 16th c. and much increased by every influx of foreign weavers, especially after 1685.

SILK DAMASCENE. 1876. A silk and wool fabric with fine stripes of wool and satin alternating.

SILK DELAINE. 1830's. A textile of silk and worsted.

SILK SERGE. 19th c. A thin twilled silk textile much used for coat linings.

SILVERETS. 18th c. A material used for mourning.

SINDON. 16th c. A linen or silk. Possibly same as the mediaeval Cendal.

SIPERS. A synonym for CYPRESS (*q.v.*).

SIRGE DEBARAGON. 17th c. A light variety of serge.

SIRSAKA. 1835. 'A silk striped lengthwise in narrow light-coloured stripes and traversed horizontally by dark ones.'

SISKIN. 14th c. A Flemish cloth of a green colour.

SISTER'S THREAD. *See* NUN'S THREAD.

SKIVER. 18th c. A thin kind of dressed leather.

SLEASY HOLLAND. 18th c. A name given to 'all thin, slight, ill-wrought hollands'. (1741, Chambers.)

SLEAVED SILK. 16th c. Raw floss silk.

SLESIA LAWN. 17th c. A fine linen resembling cambric.

SOOSEY. 18th c. A mixed striped fabric of silk and cotton, from India.

SOYEUX LINSEY. 1869. A light and brilliant woollen poplin.

SPANGLES. 16th to 19th c's. Small pieces of glittering material usually metallic; originally lozenge-shaped; later, circular, sewn on garments as decoration.

SPANISH CRAPE. 18th c. An all-worsted textile made at Norwich.

SPANISH MEDLEY. 17th and 18th c's. A Dorset broadcloth made of Spanish (merino) wool mixed with English.

SPARTA VELVET. 17th c. Another name for NAPLES FUSTIAN.

SPIDER WORK. 19th c. A cheap machine-made lace.

SPIRAL WITNEY. 1861. 'A soft material with short curls on the face, somewhat between a napped Beaver and a Frieze.'

STAMMEL, STAMIN. Med. The earlier name STAMIN was a fine worsted textile, generally red.
16th c. Under the name oi STAMMEL, a good quality of worsted or linsey-woolsey, generally red.

STAMFORTIS. Early Med. A strong and costly cloth.

STATUTE LACE. 1571. Lace woven according to the statute of that year; probably a native-made lace to be worn by those who were forbidden to wear foreign-made lace.

STOCKINETTE. 18th and 19th c's. A closely woven woollen textile having a mesh resembling knitted material. Much used for tight-fitting pantaloons. Occasionally of silk, e.g. 'superfine silk stocking-breeches'. (1766).

STOCKING-KERSEYMERE. 1836. 'Has the face and firmness of a Saxony cloth and the elasticity of stocking.' Used for evening-dress trousers.

STRAIT. 15th and 16th c's. Term denoting any 'strait' or narrow cloth as opposed to broadcloths; their dimensions fixed by statute in 1464.

STRANLYNG. Med. The autumn fur of the squirrel.

STRASBURG CLOTH. 1881. A cotton textile resembling corduroy but without the plush face.

STRIPED PLUSH. 1865. Plush with narrow stripes alternatively dull and shining.

STUFF. A mediaeval name, still surviving, for worsteds made 'of long or combing wool'. (Caulfield and Stewart.) 'Distinguished from other woollen cloths by the absence of any nap or pile.' The distinction was well recognised early in the 17th c.

SULTANE. 1866. A fabric of silk and mohair resembling fine alpaca, in alternate stripes of clear or satin or chiné.

SUPERFINE. 18th c. A superior quality of broadcloth, made of Spanish merino wool.
19th c. A West of England broadcloth of merino yarn, fairly heavy, heavily felted, raised and cropped, with a soft firm handle and lustrous face. Much used for men's clothing until c. 1880.

SURAH. 1873. A soft and brilliant Indian silk twilled on both sides, more substantial than foulard.

SUSSAPINE. 16th c. A costly silk textile.

SWANSDOWN. 18th c. and 19th c. (1) The fine down feathers of the swan, used chiefly for muffs and pelerines.
(2) 19th c. A material, originally of wool and silk; later, of wool and cotton.

SWANSKIN. 18th and 19th c's. A thick twilled flannel with a downy surface; used by working men for trouser-linings.

SWARRY-DOO. 1893. 'A very bright twilled silk' (*Tailor & Cutter*) used for facings of frock-coats.

SYLVESTRINE. 1831. A material imitating silk, manufactured from wood; the first known attempt to make 'artificial silk'.

TABARET. 18th c. 'Worsted Tabaritts, the newest fashion; in imitation of a rich Brocaded Silk.' (1749, *Boston Gazette*.) Similar to Tabbinet. A glazed brocaded woollen.

TABBINET. Late 18th and 19th c's. A watered poplin.

TABBY. 17th c. on. A coarse kind of thick taffeta, glossy and watered.

TAFFETA. From 14th c. on. Originally a plain glossy silk textile; later, a thin glossy silk with a wavy lustre.
    Many varieties; 'changeable taffeta' (16th c.) was shot taffeta. 'Glacé silk' was a taffeta with a very glossy face.

TAFFETA COUTIL. 1847. A mixed fabric of silk and cotton in blue or lilac stripes on a white ground.

TAFFETALINE. 1876. A mohair material.

TAMATIVE. 1863. A light woollen material resembling Grenadine but thicker; the warp twisted once between each shoot of the weft, i.e. the gauze weave.

TAMBOUR. 18th and 19th c's. A form of embroidery worked on a drum-shaped frame.

TAMETT. 17th c. A Norwich cloth.

TAMINE. 16th c. A fine silk and wool fabric.
    17th c. A fine worsted with a glazed finish.

TAMISE. 1876. A soft woollen fabric with a little silk in it.

TAMMY. 17th to 19th c. A worsted stuff apparently identical with Tamine.

TAPE. Med. on. A narrow flat woven braid of flax or, later, of cotton.

TARLATAN. 1830's. A thin gauze-like muslin much stiffened.

TARTARIAN CACHMERE. 1823. 'For ladies' dresses, soft and light; never creases; in all colours.'

TARTARYN. Med. A costly textile, the nature unknown.

TATTERSALL. 1891. A cloth in vivid checks resembling a horse-cloth.

TAUNTON. 16th c. A broadcloth made in that town.

TAVISTOCK, or WESTERN DOZENS. 16th c. A species of Kersey made in that town.

TAWDRY. 16th and 17th c's. A silk lace, originally St. Audry's lace.

TAWNY. 17th c. A woollen cloth usually yellowish brown in colour.

TERRENDAM. 18th and 19th c's. An Indian cotton fabric.

TERRY VELVET. 19th c. At first an uncut velvet; later, a silk textile having a fine corded surface, with no resemblance to velvet.

THE UNION. 1815. A silk and cotton shot textile.

THIBET CLOTH. 1874. A soft thick flannel-like cloth with long goat's hair surface. The name also given, early in the century, to an imitation cashmere first made in Yorkshire and in 1824 at Paisley.

THICKSET. 18th c. A coarse fustian worn by the lower classes.

THREAD. From Med. on. Made of twisted flax; many named varieties; e.g.: AXMINSTER. 17th c.; BARAGGAN. 18th c. In Renfrewshire; BRUGES. 15th, 16th, 17th c's.; COLEYN. 15th c. From Cologne; COVENTRY. 16th c. Of a vivid blue and used chiefly for embroidery; NUN'S THREAD, SISTER'S THREAD, OUNCE THREAD. 16th c. A fine white thread chiefly used in lace-making; OUTNAL THREAD, WOTE-NALL THREAD. 16th c. Thought to be 'the Flemish brown flaxen thread'; UTNARD THREAD. 15th and 16th c's. Thread spun at Oudenarde, in Flanders.

THUNDER AND LIGHTNING. 18th c. A serge made of worsted warp and woollen weft; also known as German Serge.

TICKING. 15th c. on. A linen fabric.

TICKLENGBURGS. 17th and 18th c's. A coarse linen cloth from Tecklenburg.

TIFFANY. 17th c. on. A transparent silk gauze.

TIGRINE. 1834. A mixture of silk and cashmere resembling twilled satin, very soft and supple.

TINSEL, TYLSENT, TILSON. 16th c. A rich sparkling fabric of silk inter-woven with gold or silver thread.

TIRETAINE. 13th c. A fine woollen cloth generally scarlet, much used for ladies' dresses.

TISSUE. Med. A fabric of twisted metal threads. Also applied to any woven stuff especially cloth of gold, or silver, or of coloured silk. 'Eight yerde of sea greene tyssue for double slevis for ridinge gownes.' (1612–13, Part of trousseau of the Princess Elizabeth.)

TISSUE MATALASSÉ. 1839. A cloth of which the surface was 'in small squares resembling quilting'. Used for gentlemen's overcoats.

TOBIN, TOBINE. 17th, 18th and 19th c's.
17th c. A striped woollen cloth made at Norwich; also of silk. 'A silke tobine jerkyn.' (1611, Will of Jeremy Wayman.)
18th c. A twilled silk resembling Florentine.
19th c. A heavy twilled silk.

TOILE DE SOIE. 1898. A thick silk and cotton fabric shot of 2 colours, and having a thick rib.

TOILINET, TOILONETTE. End of 18th c. A fine woollen cloth, plain, striped or checked; somewhat like merino.
19th c. 'The warp of cotton and silk, the weft of woollen.' Much used for waistcoats in the 1st half of 19th c.

TREILLIS. 18th c. 'Otherwise called Buckram.'

TRICOT. 19th c. The French name for knitted fabric; used in England in 1838 for 'a new material for panta-loons' resembling stockinette.

TRICOT DE BERLIN. 1808. A very light form of knitted fabric said to have resembled cotton gauze; used for ladies' walking dresses. In 1835 'Shawls of silk net called Tricot de Berlin'.

TRIPE. 15th to 17th c. An imitation velvet made of wool or thread. Also called Mock Velvet, Naples Fustian, Velure.

TRIPOLINE. 1874. A twilled Satin Turc.

TROLLY LACE. 17th and 18th c's. A coarse Flanders bobbin lace; the pattern outlined with thicker thread or with a flat narrow border com-posed of several thicker threads.

TUFTED CANVAS. 17th c. 'Stript or tufted canvas with thread', the 'striping' or 'tufting' done with linen thread or with silk.

TUFTED DIMITY. 18th c. A fustian with a tufted surface; used for under-petticoats.

TUFT MOCKADO. 16th and 17th c's. A Mockado, of woollen or silk, in which the pattern, instead of being figured, consisted of a geometrical arrangement of tufts.

TUFTTAFFETA. 16th and 17th c's. A Taffeta with a pile left on it.

TUKES. 16th c. A kind of Buckram.

TULLE. 18th and 19th c's. A fine silk bobbin net. First made by machinery in 1768 at Nottingham.

TULLE ARACHNE. 1831. A very clear Tulle embroidered in light patterns with a mixture of gold and silk threads.

TULY. 16th c. The name of a silk or thread fabric (Beck).

TURCO POPLINNES. 1867. A woollen fabric with a soft silky sheen.

TURIN GAUZE. 19th c. A gauze woven of raw silk.

TURIN VELVET. 1860. A silk and wool textile imitating Terry Velvet.

TURKISH VELVET. 1845. A silk velvet ribbed across the stuff; 'a group of ribs separated from another group by a plain satin bar'.

TUSSORE. 1869. A textile, half wool, half cotton, looking like poplin. Later the name invariably indicated Tussore silk.

TUSSORE SILK. 19th c. Wild silk, brownish in colour, imported from India and China. Much used for dress materials at the end of the 19th c.

TWEED. 1825 on. A woollen cloth originating in Scotland; the texture open and elastic. 'The word "tweel" on an invoice being misread as "tweed" in 1825 led to the adoption of the latter as the trade name.' (1875, *The Tailor & Cutter*.)
    All grades from the coarsest homespun to the finest saxony in named varieties: (1) Homespuns made locally in the Western Highlands and Ireland; (2) HARRIS TWEEDS, *q.v.*; (3) DONEGAL TWEED, *q.v.*; (4) West of England Tweed; made from medium spun yarns and fine soft wool.

TWIST. 16th c. Thread composed of filaments of textile material wound round one another.

TYLESENT. 16th c. Synonymous with Tinsel as some kind of fabric glittering with metallic fibres.

UMRITZUR. 1880. A rough-faced textile of camel's hair, soft and light, in art colours; introduced by Liberty and Co.

UNION. 19th c. A stout textile of cotton and linen, much dressed and stiffened.

URLING'S LACE. *See* PATENT THREAD.

VAIR. Med. Thought to have been the fur of the polecat. The whole fur or 'gros vair' meant the back and belly fur; the 'mean vair' (hence Miniver) meant the belly fur alone.

VALENCE. 14th c. A thin textile, possibly a kind of SAY.

VALENCIA. C. 1830–40. A textile the warp of cotton, the weft of worsted; much used for waistcoats (Perkins).
    1850. The name given to a kind of Habit cloth.

VALENTINE. 1833. A slight shaded silk textile.

VANDALES. 17th c. Coarse linens imported from France and the Netherlands.

VELETINE. 1812. A small figured silk textile.

VELLUTO. 1883. A cloth imitating Genoa velvet.

VELOURS BROCHÉ. 19th c. A velvet having a satin broché pattern on it.

VELOURS DE LAINE. 1894. A fabric with velvet stripes or checks on a woollen ground.

VELOURS DU DAUPHIN. 1777. Velvet with small stripes of different colours. Made at Spitalfields.

VELOURS DU NORD. 1881. A textile with a black satin ground shot with a colour, and covered with velvet flowers stamped in relief.

VELOURS ÉPINGLÉ. 19th c. Terry velvet.

VELURE. 17th c. Imitation velvet. 'My velure (breeches) . . . that you thought had been velvet.' (1604, *The London Prodigal.*)

VELVERET. 18th c. A variety of fustian with a velvet-like face.

VELVET. Med. on. A silk fabric having a short dense pile. Made in this country from 1685 (Spitalfields).

VELVET IMPERATRICE. 1860. A kind of dark Terry velvet.

VELVETEEN. 1880's. An imitation of silk velvet, the pile being silk on a cotton back.

VENETIAN. 18th c. A closely woven twilled cloth.
19th c. A fine worsted fabric with a lustre finish.

VERANO CLOTH. 1880. A kind of ribbed Cretonne.

VERDOURS. 16th c. Thought to have been green Baize.

VERGLAS. 1894. A moire with a peculiar form of watering resembling reflections on water.

VERMILION. 17th c. A cotton cloth dyed scarlet. Sometimes called BAR-MILLION.

VERVISE. Med. A blue cloth similar to PLUNKET.

VESSES. 16th c. A sort of worsted.

VICTORIA CLOTH. 1865. A substantial cloth 'replacing meltons or undressed cloths', for men's overcoats.

VICTORIA CRAPE. 19th c. A crepe made entirely of cotton.

VICTORIA SERGE. 1893. Resembled silk serge; used as a lining for lounge jackets.

VICTORIA SILK. 1893. A silk and wool mixture for petticoats 'guaranteed to rustle'.

VICUGNA, VICUNA. 1877. A very soft textile of llama wool; generally plain. Later, of worsted warp and woollen weft.

1888. 'A fine material known as Vicuna though different houses call it by different names such as "Saxony Melton", "Meltonia", etc.' (*Tailor & Cutter.*)

VIGOGNE. 19th c. An all-wool cloth, twilled, and in neutral colours.

VIGONIA CLOTH. 1809. Of Spanish wool, 'soft and warm resembling the texture of the Indian shawl'. Used for ladies' dresses.

VIRLY. Late 13th and early 14th c's. A green cloth made at Vire in Normandy.

VOILE. 1885. A very thin woollen fabric, very similar to, or identical with, Nun's veiling.

WABORNE LACE. 16th c. A braid lace made at Waborne, Norfolk.

WADMOL. Med. A coarse woollen cloth, used chiefly by the poor for their doublets, jerkins, etc.

WASH-LEATHER. 15th c. on. Very soft pliable leather, buff colour; made by splitting sheepskin.

WATCHET. Med. A kind of blue cloth.

WATERED STUFFS. Stuffs impressed with close wavy lines and generally known as Tabbies (18th c.) and Moire (19th c.).

WATERPROOF. 19th c. The use of indiarubber solution applied to a textile was patented by Charles Mackintosh in 1823. 'The cloth called *waterproof* is generally lined with calico or figured cotton; these materials are well imbued and stiffened with gum and firmly sewn together. The smell of the gum is not the only unpleasant quality in this kind of cloth for on approaching the fire the lining shrinks.' (1829, *The Gentleman's Magazine of Fashion.*)

WHALEBONE. Med. on. A cartilaginous material from the upper jaw of the whale; a flexible material used especially for the ribs of women's stays.

WHIPCORD CLOTH. 1863. A large-diagonal ribbed cloth, heavy and stiff. Used for riding breeches.

WHITE WORK. 16th c. A synonym for Cut-work.

WHITES. Med. Undyed cloth in general, particularly so called in the Middle Ages.

WILDBORE. 18th c. A stout Tammy closely woven.

WILDWARE. Med. Imported furs of various animals.

WILTON. (1) Med. A linen from Wilton, Wilts.
(2) 18th c. A woollen cloth.

WINSEY. 19th c. A cotton and wool mixture resembling Linsey.

WITNEY BLANKET. 1844. A heavy cloth produced at Witney and used for men's overcoats.

WOOL. Med. on. The hair of the sheep, the quality varying according to the breed of the animal and the locality where it was bred. English, the staple mediaeval industry; Saxony from the second half of 18th c. Spanish from near the end of 16th c. Australian ('Botany') from c. 1840. (*See* BOTANY, MERINO, SAXONY.)
The wool is divisible into two principal groups according to the length of the hairs; producing the long-stapled textiles, 'Worsteds', and the short-stapled, 'Woollens'. Blends of the two sorts or with other materials, such as silk, cotton, hair of goats, mohair, etc., have produced innumerable textiles having distinctive names or given fancy titles.

WOOL BAREGE. 1850's. A barege made of fine wool; used for shawls.

WORCESTERS. 15th and 16th c's. A cloth, usually white, made in that county.

WORSTED. Med. on. At first known as 'Cloth of Worthstede' (13th c.). A cloth made of long-stapled wool combed straight and smooth before spinning.

YAK LACE. 19th c. A coarse and rather heavy lace made of the hair of the yak. Fashionable for shawls, etc., c. 1870–80.

YEDDO CREPE. 1880. A cotton fabric thick as linen but soft; printed in Chinese designs.

YEDDO POPLIN. 1865. Of pure llama wool, resembling French merino.

YOKOHAMA CREPE. 1880. A cotton textile printed in stripes with Japanese floral designs.

ZEPHIRINA. 1841. 'A new material for coats; a mixture of various colours.'

ZEPHYR. 1880's. A light fine gingham, thin and silky, often with coloured warp and finer weft.

ZEPHYR SHIRTING. 1880's. A very fine flannel with silk warp; for hot climates.

ZEPHYR SILK BAREGE. 1840's. Of silk and wool; gauze weave.

ZIBELINE, ZIBELLINE. 1856. A textile between a barege and a paramatta; apparently a mixture of wool and cotton.

OBSOLETE COLOUR NAMES
(PRIOR TO 1800)

ABRAHAM or ABRAM. 16th c. Brown.

BOWDY. 17th c. Scarlet. From the dye house established at Bow for dyeing scarlet by a new method.

BRASSEL. 16th c. A red colour obtained from the wood of an East Indian tree.

BRISTOL. 16th c. Red.

CARNATION. 16th c. A colour 'resembling raw flesh'.

CROCUS. 17th c. A yellow dye obtained from Saffron.

FALWE. Med. Yellow.

GINGERLINE. 16th c. Reddish-violet.

GOOSE-TURD. 16th c. Yellowish-green.

HAIR. 16th c. Bright tan.

INCARNATE. 16th c. Red.

INDE. Med. Azure blue.

ISABELLE. 16th c. Yellow or light buff.

LUSTIE-GALLANT. 16th c. Light red.

MAIDENHAIR. 16th c. Bright tan.

MARBLE. 16th c. Parti-coloured.

MEDLEY. 16th c. A mixture of colours.

MILK-AND-WATER. 16th c. Bluish-white.

MURREY. 16th c. Purplish-red.

ORANGE TAWNY. 16th c. Orange-brown.

PEAR. 16th c. Russet red.

PERSE. Med. Bluish-grey.

PLUNKET. 16th c. Light blue or sky blue.

POPINJAY. 16th c. Green or blue.

PUKE. 16th c. A dirty brown.

RATS COLOUR. 16th c. Dull grey.

ROY. 16th c. A bright tawny.

RUSSET. Med. A dark brown.

SAD. 16th c. A dark tint of any colour.

SANGUIN. 16th c. Blood red.

SHEEPS COLOUR. 16th c. A neutral colour.

STAMMEL. 16th c. Red.

TAWNY. Med. A dusky brown-orange.

TOLEY. Med. Scarlet.

VERMEL. Med. Vermilion.

WATCHET. Med. Pale blue inclining towards green.